T0396859

Frontiers in African Business Research

Series Editor

Almas Heshmati, Jönköping International Business School, Jönköping, Sweden

This book series publishes monographs and edited volumes devoted to studies on entrepreneurship, innovation, as well as business development and management-related issues in Africa. Volumes cover in-depth analyses of individual countries, regions, cases, and comparative studies. They include both a specific and a general focus on the latest advances of the various aspects of entrepreneurship, innovation, business development, management and the policies that set the business environment. It provides a platform for researchers globally to carry out rigorous analyses, to promote, share, and discuss issues, findings and perspectives in various areas of business development, management, finance, human resources, technology, and the implementation of policies and strategies of the African continent. Frontiers in African Business Research allows for a deeper appreciation of the various issues around African business development with high quality and peer reviewed contributions. Volumes published in the series are important reading for academicians, consultants, business professionals, entrepreneurs, managers, as well as policy makers, interested in the private sector development of the African continent.

Binyam Afewerk Demena ·
Peter A. G. van Bergeijk
Editors

Trade and Investment in East Africa

Prospects, Challenges and Pathways to Sustainability

 Springer

Editors
Binyam Afewerk Demena
International Institute of Social Studies
Erasmus University Rotterdam
The Hague, The Netherlands

Peter A. G. van Bergeijk
International Institute of Social Studies
Erasmus University Rotterdam
The Hague, The Netherlands

ICEA
International Centre for Economic Analysis
Waterloo, Canada

ISSN 2367-1033   ISSN 2367-1041 (electronic)
Frontiers in African Business Research
ISBN 978-981-19-4210-5   ISBN 978-981-19-4211-2 (eBook)
https://doi.org/10.1007/978-981-19-4211-2

Acknowledgements

This publication was produced with the financial support of the European Union, through the EU-ACP TradeCom II Programme, as part of the 'Targeted support to strengthen capacity of policy makers, exporters, and trade associations to assess and review trade and related economic policies to promote trade competitiveness and diversification for widening trading opportunities with the EU' project implemented by REPOA and ISS-Erasmus. We would like to acknowledge the financial support of the African Caribbean and Pacific Group of States (ACP Group) of this project, grant number FED/2019/408-112.

We are particularly grateful to Springer's patience towards the research progress at various stages of the publication process. We greatly recognise the feedback and guidance of Saranya Balasubramanian, Anushangi Weerakoon, Suresh Dharmalingam, William Achauer, Shinko Mimura and the Springer's Africa book series 'Frontiers in African Business Research' editor Almas Heshmati for timely review and acceptance of our proposed project.

We are especially grateful to Donald Mmari, Jamal Msami, Stephen Mwombela, Khadijah Omari, Rehema Losiru, Berhane Ghebretnsaie, Veronika Goussatchenko, Fauzul Muna and Evans Langat for their continuous support at various stage of the process. Our appreciation also goes to Brandon Sommer for the editorial support and feedback across all the chapters of the book.

EU Disclaimer

This publication was produced with the financial support of the European Union, through the EU-ACP TradeCom II Programme, as part of the 'Targeted support to strengthen capacity of policy makers, exporters, and trade associations to assess and review trade and related economic policies to promote trade competitiveness and diversification for widening trading opportunities with the EU' project implemented by REPOA and ISS-Erasmus. Its contents are the sole responsibility of the authors and do not necessarily reflect the views of the European Union, the EU-ACP TradeCom II Programme, REPOA or ISS-Erasmus.

The Member States of the European Union have decided to link together their know-how, resources and destinies. Together, they have built a zone of stability, democracy and sustainable development whilst maintaining cultural diversity, tolerance and individual freedoms. The European Union is committed to sharing its achievements and its values with countries and peoples beyond its borders.

Contents

Part I
Introduction, Policy Framework and Challenges

Chapter 1
Trade and Investment in East Africa: Introduction, Overview, and Implications

Binyam Afewerk Demena and Peter A. G. van Bergeijk

1.1 Introduction

East Africa as a region is increasingly attracting attention, especially in view of its significant achievements since the turn of the Millennium. Figure 1.1 illustrates these steady improvements in the level of development in terms of Gross National Income (GNI) for the African Great Lakes region, where (with the clear exception of Burundi) the standard of living markedly improved. In particular, the outperformance of the average for Eastern and Southern Africa is noteworthy.

Based on these developments, reclassification into 'higher' income groups is to be expected, such as in Kenya in 2014, and in 2020 when the World Bank upgraded Tanzania to the status of a lower middle-income country.[1] The reclassifications first of all are achievements and will enhance Kenya's and Tanzania's country profiles. This is an asset for attracting Foreign Direct Investment (FDI) and will also add further strength to the key productive sectors with considerable trade potential. The upgrade from lower to middle-income country will, however, have an impact on concessional finance as well, because donor countries may prioritize other countries for their Official Development Assistance (ODA) and the World Bank uses income

---

[1] Although National Accounts revisions also played a role, the achievement mainly reflected Tanzania's economic track record of on average a bit more than six per cent real growth of Gross Domestic Product over the past decade. See also Fialho and van Bergeijk (2017) on World Bank country classifications.

B. A. Demena · P. A. G. van Bergeijk (✉)
International Institute of Social Studies (ISS), Erasmus University Rotterdam, The Hague, The Netherlands
e-mail: bergeijk@iss.nl

B. A. Demena
e-mail: demena@iss.nl

P. A. G. van Bergeijk
ICEA, International Centre for Economic Analysis, Waterloo, Canada

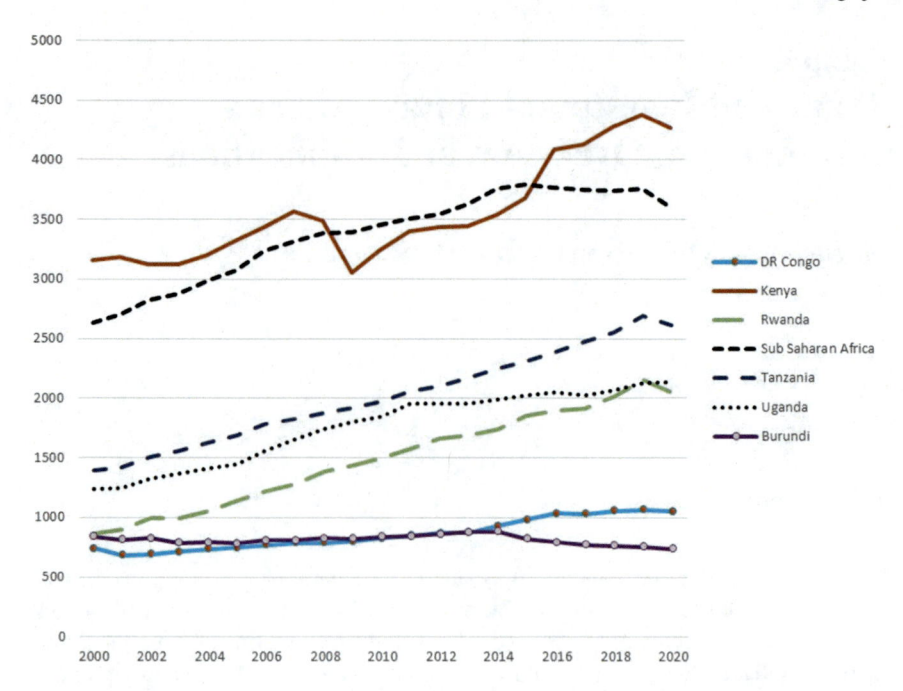

Fig. 1.1 Gross national income per head of population, purchasing power parity, constant 2017 international dollars, 3-year centred moving average 2000–2019. *Source* World Bank, World Development Indicators, accessed April 1, 2022

per head as one of the variables that informs its decision on whether or not a country is eligible for World Bank (IDA—International Development Association) zero to low-interest credits and grants. In the longer term, access to concessional finance will thus decrease, but this change will not occur overnight as shown by the experience of the 35 low-income countries that upgraded from low to middle-income status over the past 15 years (Engen and Prizzon 2019). Typically, there is a window of some 5–6 years in which new middle-income countries have a 'blended' status. The challenge is to use this period wisely and for a financial and economic strategy to be formulated to facilitate the change from concessional lending to financing at market conditions. An important element in such a strategy is to also look beyond borrowing because the financial requirements can be reduced by an improvement in the trade balance and the increase in FDI inflows.

From this perspective, it is hopeful that policymakers have recognized that one of the growth driving forces has been the reorientation towards openness, international trade, and FDI. Figure 1.2 shows by way of illustration the average growth rate for exports and again the outperformance of the African Great Lakes region (with the exception of Burundi) is noteworthy.

This resilience of the African Great Lakes region is remarkable in view of the tsunami of negative foreign trade and investment shocks of the last decade, including Brexit, COVID-19, and adverse geopolitics that all affect the flows of goods and

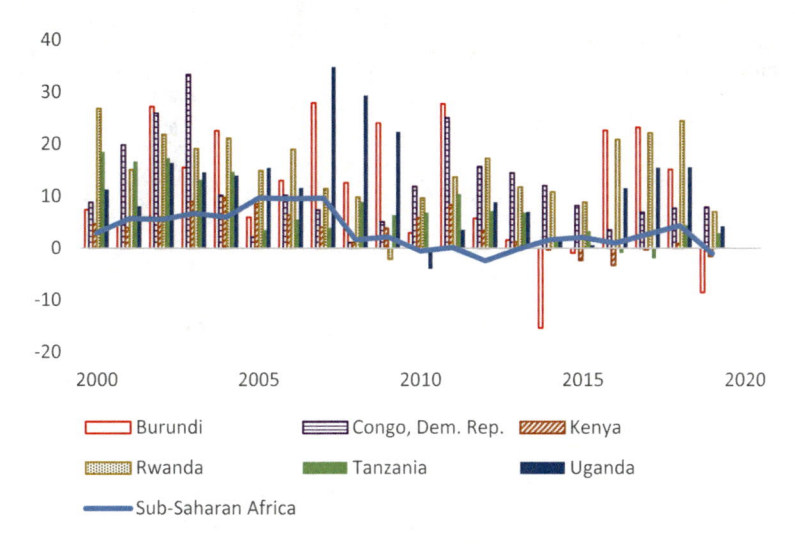

Fig. 1.2 Export growth rates (centred three years moving average). *Source* World Bank, World Development Indicators, accessed April 1, 2022

finances, most notably in the sectors that are heavily dependent on global demand, such as tourism.[2] There is a need to strengthen resilience by diversifying beyond minerals, tourism, and traditional cash crops, boosting private sector backed growth and competitiveness, and preparing for competitiveness-led export growth. There is a need to ensure that the benefits of international specialization trickle down not only to strengthen economic growth but also to create jobs and reduce poverty.

1.2   Strengthening Trade Capacities

This edited volume takes stock of recent research and aims to strengthen the capacity of policymakers, exporters, and trade associations to promote trade competitiveness and diversification for widening trading opportunities mainly within the East African Community (EAC) and between the EAC and the EU.[3] It largely focuses on the capacity of EAC member countries to formulate and implement suitable trade and investment policies to harness the opportunities arising from the effective implementation of regional and international trade agreements. Strengthening export capacity is a broad topic, and its relevancy is illustrated by the scores in the World Bank's Ease of Doing Business ranking (Table 1.1).

---

[2] For instance, it has now become clear that the prospect of achieving the SDGs by 2030 is significantly worsened by the spread of the COVID-19 pandemic across the globe (Eden and Wagstaff 2021); see also van Bergeijk (2021).

[3] Where relevant, we make a distinction between EAC-6 and EAC-7, the latter including the Democratic Republic of Congo (DRC).

Table 1.1 EAC-7 ease of doing business ranking

Location	Score	Border type	Rank
Rwanda	75.0	Land	88
Kenya	67.4	Land	117
Uganda	66.7	Land	121
P.M. Sub-Saharan Africa	*53.6*		*140*
Burundi	47.3	Land	169
South Sudan	26.2	Land	180
Tanzania	20.2	Port	182
Congo, Dem. Rep	3.5	Port	187

Source World Bank World Development Indicators, accessed April 5, 2022

As reported in Table 1.1, Rwanda, Kenya, and Uganda outperform the average for Sub-Saharan Africa. The other four EAC member countries do not do so well. It is important to note that good performance by some member countries holds great promise for the other member countries as best practices could spill over and often with comparatively small investments. For example, as illustrated in Chap. 6, reducing the costs and time of border procedures and documentary compliance could significantly enhance trade flows. Streamlining and reducing the red tape of international trade is of course not a free lunch, but at the same time improvements in port management, one-stop shops, and efficient border procedures do not require major investments in infrastructure.

An important issue is the geographical scope of the contributions. Some contributors focus specifically on one or two countries, others broaden the scope to include other Sub-Saharan African (SSA) countries as well (Table 1.2). Moreover, the emphasis of the contributions in this edited volume is on how trade policies constrain competitiveness so as to identify concrete options for policy action. The analysis is thus by design mainly restricted to the period up to and including 2019 so as to avoid

Table 1.2 Country coverage of the contributions

Country under examination	Chapter
The entire group of ACP countries	3
EAC-7 and other major trading partners	6
EAC-7	2, 15
EAC-5 (DRC, Kenya, Rwanda, Tanzania, and Uganda) and Malawi and Zambia	7
China, Ethiopia, India, Tunisia, Kenya, and Tanzania	11
Burundi, Kenya, Rwanda, Tanzania, and Uganda	9
Kenya, Rwanda, Tanzania, and Uganda	4, 8
Tanzania	5, 10, 12, 13, 14

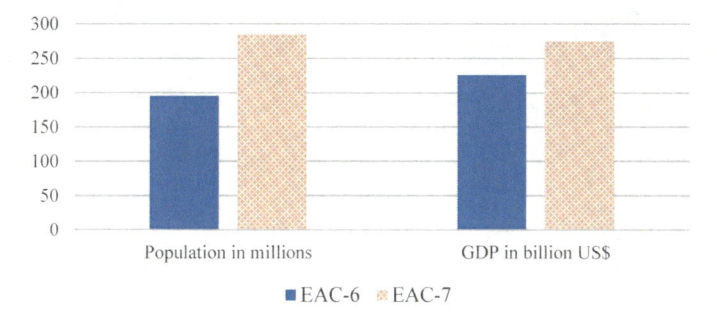

Fig. 1.3 Population and production in EAC-6 and EAC-7 (2020). *Source* World Bank Data, https://data.worldbank.org accessed on April 6, 2022

the impact of the COVID-19 pandemic on trade (Afesorgbor et al. 2022) also in view of the heterogeneous health responses in the region.

While this choice to restrict the research period to the years before 2020 has the benefit of avoiding analytical problems that could compromise robustness and comparability, it also carries a cost as many chapters do not explicitly reflect on the recent enlargement of the EAC, that is, the DRC joining EAC on 29 March 2022. Fortunately, five chapters already cover all member countries of the enlarged EAC-7 and especially Chap. 2 will be relevant for readers interested in the implications of the membership of the DRC as it offers a policy perspective on the enlarged EAC.

The enlargement of the EAC brings both opportunities and challenges. Access to the Atlantic Ocean (especially relevant for the landlocked EAC members) and a significant increase of the EAC market (Fig. 1.3) are both undoubtedly of strategic importance for the development of the region. Clearly, however, market integration and cross-continental transportation will require major investments in infrastructure as well as a reduction of Non-Tariff Barriers (NTBs), including a streamlining of border procedures and also of security and political barriers to trade, in particular a reduction of armed conflict and lawlessness. As discussed in Chap. 2, security issues play havoc both internally and at the external borders of the EAC-7. The EAC Treaty rightly stresses the necessity of peace and security for fostering a thriving environment for integration.

The major economic challenge of the enlargement may very well be that the focus on the enlargement of the EAC may slow down the necessary deepening of economic integration (Si Tou 2021). Deepening international integration is a key policy area, also because EAC-7 is characterized by significant heterogeneity with regard to productivity levels and the ease of cross-border economic activity (Fig. 1.4).

This heterogeneity is important for two reasons. Firstly, regional integration will have different impacts on welfare, public finance, and trade for different EAC members (this is a common finding of recent modelling exercises; see, for example, Mugume 2021; Shinyekwa et al. 2021). Secondly, the recent enlargement involves countries with significantly different levels of per capita income (Fig. 1.1) and adjustments to international specialization patterns thus can be expected to create winners

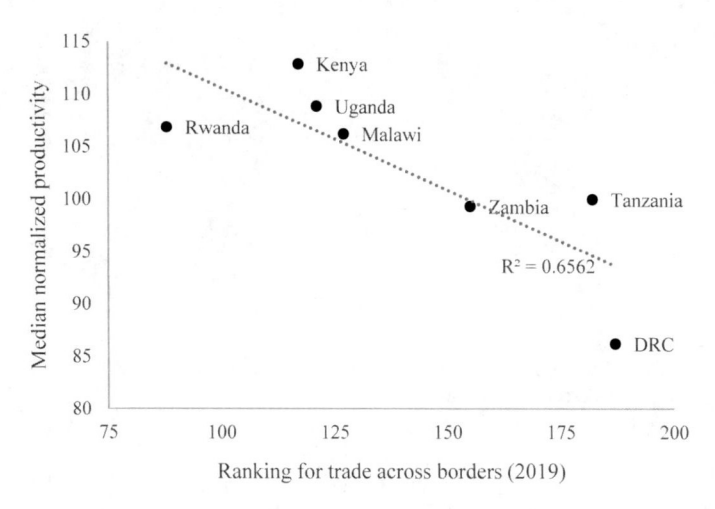

Fig. 1.4 Firm-level productivity and ease of trade across borders in the EAC. *Source* Demena et al. (2021a)

and losers, both within countries and across countries.[4] Figure 1.5 compares the productivity of the countries and their industries. The further away from the origin, the higher the normalized productivity level. For example, for garments and furniture, we see that firm-level productivity in Kenya is higher than in Tanzania, DRC, Uganda, and Rwanda. Rwanda for non-metallic manufactured products outperforms other EAC countries. In the same vein, Uganda has higher productivity for chemicals and DRC for textiles.

It is important to note that due to data limitations, Fig. 1.5 provides a snapshot only and the snapshot is somewhat dated (2014 is the most recent year for which we have observations) and somewhat unsharp because we look at comprehensive aggregates that may hide underlying heterogeneity and because the sample size at the country level is relatively small. Therefore, the radar diagram needs to be interpreted with caution and cannot be used to set policy priorities without a detailed evaluation of current conditions on the ground.

This being said, two robust and important conclusions emerge. First, the radar diagram shows that beneficial international specialization on the basis of comparative and competitive advantage is possible when these countries get more integrated economically because of the different patterns of strong and weak sectors. Second,

---

[4] Incidentally, such problems are not unique for African Integration. A similar trade-off for example occurred by the enlargement of the European Union after the fall of the Iron Curtain in 1990. Originally, many economists doubted the validity of integrating Eastern Europe in the EU but that skepticism was based on *absolute* cost differences and thus neglected the potential for international specialization based on *comparative* advantage as well as the importance of non-traditional exports (Oldersma and van Bergeijk 1992).

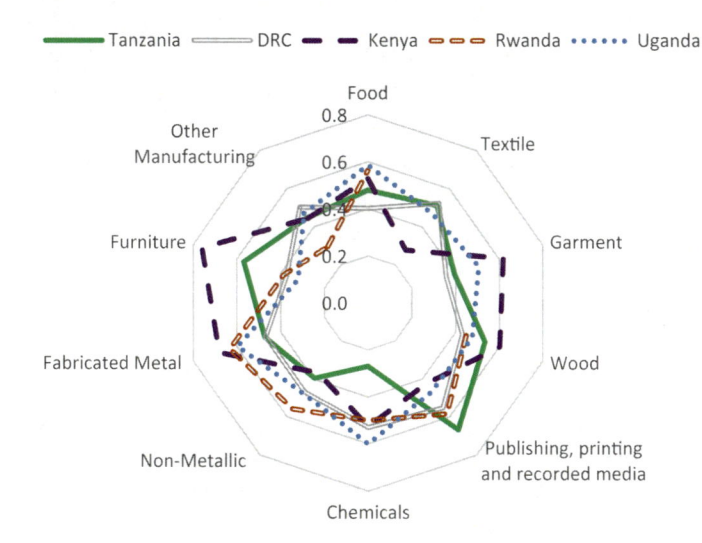

Fig. 1.5 Normalized productivity levels by product and country (2014). *Source* Data underlying Chap. 7

for all countries there are winners and losers from stronger international competition. Still, the message is clear: not all sectors can benefit if (non tariff) barriers to international trade are reduced.

In addition to findings that are relevant for the individual countries and country groupings, *Trade and Investment in East Africa—Prospects, Challenges and Pathways to Sustainability* may also serve as a base for a deeper understanding of the challenges, opportunities, and requirements of the intra-continental trade agreement which is now in sight with the ratification of the Tripartite (EAC-COMESA-SADC) Free Trade Area that is critical in addressing key constraints to trade in the African continent. Moreover, the lessons from this edited volume may also extend to the challenges and opportunities of the African Continental Free Trade Area and other long-term issues (Moyo and Chikwanha 2022).

The individual chapters were developed as part of a research and capacity-building programme under the aegis of ACP and EU that we implemented in 2020–2022.[5] The research project well fits into the Frontiers in African Business Research series as we have many African contributors.[6] In this regard, the contributors know the EAC context very well as their engagement in policymaking goes beyond the context of the

---

[5] The full title of the project is targeted support to strengthen capacity of policymakers, exporters, and trade associations to assess and review trade and related economic policies to promote trade competitiveness and diversification for widening trading opportunities with the EU. The authors acknowledge the financial support of the African Caribbean and Pacific Group of States (ACP Group) of this project, grant number FED/2019/408-112.

[6] The call for research proposals that constitute the main part of this edited volume with small research grants to carryout research in selected thematic areas is available at: (http://www.repoa.or.tz/?p=4584).

Table 1.3 Overview of methods and methodologies

Research method	Chapter
Secondary analysis of literature and data	2, 11, 15
Primary data and analysis	12, 14, 15
Revealed comparative (trade) advantage	5
Firm level panel data	4, 7, 8, 9
Constant market share analysis	10
Time series data analysis	13
Econometric gravity trade model	3, 6

papers they are writing about. The contributions matter to policymakers and academic circles. All chapters have been peer-reviewed. The chapters use a combination of quantitative and qualitative methods (Table 1.3) and thereby the collective effort provides a multi-method approach using comprehensive applied empirical tools to generate the knowledge needed to identify key constraints as well as opportunities.

1.3 Overview and Structure of the Chapters

We have organized the contributions into four parts. Following this introduction, two contributions set out a common policy framework that serves as a point of reference for the other chapters. Against the background of major shocks to the world economic system, including Brexit, COVID-19, and the Ukraine war, giving policy advice is complicated. At the same time, *evidence-based policy* is more necessary than ever.

Chapter 2 by Donald Mmari, Jamal Msami, Stephen Mwombela, Binyam Afewerk Demena, Jane Mpapalika, and Peter A. G. van Bergeijk discusses the history of the EAC, its ups and downs, and its outlook. Here, a useful overview of protocols for the different stages of economic integration (from customs union via common market, and monetary union to political federation) and a listing of recent new commitments are provided. These help to identify key challenges to the EAC. For policymakers, it is important that the economic bottlenecks that are the lens through which this books studies competitiveness are one aspect only (although important), and therefore this chapter also addresses the challenges in the legal, political, institutional, and cultural domains offering suggestions and policy proposals on how to deal with these issue in a comprehensive manner.

In Chap. 3, Sylvanus Kwaku Afesorgbor focuses on the potential for export-led growth in the context of the EU-African Caribbean and Pacific (ACP) preferential market access arrangements. This chapter addresses two salient issues: first, it considers the relevance of preferential trade agreements in fostering exports to developed countries' markets and then examines the effectiveness of foreign aid in reducing the supply-side constraints in the beneficiary countries to enable them to utilize the granted market access opportunity effectively. The research is based on the entire group of ACP countries and their annual trade with the EU preference-giving countries starting in 1970. Using a gravity model to examine the trade effect of EU-ACP agreement conditional on foreign aid he finds EU-ACP is effective in promoting exports, but in itself not a sufficient condition. Importantly, improvements in the level of economic development require a sufficient level of foreign aid complemented with technical and development assistance.

1.3.1 The Potential for Trade and Investment

Next follows Part II that focuses on the identification of the trade and investment potential of East Africa. Chapter 4 by Binyam Afewerk Demena analyses at the micro level of private firms how the business environment (investment climate) and firm characteristics impact the internationalization strategies in Sub-Saharan Africa. This is an important policy dimension as government interventions to ease trade obstacles to support export competitiveness and diversification can address the key factors that are responsible for constraining supply capacity across countries in the EAC.[7] The data allow for the analysis of firms' views and perceptions, also related to how institutional and trade policy obstacles affect international integration for firms in the EAC. For most EAC countries, firms tend to see many areas of the investment climate as bottlenecks to business. Access to formal and informal finance, custom and trade regulations, and telecommunication opportunities tend to pose serious constraints to the investment climate.

Huda Ahmed Yussuf and Masoud Mohammed Albiman in Chap. 5 deploy a macroeconomic lens but focus on a specific country as it investigates movements in Tanzania's comparative advantage (Balassa and Volrath indices) and intra-industry trade (Grubel-Lloyd index) in order to identify opportunities for trade with Europe. The research is based on Harmonized System (HS) 2-digit classification and data from 2009 to 2018, inclusive. Based on their findings on comparative specialization patterns, they identify trade complementarities between Europe and Tanzania, indicating that trade agreements will lower the cost of production for local industries. The implication is that trade between Tanzania and the rest of the world is found to be inter-industry as opposed to intra-industry except for textile products. Sectors with export potential are the processing of animal products, textile, and leather industries.

Chapter 6 by Binyam Afewerk Demena and Peter A. G. van Bergeijk also addresses trade and competitiveness at the macro-economic level but from a broader perspective and investigates the trade impact of the time and costs that firms incur when they comply with documentary requirements and border procedures which still is an important bottleneck for intra-EAC trade. The research is based on the seven

---

[7] More specifically, Demena et al. (2021a, b, c) argued that dealing with the emerging micro data-driven research in investigating the relationship between internationalization and firms enhances our empirical understanding and policy relevance.

EAC member countries and other trading partners and a panel dataset for 80 countries during the period 2015–2018. An applied structural gravity trade model shows that reducing time and costs by streamlining procedures, one-stop portals, reducing handling time, as well as the use of common standards that facilitate EAC internal trade flows do not require large financial investments but do have a high payoff.

1.3.2   Productivity and Competitiveness

The third part deals with competitiveness and the contributions have also been organized from micro (firm level) to macro (country level). While countries do not actually trade (firms after all have to do the work) and competition is essentially taking place at the level of individual firms, the development of a country's international competitiveness is an important policy parameter that complements findings and policy implications at the firm level.

Chapter 7 by Binyam Afewerk Demena, Jamal Msami, Donald Mmari, and Peter A. G. van Bergeijk argues that productivity development is a key issue for export-driven growth and development. The investigation of firm-level productivity differences involves seven countries that are part of the COMESA-EAC-SADC tripartite free trade area (TFTA, namely Democratic Republic of Congo, Kenya, Malawi, Rwanda, Tanzania, Uganda, and Zambia). The data consists of firm-level information for 4,488 observations. While most existing empirical studies only focus on the manufacturing sector, the research separately incorporates the service sectors in the analysis. The analysis uncovers a clear export productivity premium for national firms (both in manufacturing and service sectors); foreign-ownership productivity premia for both domestic and exporting firms exist in manufacturing sectors (but less so in services sectors). Productivity premia are also related to firm size, training programmes, and the country's level of development in the manufacturing firms.

In Chap. 8, Gerald P. Lesseri and Kauthar S. Salum delve further into this issue in order to find out whether learning by exporting drives the productivity differences. The analysis involved a panel dataset of 876 firms compiled from two waves of the survey in each country collected between 2006 and 2013. Exporting firms in Tanzania, Kenya, Uganda, and Rwanda are more productive, pay higher wages, and employ more workers relative to non-exporting firms, and this offers an alternative indication of export premium. In line with this, exporters exhibit higher growth of labour productivity relative to non-exporters which supports the learning by exporting hypothesis, especially for domestically owned firms where learning effects accumulate with a length of export. The authors suggest that well-targeted export promotion activities should aim at stimulating firms to participate in international trade and tap the export premium.

Masoud Mohammed Albiman, Huda Ahmed Yussuf, and Issa Moh'd Hemed in Chap. 9 examine the effect of FDI and trade openness on competitiveness and diversification among EAC members. The research is based on 5 member countries of the EAC using a panel dataset for the period 2010–2019, inclusive. The effect of FDI on a firm's export competitiveness and trade diversification is positive and statistically significant. The authors argue that policy reforms to improve economic freedom, technological development, and strengthening the inter-relationship of the domestic sector with FDI and trade openness are needed to improve export competitiveness and diversification. An intriguing finding is that the effect of trade openness is positive and statistically significant for export diversification but insignificant for export competitiveness. This suggests the need for a closer look at the export competitiveness of the EAC member countries.

Harry Thomas Silas Achentalika and Dorah Teddy in Chap. 10 provide such an analysis deploying the Constant Market Share method to disentangle the contribution of changes in competitiveness and structural factors, including commodity composition and development of world trade based on a comparison of the years 2009–2013 and 2014–2018. Controlling for the overall development of world trade and the trade composition, they find a strengthening of Tanzania's competitive position in comparison to the other EAC-6 member states.

1.3.3 Industries, Cooperatives, and Value Chains

The fourth part showcases five case studies that add an important dimension to the predominantly quantitative analyses of secondary data in the parts on trade and investment potential, productivity, and competitiveness. The methodologies in this chapter allow for more discussion of context and institutions, drawn from primary data collection and the voices of producers, traders, and policymakers in order to get a better understanding of East African integration on the ground.

Fauzul Muna in Chap. 11 reviews the literature on the leather value chain in Tanzania. Tanzania has significant livestock, but the contribution of the leather industry to the economy is minimal due to various problems in downstream and upstream activities. The research is based on a mixed research method combining a review of the literature and analytical descriptive statistics of secondary data. The literature systematically discussed in this chapter extends beyond academic literature, as also non-academic literature such as government documents are included. The chapter identifies best practices for the leather industries development policies of China, India, Tunisia, Ethiopia, and Kenya that have higher quality supporting facilities such as tax incentives, leather research institutes, grading institutions, innovation, and dedicated training facilities. These elements may be a vital element of Tanzania's policies for the leather industry aimed at strengthening the capacity for effective implementation of export competitiveness and diversification. The study emphasizes that particular attention should be paid to the production of finished products since Tanzania does not have adequate leather manufacturing.

Chapter 12 by Eliaza Jones Mkuna takes a more detailed look focusing on the impact of horticulture export promotion on common bean farmers' welfare in Arusha, Tanzania. This study employed a cross-sectional design collecting primary data from a variety of common beans farmers in the study area. The information brought deeper insights and a better understanding of the problems. The study reflects a mix of both qualitative and quantitative data and methodological treatments. These farmers are aware of the significant potential of exporting their crops (rather than trading only locally). Socio-economic, production, and institutional factors influence both the decision on and extent of the export of common bean by smallholders. The chapter recommends that policy attention needs to shift from supporting and regulating particular trade policies to focusing on how farmers will be trained to utilize available opportunities in the common beans export market.

The next chapter adds an important macroeconomic dimension to international competitiveness of the horticultural sector. William George in Chap. 13 investigates determinants of Tanzanian horticultural export performance from 1988 to 2018, inclusive. In the long run, real exchange rates, agricultural value added, and foreign demand significantly influence horticultural export performance. An important policy implication is that flexibility of the exchange rate in line with the fundamentals of the economy is necessary. Efficient policies for stabilization of interest rates should be put in place (e.g., ceiling on lending rates and lowering inflation rate). These findings may also be relevant for other value chains.

Chapter 14 by Wahida Hamza Makame provides a detailed multimethod analysis of the seaweed sector in Zanzibar, studying the livelihood aspects of the seaweed value chain in 32 villages on the islands of Unguja and Pemba with focus group discussions, a large survey, key informant interviews, and field observations. Nearly half of the surveyed farmers had no formal education. Low formal education leads to challenges including low technology uptake and innovation, wide information and knowledge gaps, and low income and productivity. Quality, an important factor for determining price and export competitiveness, does not receive much attention. Besides, seaweed is highly impacted by climate change, and movement in search for new farming areas was taken as the main adaptation strategy. Other challenges were infrastructure, high taxation, and conflicts of space between seaweed sector, tourism, and fishing. To increase export competitiveness of the seaweed, Zanzibar needs to invest in education and research, quality management, tailor-made trainings, physical infrastructure, strong coordination with stakeholders and also to strengthen the policy and institutional framework.

Gerard Dushimimana in Chap. 15 studies the role of cross-border cooperatives. A structured review informs follow-up interviews with key informers in Rwanda. Cross-Border cooperatives improve regional trade and address challenges of small-scale cross-border traders. Synthesizing 15 primary studies that explore the role played by cross-border cooperatives in the EAC, it is found that cross-border cooperatives improved the socio-economic conditions of members through pooling resources, reduction of transaction cost, and representation of traders in public space. The study suggests knowledge gaps need to be addressed by future research, focusing on the specific roles and effects of cross-border cooperatives on cross-border trade, and (as Kenya and Uganda have been covered already quite well) a shift in geographical focus would add value.

1.4 What Next?

The contributions to this book sketch a rich up-to-date and multidimensional picture of the challenges and opportunities of further economic integration in (East) Africa. All contributors agree that significant potential for international trade and investment exists, and this robust finding is all the more telling since their approaches differ and cover a diverse set of observation units including firms, industries, and value chains as well as the macroeconomic point of view. The contributors also agree that the growth of trade is not a *fait accompli*, and that a concerted, comprehensive, and coherent policy effort will be necessary to make the best out of East African economic integration.

1.4.1 Deepening Economic Integration

The need for a major policy initiative while deepening economic integration does not come as a surprise: all major economic integration projects have had to address the heterogeneity and contradictions that emerge and/or become more transparent when countries become increasingly integrated. From history, we know that adjustment is necessary and sometimes costly as less productive industries and firms are replaced by more productive counterparts elsewhere in the economic integration area. Economic integration so to say magnifies the distortions that make domestic firms less productive—it also magnifies the potential welfare gains for the productive sectors, industries and firms that can benefit both from a larger internal market and, thanks to economies of scale, improve their international competitive advantage.

East African integration, however, has an extra dimension as often missing firms, missing industries, and missing institutions can be identified that are bottlenecks to moving up the value chain. Also, excessive regulation, institutional deficiencies, and incoherent policies drive a wedge between productivity and costs that significantly hinder the private sector's contribution to growth and development. It is vital to strengthen policies to avoid costly distortions on the road to further integration.

1.4.2 Implications and Key Messages

From this perspective, what are the most important policy conclusions that follow from this edited volume? Based on each of the book chapters, we collectively draw the following implications and common key messages.

1.4.2.1 Evidence-Based Policy Needs Robust Research

Evidence-based policy can be defined as 'a fundamental principle of good public services that decisions are made on the basis of strong evidence and what we know works' (Cabinet Office 2013). The first practical implication (and also conclusion) is analytical, but it contains a major message for policymakers: the issues are multidimensional (this is even true within the specific domain that is the focus of *Trade and Investment in East Africa—Prospects, Challenges and Pathways to Sustainability*). For instance, a major challenge to advancing sustainable development in the past has been the lack of multidimensional evidence-based approaches that enable comprehensive dimensions of development (Allen et al. 2018; Scrieciu 2007). Evidence-based policymaking thus cannot be based on a single finding, a single approach, or a single analysis. Policies need to be robust and therefore robustness of the evidence is key to the success or failure of considered policies.

Policy Message 1: The growing agenda for policymaking requires a marked shift in focus from a single approach or finding to multidimensional evidence-based policymaking. Policymakers require a systematic and multi-research approach and knowledge synthesis in order to support and employ informed decisions on expected outcomes, especially, on whether a particular policy programme can(not) achieve or is (not) achieving its desired outcomes.

1.4.2.2 East Africa's Trade Potential Is Significant

For the macroeconomy (macro revealed comparative advantage, gravity analysis), for industries and value chains (horticulture, seaweed, leather) and at the firm level (importantly for both primary and secondary data) the quantitative evidence agrees that significant export premia exist (trade is associated with higher productivity and/or income). This consensus is also supported by qualitative evidence such as key stakeholder interviews and focus group discussions. Therefore, our second key message is as follows.

Policy Message 2: Trade competitiveness is a key issue for export-driven growth and development. A solid understanding of the drivers of productivity development (and thus on the size of the export premium) are therefore a prerequisite for any sound policy-oriented arguments and policy parameters for economic diplomacy and trade policy. Unblocking the trade barriers among the EAC member countries can pave the way for a rapid utilization of East Africa's trade potential and growth in key productive sectors. Alongside the removal of trade barriers, the ratification of the so-called tripartite free trade area (TFTA) that constitutes countries that are part of the Common Market for Eastern and Southern Africa (COMESA), the Southern African Development Community (SADC) and EAC is an important step towards maximizing trade potential in the region.

1.4.2.3 East Africa Is Very Heterogeneous

This lesson is clear from all comparative analyses as shown by the productivity analyses between and within countries, the best (and worst) practices identified in chapters that use macroeconomic trade modelling and value chain analysis, as well as in the detailed analyses of trade patterns and trade structures. Heterogeneity is not a problem per se: often, differences create comparative and competitive advantages and are thus a basis for trade. After all, in a perfectly homogeneous world no *raison d'être* exists for international trade and investment. The policy implication of the large extent of heterogeneity is essentially that this heterogeneity indicates that policymakers need to prepare for potential drastic short-term adjustments along the road to further economic integration.

Policy Message 3: The analysis in this book cautions that the process towards an export-led competitive economy will not be a free lunch and that next to winners, there will also be sectors that will lose from trade integration and international competitiveness. This requires targeted policy to adapt and mitigate against losses from increased integration.

1.4.2.4 Rebalancing Private and Official Capital Flows

Although East Africa can also facilitate trade by streamlining the bureaucracy and better management of transport hubs, in the midterm it also needs foreign finance to speed up the transformation of the economy. In view of the adjustment costs, external finance, either in the form of FDI or by means of continued concessional finance from donor countries and international organizations, is needed to prevent a situation that short-term costs stand in the way of reaching the longer term benefits of further economic integration. In the midterm, a shift away from official capital flows and towards private capital flows is both unavoidable and possible. It is unavoidable given East Africa's development—witness the upgrading of Kenya and Tanzania to middle-income country states—that will make the region less eligible for concessional finance. It is also possible to make this shift, given the existing potential and the commitment of East Africa to international trade as an engine for growth.

Policy Message 4: FDI should further be reinforced as a major priority of private capital flows. FDI is not only important as a source of external macroeconomic finance, but also and especially for the indirect effects that it generates for the local economy and in the process of internationalization strategy. FDI is important as a policy guideline for implementation of the Substantial Development Goals (SDGs) as it strengthens FDI-related direct and indirect effects (United Nations 2015a, b).[8]

---

[8] Recently, the importance of FDI was re-emphasized through two major global development events in 2015: the Global Summit on Post-2015 Development Agenda in September 25 and the third International Conference on Financing for Development in July. These two major events have ushered in new global agendas and identified how these should be implemented (UNECA et al. 2015). The former event provides a global framework for achieving 17 Sustainable Development Goals (SDGs), and the latter introduces implementation policy guidelines.

In terms of sustainable development, FDI remains an important source of finance for most developing countries.

Acknowledgements The authors acknowledge the financial support of the African Caribbean and Pacific Group of States (ACP Group) of this project, grant number FED/2019/408-112.

References

Afesorgbor SK (2022) Preferential market access, foreign aid and economic development. A case of the EU-ACP preferential trade agreement. (Chap 3)

Afesorgbor SK, van Bergeijk PAG, Demena BA (2022) COVID-19 and the threat to globalization: an optimistic note. In: Papyrakis E (ed) Covid-19 and international development. Springer, Cham. https://doi.org/10.1007/978-3-030-82339-9_3

Albiman MM, Yussuf HA, Hemed IM (2022) Trade complementarities between Europe and Tanzania. (Chap 9)

Allen C, Metternicht G, Wiedmann T (2018) Initial progress in implementing the sustainable development goals (SDGs): a review of evidence from countries. Sustain Sci 13(5):1453–1467

Cabinet Office (2013) What works: evidence centres for social policy. Cabinet Office, London

Demena BA (2022) Investment climate and international development of firms: what matters for sub-Saharan African firms. (Chap 4)

Demena BA, van Bergeijk PAG (2022a) Trade and investment in East Africa: introduction, overview, and implications. (Chap 1)

Demena BA, van Bergeijk PAG (2022b) Trade potential and bottlenecks in East Africa: a gravity approach. (Chap 6)

Demena BA, Msami J, Mmari D, van Bergeijk PAG (2021a) Trade, productivity and competitiveness. African portal and policy brief no 18/2021a, Research on Poverty Alleviation

Demena B, Msami J, Mmari D, van Bergeijk PAG (2021b) Trade, productivity and competitiveness. Repoa policy brief no 18

Demena B, Msami J, Mmari D, van Bergeijk PAG (2021c) Productivity premia and firm heterogeneity in Eastern Africa. ISS WP no 680

Demena BA, Msami J, Mmari D, van Bergeijk PAG (2022) Productivity premia and firm heterogeneity in Eastern Africa. (Chap 7)

Dushimimana G (2022) The role of cross border cooperatives in the EAC: a structured review. (Chap 15)

Eden L, Wagstaff MF (2021) Evidence-based policymaking and the wicked problem of SDG 5 gender equality. J Int Bus Policy 4(1):28–57

Engen L, Prizzon A (2019) Exit from aid: an analysis of country experiences. ODI report, Overseas Development Institute (ODI), London

Fialho D, van Bergeijk PAG (2017) The proliferation of developing country classifications. J Dev Stud 53(1):99–115

George W (2022) Export performance of the horticultural sub-sector in Tanzania. (Chap 13)

Lesseri GP, Salum KS (2022) Export status changes and firm productivity: evidence from EAC. (Chap 8)

Makame WH (2022) The seaweed sector in Zanzibar: a multimethod approach to value chain analysis. (Chap 14)

Mkuna EJ (2022) Determinants of horticultural export and welfare impact of smallholder farmers: evidence from common beans (Phaseolus vulgaris L) farming in Arusha Tanzania. (Chap 12)

Mmari D, Msami J, Mwombela S, Demena BA, van Bergeijk PAG, Mpapalika J (2022) EAC integration: evidence-based policy in difficult times. (Chap 2)

Moyo T, Chikwanha AB (2022) African agency for development: progress, contradictions, and complexities in the era of globalisation. Int J Afr Renaiss Stud-Multi-, Inter-and Transdiscipl 1–20

Mugume R (2021) How will the Democratic Republic of Congo's joining the EAC bloc affect regional trade?. EPRC, Economic Policy Research Centre, Kampala

Muna F (2022) The Tanzania's leather value chain: a review of the literature. (Chap 11)

Oldersma H, van Bergeijk PAG (1992) Potential for an export-oriented growth strategy in Central Europe. J World Trade 26:47

Scrieciu SS (2007) The inherent dangers of using computable general equilibrium models as a single integrated modelling framework for sustainability impact assessment. A critical note on Böhringer and Löschel (2006). Ecol Econ 60(4):678–684

Shinyekwa IM, Bulime EN, Nattabi AK (2021) Trade, revenue, and welfare effects of the AfCFTA on the EAC: an application of WITS-SMART simulation model. Bus Strat Dev 4(1):59–74

Si Tou WK (2021) Enhancing export competitiveness by deeper integration: the case of the East African Community. Dev Policy Rev 39(3):493–507

Silas HT, Teddy D (2022) Competitiveness of East African exports: a constant market share analysis. (Chap 10)

UNECA, AUC, AfDB, UNDP (2015) MDG report 2015: assessing progress in Africa toward the millennium development goals. UN Economic Commission for Africa, Addis Ababa

United Nations UN (2015a) Outcome of the third international conference on financing for development: Addis Ababa Action Agenda. United Nations, Addis Ababa

United Nations UN (2015b) Report on the third international conference on financing for development. United Nations, New York

Van Bergeijk PAG (2021) Pandemic economics. Edward Elgar, Chatenham

Yussuf HA, Albiman MM (2022) Trade complementarities between Europe and Tanzania. (Chap 5)

Chapter 2
EAC Integration: Evidence-Based Policy in Difficult Times

Donald Mmari, Jamal Msami, Stephen Mwombela, Jane Mpapalika, Binyam Afewerk Demena, and Peter A. G. van Bergeijk

Abstract This chapter addresses challenges in the legal, political, institutional, and cultural domains offering suggestions and policy proposals based on a discussion of the history of the EAC, its ups and downs, and its current outlook. We provide an overview of protocols for the different stages of economic integration from a customs union via a common market, and a monetary union to the ultimate goal of a political federation. Progress has been slower than originally planned and asymmetries threaten to undercut support towards integration, among the citizens of some partner states and sometimes to local apathy towards the EAC and a lack of policy coherence. A shared history, customs, geography, the need to re-evaluate and balance sovereignty in a federation, as well as the need to invest in transboundary resources and infrastructure incentivize greater integration by enabling the building of an economic and political rationale for improved regional prosperity, employment, trade, security, and stability. The EAC's willingness to take up new challenges is a reason for cautious optimism.

2.1 Introduction

In recent decades, increased globalization has resulted in a more interconnected world characterized by intensified international trade, wireless communications, and high mobility of people and products. At a macro level, integration has often materialized through increased regionalization and cooperation between neighbouring states. The integration process in Eastern Africa combines both trends as is demonstrated by our discussion of the history of the East African Community (EAC) from the original EAC-3 (Kenya, Tanzania, and Uganda) to the current EAC-7 and its current outlook. The aim of this chapter is to take stock of these developments from

D. Mmari · J. Msami (✉) · S. Mwombela · J. Mpapalika
REPOA, Development Policy Research Institute in Tanzania, Dar es Salaam, Tanzania
e-mail: jamal@repoa.or.tz

B. A. Demena · P. A. G. van Bergeijk
International Institute of Social Studies (ISS), Erasmus University Rotterdam, The Hague, The Netherlands

B. A. Demena and Peter A. G. Van Bergeijk (eds.), *Trade and Investment in East Africa*, Frontiers in African Business Research, https://doi.org/10.1007/978-981-19-4211-2_2

the perspective of EAC and to identify key challenges to the Community to provide the necessary context to the international economics lens through which the book's other contributions study. Such context is key to understanding the broader analysis of trade and competitiveness in the book, and their corresponding policy prescriptions. This chapter is organized as follows. Section 2.2 discusses the historical roots of the Community, its collapse in 1977, re-establishment in 2000, and consequent enlargements. Section 2.3 provides an overview of the current status demonstrating progress in deepening the EAC's integration processes by means of evaluating the progress of forming the Protocols for the Customs Union, the Internal Market, the Monetary Union and the Political Federation as well as the geography of the EAC's major institutions. Section 2.4 zooms in on the enabling environment: the laws, regulations, procedures, customs, and norms that form the EAC's institutional framework. Having laid the groundwork, Sect. 2.5 identifies the key political, legal, economic, social, and cultural challenges ahead, while Sect. 2.6 pinpoints measures to address these challenges. Section 2.7 concludes.

2.2 A Short History of East African Community Integration

EAC is a regional intergovernmental organization headquartered in Arusha, Tanzania, with the mission of widening and deepening socio-economic, political, and cultural integration to improve the quality of life of the people of East Africa through increased competitiveness, value addition, trade, and investments.

2.2.1 The Defunct East African Community

The Community can be traced back to the late nineteenth century when the Kenya-Uganda railway was constructed between 1897 and 1901 and the establishment of a Postal Union in 1905 along with the Customs Collection Centre in Kenya in 1900. Colonial authorities instituted a Custom Union between Kenya and Uganda in 1917, which Tanzania (then Tanganyika) later joined in 1927; followed by the East African High Commission (EAHC) from 1948 to 1961; and the East African Common Services Organization (EACSO) between 1961 and 1967.

In 1967, a treaty for East African Cooperation was signed by the three founding members including the Republic of Kenya, the United Republic of Tanzania, and the Republic of Uganda establishing the East African Community and the resulting EACSO. Under the Treaty, these founding nations agreed to cooperate on various issues such as trade and investment, infrastructure, agriculture and manufacturing, transport, and communication, with the aim of developing the wider economy. However, over time, the Community collapsed in 1977 barely a decade after its formation for a number of reasons including a lack of leadership, the unfair allocation of benefits, and disagreements with the then Ugandan dictator, Idi Amin, who blamed Tanzania for trying to topple his dictatorial regime and the antagonistic economic paths of capitalist Kenya and socialist Tanzania.

2.2.2 Re-Establishment of the EAC in Context

The Community re-established itself in 2000 when the three founding member states—Kenya, Tanzania, and Uganda—agreed to cooperate on a wide range of socio-economic and political issues. It witnessed its first expansion in 2007 with the accession of the Republics of Rwanda and Burundi, which were later joined by South Sudan and DR Congo in 2016 and 2022, respectively. Noting its strategic position, with an estimated nominal GDP of US$ 240 billion, a population of 265 million, and an area of 4.8 million square kilometres, Sippy (2022) expects that the Community may sustainably improve its socio-economic development. The Community's organizational structure is headed by the Summit of the Heads of State, followed by the Council of Ministers, the Co-ordinating Committee, the Sectoral Committees, the East African Court of Justice, the East African Legislative Assembly, and the Secretariat. All member states adhere to the EAC principles and values as well as share their regional socio-economic development and political views through the Summits. Thereafter, summit views or priorities are submitted by the Council of Ministers as guided by provisions in Article 3 of the EAC Treaty.

Following the Community's collapse in 1977, the member states negotiated a Mediation Agreement that would ensure future cooperation with the common goal of having a united EAC. Subsequent meetings of the then three Heads of State led to the signing of the Agreement for the Establishment of the Permanent Tripartite Commission for East African Co-operation in 1993 that paved the way for the operations of East African Co-operation in March 1996 starting with the Treaty for the Establishment of the EAC which was signed in Arusha, Tanzania, in 1999 and became operational in early 2000. This re-integration process entailed tripartite programs of cooperation in socio-economic, political, and cultural aspects, research, innovation, and technology, defence measures, as well as legal issues.

At the continental level, just like other regional blocs such as the Southern African Development Community (SADC), the Economic Community of West African States (ECOWAS), and the Common Market for Eastern and Southern Africa (COMESA), the EAC is an integral part of the African Economic Community (AEC) that was founded through the Abuja treaty, signed in 1991 by all members of the African Union (AU) and entered into force in 1994 to achieve a single market, common currency, customs union, and free trade areas.[1] East African economies have been growing at an impressive rate, with regional GDP expanding by an estimated 6.6%

---

[1] The newly created Africa Continental Free Trade Area (AfCFTA) acts as a catalyst in deepening the regional integration by developing regional value chains to transform the manufacturing sector.

in 2020. The high growth rate is set to continue, with improvements in agricultural production, buoyant domestic consumption, and infrastructure investment sustaining growth (ECA 2020).

On the political front, there are plans in the pipeline for the EAC to take a more central role in attaining regional security and stability. Moreover, member states' borders are still porous and lack the necessary monitoring technologies, and thus illegal activities such as the smuggling of goods and services continue. Kenyan's borders with Somalia, Sudan, and Ethiopia are areas of insecurity due to the instability in those countries. In addition, Kenyan's maritime waters have been qualified as troubled waters with high risk as the coastal line was marred by pirates in 2009. Likewise, continued political instability in Burundi and the Democratic Republic of Congo pose a significant threat to the bloc's founding principles as well as the welfare of neighbouring countries.

Thus, article 124 of the Community's Treaty prioritizes the necessity of peace and security to foster a thriving environment for integration. The shared vision for a politically united East Africa is commendable and a potential driver for change. Generally, a glimmer of hope for the imminent political union is impractical. From the economic perspective, Tanzania has been concerned about the establishment of a common market that implies the free movement of labour and capital without any restrictions. Interestingly, the free movement of labour may be perceived as a highly desirable step towards greater integration in Uganda and Kenya, but on the contrary, Tanzania deems it as a cost because the country has more land than all other member states other than DR Congo. Agreeing to the common market would lead to foreign exploitation of existing land policies which have encouraged low-cost indigenous ownership and supported the country's Local Content policy that underscores the prioritization of locals in all the ensuing opportunities and resources.

2.3 Progress Made on Deepening the EAC Integration

Progress in implementing the bloc's three protocols for integration, namely a Customs Union, a Common Market, and a Monetary Union process, has been slower than planned. The progress of the various protocols is still faltering. For instance, a protocol for the common market has been in force for a decade ago but still, national implementation is a challenge. As for the customs union, businesses are still experiencing obstacles under all the six Non-Tariff Barriers (NTBs) clusters.[2] Kenya has more Tariff and NTBs than any other member state thus discouraging inter- and intra-regional trade. Another example is the Monetary Union protocol: member states still

---

The objective of the AfCFTA is to create a single continental market in Africa in turn, accelerating the establishment of Africa-wide customs union.

[2] NTBs clusters include Customs procedures, Immigration and work permits, Business registration and licensing, Police roadblocks, Weighbridge stations, and Quality standards and export certification (EABC 2007).

have inconclusive views on harmonizing financial sector policies, systems, practices, and standards and establishing a united East African reserve bank. On all these issues efforts need to be stepped up.

Deliberate efforts should, however, first and foremost be geared towards strengthening the customs union, with an emphasis on the removal of NTBs while at the same time member states should be pressured to create a conducive environment for the effective implementation of the common market and the customs union. Priority should be given to strengthening regional industrial growth and infrastructure development to improve the transport network. This, in turn, will stimulate the development of the customs union and the common market. Such measures will further integrate the EAC member countries to promote their exports and raise the export earnings.

2.3.1 Customs Union Protocol

The customs union (a free trade area with zero duty on goods and services) was the first pillar of integration which started operating in 2005. The EAC summit signed the protocol for introducing the customs union in 2004 as defined in Article 75 of the EAC Treaty that entails the gradual removal of import duties on goods among member states and agreed on a common external tariff (CET) within the bloc (imports from outside the bloc are subjected to the same tariff when sold to any other EAC member state). NTBs are still a challenge and further efforts are being considered to deal with NTBs. However, goods moving freely within the EAC must comply with the EAC Rules of Origin and with certain provisions of the EAC Protocol.

Sectors under the customs union include Agriculture (emphasis is on the harmonization of the sector's policies and the execution of joint programs for efficient and effective production); Customs (the establishment of a single custom territory); Health (the sector's aim is to consider joint action towards the prevention and control of communicable and non-communicable diseases and to control pandemics and epidemics, with the current public health concern being the COVID-19 pandemic); Immigration and Labour (the promotion of free movement of people and labour without restrictions through the adoption of common policies and procedures); industrialization and entrepreneurial development (aim to foster competitiveness of the manufacturing sector to encourage domestic industries and Micro, Small, and Medium-scale Enterprises (MSMEs)); Infrastructure (the coordination and harmonization of transport and communications policies); Tourism and wildlife management (a single-tourist destination while sustainably conserving wildlife and other tourist sites); and Trade (the harmonization of trade policies, investment incentives, and product standards aiming at achieving a single investment area).

Major ongoing initiatives under the customs union are the single customs territory (particularly the operationalization of One-Stop Border Posts—supported by Trade-Mark East Africa), African Growth Opportunity Act (AGOA), the COMESA-EAC-SADC Tripartite, the EAC-EU Economic Partnership Agreement, EU Everything But Arms (EBA), and harmonization of tariffs with the newly established AfCFTA.

2.3.2   Common Market Protocol

The common market is the second regional pillar of integration after the Customs Union. Its protocol was operationalized in 2010 following ratification by all the then five EAC member states. However, its national implementation is still faltering in terms of the free movement of goods and services, persons, factors of production—labour and capital, right of residence, and establishment. In essence, cross-border trade within the bloc is still weak and dominated by Kenya. Geographical conditions also hinder the exchange of goods because of poorly developed regional infrastructure to smoothly transport goods.

Several sectors are under the Common market, namely agriculture, culture, customs, education, science and technology, energy, environment, and natural resources, gender-based issues, health, immigration of persons, industrialization, infrastructure, and investment, peace, and security as well as trade.[3]

2.3.3   Monetary Union Protocol

This Protocol was signed in 2013 and entails the attainment of a single currency for daily transactions within the Common Market. As part of having a single currency, the EAC Partner States aim to harmonize monetary and fiscal policies; financial accounting and reporting practices as well as policies and standards on statistical information; and envision the setting up of a united reserve bank for the region. Currently, three sectors fit under the Monetary Union: the financial sector, investment promotion, and private-sector development (creating an enabling business environment for the private sector and enhancing investor sentiment in the region that will ultimately result in improving the member states credit ratings) and trade (harmonization of trade policies and the promotion of a single investment area).

---

[3] The African Growth Opportunity Act (AGOA) and the EU Everything But Arms (EBA) fit under this protocol.

2.3.4 Political Federation Protocol

The EAC member states envisage a supranational governing entity under a single political authority or government provided for under Article 5(2) of the EAC Treaty. This protocol is founded on common foreign and security policies and good governance. In 2004, the EAC Heads of State agreed to deepen and accelerate political unity among member states. In response, they set up a Committee to Fast-Track the EAC Political Federation, coined as the *"Wako Committee"*, to consult stakeholders using a participatory approach. Since 2004, the EAC has been putting in place initiatives to fast-track political integration leading to the EAC Heads of State adoption of the political confederation as a transitional model of the East African Political Federation in 2017. It is apparent that the strengthening of political unity indirectly creates a conducive environment for socio-economic development.

2.3.5 EAC Institutions

All member states host one of the EAC's institutions except the newest members of the Community—South Sudan and DR Congo.

a. **Tanzania**

Tanzania is one of the three founding members of the Community that joined in 2000 and hosts the EAC Headquarters constituting the EAC Secretariat[4] situated in Arusha. The country also hosts the temporary seat of the East African Legislative Assembly (EALA)—the legislative Organ of the Community, the East African Court of Justice (EACJ)—the judicial Organ of the Community and the East African Kiswahili Commission (EAKC)

b. **Uganda**

Uganda is another founding member that joined the Community in 2000 and hosts the East African Development Bank (EADB) mandated to promote sustainable socio-economic development in the region by providing development finance, support, and advisory services; the Civil Aviation Safety and Security Oversight Agency (CASSOA) that aims at making air transport services safe, efficient, and profitable through the adoption of common policies for the development of civil air transport in the region; and the Inter-University Council for East Africa (IUCEA) that coordinates inter-university cooperation in East Africa.

---

[4] EAC Secretariat is the executive body of the community that houses 6 offices, namely The Executive Office of the Secretary-General, Customs and Trade, Planning and Infrastructure, Productive and Social sectors, Co-operation in political matters, as well as the Finance and Administration.

c. **Burundi**

The country joined the Community later in 2007 and hosts the East African Health Research Commission (EAHRC), a research institution mandated to coordinate and promote public health research aiming at enhancing the quality-service delivery and well-being of the people in the sub-region of the continent.

d. **Rwanda**

The country joined the Community at the same time as Burundi in July 2007 and hosts the East African Science and Technology Commission (EASTC). EASTC promotes the use of science-based innovations and technologies among member states.

e. **Kenya**

As for the case of Tanzania and Uganda, Kenya is also a founding member of the Community that joined in 2000 and hosts the Lake Victoria Basin Commission (LVBC) and the Lake Victoria Fisheries Organization (LVFO); both institutions of the EAC are mandated with coordinating sustainable development in the Lake Victoria Basin and its surroundings.

f. **South Sudan and DR Congo**

South Sudan joined the Community in April 2016 and has not yet been assigned additional commitments and the same is true for the **newest**, most populous, and largest member of the bloc, DR Congo that joined in March 2022 (four years after it first applied). The EAC started the process of reviewing its founding treaty for a more equitable distribution of roles and responsibilities among members.

2.4   Enabling Environment

2.4.1   Governance Institutions

The EAC's institutional framework comprises laws, regulations, and procedures, customs, and norms that guide the pursuit of the Community's aims and objectives (EALA 2014; Kaahwa 2017). As per the EAC Treaty and its Protocols, the bloc's institutional framework is divided into the Executive, Legislative, and Judicial components. The executive branch of the EAC includes the Summit of Heads of State; the Council of Ministers; the Coordination Committee; the Sectoral Committees; and the Secretariat, and other designated EAC Institutions. Legislative institutions of the EAC include the East African Legislative Assembly (EALA), and the East African Court of Justice (EACJ), which provides judicial oversight for the EAC. The Summit is responsible for policy guidance and spearheading of policy development and achievement of the EAC. The Council of Ministers is the policy organ of the EAC and is responsible for the general implementation of the Community's programs, projects, and activities. These apex authorities are supported by a number of sector-specific organizations responsible for policy setting and oversight across the region.[5] As per the EAC treaty, the EAC Secretariat is the designated body for the development and implementation of the bloc's trade policies. In addition to trade, the Secretariat is also responsible for customs, planning, and infrastructure, productive social sectors, and political cooperation (EAC 2017). However, the EAC has not yet established many of the formal institutions required for policy implementation (EAC 2017, 2021a; Mathieson 2016).

In addition to shortages or complete lack thereof of implementing regional agencies, the EAC also faces challenges in enforcing partner states' compliance with regional policies due to institutional weaknesses and limited jurisdiction of the EACJ (Apiko 2017; EAC 2021a). The authority of the EACJ is often circumscribed by the primacy of national courts which have limited its effectiveness.[6] Despite multiple violations of the founding Treaty by the members, no EAC country has to date been sanctioned. The absence as well as weaknesses of existing EAC institutions have de facto delegated implementation responsibilities to partner states. The latter primarily engage at the EAC level through line ministries, the bulk of which lack key expertise and resources on the core issues of focus for the EAC and are prone to nationalist influences. Consequently, the governance of the EAC has generally been characterized by institutional impasses as partner states' contest policy and legislation which have been met with weak mediation at the regional level. Weaknesses in the bloc's key institutions of governance undermined integration as overly generous allowances have been made for partner states—for example, the 8-year-long delay by Tanzania in ratifying the EAC's Sanitary and Phytosanitary Protocol (SPS) or the 10-year failure to ratify amendments to Article 24(2) of the Customs Union Protocol that has stifled the resolution of the region's NTBs—at the expense of a collective bloc trade and other policy priorities.

2.4.2 Legal and Regulatory Framework

The EAC legal framework consists of the Treaty and protocols agreed upon by the Partner States to enhance their cooperation. In principle, each protocol spells

---

[5] These include the: East African Science and Technology Commission (EASTECO) responsible for promotion, development, management, and application of Science and Technology; Lake Victoria Fisheries Organization (LVFO), responsible for the development and adoption of conservation and management measures including in fisheries and aquaculture resources of the EAC; Lake Victoria Basin Commission (LVBC), responsible for sustainable development and management of the Lake Victoria Basin; Civil Aviation Safety and Security Oversight Agency (CASSOA); Inter-University Council for East Africa (IUCEA) for collaboration and harmonization of standards in higher education; East African Kiswahili Commission (EAKC) for promotion of a common language; East African Parliamentary Institute (EAPI); East African Development Bank (EADB); East African Human Rights Council (EAHRC); and the East African Community Competition Authority (EACCA) tasked with regulation of trade practices in the region.

[6] As of March 2022, the court has issued 79 judgements, 50 other rulings, 20 taxation rulings, and two advisory opinions (EACJ 2022).

out its objectives, scope, and any institutional framework needed for cooperation and integration as articulated in Article 151 of the EAC Treaty. So far, most of the protocols have been ratified and are implemented. Most importantly, it is underscored that country-specific legal variations should be considered to single out instruments that will harmonize laws and in addition, the areas that need harmonization should be highlighted to ease the process. In practice, it was suggested the focus should be on the mobility of factors of production to further EAC Common market, constitutional laws to deepen integration, rule of law as a cornerstone for the law-based integration process, and a strong political will concerning the integration process. Harmonization of all the national laws in EAC is a requirement of the EAC Treaty under Article 126(2)(b) (Doveling et al. 2018). On the other hand, five of the six[7] Partner States have initiated regulatory reform programs, although the individual members' speed and success of implementation vary. It is widely believed that the cost of doing business is relatively high in the EAC largely due to poor regulatory practices and weak enforcement capabilities (see also Chap. 6 of this volume).

2.4.3 Policy Space

In a bid to attain the Community's objective of deepening the integration pursuant to Article 5 of the Treaty, the members should attempt to coordinate and harmonize different policies on various issues of mutual interest to the Community such as labour policies, culture and traditions, monetary policies, transport and communications policies, research and technology, defence, security, and legal and judicial affairs.

2.5 Challenges in the EAC

As already alluded to before, challenges within the EAC have existed for a long time. Of course, after the original East African Community was established by the Treaty for East African Co-operation in 1967, it lasted 10 years before it dissolved in 1977. This was due to many factors including (but not limited to) demands by Kenya for more seats than Uganda and Tanzania in decision-making organs (Petersen and Bech 2005), disagreements with Ugandan dictator Idi Amin who demanded that Tanzania as a member state of the EAC should not harbour forces fighting to topple the government of another member state, and the disparate economic systems of socialism in Tanzania and capitalism in Kenya (McLaughlin 2006). According to the report by the team of experts on addressing the fears, concerns, and challenges of the East African Federation (EAC 2011; EAC and Kaahwa 2003), they can be classified into three thematic areas: political and legal; economic; and socio-cultural; while

---

[7] Excludes DR Congo which formally joined the bloc in March 2022.

at the same time they identified cross-cutting issues that are recurrent and underpin successful implementation of EAC regional integration.

2.5.1 Political and Legal Challenges

Challenges related to political and legal issues are linked with the fear of losing national sovereignty and its associated political economy (Mathieson 2016; Verhaeghe and Mathieson 2017). The ultimate goal of EAC integration remains the attainment of a political federation that will see the establishment of a new supra-national governing entity. The anticipated loss of political and legislative powers associated with this goal continues to create constituencies within and across partner states both in favour and against the ceding of sovereignty. Since the partner states have acquired an international legal identity as independent sovereign states, federating would entail ceding or sharing sovereignty. This is potentially problematic because each sovereign state has its own doctrines, policies, and priorities. If partner states cease to be subjects of international law, challenges will arise out of the Vienna Convention of State Succession to Treaties and the Vienna Convention to Succession of Debts, State Property and Archives (EAC 2011). Further, the consequences of creating a political federation will place an added dimension to the balance of political power in individual partner states as political representation and marrying of federal policy objectives with national priorities will affect the status quo governing the distribution of political rents and other resources.

Other political and legal challenges facing the EAC include disparities in the governance of partner states, particularly in national constitutions and practices of democracy and good governance, also, the lack of uniformity in doctrine, discipline, and accountability, and the fear of replication and spillover of bad national practices. The process is not truly people-centred; people are not adequately informed, nor do they play an active role in making major decisions that affect their livelihoods. The federation and integration agenda is driven by the political leadership and external forces. Citizens feel left out of the integration process, particularly their representation and participation in regional decision-making institutions such as the EALA. Additionally, most of the EAC decisions are not fully implemented, and the current decision-making structure is too costly and inefficient because of the limited mandate of EAC institutions.

Partner states lack policy cohesion, particularly regarding foreign, defence, and security policies. The Customs Union and Common Market require a common external trade policy. Besides the issue of policy cohesion, there is no clarity on the model of federation that East Africa will adopt. There are also unique challenges facing some partner states, such as internal tensions and conflicts like the power struggle in South Sudan, internal strife in Uganda, tensions in the union between Tanzania Mainland and Tanzania Zanzibar, and ethnic tensions in Kenya, Burundi, Uganda, and Rwanda. The fear is that some of these internal conflicts may spill over to other partner states.

2.5.2 Economic Challenges

Economic challenges are largely centred on economic imbalances, where weaker economies in the region feel they will be dominated by stronger economies. Unequal distribution of costs and benefits is one of the major factors that tends to undermine efforts by federal arrangements to produce stability and prosperity. Likewise, people of East Africa fear the domination of the East African labour market by more skilled and qualified labour endowments in some of the partner states to the disadvantage of nationals of the less labour-endowed partner states.

The issue of loss of land and disparities in land tenure systems is also challenging. Partner states have different land policies and laws, and land management systems. There is skewed land ownership and a prevalence of disputes aggravated by population density and resource constraints for land use planning, survey, and demarcation in the partner states. There is also the concern of sustainable exploitation of natural resources which is linked to environmentally sustainable development. Moreover, there is fear of increased costs as well as the distribution of benefits from integration. The concern is that a political federation will lead to increased taxation, and disproportional sharing of the financial burden and benefits between the states. Concerns about the economic costs and benefits of the EAC are further compounded by a limited understanding of the bloc by its own citizens (see, for example, Knowles 2014). Information symmetry of this scale not only affects the popular legitimacy of the EAC but also creates room for the distortionary application of common rules—for example, through the imposition of arbitrary bottlenecks in trade facilitation and rent seeking—further undermining the pursuit of the bloc's economic goals.

Information asymmetry is also partially responsible for the failure of partner states to fully institutionalize key aspects governing the bloc's economic relations including those related to budgeting and the financing of the bloc's operations (Mathieson 2016). Asymmetry has promoted popular indifference to the EAC (Balongo 2015; Katera 2008) constraining the accountability of partner states to commitments under the EAC treaty (Anami 2022; Shaban 2020). Due to late and occasionally unpaid member contributions, the EAC continues to face budget constraints, placing an undue dependence on its external development partners who currently support 41% of its budget (Anami 2022). Donor dependency on this scale undermines meaningful integration and heightens the bloc's vulnerability to influence from external actors.

The Customs Union is faced with several operational problems that need to be addressed including the derogation from the EAC common external tariff (EAC CET); dual membership in other RECs; non-tariff and technical barriers to trade (NTBs and TBTs); inadequate physical infrastructure; weak private sector participation; and extra-region export volatility. Other challenges are the management of the integration process towards a federation and the need for mechanisms to address liabilities contracted by the partner states before the federation. The challenges with benefits and costs of a federation arrangement will have two basic financial implications, namely administrative costs and adjustment costs.

2.5.3 Social and Cultural Challenges

Social and cultural challenges are diverse. One is the loss of gains already attained at the national level regarding affirmative action for marginalized groups. Partner states have different policies on affirmative action, some more advanced than others. The issue of regional social and cultural cohesion is also important for successful integration—diversity in unity. Cultures, traditions, and norms are part and parcel of what East Africans count as heritage, some value systems may dominate or dilute others, and social and cultural lives are not homogenous. Another issue of concern is that women may have a diminished voice and influence at the EAC level due to fewer women being involved in the decision-making at the partner state level, and there is inadequate gender-sensitive legislation in some partner states. There are some laws and actions that are perceived as contrary to the spirit of integration such as isolated cases of expulsions of persons from some partner states. Border communities and others crossing borders are concerned that the way they are treated is not consistent with the spirit of integration.

Priority given to health programs and services in the region means that some partner states have comprehensive health and social insurance schemes while others do not. These disparities are a concern for integration. The free movement of people increases the risk of the spread of epidemics and other infectious diseases. The difference in education curriculum and training systems, as well as variations in academic or professional training among partner states, is another issue of concern.

Often overlooked is that conditions on the ground rooted in historical and cultural differences may strongly impact the ease of integration. A clear example is a differentiated access to identification documents which are machine-readable. This is an important impediment to integration. The identification can be used for intra-East Africa free movement of people, but while some partner states are up to this standard, some partner states do not have a widespread use of identification documents while others do, but not in machine-readable format.

2.6 Measures to Address Challenges in the EAC Integration

2.6.1 Measures to Address Political and Legal Challenges

To address the issue of loss of sovereignty, the people of East Africa should be sensitized to appreciate how a political federation involves ceding some sovereignty and that benefits should be highlighted and disseminated. The EAC should implement fully the stages of integration preceding the political federation to realize tangible benefits to build confidence in the federation. As a transitional measure, before the establishment of the political federation and to enable the gradual ceding of sovereignty to the regional level, some more powers of exclusive competence should be given to the Secretariat, for example, in external trade and investment. Partner states should be prepared to cede their international legal status to federate.

To address disparities in governance, EAC partner states should expedite the conclusion of the Protocol on Good Governance and establish a strong implementation mechanism. The EAC secretariat should become a Commission that would spearhead the federal institutions. Such a Commission needs to have strict accountability measures and work on a performance contract basis to avoid further loss of confidence of citizens. Furthermore, partner states should harmonize their constitutions to ensure the existence of presidential term limits, and harmonize the length of the presidential term, electoral cycles, and electoral processes management.

There's also a need to empower the EACJ to be a strong regional institution that should guarantee compliance to all agreed regional standards on good governance including extending the jurisdiction to cover human rights. Moreover, it is essential to develop regional monitoring and evaluation mechanisms on issues of constitutionalism and good governance, for example, an EAC peer-review mechanism. Finally, beyond economic arguments, it is important to identify specific imperatives that will drive the political integration process. These should be popularized, debated, and owned by the citizenry of East Africa. It is only then that the political federation will be seen as a strategic necessity. EALA members should be directly elected by the people. Partner states should amend the treaty to strengthen the accountability of the Council to EALA.

In addressing issues of policy cohesion and a clear model of the federation, partner states must negotiate the Treaty for the establishment of the EAPF based on concrete principles and also clearly define the model of the EAPF. There's a need to expedite the harmonization of the partner states' foreign, security, and defence policies and practices, and expedite the conclusion of the Conflict Prevention, Management and Resolution (CPMR) and implementation of the Conflict Early Warning Mechanism. Partner states should also solve national conflicts in a way that does not undermine the EAC integration process by avoiding ethnic constituencies, and international best practices in conflict resolution should be recognized at the regional level.

2.6.2 Measures to Address Economic Challenges

To address the existing economic challenges it is imperative to expedite the finalization of the EAC Study on Equitable Sharing of Costs and Benefits of the East Africa Integration and the EAC Industrialization and Investment Promotion Strategy to inform decision-makers on how best to address this challenge and institute an appropriate mechanism. Federal institutions should be designed on the basis of cost-effectiveness, efficiency, and sustainability; in the short- and medium terms, the EAC partner states should effectively implement the fundamental stages of integration, grounded on the adoption of policies and strategies focusing on the primacy of accelerated economic growth and sustainable development; in line with their obligations, under Article 8 (4) and (5), the partner states should align their relevant national policies with regional priorities within the regional policy frameworks; and lastly partner states need to meet their financial commitments necessary for the functioning of the Secretariat and other Community institutions so that financial sustainability is established a-priori.

Additionally, there is a need to expedite the establishment of the EAC Development Fund, devise concrete alternative mechanisms for financing EAC projects and programs, and effectively implement the EAC Customs Union and the Common Market Protocols by putting in place a robust enforcement and evaluation mechanism for assessing if the benefits of integration are trickling down to weaker economies demonstrated by accelerated economic growth and development. Lastly, the Summit should set a deadline within which partner states should streamline their national laws and policies to conform to the Common Market Protocol.

To tackle the fear of domination by more skilled and qualified labour endowment in some of the partner states to the disadvantage of nationals of the less labour-endowed partner states—in the short to the medium term; the fear of loss of employment must be addressed through the following immediate deliberate measures: facilitating nationals of partner states who are skillful in Kiswahili, English, and French to take up teaching positions respectively in Partner States; and developing specific programs for unskilled labour and MSMEs, in particular also to develop an EAC-wide Strategy for Skills and Competitiveness Development to enhance productivity through vocational training, science and technology; and expedite the harmonization of curricula and certification across the region.

For addressing the issue of loss of land and disparities in land tenure systems, it is vital to maintain national jurisdictions regarding the use and distribution of land. Partner states should survey land to provide basic instruments that provide security of tenure to the people and, likewise, partner states must work towards equitable distribution of land within their own countries, and partner states must also initiate actions towards harmonization of land policies and laws, and work towards eventual convergence. Finally, partner states must initiate socio-economic transformation programs in order to be able to reduce the necessary subsistence use of land. To address concerns of sustainable exploitation of natural resources which is linked to environmentally sustainable development, there is a need to strengthen the Lake Victoria Basin Commission (LVBC) as an oversight agency of the Community in respect of the sustainable utilization of the resources of Lake Victoria basin and other water bodies.

To address the fear of increased costs or sharing of benefits of integration; where the concern is that a political federation will lead to increased taxation, disproportional sharing of the financial burden and benefits between the states, as well as donor dependency—partner states must be willing to design institutions that will address cost-effectiveness, efficiency, and sustainability for accelerated economic growth and sustainable development. In line with partner states' obligations, under Article 8 (4) and (5), they should align their relevant national policies with regional priorities within the regional policy frameworks; and the Summit should agree on sustainable financing arrangements for the EAC by examining the options of either introducing an integration tax, or contribution, based on the ability to pay which, in essence, shifts the burden of financing the Community to a few partner states.

In order to address Customs Union challenges, there is a need for partner states to strengthen the customs administration institutional framework; resolve existing derogations by finalizing the CET review and addressing infrastructural constraints; expedite the COMESA-EAC-SADC Tripartite FTA negotiations; review the role of the East African Business Council vis-a-vis its linkage with national sectoral private sector organizations; and expedite the finalization and implementation of the EAC Industrialization Strategy and Export Promotion, and the Agricultural and Rural Development Strategy as a matter of priority for the region.

Similarly, to address the challenge of the management of the integration process towards a federation, it is important to have the effective implementation of the fundamental stages of the EAC integration (Customs Union, Common Market) bolstered by an Economic Union for sectoral policy harmonization and convergence; an East African Customs Authority for the Customs Union, managed by competent executive and professional staff; an East African Common Market Commission for the Common Market with adequate powers for monitoring and enforcement; an East African Economic Union Commission managed by political heads; an East African Monetary Authority, leading to an East African Central Bank for the Monetary Union; and a unified Federal Treasury for the Federation.

Correspondingly, to address the need for mechanisms for addressing liabilities contracted by the partner states before the federation, the EAC Secretariat is required to source and obtain a list of multilateral, regional, and bilateral commitments of all partner states, and refer and subject them to the East African Monetary Union Negotiations process.

2.6.3   Measures to Address Social and Cultural Challenges

To address the lack of identification documents, partner states with no identification documents should be given help by states with successful ID programs so that all partner states have machine-readable identification documents. An EAC passport should be used for international travel, and a roadmap for that should be designed and implemented. Moreover, marginalized and vulnerable groups should be entrenched in a federal constitution of the EAC and represented in all EAC institutions. The federal constitution should recognize the positive cultures and traditions among the partner states, and the move towards a united entity should also be grounded in the education curriculum in schools and in socialization and sensitization programs. Partner states should promote and encourage Kiswahili as the lingua franca, and they should institute EAC cultural competitions to enhance "East Africaness".

To address the issue of women having a diminished voice and influence, there's a need to strengthen the Treaty provision on enhancing gender equality and equity; borrow the best practices from some partner states; expedite implementation of the EAC policy and strategy on gender; and outlaw traditional and cultural practices that infringe on the rights of women for equal treatment. With regard to addressing laws and actions that are perceived as contrary to the spirit of integration, Conflict Prevention Management Resolution should also include building the capacity of partner states to manage conflict. There's a need to develop joint programs for border regions and communities to give them a chance to reap the benefits of integration.

Partner states should expedite reviewing and harmonizing their national social security policies, laws, and systems. Examples include, the need to accelerate the adoption and implementation of such protocols as the East African Integrated Disease Surveillance (EAIDS). As for addressing differences in education curriculum and training systems, as well as variations of academic or professional among partner states, they must expedite the process of harmonizing education curricula and establish a professional accreditation system in the region.

2.7 Conclusions

This chapter has historically examined the EAC integration agenda through a political economy framework. Analysis has revealed that regional integration has largely followed an economic agenda and been driven by trade and related institutional reforms. The EAC continues to be the most integrated of Africa's nine regional economic communities, having already attained a customs union, and is on course towards establishing a common market, monetary union, and a political federation. The bloc's shared history, customs, geography, and concerns about the loss of sovereignty as well as transboundary resources have both incentivized and disincentivized the evolution of the EAC. These key attributes have incentivized greater integration by enabling the building of an economic and political rationale for improved regional prosperity, employment, trade, security, and stability. However, the shared traits have also informed constituencies in the partner states as opposed to integration on account of the potential losses of sovereignty. The political management of these forces has proved challenging to partner states, many of which have failed to effectively communicate the regional integration agenda to their citizens, creating an information asymmetry. The effect of the asymmetry has been two-fold. Firstly, there has been a generalized fear and reluctance among citizens of some partner states towards integration, which has provided Governments with a pretext for delayed or non-compliance aspects of the EAC Treaty. Secondly, asymmetry has fostered local apathy towards the EAC, and abdicated decision-making to line ministries. As a result, national-level decision-making has been less inclusive, and more dependent on the political expediency of line ministers. A corollary has been a weak institutionalization of the EAC through resource scarcities that have impacted the implementation of the Treaty.

Notwithstanding these challenges, the EAC has witnessed an unprecedented expansion of regional trade in recent years (EAC 2021b),[8] and increased focus by other regional trading blocs seeking to emulate its success. The improved intra-regional trade and recent admission of the chaotic but $54.8 billion-strong DR Congo market are likely to further add to the political and economic rationale for the realization of the EAC Treaty. However, the extent to which the EAC successfully harnesses these emerging opportunities will remain conditioned on the resolution of existing historically grown institutional bottlenecks discussed above.

References

Anami L (2022) EAC in crisis once again as funding model splits partner states. The East African. https://www.theeastafrican.co.ke/tea/news/east-africa/eac-in-crisis-once-again-fun ding-model-splits-partner-states-3761164. Accessed 28 March 2022

Apiko P (2017) Understanding the East Court of Justice: the hard road to independent institutions and human rights jurisdiction. European Centre for Development Policy Management (ECDPM), Maastricht, Netherlands

Balongo S (2015) Support for the formation of a federation of East African states: citizens' atti-tudes in Kenya and Tanzania. Afrobarometer (Afrobarometer policy paper no 16). https://afroba rometer.org/sites/default/files/publications/Policy%20paper/ab_policypaperno16.pdf. Accessed 30 September 2021

Doveling J, Majamba H, Oppong R, Wanitzek U (2018) Harmonization of laws in the East African Community. Law Africa Publishing Ltd., Nairobi

EABC (2007) East African Community 2006/07 business climate index survey. East Africa Business Council (EABC)

EAC (2011) Report of the team of experts on addressing the fears, concerns and challenges of the East African Federation. East African Community (EAC)

EAC (2017) EAC development strategy (2016/17 – 2020/21). East African Community, Arusha, Tanzania

EAC (2021a) Sixth EAC development strategy, 2021a/22 - 2025/26. Secretariat of the East African Community, Arusha, Tanzania

EAC (2021b) East African Community trade and investment report 2020. East African Community Secretariat, Arusha, Tanzania

EAC and Kaahwa WTK (2003) EAC treaty and challenges to the community. East African Community Secretariat, Arusha, Tanzania, occasional paper no 3

EACJ (2022) Recent decisions. East African Court of Justice (EACJ). https://www.eacj.org/? page_id=2298. Accessed 30 March 2022

EALA (2014) Report of the committee on legal, rules and priviledges on the assessment of adherence to good governance in the EAC and the status of the EAC political federation.Clerk's Chambers, Kampala, Uganda

ECA (2020) Macroeconomic and social developments in Eastern Africa 2020: benchmarking perfor-mance towards national, regional, and international goals. Office for Eastern Africa, Kigali, Rwanda

Kaahwa W (2017) The institutional framework of the EAC: East African Community Law. Brill, Uganda

---

[8] From $4.8bil in 2016 to a pre-COVID-outbreak high of $6.3bil in 2019 and a pandemic affected high of $5.9bil in 2020 (see EAC 2021b).

Katera L (2008) East African Federation: Tanzanians favour economic integration but wary of stronger political links. Afrobarometer (Afrobarometer briefing paper no 54). https://afroba rometer.org/sites/default/files/publications/Briefing%20paper/AfrobriefNo54.pdf. Accessed 30 September 2021

Knowles J (2014) East African Federation: Tanzanian awareness of economic and political integration remains poor, but there is growing support for political links. Afrobarometer (Afrobarometer briefing paper no 146). https://afrobarometer.org/sites/default/files/publications/Briefing%20paper/afrobriefno146.pdf. Accessed 30 September 2021

Mathieson C (2016) The political economy of regional integration in Africa: The East African Community (EAC). European Centre for Development Policy Management (ECDPM), Maastricht, Netherlands

McLaughlin A (2006) East Africa trade zone off to a creaky start. The Christian Science Monitor, Boston, US, March 9

Petersen TL, Bech M (2005) East Africa: born in anonymity. The Arusha Times. https://allafrica.com/stories/200505230643.html. Accessed 28 November 2021

Shaban ARA (2020) Burundi, South Sudan risk expulsion from East Africa bloc. Africa News. https://www.africanews.com/2020/07/07/au-sanctions-south-sudan-for-non-payment-of-over-9m-dues//#:~:text=EAC%20members%20are%20supposed%20to,South%20Sudan%20owes%20%2410%20million. Accessed 30 September 2021

Sippy P (2022) The Democratic Republic of Congo becomes the biggest country in East Africa's trading bloc. Quartz Media, Inc., Quartz Africa. https://qz.com/africa/2147718/the-drc-is-now-officially-part-of-the-east-africa-Community/. Accessed 29 March 2022

Verhaeghe E, Mathieson C (2017) Understanding the East African Community and its transport agenda: informal adaptation in regional trade and transport cooperation. European Centre for Development Policy Management (ECDPM), Maastricht, Netherlands

Chapter 3
Preferential Market Access, Foreign Aid, and Economic Development. A Case of the EU-ACP Preferential Trade Agreement

Sylvanus Kwaku Afesorgbor

Abstract Several studies highlight that exporters in developing countries (LDCs) face substantial trade costs when exporting to developed countries (DCs). Thus, granting preferential market access to LDCs by DCs is expected to play a pivotal role, especially in reducing trade costs and ultimately promoting development in LDCs. Focusing on the EU-African, Caribbean and Pacific (ACP) preferential market access, we use the gravity model to examine the trade effect of EU-ACP agreement conditional on foreign aid. Our results show that EU-ACP is effective in promoting exports; however, only improves economic development if it is complemented with a sufficient level of foreign aid.

3.1 Introduction

Many developing countries in African, Caribbean, and Pacific (ACP) regions depend largely on the European markets to sell their products abroad. Their dependence on the European market is informed by two main reasons. First, intra-regional trade flows among these countries are low and thus, their market access is mostly targeted abroad. For example, intra-regional Africa flow remains low and about 15% (see, e.g., Afesorgbor 2017; Ngepah and Udeagha 2018). Intra-regional trade is low mostly because the structure of supply is similar and the value-added in most primary commodities is low (Afesorgbor and van Bergeijk 2014). Second, the European Union (EU) has also provided duty-free and quota-free market access for almost all products emanating from the ACP countries. This therefore makes producers in the ACP regions more competitive in the European market.

S. K. Afesorgbor (✉)
Department of Food, Agricultural and Resource Economics, University of Guelph, 50 Stone Road E., Guelph, ON N1G 2W1, Canada
e-mail: safesorg@uoguelph.ca

International Associate, Environment and Natural Resource Research Initiative (ENRRI-EfD Ghana), Accra, Ghana

© The Author(s), under exclusive license to Springer Nature Singapore Pte Ltd. 2022
B. A. Demena and Peter A. G. Van Bergeijk (eds.), *Trade and Investment in East Africa*, Frontiers in African Business Research, https://doi.org/10.1007/978-981-19-4211-2_3

The EU-ACP agreement involves more than just market access as it captured EU's total commitment to its development and foreign aid policies towards the ACP groups of countries (Dearden and Mira Salama 2002). According to Dearden and Mira Salama, the intention of the EU was to move away from the non-reciprocal free trade agreement (FTA) of the Lomé Convention to rather a reciprocal FTA under the Cotonou Agreement with emphasis on good governance, strong institutions and allocation of foreign aid to enable the ACP countries utilize the market access opportunities provided by the EU. Within the EU—ACP program, the ACP countries received a larger share of EU aid compared to other regions such as Asia, Latin America, and the Mediterranean (Dearden and Mira Salama 2002). The combined market access and foreign aid received by the ACP countries was expected to spur higher economic growth and development in the ACP group of countries.

Myriad channels have been identified through which market access can promote economic development in LDCs. Collier and Venables (2007) emphasize two main channels; transfer of rent through import tariff not received by DCs and export supply response through job-creating opportunities for exporting firms in LDCs. Acemoglu et al. (2005) emphasize that greater market access may facilitate economic development through the adoption of DCs' institutions. At the firm level, various channels have been identified through which foreign market access can affect economic development. For instance, exporting firms' productivity is enhanced through learning by exporting and higher wages for employees working in exporting firms. To this end, preferential market access remains a viable and relevant trade policy tool to improve market access for LDCs.

However, granting preferential market access may be necessary but not a sufficient condition to promote economic development in the case of LDCs. Stiglitz and Charlton (2005) emphasize that unless complementary policies geared towards minimizing the structural constraints that are endemic in LDCs, market access would create opportunities but not effectively produce development. These constraints mostly undermine the supply capacity of the LDCs and they include, for example, technological backwardness, high transport costs, poor infrastructure, and weak government institutions.

To this end, foreign aid taking the forms of development and technical assistance may play a pivotal role, especially in reducing the supply-side constraints that most LDCs face. It is expected that the use of foreign aid targeted at trading activities to support trade-related or economic infrastructures would minimize some of the structural bottlenecks endemic in the ACP countries. Reducing these supply-side constraints should translate to lower trade costs for LDCs' exporters as Hoekman and Nicita (2011) emphasize that the behind-the-border trade barriers, which take the forms of poor infrastructure and high transports costs constitute a substantial disincentive for LDC exports to DCs.

Focusing on supply-side constraints, Silva and Nelson (2012) argue that foreign aid used in the provision of trade-related projects and trade-supportive infrastructures would improve allocative efficiency and production capacity to enhance trade and development. For instance, aid-funded projects could help reduce the procedural and regulatory trade obstacles that exporters faced in exporting to advanced foreign markets. Alternatively, the aid funds can directly be used to enhance the capacity of producers or farmers to tailor their products to the high-quality standards of more advanced countries. Conversely, another strand of literature argues that foreign aid may cause the Dutch disease and price distortions that are inimical to the export competitiveness of aid-receiving countries (Rajan and Subramanian 2011).

To test the role of market access with or without complementary policies, we use the European Union (EU) preferential market access granted to ACP countries. Exemplified in the EU—ACP preferential trade agreement (PTAs) is the granting of non-reciprocal preferential market access in addition to complementary policies, wholly targeted at reducing the supply-side constraints. In one instance, the complementary policy involves the provision of development and technical assistance through the European Development Fund (EDF). This EDF was established solely for the purpose of providing funding and support for trading activities in the ACP preference-beneficiary countries. In addition, various members of the EU provide aid for infrastructural activities in the ACP states. In this sense, foreign aid would complement market access by reducing the supply-side constraints to help preference-receiving countries utilize their market access opportunity more effectively.

In the second instance, the EU-ACP framework extends beyond just creating market access as it incorporates mechanisms targeted at promoting industrialization, food security and self-sufficiency, diversification of ACP economies, promotion of the private sector and increasing regional cooperation. It also focuses on building strong institutions such as human rights, democracy and good governance, strengthening the position of women, protection of the environment, and decentralized cooperation. The EU-ACP preferential framework is consistent with the popular Generalized System of Preferences (GSP) under the United Nation Conference for Trade and Development (UNCTAD) arrangement that seeks to raise export earnings and promote industrialization and development in the preference-receiving countries.

From the empirical perspective, separate studies that focus on the effectiveness of non-reciprocal PTAs in promoting exports have produced mixed results. Bureau et al. (2007) and Frazer and Van Biesebroeck (2010), by focusing on product coverage and preferential margins, find high utilization rates of the EU and US preferential schemes. Without focusing on any donor-specific PTAs, Rose (2004) and Aiello et al. (2010), using the gravity model, conclude that PTAs have a strong positive effect by doubling trade. Comparing specific PTAs, Nilsson (2002) and Manchin (2006) find a significant and positive effect on exports in contrast to Lederman and Özden (2004), who find the US PTA to have a negative effect on imports. On the other side, are studies that have looked separately at the effect of foreign aid or market access on economic development (see, e.g., Doucouliagos and Paldam 2011; Bosker and Garretsen 2012).

While all these studies have looked separately at the effectiveness of preferential market access and foreign aid on trade and development, we connect these two different strands of literature. Thus, we follow the conditional approach like Burnside and Dollar (2000) by investigating whether market access would be more effective in preference-beneficiary countries that received more foreign aid. The principal contributions of our paper are twofold. First, we extend the effectiveness measure of the

PTAs from trade to economic development. This is important because one of the core objectives of the PTAs according to UNCTAD is to accelerate economic development of the preference-receiving countries. Second, we examine the role of foreign aid as an important element that could enhance the effectiveness of preferential market access.

Thus, we analyze whether there exists any differential effect of market access on economic development between low-aid and high-aid receiving countries using the EU preferential access granted to the ACP countries. The EU-ACP framework provides a unique opportunity to test whether granting market access in addition to providing development and technical assistance for LDCs would produce more of a positive synergy impact on economic development.

In this paper, we adopt a three-step procedure in the empirical strategy. In the first step, we use the gravity model to examine the effectiveness of EU-ACP PTA on bilateral trade. In using the gravity model, we deal with basic econometric concerns—zero trade flows and the multilateral resistance term (MRT). These concerns are relevant econometric concerns because, if not adequately dealt with, they can lead to biased and inconsistent results (see, e.g., Anderson and van Wincoop 2003; Santos-Silva and Tenreyro 2006). In the second step, we construct a market access index from the gravity model based on the standard approach. This follows the new economic geography approach exactly as used in several studies (Redding and Venables 2004; Head and Mayer 2011; Bosker and Garretsen 2012). In the third step, we examine the effectiveness of market access conditional on the level of foreign aid allocated to preference beneficiary countries. The estimation method in the third step strictly follows the Clemens et al. (2012) approach to correct for endogeneity. They emphasize the methods of lagging and differencing as more transparent and efficient rather than using weak instruments. This approach also corrects for autocorrelation, thus avoiding spurious results as our data consist of a large panel with long time series.

Our results indicate that non-reciprocal preferential market access granted by the EU has a large positive and significant impact in fostering exports from ACP countries to the EU; however, this trade-enhancing impact does not translate unconditionally into improving economic development. In particular, we find that the impact of market access on economic development is conditional on the level of foreign aid. In that, the impact of market access on economic development is a positive function of the level of foreign aid. More precisely, there is a differential effect of market access between high-aid and low-aid receiving countries. High-aid receiving ACP states experience a greater but modest positive impact of market access on GDP per capita compared to low-aid receiving ACP countries.

The rest of the chapter proceeds as follows. Section 3.2 describes the data and main variables. Section 3.3 provides the empirical framework. Section 3.4 discusses the estimation results. Section 3.5 concludes.

3.2 Data

We focus on the entire group of ACP countries and their annual trade with the EU preference-giving countries from 1970 to 2009. Restricting the scope to this period is appropriate considering newly introduced economic partnership agreements between the EU and the ACP countries in 2009. In addition, stopping at 2009 is important to avoid the financial crisis and the onset of deglobalization that set in from 2009 (see, e.g., van Bergeijk 2018). The focus is delimited to ACP countries as they enjoyed a more favorable preferential market access among all developing countries (Persson and Wilhelmsson 2013). Unlike similar preferential market access schemes granted by the US, Canada, and Japan the EU-ACP PTA provides a more extensive concession in terms of product coverage. A study by UNCTAD (2001) indicates an extremely high trade-weighted coverage of 99.9% for EU-ACP PTA. Further, it has a contractually binding element, and hence limiting unilateralism, which makes it distinct from other schemes. This is important because Pomfret (2007) points out that the unilateral and revocable nature of the PTAs made them feeble instruments in promoting exports.

The main dataset used in this paper comes from IMF's Direction of Trade Statistics.[1] The dataset provides information on export flows from 61 ACP countries to 27 EU member countries. The use of all ACP and EU countries on which data was available gives us an added advantage of avoiding selection bias as we consider trade flows between the same trading partners over the time period. The variation in the sample emanates from the fact that trading countries joined the EU or ACP group of states at different times. Thus, our control group is the same trading partners but at a point in time they were not members of EU or ACP. To capture the fact that the EU-ACP framework was an integrated scheme and not targeted towards promoting exports in specific sectors or products, we measure trade at an aggregated level rather than a disaggregated product level. Furthermore, data on gravity model variables such as bilateral distance; gross domestic product (GDP); population; geographical area; colonial ties and trade agreements comes from the CEPII database.[2]

Aidt and Gassebner (2010) argue that political regimes influence countries' involvement in international trade. Given that ACP countries have substantially different political regimes, there is a need to control for the stability of political and institutional quality. For this purpose, we rely on the data constructed by Cheibub et al. (2010) on whether a particular country is democratic or autocratic to control political regimes. Relatedly, we control for institutional and policy quality using data from Polity IV database developed by Marshall et al. (2013).

We also use the OECD database for information on actual net foreign aid disbursement rather than commitments.[3] In line with the aid literature, we account for the

---

[1] http://data.imf.org/?sk=9D6028D4-F14A-464C-A2F2-59B2CD424B85&sId=1390030341854, accessed January 31, 2020.

[2] http://www.cepii.fr/CEPII/en/bdd_modele/presentation.asp?id=8, accessed January 31, 2020.

[3] https://data.oecd.org/oda/net-oda.htm, accessed January 31, 2020.

size of recipient by using aid/GDP ratio, and this underlines a striking heterogeneity in level of aid/GDP among the ACP countries.[4]

Information on basic control variables such as gross primary school enrollment (proxy for human capital); gross domestic saving as percentage of GDP (proxy for physical investment) and population growth rate, percentage of urban population; value added of agriculture to GDP and value added of oil to GDP are obtained from the World Bank Development Indicators (WDI) database.

3.3 Empirical Framework

To examine the trade and economic development effects of preferential market accesses, we proceed in three steps. In the first step, we use the gravity model to assess the effectiveness of the EU-ACP PTA on exports from an ACP member state to an EU member. Following Anderson and van Wincoop (2003), we base our estimation on the benchmark gravity model specified in Eq. (3.1).

$$ln\left(X_{ijt}\right) = \alpha_i + \alpha_j + \alpha_t + \beta_1 lnM_{it} + \beta_2 lnM_{jt} + \eta T_{ij(t)} + P_{it} + \Pi_{jt} + \varepsilon_{ijt} \tag{3.1}$$

X_{ijt} is export flow from country i to country j; α_i and α_j are exporter and importer fixed effects, respectively, and α_t are the time dummies, β is a vector of estimated coefficients, and ε_{ijt} is the error term. M_{it} and M_{jt} are vectors of monadic variables of the exporter and importer, respectively. The monadic variables consist of GDP, population, geographical area, and democracy indicator. P_{it} and Π_{jt} are the multi-lateral resistance term. $T_{ij(t)}$ is the trade cost variable which includes a vector of dyadic time-invariant (variant) variables such as distance between countries i and j, and indicator variables that equal one if countries i and j have colonial ties, share a common language or both are members of PTA or GATT/WTO. The PTA variable in $T_{ij(t)}$ is our main variable of interest and it is an indicator variable that equals one if countries i and j are members of the EU and the ACP group of states, at time t and 0 otherwise. The main difficulty in estimating Eq. (3.1) is due to potential bias that may emanate from simultaneity between export flows and PTA formation. In the estimation, we lag the PTA variable to account for the phased-in agreements and lagged terms of trade effect by virtue of the institutional design of trade agreements (Baier et al. 2008). By lagging the PTA variable, we also minimize the endogeneity problem in this exercise. This approach may be more efficient especially when instrumental variables are weak. Other alternatives such as using colonial ties as an instrumental

---

[4] For instance, aid as percentage of GDP from EU and all donors has a mean (standard deviation) of 5% (6%) and 12% (13%), respectively. There are countries like Cabo Verde, Guinea Bissau, where the average size of foreign aid is above 30% of the size of their economy, whereas it is below 5% for countries such as Fiji, Gabon, and Jamaica.

variable as in Egger et al. (2011) do not fit our panel data setting mainly because this variable does not change over time.

In the second step, we construct a market access index for each of the ACP countries to individual EU member countries. The construction of the markets access index follows from the gravity model that relates bilateral exports between countries i and j to supply potentials (s_{it}) of country i, market demand potentials (m_{jt}) of country j and trade cost (T_{ijt}) between them. This relationship is given by Eq. (3.2).

$$X_{ijt} = s_{it}[\underbrace{m_{jt} T_{ijt}^{\eta}}_{MA}] \qquad (3.2)$$

The market access (MA) index is captured by market demand potentials (m_j) of country j and trade cost (T_{ij}). The market demand potentials of a country encompass mainly monadic variables for the importer in the gravity model such as GDP and population that make the importer a potential buyer of goods from the exporter. The trade cost is captured by a vector of dyadic variables including distance, common language, colonial ties and preferential trade agreement. Bilateral distance has a negative relationship with market access, in that, a longer bilateral distance would result in a higher trade cost emanating from higher costs of transport. A common language and colonial ties are supposed to have a reducing impact on trade costs as common language and culture would reduce the administrative costs associated with trade transactions. PTA takes a focal point in these dyadic determinants of trade cost as they can be used effectively to eliminate non-tariff and tariff barriers. The market potentials are captured using the estimated importer fixed effects (α_j) and trade cost estimated from the dyadic variables.

Thus, we construct the market access index separately for each ACP country to each PTA donor and sum over all the donor countries for each year as in Bosker and Garretsen (2012). More specifically, the MA index is given by Eq. (3.3).

$$MA_{it} = \sum_j \exp(\alpha_{jt}) T_{ijt}^{\eta} \qquad (3.3)$$

Following the approach of Redding and Venables (2004), Head and Mayer (2011), and Bosker and Garretsen (2012), parameters of Eq. (3.3) are obtained from estimating the gravity model as in Eq. (3.1) but separately for each year, and the estimated market access variable is constructed as follows in Eq. (3.4).

$$\widehat{MA}_{it} = \sum_j \left[\exp(\hat{\alpha}_{jt}) distance_{ij}^{\hat{\eta}_{1t}} exp(\hat{\eta}_{2t} coloniality_{ij} + \hat{\eta}_{3t} language_{ij} + \hat{\eta}_{4t} PTA_{ijt}) \right] \qquad (3.4)$$

In the third step, the constructed MA index is used as the main variable of interest in cross-country regressions to explain the differences in the level of economic development. Head and Mayer (2011) have shown empirically that the NEG framework is relevant and applicable to LDCs. In this framework, the wage rate any given firm is willing and able to pay is a function of distance-weighted market access to foreign markets (Redding and Venables 2004). In line with the Head and Mayer (2011) assertion of a broader applicability of wage equation, we specify the wage equation similarly but augmented with human capital and other country-specific characteristics as in Boulhol and de Serres (2010) in Eq. (3.5). Given that we use total exports rather than manufacturing exports, we measure economic development in terms of GDP per capita (GDPpc) as in Head and Mayer (2011). The use of total exports enables the measurement of the overall impact of preferential market accesses, which basically covers both the primary and manufactured goods that ACP countries export to EU countries.

$$lnGDPpc_{it} = \delta_i + \delta_t + \tau \, ln\left(\widehat{MA}_{it}\right) + \gamma ln(C_{it}) + \epsilon_{it} \qquad (3.5)$$

C_{it} is a vector of control variables as in Bosker and Garretsen (2012), δ_i and δ_{tt} are the country and time fixed effects, respectively. We do not rely solely on the use of fixed effects as solutions to the endogeneity problems that characterized regression analyses of growth models. Head and Mayer (2011) also pinpoint to endogeneity arising from circular dependence in the domestic market access index construction as the construction involves the use of income levels. Although, this would not be problematic as our central focus is on foreign market access, we rely on first-differencing and lagging as used in Clemens et al. (2012) to solve any potential endogeneity. In addition, we introduce an interaction term between the market access index and the aid variable. In line with Burnside and Dollar (2000), we introduce an aid square term to test whether there is a diminishing return to the level of aid.

$$lnGDPpc_{it} = \delta_i + \delta_t + \tau ln\left(\widehat{MA}_{it}\right) + \zeta Aid_{it} + \xi ln\left(\widehat{MA}_{it}\right) * Aid_{it}$$
$$+ \rho ln\left(\widehat{MA}_{it}\right) * (Aid_{it})^2 + \gamma ln(C_{it}) + \epsilon_{it} \qquad (3.6)$$

3.4 Estimation, Results, and Discussion

3.4.1 Assessment of the EU-ACP PTA

Estimating Eq. (3.1) brings to the fore two main econometric concerns—the multilateral resistance term and the zero flows. The multilateral resistance term highlights the fact that the trade flow between any two countries is not solely determined by the bilateral variables between these two countries but also by their relative position to the rest of the world. Anderson and van Wincoop (2003) indicate that the MRT is theoretically consistent with the microeconomic derivation of the gravity model. Anderson and van Wincoop (2003) have shown that ignoring this term produces inconsistent estimates of standard gravity model coefficients. To best handle the omission, Feenstra (2004) recommends including time-varying fixed effects in the gravity regression. However, the inclusion of the exporter-year and importer-year fixed effects leads to high-dimensional fixed effects and also many policy-relevant variables are differenced away (see, e.g., Baier and Bergstrand 2010). To overcome these shortcomings, we follow the Baier and Bergstrand (2010) proxy variable approach.[5]

The second econometric concern comes from the fact that there are substantial zero flows in the bilateral trade data, 35% in our case. Unless these zero flows are randomly distributed, they introduce self-selection bias into the model resulting in inconsistent estimates. Several studies such as Lederman and Özden (2004) and Gamberoni (2007) deal with the zero flows using the Tobit estimator.[6] Alternatively, Santos-Silva and Tenreyro (2006, 2011), Martinez-Zarzoso (2013), and Head and Mayer (2013) recommend the use of the PPML estimator.[7] Exports (X_{ijt}) are now measured at level and Z_{ijt} is a vector of explanatory variables similar to Eq. (3.1).

PTAs can effectively affect the economic development if they significantly improve the market access through increased bilateral exports to the PTA donors. Using the PPML estimator, we estimate Eq. (3.1).

In Table 3.1, column 1 shows the PPML estimates without using fixed effect and multilateral resistance term. Although the coefficients are significant and have the expected signs, this does not deal with the omitted variable bias. The results in column 2 control for the time-invariant heterogeneity by including the importer and exporter fixed effects, however, the fixed effects cannot adequately control for the time-varying MRT. Thus, in column 3, we included the computed Baier and Bergstrand (2010) proxy for MRT. Including the MRT terms reduces the magnitude of elasticities.[8] Anderson and van Wincoop (2003) show that without controlling for MRT there is upward bias in the elasticities. In column 4, we correct for any possible cross-sectional and temporal dependence as we have a large time dimension by using the population-averaged Poisson estimator. The results in columns 2 to 4 indicate that the EU PTA has large economic and statistical effects in increasing bilateral exports from the ACP countries to the EU member states. UNCTAD (2001) explains unique features

---

[5] In this approach the multilateral resistance term is derived from the first-order log-linear Taylor expansion of the multilateral price equations within the theoretical gravity equation which yields an empirical reduced-form equation: $[P_{it} + \Pi_{jt} = \frac{1}{N}\left[\sum_i^N \theta_{it}\ln T_{ijt} + \sum_j^N \theta_{jt}\ln T_{ijt} - \frac{1}{N}\left(\sum_k^N \sum_m^N \theta_{kt}\theta_{mt}\ln T_{ijt}\right)\right]$. This measure is simple averages of multilateral relative to world trade costs (T_{ijt}), where T_{ijt} is replaced with observable trade costs such as distance, common language, colonial ties etc. This approach has been used in recent studies: Egger and Nelson (2011), Hoekman and Nicita (2011), and Silva and Nelson (2012).

[6] Left-censoring at zero as employed in the Tobit estimator for trade data is not a plausible assumption. Santos-Silva and Tenreyro (2006) indicate that the Tobit estimator produces inconsistent estimates.

[7] This estimator has been extensively used in recent studies such as Persson and Wilhelmsson (2013) and Afesorgbor and van Bergeijk (2014). It solves the zero flows and is also consistent in the presence of heteroscedasticity.

[8] The elasticities must be converted by using, $exp^{\eta} - 1$.

Table 3.1 Effect of EU-ACP PTA on bilateral trade

	(1)	(2)	(3)	(4)
Estimator:	Poisson	Poisson	Poisson	Poisson
EU-ACP PTA indicator	0.144	0.513**	0.495**	0.407***
	(0.150)	(0.212)	(0.220)	(0.143)
Log exporter GDP	1.401***	0.518***	0.494***	1.054***
	(0.0971)	(0.186)	(0.181)	(0.0985)
Log importer GDP	0.884***	0.249	0.177	0.872***
	(0.175)	(0.214)	(0.202)	(0.101)
Log exporter population	−0.262***	0.295	0.641*	−0.253***
	(0.0934)	(0.406)	(0.352)	(0.0754)
Log importer population	0.206	4.330***	4.603***	0.278
	(0.243)	(1.532)	(1.240)	(0.172)
Exporter democracy indicator	−0.158	0.0513	0.0663	−0.237*
	(0.204)	(0.107)	(0.101)	(0.142)
Importer democracy indicator	1.269***	0.852***	0.808***	0.425***
	(0.284)	(0.232)	(0.244)	(0.114)
GATT/WTO participants indicator	0.197	0.0819	0.0716	0.292**
	(0.182)	(0.144)	(0.139)	(0.149)
Log distance	−0.920***			
	(0.211)			
Common language	0.478			
	(0.311)			
Colonial ties	0.344			
	(0.359)			
MRT for distance			−1.164***	−1.033***
			(0.177)	(0.265)
MRT for common language			−0.0424	−0.0283
			(0.264)	(0.406)
MRT for colonial ties			1.270***	0.370
			(0.310)	(0.291)
Constant	1.916	−1.500	−1.629	−2.968***
	(2.423)	(4.016)	(3.459)	(1.071)
Observations	44,927	44,927	44,927	41,415
Time fixed effects	Yes	Yes	Yes	Yes
Country-pair fixed effects	No	Yes	Yes	Yes
Correction for autocorrelation (AR1)	No	No	No	Yes
MRT controls	No	No	Yes	Yes

The dependent variable is exports and is given in levels. Robust standard errors clustered at the level of country-pairs in parentheses, ***$p < 0.01$, **$p < 0.05$, *$p < 0.1$

of the EU-ACP that could be plausible explanations for this significant effect. Apart from the more generous market access arrangement compared to other EU GSPs, the EU-ACP agreement is contractual and legally binding on preferential market access matters as this minimizes unilateral revocation of preferences. The contractual nature guarantees stability and security of the preferential market access.[9]

3.4.2 Market Access and Economic Development

In this section, we focus on how market access can explain the cross-country differences in the level of development. In this development accounting, we hypothesize market access as a basic determinant of income level. Just as argued by Acemoglu et al. (2005) that the historically rapid economic development of Western Europe was due to access to Atlantic trading countries, we also argue the reversal that market access to these European countries can explain the income level differences.

In estimating Eq. (3.5), reverse causality could be a problem if market access does not only influence GDP per capita, but in turn GDP per capita influences market access. For instance, a country with relatively higher income per capita and productivity would enjoy greater market access to DCs as it can tailor goods of high quality to meet the high tastes and preferences of consumers in DCs. Hoekman and Nicita (2011) confirm this argument in which they indicate that middle income countries enjoy more favorable market access in DCs.[10] By and large, the problem of endogeneity resulting from reverse causality requires more than the use of fixed effects in accounting for it. In many cases, the recommended standard approach is the use of instrumental variables in a two-stage regression. In relation to NEG literature, some of the proposed instrument variables included geographic centrality proposed by Head and Mayer (2006). Bosker and Garretsen (2012) also use distance to most important markets as an instrument. However, the use of these instrumental variables is limited to cross-sectional data as they do not vary over time.

Considering the unsuitability of these aforementioned instruments in case of panel data, we resort to the use of methods of lagging and differencing. Clemens et al. (2012) identify these methods as more transparent and efficient than using weak instruments. Wooldridge (2010) indicates that weak instruments can result in a more asymptotic bias compared to using the endogenous variables in structural estimations. Using these methods do not only control for potential simultaneity and reverse causality

---

[9] The contractual and legally binding preferential market access matters as this can minimize unilateral revocation of preferences. For example, the US PTA also unilaterally drops beneficiary countries, culminating in about 42 LDCs withdrawals. The US scheme was also characterized by instability as the scheme elapsed on some occasions (Romalis 2007). The anticipation of these uncertainties can dampen exports to US markets.

[10] However, in the ACP group of states, we are looking at a group of countries about the same level of development. This is evidenced in the low standard deviation (1.03) of log GDP per capita, which is six times the mean (6.21).

but also for serial correlation. Thus, the first differencing and lagging corrects for any potential reverse causality.

To differentiate the first-differencing from other estimation methods, we estimate Eq. (3.5) using ordinary least squares (OLS), fixed effect (FE) and first-differencing (FD) estimators. We lag the market access variable by one period to account for the fact that market access may not have a contemporaneous effect on economic development. Additionally, we control for market potential to the rest of the world (RoW) by using the sum of GDP of major trading partners (US, Canada, China, and Japan)[11] weighted by the inverse of bilateral distance as in Boulhol and de Serres (2010).

Under the general assumption that unobserved individual country heterogeneity is uncorrelated with the regressors, we estimate Eq. (3.5) using OLS as reported in columns 1 and 2 of Table 3.2. We find that, in the exception of market access which is significant but negative, all the other variables have expected signs and are strongly significant. However, excluding the country fixed effects would produce bias results because of possible endogeneity, in the sense that country-specific characteristics such as cultural, historical, and social factors are not explicitly controlled for in the model. These factors would be subsumed into the idiosyncratic error term, leading to a breakdown of the exogeneity condition. Accounting for the endogeneity using observable country-specific characteristics does not adequately deal with the problem as cultural and historical values which are unobserved cannot be explicitly controlled for. Although the adjusted R-square increased significantly under column 2, which is indicative of a good measure of fit of the model, the use of these observed time-varying country-specific characteristics does not suffice. In column 2, the size of the elasticities changes but the signs and significance are very similar to column 1. In column 3, we include the country fixed effects and in column 4, we add the time-varying observable country characteristics. The results in columns 3 and 4 delineate that market access to EU is both of economic and statistical significance in determining the level of economic development in the ACP states. However, this may be spurious because of the non-stationarity of our main dependent variable.

Using the methods of lagging and first-differencing, we present estimates in columns 5 and 6, which basically control for serial correlation, time-invariant omitted variables, and possible reverse causality. The results indicate a positive effect of market access on GDP per capita but the effect is statistically insignificant. This is consistent with Bosker and Garretsen's (2012) result in terms of the effect of foreign market access. Although Bosker and Garretsen find a positive effect of market access on economic development when market access was decomposed further, they fail to find a significant and positive effect of foreign market access on economic development for a group of Sub-Saharan African (SSA) countries.

Turning to the controlling variables, they all have their expected signs, but physical capital and urbanization rate are the only variables that are statistically significant determinants of economic development. Finding that market access cannot significantly explain the differences in the level of development, we move further to

---

[11] These countries have also provided preferential schemes to most ACP members.

Table 3.2 Effect of market access on economic development

	(1)	(2)	(3)	(4)	(5)	(6)
Estimation method:	OLS	OLS	FE	FE	FD	FD
Log market access (lag)	−0.0283**	−0.0555***	0.0374**	0.0373**	0.00666	0.0101
	(0.0126)	(0.0102)	(0.0161)	(0.0152)	(0.00770)	(0.00778)
Log physical capital	0.332***	0.140***	0.0705***	0.0528***	0.0184*	0.0194*
	(0.0201)	(0.0167)	(0.0115)	(0.0106)	(0.0100)	(0.0106)
Human capital	0.00901***	0.00236***	−0.00263***	−0.00203***	0.00116	0.00127
	(0.000729)	(0.000633)	(0.000925)	(0.000672)	(0.000799)	(0.000802)
Log population growth	−0.564***	−0.339***	−0.0140	−0.00876	0.0322	0.0278
	(0.0326)	(0.0274)	(0.0286)	(0.0251)	(0.0253)	(0.0279)
Log market potential to ROW		0.487***		0.518		0.837
		(0.0659)		(0.451)		(0.707)
Agriculture as % of GDP		−0.0248***		−0.0120***		−0.000276
		(0.00142)		(0.00208)		(0.00243)
Urbanization rate		0.00636***		0.00783**		0.0484***
		(0.00124)		(0.00312)		(0.0165)
Polity IV		0.00871***		−0.00153		0.00343
		(0.00307)		(0.00250)		(0.00217)
Oil as % of GDP		0.00859***		0.00389	0.0540***	−0.0347
		(0.00130)		(0.00279)	(0.00898)	(0.0565)
Constant	3.562***	1.592***	6.592***	4.173*	0.00666	0.0101
	(0.418)	(0.494)	(0.532)	(2.445)	(0.00770)	(0.00778)
Observations	1,104	1,050	1,104	1,050	964	913
Adjusted R-squared	0.632	0.795	0.933	0.939	0.540	0.551
Countries fixed effects	No	No	Yes	Yes	Yes	Yes
Time fixed effects	Yes	Yes	Yes	Yes	Yes	Yes
Panel unit root corrected	No	No	No	No	Yes	Yes

Robust standard errors clustered at the level of countries in parentheses, ***$p < 0.01$, **$p < 0.05$, *$p < 0.1$

investigate whether the impact of market access conditional or supported by a given level of foreign aid would produce a different outcome.

3.4.3 Market Access, Foreign Aid and Economic Development

Foreign aid can make market access effective if it is efficiently directed at supporting trading activities or directed at providing trade-related infrastructures that would reduce the supply-side constraints that producers or farmers in ACP states face. Thus, we hypothesize that the effect of market access is conditional on the level of foreign aid and test this using Eq. (3.6). In accordance with aid literature, we account for the size of recipient by using aid/GDP ratio and we include its square term to account for any quadratic relationship aid may have on economic development. Also, the aid variable is lagged by one period in accordance with Clemens et al. (2012) as we specifically look at aid which can affect development in a short time.

Reported in Table 3.3 are the effects of market access conditional on the level of foreign aid received by an ACP country. Interestingly, we find that aid interacted with market access has a strong economic and statistical significance on economic development. The coefficient for the interacted term is positive and significant, which implies that the impact of market access on economic development is a positive function of the level of foreign aid. In columns 1 and 2, we differentiate the effect when aid disbursement is from EU and in columns 3 and 4 when aid disbursement is from all donors. With the multiplicative interaction terms, the conditional marginal effects provides a more nuanced result, so we present the conditional marginal effect of market access at different levels of aid in Table 3.4. The economic and statistical significance of the conditional marginal effects tend to increase with the level of foreign aid. The results are robust to the source of aid and when we include the quadratic terms for the aid variable. These results suggest that developing countries can utilize the foreign market access opportunity under preferential trade agreements more effectively when this market access is complemented with foreign aid targeted at tackling structural constraints in exportable sectors of the developing countries.

3.4.4 Robustness

For robustness, we estimate the effect of market access conditional on foreign aid defined by an indicator variable instead of the continuous variable we employed in the previous section. The aid variable is converted into an indicator variable by using the threshold that if aid as a percentage of GDP received by a country in a particular year is greater than the 50th or 75th percentile for all countries in each year, then that country is labeled as a high-aid receiving country (the indicator variable takes the

Table 3.3 Effects of market access interacted with foreign aid on economic development

	(1)	(2)	(3)	(4)
Estimation method:	FD	FD	FD	FD
Log market access (lag)	0.0147*	0.0157*	0.0147*	0.0148*
	(0.00863)	(0.00883)	(0.00828)	(0.00828)
Aid/GDP (lag)	0.430*	0.376	0.226**	0.218*
	(0.234)	(0.242)	(0.109)	(0.108)
Log market access × aid/GDP (lag)	0.0217**	0.0337**	0.0124***	0.0140*
	(0.0100)	(0.0166)	(0.00383)	(0.00790)
Log market access × (EU aid/GDP)^2 (lag)		−0.0635		−0.00437
		(0.0516)		(0.0146)
Log physical capital	0.0194*	0.0188*	0.0199*	0.0198*
	(0.0106)	(0.0108)	(0.0105)	(0.0107)
Human capital	0.00106	0.00108	0.00118	0.00118
	(0.000765)	(0.000767)	(0.000771)	(0.000770)
Log population growth	0.0268	0.0273	0.0255	0.0256
	(0.0287)	(0.0283)	(0.0270)	(0.0271)
Log market potential to RoW	0.939	0.931	0.973	0.972
	(0.673)	(0.673)	(0.690)	(0.691)
Agriculture as % of GDP	−0.000325	−0.000382	−0.000347	−0.000372
	(0.00240)	(0.00239)	(0.00240)	(0.00241)
Urbanization rate	0.0484***	0.0485***	0.0480***	0.0479***
	(0.0168)	(0.0169)	(0.0165)	(0.0166)
Polity IV	0.00328	0.00338	0.00342	0.00345
	(0.00224)	(0.00222)	(0.00228)	(0.00230)
Oil as % of GDP	−7.35e−05	−5.36e−05	−1.01e−05	−5.71e−06
	(0.00207)	(0.00208)	(0.00210)	(0.00210)
Constant	−0.0481	−0.0492	−0.0508	−0.0509
	(0.0539)	(0.0537)	(0.0554)	(0.0554)
Observations	913	913	913	913
Adjusted R-squared	0.552	0.552	0.553	0.552
Source of aid	EU	EU	All donors	All donors

Robust standard errors clustered at the level of countries in parentheses, ***$p < 0.01$, **$p < 0.05$, *$p < 0.1$

Table 3.4 Conditional marginal effects of market access

	Simple interaction terms			Simple and quadratic interaction terms		
Aid/GDP=	Median	Mean	Mean + 3*std. deviation	Median	Mean	Mean + 3*std. deviation
Market access × EU aid/GDP	0.015*	0.016*	0.020**	0.016*	0.017*	0.020**
	(0.009)	(0.009)	(0.009)	(0.009)	(0.01)	(0.010)
Market access × all aid donor/GDP	0.016*	0.016*	0.021**	0.016*	0.016*	0.021**
	(0.008)	(0.008)	(0.01)	(0.008)	(0.009)	(0.009)

Robust standard errors clustered at the level of countries in parentheses, $***p < 0.01$, $**p < 0.05$, $*p < 0.1$

value of 1). Otherwise, the country is a low-aid receiving country with the indicator taking the value zero. Using the indicator variable makes it more convenient to interpret the results as we simply have to compare the effect of market access in low-aid and high-aid receiving countries. This also helps in avoiding some arbitrariness as we do not have to look at the impact of market access at some value of aid/GDP such as the median, mean, or any arbitrary value.

In Table 3.5, we present the results using the aid indicator variable which indicates that market access has differential effect in low-aid and high-aid receiving countries. In that, market access has a stronger effect in preference-receiving countries that receive higher amounts of foreign aid from the EU and all donors compared to low-aid receiving countries. In columns 1 and 3, we use the 50th percentile threshold for classifying a country as high-aid or low-aid receiving and we find a positive effect but not economically and statistically significant. Increasing the threshold for the aid indicator variable from 50 to 75th percentile changes the results quantitatively as the size and significance of the coefficient for the interaction term increases as shown in columns 2 and 4. This suggests that for foreign aid to complement market access more effectively, the level of foreign aid targeted to support trade-related projects and trade-supportive infrastructures significantly matters. This is consistent with Silva and Nelson's (2012) assertion that higher amounts of foreign aid used to support trade-related projects and built infrastructures would enhance the export competitiveness.

Although the marginal effects presented here indicate a strong statistical effect, their economic significance is less pronounced or quite modest if compared to other determinants of the level of economic development. However, we must emphasize the fact; the estimates are very comparable to other studies that analyze the impact of market access on economic development. For example, Bosker and Garretsen (2012) find an impact ranging from 0.01 to 0.03 percentage increase in income level when market access increases by 1 percentage for SSA. Similarly, for a group of OECD countries, Boulhol and de Serres (2010) find elasticities ranging from

Table 3.5 Effects of market access and foreign aid on economic development, using an indicator variable for aid

	(1)	(2)	(3)	(4)
Aid classification threshold:	50th percentile	75th percentile	50th percentile	75th percentile
Log market access (lag)	0.011	0.013	0.013	0.012
	(0.0081)	(0.0079)	(0.0080)	(0.0074)
Aid dummy (lag)	−0.018	0.035*	0.0092	0.037**
	(0.024)	(0.018)	(0.013)	(0.016)
Log market access × aid dummy (lag)	0.00028	0.0018***	0.0010*	0.0020***
	(0.00073)	(0.00062)	(0.0005)	(0.0006)
Log physical capital	0.019*	0.020*	0.019*	0.019*
	(0.011)	(0.011)	(0.011)	(0.010)
Human capital	0.0014*	0.00098	0.0013	0.0012
	(0.00076)	(0.00076)	(0.00077)	(0.00079)
Log population growth	0.029	0.028	0.028	0.028
	(0.028)	(0.028)	(0.028)	(0.027)
Log market potential to RoW	0.86	0.92	0.87	0.94
	(0.69)	(0.69)	(0.71)	(0.72)
Agriculture as % of GDP	−0.00027	−0.00032	−0.00039	−0.00035
	(0.0024)	(0.0024)	(0.0024)	(0.0024)
Urbanization rate	0.049***	0.048***	0.048***	0.047***
	(0.016)	(0.017)	(0.016)	(0.017)
Polity IV	0.0033	0.0032	0.0035	0.0031
	(0.0022)	(0.0022)	(0.0022)	(0.0022)
Oil as % of GDP	0.00021	−0.000099	0.000059	−0.00010
	(0.0021)	(0.0020)	(0.0021)	(0.0020)
Constant	−0.038	−0.044	−0.041	−0.045
	(0.055)	(0.055)	(0.057)	(0.057)
Observations	913	913	913	913
Adjusted R-squared	0.551	0.553	0.551	0.553
Source of aid	EU	EU	All donors	All donors

Robust standard errors clustered at the level of countries in parentheses, $***p < 0.01$, $**p < 0.05$, $*p < 0.1$, time, and country dummies are included

0.05 to 0.086. A plausible explanation for finding a modest effect of market access on economic development while we see a large effect on trade could be that the composition of exports is dominated by primary and low-value agricultural produces. For instance, Persson and Wilhelmsson (2013) find that EU-ACP preferences increase export concentration without any significant export diversification.

3.5 Conclusion

This paper addresses two salient issues. It first considers the relevance of preferential trade agreements in fostering LDCs' exports to DCs' markets. Then, it examines the effectiveness of foreign aid in reducing the supply-side constraints in the beneficiary countries to enable them to utilize the granted market access opportunity effectively. In our analysis, we focus on the EU-ACP preferential trade scheme mainly because it is a relatively more generous, stable, and binding trade arrangement for ACP states countries to access to EU market. Additionally, the scheme involves the provision of complementary developmental and technical support aimed at improving the productive capacities of the beneficiary countries.

We find that non-reciprocal preferential market access granted to ACP by the EU is an important determinant of export flows vis-à-vis other determining variables within the gravity model. Interestingly, we find that market access to the EU, although positive, does not play a significant role in explaining differences in the level of economic development across beneficiary countries. However, we find that market access has a positive and significant effect in high-aid receiving preference beneficiary countries compared to low-aid receiving counterparts. This feature strongly suggests that complementing preferential market access with foreign aid targeted at trading activities would effectively benefit the preference-receiving countries. The results from our paper provide an interesting flipside to the aid effectiveness debate as we have demonstrated that foreign aid can be more effective if it is combined with a granting of preferential market access that is contractually binding, more secure and with extensive product coverage. The direct policy implication is that granting any form of preferential market access opportunities to least developed countries without complementary technical and development assistance directed specifically at reducing production capacity constraints or other structural constraints may be ineffective in promoting economic development.

Appendix: ACP Beneficiaries

Angola	Madagascar
Bahamas	Malawi

(continued)

(continued)

Barbados	Mali
Belize	Mauritania
Benin	Mauritius
Burkina Faso	Mozambique
Burundi	Niger
Cameroon	Nigeria
Cape Verde	Papua New Guinea
Central African Republic	Rwanda
Chad	Saint Kitts and Nevis
Comoros	Saint Lucia
Congo	Saint Vincent and the Grenadines
Côte d'Ivoire	Samoa
Djibouti	Sao Tome and Principe
Dominica	Senegal
Dominican Republic	Seychelles
Ethiopia	Sierra Leone
Equatorial Guinea	Solomon Islands
Fiji	Somalia
Gabon	Sudan
Gambia	Suriname
Ghana	Tanzania (United Republic of)
Grenada	Togo
Guinea	Tonga
Guinea-Bissau	Trinidad and Tobago
Guyana	Tunisia
Haiti	Uganda
Jamaica	Zambia
Kenya	Zimbabwe
Liberia	

References

Acemoglu D, Johnson S, Robinson J (2005) The rise of Europe: Atlantic trade, institutional change, and economic growth. Am Econ Rev 95(3):546–579

Afesorgbor SK (2017) Revisiting the effect of regional integration on African trade: evidence from meta-analysis and gravity model. J Int Trade Econ Dev 26(2):133–153

Afesorgbor SK, van Bergeijk PAG (2014) Measuring multi-membership in economic integration and its trade impact: a comparative study of ECOWAS and SADC. S Afr J Econ 82(4):518–530

Aidt TS, Gassebner M (2010) Do autocratic states trade less? World Bank Econ Rev 24(1):38–76

Aiello F, Cardamone P, Agostino MR (2010) Evaluating the impact of nonreciprocal trade preferences using gravity models. Appl Econ 42(29):3745–3760

Anderson JE, van Wincoop E (2003) Gravity with gravitas: a solution to the border puzzle. Am Econ Rev 93(1):170–192

Baier SL, Bergstrand JH (2010) Approximating general equilibrium pacts of trade liberalizations using the gravity equation. In: Van Bergeijk P, Brakman S (eds) The gravity model in international trade: advances and applications. Cambridge Univ Press, pp 88–134

Baier SL, Bergstrand JH, Egger P, McLaughlin PA (2008) Do economic integration agreements actually work? Issues in understanding the causes and consequences of the growth of regionalism. World Econ 31(4):461–497

Bosker M, Garretsen H (2012) Economic geography and economic development in Sub-Saharan Africa. World Bank Econ Rev 26(3):443–485

Boulhol H, de Serres A (2010) The Impact of economic geography on GDP per capita in OECD countries. In: Van Bergeijk P, Brakman S (eds) The gravity model in international trade: advances and applications. Cambridge University Press, pp 323–353

Bureau JC, Chakir R, Gallezot J (2007) The utilization of trade preferences for developing countries in the agri-food sector. J Agric Econ 58:175–198

Burnside C, Dollar D (2000) Aid, policies and growth. Am Econ Rev 90(4):847–868

Cheibub JA, Gandhi J, Vreeland JR (2010) Democracy and dictatorship revisited. Public Choice 143(1–2):67–101

Clemens MA, Radelet S, Bhavnani RR, Bazzi S (2012) Counting chickens when they hatch: timing and the effects of aid on growth. Econ J 122(561):590–617

Collier P, Venables AJ (2007) Rethinking trade preferences: how Africa can diversify its exports. World Econ 30(8):1326–1345

Dearden S, Mira Salama C (2002) The new EU ACP partnership agreement. J Int Dev 14(6):899–910

Doucouliagos H, Paldam M (2011) The ineffectiveness of development aid on growth: an update. Eur J Polit Econ 27(2):399–404

Egger P, Nelson D (2011) How bad is antidumping? Evidence from panel data. Rev Econ Stat 93(4):1374–1390

Egger P, Larch M, Staub KE, Winkelmann R (2011) The trade effects of endogenous preferential trade agreements. Am Econ j: Econ Pol 3(1):113–143

Feenstra RC (2004) Advanced international trade: theory and evidence. Princeton University Press

Frazer G, Van Biesebroeck J (2010) Trade growth under the African growth and opportunity act. Rev Econ Stat 92:128–144

Gamberoni E (2007) Do unilateral trade preferences help export diversification? An investigation of the impact of European unilateral trade preferences on the extensive and intensive margin of trade. HEI working paper # 17/2007

Head K, Mayer T (2006) Regional wage and employment responses to market potential in the EU. Reg Sci Urban Econ 36(5):573–594

Head K, Mayer T (2011) Gravity, market potential and economic development. J Econ Geogr 11:281–294

Head K, Mayer T (2013) Gravity equations: workhorse, toolkit, and cookbook. Science Po Economics Discussion Papers 2013-02

Hoekman B, Nicita A (2011) Trade policy, trade costs, and developing country trade. World Dev 39(12):2069–2079

Lederman D, Özden Ç (2004) U.S. trade preferences: all are not created equal, unpublished. World Bank, Washington, DC

Manchin M (2006) Preference utilization and tariff reduction in EU imports from ACP countries. World Econ 29(9):1243–1266

Marshall MG, Gurr TR, Jaggers K (2013) Polity IV project: political regime characteristics and transitions, 1800-2012

Martínez-Zarzoso I (2013) The log of gravity revisited. Appl Econ 45(3):311–327

Ngepah N, Udeagha MC (2018) African regional trade agreements and intra-African trade. J Econ Integr 33(1):1176–1199

Nilsson L (2002) Trading relations: is the roadmap from Lomé to Cotonou correct? Appl Econ 34(4):439–452

Persson M, Wilhelmsson F (2013) EU trade preferences and export diversification. IFN working paper # 991

Pomfret R (2007) Is regionalism an increasing feature of the world economy? World Econ 30:923–947

Rajan RG, Subramanian A (2011) Aid, Dutch disease, and manufacturing growth. J Dev Econ 94:106–118

Redding S, Venables AJ (2004) Economic geography and international inequality. J Int Econ 62:53–82

Romalis J (2007) Market access, openness and growth. NBER working paper # 13048

Rose AK (2004) Do we really know that the WTO increases trade? Am Econ Rev 94(1):98–114

Santos-Silva J, Tenreyro S (2006) The log of gravity. Rev Econ Stat 88:641–658

Santos Silva JMC, Tenreyro S (2011) Further simulation evidence on the performance of the Poisson pseudo-maximum likelihood estimator. Econ Lett 112(2):220–222

Silva SJ, Nelson D (2012) Does aid cause trade? Evidence from an asymmetric gravity model. World Econ 35(5):545–577

Stiglitz JE, Charlton A (2005) Fair trade for all: how trade can promote development. Oxford University Press, New York

UNCTAD (2001) Improving market access for least developed. UN, New York and Geneva. http://unctad.org/en/Docs/poditctncd4.en.pdf

van Bergeijk PA (2018) On the brink of deglobalization...again. Camb J Reg Econ Soc 11(1):59–72

Wooldridge JM (2010) Econometric analysis of cross section and panel data. MIT press

Chapter 4
Investment Climate, Firm Heterogeneity, and Internationalization of Firms: What Matters for EAC Firms?

Binyam Afewerk Demena

Abstract This chapter investigates several investment climate measures and firm characteristics on the internationalization of domestic firms using the World Bank Enterprise Surveys firm-level data in sub-Saharan Africa (SSA). I first build an empirical framework on how firms' views and perceptions of investment climates related to institutional and trade policy obstacles affect international integration for firms in the East African Community (EAC). Next, I demonstrate the application of more objective indicators to capture firm-level heterogeneity aspects in explaining international integration at a finer level. Based on the availability of micro-level data, the research deals with four of the seven EAC countries. For most EAC countries, firms tend to see many areas of the investment climate as bottlenecks to business. I find that access to formal and informal finance, custom and trade regulations, and telecommunication opportunities tend to pose serious constraints to the investment climate. Regarding firm-level determinants, the study reveals that all the considered factors are substantially significant across all specification and estimation approaches.

4.1 Introduction and Background

The role of international integration[1] in the process of industrialization of developing countries, or in enhancing the ability to participate effectively in the foreign market is an important policy issue for many developing countries. Internationalization could play a role by facilitating the introduction of new export items (growth at an extensive margin). Internationalization could also contribute to productivity growth by intensifying the competitiveness or expansion of existing exports to the existing market (growth at the intensive margin).

Although most sub-Saharan African (SSA) countries have placed significant efforts on promoting internationalization of domestic firms, the region is well recognized for its low competitiveness in international markets (Djankov et al. 2010;

B. A. Demena (✉)
International Institute of Social Studies, Erasmus University Rotterdam, Hague, Netherlands
e-mail: demena@iss.nl

---

[1] I use international integration and internationalization interchangeably throughout the chapter.

© The Author(s), under exclusive license to Springer Nature Singapore Pte Ltd. 2022   65
B. A. Demena and Peter A. G. Van Bergeijk (eds.), *Trade and Investment in East Africa*,
Frontiers in African Business Research, https://doi.org/10.1007/978-981-19-4211-2_4

Hoekman and Shepherd 2015). Moreover, it has been argued that the region will not be able to achieve a sustainable path to growth and poverty reduction, unless trade increases (UNECA, Economic Commission for Africa 2015). Furthermore, over the past 30 years, the share of Africa's exports in the world market has halved, and considering its population, income, and other characteristics, Africa's exports are less than expected (Freund and Rocha 2011). However, some countries of the region performed better while others remained marginalized in promoting exports and developing new markets abroad.

Investment in production for export markets is, therefore, likely to offer great potential. The challenge is how to identify constraints that impede export performance or international integration and determine how they could be resolved. In general, there are demand-side and supply-side constraints. Existing studies argue that SSA countries have faced relatively fewer barriers or constraints in accessing external markets than other developing countries (e.g., see, Bacchetta 2007; Freund and Rocha 2011; Morris and Fessehaie 2014; Hallward-Driemeier and Pritchett 2015). Notedly, Morris and Fessehaie (2014) argued that strengthening supply capacity enhances the ability to capture a greater share of trade in African countries. It is therefore plausible that poor export performance is concomitant with weak export supply responses that prevent SSA countries from full utilization of international market access opportunities. Some of the supply-side bottlenecks are associated with trade policy obstacles related to investment climate that hinder strengthening supply capacity, while others are underlying economic conditions (Morris and Fessehaie 2014; Demena et al. 2021a).

These bottlenecks have particular relevance in explaining how institutional infrastructure influences the international development of firms. In the context of developing countries, this is more important as institutional infrastructures are generally less developed (Freund and Rocha 2011; Hallward-Driemeier and Pritchett 2015). This observation begs the main question, what are the main investment climate related constraints hampering international integration? Empirical evidence suggests that a weak investment climate in developing countries is a key constraint for utilizing foreign market access opportunities (Morris and Fessehaie 2014; Hallward-Driemeier and Pritchett 2015). For instance, a recent survey of 65 Nordic-affiliated firms operating in Tanzania conducted in 2019 shows that various constraints in the investment climate resulted in setbacks to Tanzania in its reputation as an investment haven (Jahari 2021). As noted earlier, the challenge is to identify a comprehensive representation of the constraints that impede internationalization and to determine how they could be relieved. This is an important policy dimension as government interventions to ease trade policy obstacles to support export competitiveness and diversification can address the key factors that are responsible for constraining supply capacity across countries in the SSA.

It is difficult to precisely define investment climate[2], however, I follow Stern (2002) who noted that it is the policy, institutional, and behavioral environments and thus argued that improving the investment climate is the central challenge in reaping greater benefits from international integration and globalization. More broadly, this includes "…providing sound regulation of industry, including the promotion of competition; in overcoming bureaucratic delay and inefficiency; in fighting corruption; and in improving the quality of infrastructure" (Stern 2002:52). In the globalization literature, more specifically, the term is used to refer to the regulatory environment and institutional policy through which firms operate (Hallward-Driemeier and Pritchett 2015).

Accordingly, this chapter has the following goals. First, it builds an empirical framework on how investment climate relates to institutional and trade policy obstacles which subsequently affect international integration. The main analytical framework is that the various elements of the investment climate are mediating factors in making it easy or difficult for foreign market activities, representing an indirect kind of trade bottlenecks. Second, it will demonstrate the application of more disaggregated data to capture the role of the investment climate along firm-level heterogeneity aspects on international integration at a more specific level than macro-level explanation alone. Existing studies on firm performance literature (e.g., see Freund and Rocha 2011; van Bergeijk and van Marrewijk 2013; Chang and van Marrewijk 2013; Demena 2017; Demena and Murshed 2018; Demena et al. 2021b) show the relevance of micro-data-driven research that underlies the nature of firm heterogeneities. They argue that building an empirical framework based on macro-level cross-country or country-level analysis implicitly assumes aspects of heterogeneity to have the same impact in each country under consideration. More specifically, van Bergeijk et al. (2011) argued that dealing with the emerging micro-data-driven research in investigating the relationship between internationalization and firms enhances our empirical understanding and policy relevance.

I use East African Community (EAC) firm-level data analysis that goes beyond a single country case study to explore several investment climate measures along with individual firm characteristics on internationalization and provide policy advice in which reforms improve foreign market performance. Based on the availability of micro-level data, I consider firms in Tanzania, Kenya, Rwanda, and Uganda comprising four out of the seven EAC countries.

The chapter is structured as follows: Sect. 4.2 discusses the data and Sect. 4.3 presents the empirical strategy in the context of the micro-level data. Section 4.4 provides the results of the analyses. The final section concludes the findings with a discussion on the policy implications of the findings.

---

[2] Alternatively, investment climate is viewed as synonymous to 'business environment', but it is the former that has been often used in policy discussion more frequently. In policy discussion of phasing out aid and phasing in trade, van den Berg (2015), points out that development successes need responsible business conduct, which in turn is an essential part of creating conducive investment climate or business environment.

Table 4.1 List of EAC countries and distribution of private enterprise by ownership status

EAC countries	Year of survey	Domestically owned firms	Foreign-owned firms	Total firms	Percentage of exporters
Kenya	2013	635	78	713	22.02
Rwanda	2011	191	50	241	4.15
Tanzania	2013	686	37	723	4.98
Uganda	2013	556	84	640	7.50
Total		2068	249	2317	10.83

Source Author's own compilation from the RPED World Bank enterprise survey 2014

4.2 Data

The data come from the Regional Program on Enterprise Development (RPED) World Bank enterprise firm-level surveys in SSA countries.[3] The firm-level data provides firm characteristics, production variables, and qualitative and quantitative perception-based investment climate indicators across SSA. The former includes information related to firm demographics (firm size and age), ownership structure (domestic vs. foreign ownership), market orientation (foreign vs. domestic market oriented), and employment pattern. Similarly, based on the perception of each firm, the investment climate as bottlenecks considers among others institutional quality, infrastructural constraints, financial problem, and availability of workforce. Based on the availability of micro-level data, I have compiled the required information from four countries of EAC carried out from 2011 to 2013 (Table 4.1).

Table 4.1 gives the distribution of the enterprise surveys included in this study. Approximately, 11% of the overall sample are exporting firms. Of these firms, the majority, about 22%, are from Kenya, whereas the other 7%, 5%, and 4% are from Uganda, Tanzania, and Rwanda, respectively. Thus, Kenya has a higher percentage of exporting firms, and the other three countries have less than the average overall sample of exporting firms. To put these figures into perspective, the total share of exporters in this study (11%) is slightly greater than the 8% reported by Demena and Murshed (2018) for SSA countries for the period 2006–2014 and marginally lower (about 0.5 percentage points) than the recent productivity premia analysis for SSA sample of firms from 2013 to 2014 (Demena et al. 2021b, Chap. 7). Beyond the region, the current figure corroborates the 11% share of exporters sampled in 2006 for 15 Latin American counties analyzed by Chang and van Marrewijk (2013).

Existing studies on Africa use firm size captured by the number of employees (Demena and van Bergeijk 2019; Chaps. 7 and 8 of this book). In general, exporters are larger in size than non-exporters (Demena et al. 2021b; Chap. 7 of this book, Demena et al. 2022). This is also confirmed in our sample. On average, exporters are

---

[3] Chapter 7 of this book provides detailed description of the RPED World Bank Enterprise Survey standard survey instruments (Demena et al. 2022).

large-sized (of exporting firms, about 23% are large-sized, whereas 10% are medium-sized). Indeed, large-sized firms are more likely to be an exporter than medium-sized firms that in their turn outperform small-sized firms.

Regarding the investment climate, both exporting and non-exporting firms across EAC countries face many constraints to business. Figure 4.1 gives the rankings of constraints based on the perception of the sampled firms. Of primary concern, access to finance and reliable electricity are highly ranked investment climate constraints. The probability that firms are more likely to be exporters increases when access to financing constraints are less binding to business (Fig. 4.2, about three-fourths are exporters when firms consider access to finance is not a serious obstacle).

Compared to these subjective perception-based assessments of the investment climate, Figs. 4.3 and 4.4 highlight more objective factors. The probability that a firm is an exporter is likely to decrease when firms rely more on informal financing for

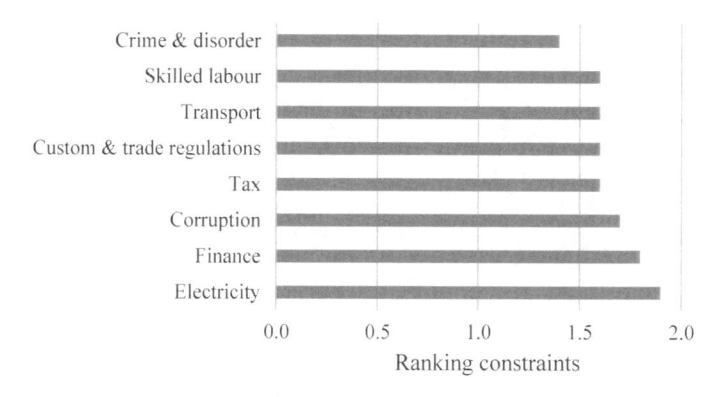

Fig. 4.1 Ranking of investment climate as binding constraints. *Source* Author's own compilation from the RPED World Bank enterprise survey 2014

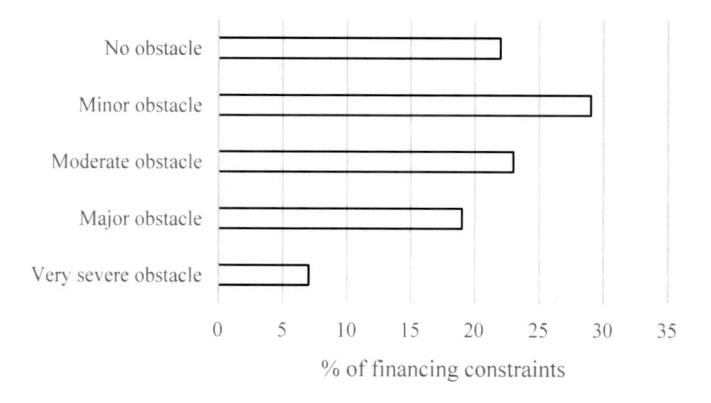

Fig. 4.2 The degree of financing constraints for exporting firms. *Source* Author's own compilation from the RPED World Bank enterprise survey 2014

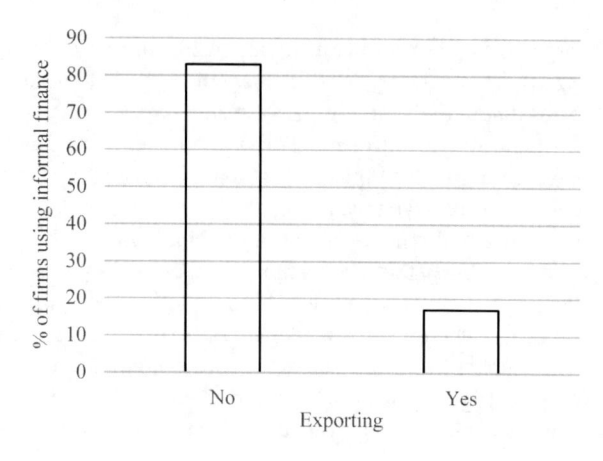

Fig. 4.3 Exporters' access to informal finance. *Source* Author's own compilation from the RPED World Bank enterprise survey 2014

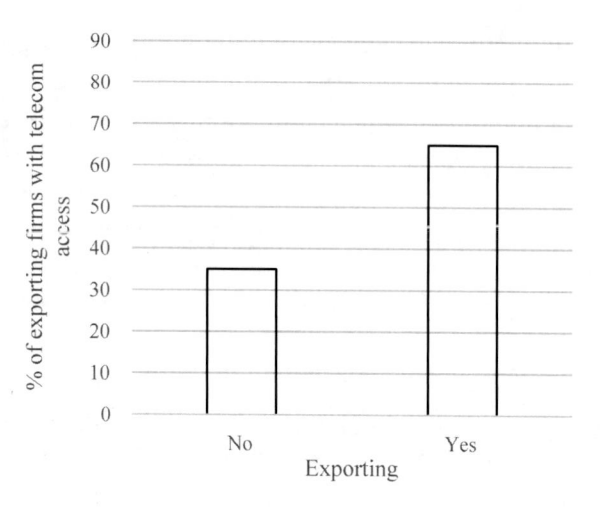

Fig. 4.4 Exporters and telecom opportunities. *Source* Author's own compilation from the RPED World Bank enterprise survey 2014

operating businesses such as sources from friends, relatives, money lenders (Fig. 4.3). Concerning, the telecommunication problem, firms are likely to be exporters where firms have access to telecoms, for instance, they use their own website for sales and product promotion for business-related activities (Fig. 4.4).

The discussion of the data above indicates that there is no single dimension that can completely elucidate the investment climate and firm-level determinants for the internationalization of firms. Indeed, the descriptive data reveals some stylized facts, but is only based on surface-level information. Accordingly, I need to simultaneously control for the various investment climates binding constraints and firm heterogeneities before I can draw any definite conclusions. The next section will present the empirical approach.

4.3 Empirical Strategy

I now proceed to build the empirical framework to investigate the probability that a particular firm participates in the export market given the firm-specific characteristics and particular investment climate indicators. The probability that a domestic firm is integrated into a foreign market depends partly on how productive the firm is and partly on trade costs that are beyond the firm's control. In this regard, the main interest in investment climate indicators will likely influence international integration (i.e., export market participation) via two channels: firm-level heterogeneities and trade costs. I will therefore examine how particular investment climate measures and firm-level characteristics affect the probability that a firm participates in the export market.

The reduced-form empirical model can be written as:

$$Y_{ijk} = \beta_0 + \beta_1(firm\ characteristics)_{ijk} + \beta_2(investment\ climate)_{ijk} + \beta_3 X_j + \beta_4 Z_k + \varepsilon_{ijk} \tag{4.1}$$

where Y_{ijk} is the dichotomous dependent variable that takes the value:

- 0, if a firm i in sector j and country k is local market oriented.
- 1, if a firm i in sector j and country k is exporter.

X and Z are a vector/matrix of country and sector-fixed effects, respectively.

Equation (4.1) estimates the effects of firm-level characteristics and investment climate measures on the probability that a domestic firm integrated into a foreign market (undertakes internationalization). Accordingly, the main hypothesis has two parts. The first bundle of hypothesis is that larger and older domestic firms can perform better to undertake internationalization as they are likely to have potential production scale and space. Similarly, I expect that foreign firms and agglomeration activities are likely to enhance internationalization. The second bundle of hypothesis is that in countries and regions of EAC countries with a better investment climate are relatively likely to enhance internationalization activities.

Table 4.2 sets out the firm-level determinants of exporting. This includes the size of the firm, the number of years since establishment, firm ownership status, and agglomeration. I control for the age and size of the firm as older and larger firms can be expected to influence export status considering that these firms may have sufficient scale and space for production. To control for firm size, I follow the Enterprise Survey that categorizes establishment size based on the number of employees: small (firms with up to 19 employees), medium (20–99 employees), and large (more than 100 employees) (World Bank 2017). I account for firm age using the number of years since inception. Foreign Direct Investments (FDI) is an important channel of international integration (Change and van Marrewijk 2013; Demena et al. 2021b; Chapter 7 of this book), thus I included whether the firm is local or foreign owned. Doing so, the analysis will help to assess whether the

Table 4.2 Potential list of variables related to firm characteristics

Variables	Description
Exports	Firm exports (at least 10% of its outputs) (Demena and van Bergeijk 2019; Demena et al. 2021a, b)
Foreign owned	Dummy variable for foreign-owned firms with at least 10% ownership (Demena & van Bergeijk, 2017; Kinuthia, 2016)
Firm size—SS (5–19 workers)	Dummy variable if the size of the firm is small (Demena and Murshed 2018; Kinda 2013)
Firm size—MS (20–99 workers)	Dummy variable if the size of the firm is medium (Demena 2016a; Chang and van Marrewijk 2013)
Firm size—LS (100+ workers)	Dummy variable if the size of the firm is large (Demena 2016b; Chaffai et al. 2012)
Agglomeration	The number of exporting firms in same the country–region–sector (Demena et al. 2021a, b; Kinda 2013)
Firm age	Number of years in operation (Demena 2016b, 2017; Kinda 2010)

degree to which the investment climate indicators affect internationalization via the FDI channel carries over into export market participation. In other words, given the constraints, would FDI be a suitable policy response to promote internationalization? Regarding agglomeration, Demena and Murshed (2018) highlight the relevance of accounting for the geographical distribution of firms. I follow the literature and control for agglomeration using the number of exporting firms in each sector, region, and country.

Concerning investment climate aspects, Table 4.3 gives the list of potential indicators. I include the perception of firms about infrastructural (physical and financial) constraints, lack of skilled labor force, custom and trade regulations, crime, and disorder. I expect that weak investment climate indicators are the main reasons constraining the utilization of available foreign market access opportunities.

Table 4.4 gives the descriptive statistics of the variables considered for the empirical strategy (Eq. 4.1). Given the empirical framework, I addressed several econometrics concerns. First, with respect to multi-collinearity issues, the WB enterprise survey questionnaire includes various variables for a specific characteristic of investment climate indicators. An example is an infrastructural constraint which is represented both by the number of electrical outages and by the financial losses due to electrical outage. To avoid collinearity concerns from including similar variables simultaneously, I constructed aggregated indices. This also avoids the problem that the choice of a single variable per investment constraint indicator may introduce (subjective) selection bias. I used Principal Component Analysis (PCA) to generate aggregated indices. Second, existing studies (e.g., Kinda 2013; Demena 2017) argue that to reduce potential endogeneity concerns, an agglomeration variable can be included. For instance, agglomeration variables can be introduced by the number of exporters in a specific sector and region which captures the average attractiveness of a region.

Table 4.3 Potential list of variables related to investment climate indicators

Variables	Description
Telecom access 1	Access to e-mail for business with clients and suppliers
Telecom access 2	Access to website for business with clients and suppliers
Electricity problems	Electricity-related business constraints
Transport problems	Transport-related business constraints
Access to finance problems	Various access to finance-related business constraints (e.g., collateral)
Informal finance problems	Problems related to informal sources of financing
Custom and trade regulations	Customs and trade-related business constraints
Crime and disorder	Crime, theft, disorder-related business constraints
Skilled labour problems	Business constraints related to skills of available workers

Source Author's compilation using World Bank Enterprise Surveys 2014

Table 4.4 Descriptive statistics

Variables	Mean	SD	Min	Max
Exports	0.11	0.31	0	1
Foreign owned	0.11	0.30	0	1
Firm size—SS (5–19 workers)	0.55	0.50	0	1
Firm size—MS (20–99 workers)	0.30	0.46	0	1
Firm size—LS (100+ workers)	0.15	0.36	0	1
Agglomeration	0.62	2.29	0	15
Firm age	16.74	14.14	1	107
Telecom access 1	0.55	0.50	0	1
Telecom access 2	0.34	0.48	0	1
Electricity problems	1.93	1.29	0	4
Transport problems	1.64	1.33	0	4
Access to finance problems	1.84	1.29	0	4
Informal finance problems	0.14	0.34	0	1
Custom and trade regulations	0.75	0.43	0	1
Crime and disorder	0.68	0.47	0	1
Skilled labor problems	1.55	1.38	0	4

Source Author's compilation using World Bank Enterprise Surveys 2014

Third, potential endogeneity could also arise from firms' response to identical investment characteristics but depend on the performance of each firm (this is also documented in the literature, for instance, Chaffai et al. 2012; Kinda 2010). For example, the most efficient or productive firms could have different perceptions of investment constraints as they could have better resources than the less efficient firms to assess and develop suitable responses to the constraints, and this can imply assessing an identical bottleneck differently. To minimize potential investment climate bias, I use sector-region averages measures as instrument variables.[4] Finally, to avoid within-country dependency, the estimation technique employs a clustered data analysis at the country level. On the basis of these econometrics concerns, the estimation method will mainly employ the instrumental variable probit model. As a method of robustness check or as a baseline estimation, the linear probability model—the two-stage least square (2SLS) estimation is provided. Given that our outcome variable is whether a firm exports or not (dichotomous variable), the probit model is preferred.

4.4   Empirical Results

A set of various estimations is presented. Firstly, I apply the reduced empirical model to estimate the impact of investment climate indicators and firm-level characteristics on the probability to export. Table 4.5 presents the results. Regressions in Columns (1) and (2) estimate the impact of infrastructural constraints (indexed from both physical and financial infrastructural information) on the probability to enter a foreign market. The preferred model (Column 2) shows that a marginal decrease in infrastructural constraints will significantly increase the probability to export. Next, I consider the breakdown of the infrastructure constraints into the physical and financial indexes separately. The results are presented in Columns (3) and (4), and I find a more nuanced picture of the infrastructure constraints. The results suggest that the financial infrastructure constraints are the main drivers of the internationalization of EAC firms but not the physical infrastructure. Because of this, the results suggest that firms in the EAC are less discouraged by the physical infrastructure index (firms' perception of electricity and transport problems) when deciding on their foreign market participation. Rather existing financial systems for their financing needs captured by firms' formal and informal sources of financing receive particular attention as investment climate constraints.

---

[4] I find that infrastructural problems (including both physical and financial infrastructural problems) and telecom access 2 (access to website) are potentially endogenous variables. That means investment climate related to these variables could be differently assessed (i.e., perceived) depending on the performance and resources of the firms. In this regard, resourceful or more productive firms could have less perception of these kind of investment climate bottlenecks relative to less resourceful or productive firms. To account for such endogeneity issue, following Chaffai et al. (2012) and Kinda (2013) I define instruments using sector–region average instead of individual firm perceptions.

Table 4.5 Results of Infrastructural and other structural variables

Variables	(1)	(2)	(3)	(4)	(5)	(6)
	2SLS	IV probit	2SLS	IV probit	2SLS	IV probit
Foreign (F)	0.111***	0.154***	0.099***	0.135**	0.108***	0.113***
	(0.012)	(0.043)	(0.008)	(0.050)	(0.011)	(0.035)
Agglomeration	0.102***		0.099***		0.103***	
	(0.013)		(0.010)		(0.013)	
Medium Firm—MF	0.014**	0.066***	0.018***	0.071***	0.013	0.060**
(20–99 workers)	(0.007)	(0.021)	(0.005)	(0.223)	(0.011)	(0.024)
Large Firm—LF	0.076***	0.179***	0.091***	0.240***	0.070***	0.183***
(100+ workers)	(0.016)	(0.043)	(0.024)	(0.055)	(0.025)	(0.053)
Firm age	0.001**	0.001**	0.000*	0.001**	0.001*	0.001**
	(0.000)	(0.0002)	(0.000)	(0.0003)	(0.000)	(0.0003)
Infrastructural problems (IP)	0.001	−0.031*				
	(0.032)	(0.016)				
Physical infra. problems (PIP)			0.022	0.014		
			(0.016)	(0.015)		
Financial infra. problems (FIP)			−0.037	−0.018*		
			(0.024)	(0.009)		
Skilled labour problems (SLP)	0.012**	−0.007	0.007	−0.016		
	(0.005)	(0.018)	(0.014)	(0.024)		
Custom and trade reg. (CTR)	0.010	−0.033*	−0.013	−0.018*		
	(0.015)	(0.018)	(0.012)	(0.009)		
Crime and disorder (CD)	−0.019*	−0.016***	−0.039***	−0.031**		
	(0.011)	(0.004)	(0.010)	(0.013)		
Telecom (website)					−0.014	0.052***
					(0.018)	(0.005)
Telecom (email)					0.026***	0.037**
					(0.008)	(0.014)
Observations	2063	2063	1742	1742	2199	2199
Number of countries	4	4	4	4	4	4
$\overline{R}^2$	0.65		0.66		0.65	

(continued)

Table 4.5 (continued)

Variables	(1)	(2)	(3)	(4)	(5)	(6)
	2SLS	IV probit	2SLS	IV probit	2SLS	IV probit
% of correct prediction		91.12		90.89		91.69
Wald test for exogeneity						
Infrastructure						
Chi^2 (1)		0.00				
p-value		0.9606				
Physical/Financial infra						
Chi^2 (2)				3.14		
p-value				0.0208		
Telecom: Chi^2 (1) p-value						12.46 0.0004

Notes Robust standard errors in parenthesis are clustered at the country level. * $p < 0.1$; ** $p < 0.05$; *** $p < 0.01$. The dependent variable is the probability to export. All regressions include country and industry-fixed effects. For probit regressions, reported coefficients are marginal effects. The control/reference for firm size is a dummy variable if the firm is small (5–19 workers). In most cases the statistical validity of the instruments is supported by the Wald test for exogeneity, rejecting the null hypothesis that the instrumented variables are exogenous, which is an important condition to have reliable findings. In addition, we apply the % correctly predicted method for the probit model for goodness-of-fit

Table 4.5 also underlies the relevance of other structural factors such as human capital constraints and institutional problems. I consider firms' perceptions of the availability skilled laborers as a proxy for human capital, whereas institutional quality is captured by firms' perceptions of customs and trade regulations, and crime, theft, and disorder. Focusing on the preferred model, Columns (2) and (4) underlie the importance of institutional quality in driving foreign market participation. I found that an increase in both crime and disorder, and in custom and trade regulations significantly discourage the probability of becoming an exporter.

Next, I incorporate additional factors of the investment climate to check if they mediate the firm-level internationalization strategy. I consider telecommunication opportunities captured by whether an establishment has its own website and access to e-mail to interact with suppliers and clients. Results are presented in Columns 5 and 6. Consistent with the existing theoretical background that a well-functioning telecommunication system enhances economic activities, I found that both these variables are positively and significantly associated with the probability of firm-level internationalization strategy.

Regarding firm-level determinants, all the considered factors are consistent and significantly drive the probability of foreign market participation. Regarding the firms' size effects, medium-sized firms are more likely to be exporters (6–7%) as opposed to small-sized firms and large-sized firms are even more exporters (18–24%). The age of firms since establishment is statistically significant, but the magnitude of the estimated coefficients is not different from zero.[5] The agglomeration impact is also positively and statistically significantly linked with the probability of internationalization of firms, capturing some externality of nearby firms in a specific region and industry (e.g., see Demena and Bergeijk 2019).

Finally, in line with the argument on the extension of a firm's international organization incorporating ownership status (Demena et al. 2021b), I find that FDI is an important dimension of firm-level internationalization strategy. The argument is that foreign affiliates may facilitate the entry or expansion of trade to foreign markets by providing knowledge of foreign product markets, transport infrastructure, and distribution channels (Demena 2017). Specifically, according to Demena (2017:181) 'firms may look for larger economies of scale and cheaper factors of production, and thus developing countries may provide better competitive advantages as a production location'. The results are consistently positive and statistically significantly associated with foreign market entry and operation of EAC firms.

As presented in Table 4.5, I consistently find that foreign ownership is another dimension of firm-level internationalization. Therefore, the next question to further investigate is whether the intensity of the foreign-ownership structure matters for international integration. In this procedure, I narrow the broader definition of foreign ownership to vary according to the degree of ownership. Accordingly, I included two additional variables in terms of majority and minority ownership to replace the previous single foreign ownership variable. The previous analyses were only based on a dichotomous specification. I now specify minority foreign ownership with a dummy value that takes 1 if ownership by foreigner ranges from 10% up to 50%. Similarly, the majority of foreign ownership takes the value of 1 if its share exceeds 50%.

Results are presented in Table 4.6 using Eq. (4.1). Estimated coefficients of the two types of firms are statistically significant across the various specifications and estimation approaches, corroborating the view that foreign ownership is a relevant factor for firm-level internationalization strategy regardless of the degree of ownership. In general, I continued to find similar results to the previous analyses (compared to the single foreign ownership variable regardless of its extent). Unlike the previous analyses, I have now provided additional statistics if the difference in the reported estimates of these two types of firms are statistically significant. The point estimates for the statistical difference are provided using the F-test and reported at the bottom of Table 4.6. The findings across most specifications and estimations (in particular in our preferred model) suggest a statistically insignificant difference in the reported estimates between minority and majority foreign-owned firms (most of the p-values

---

[5] To model the effect of age since inception more accurately (i.e., to check if age has a nonlinear relationship with internationalization of firms), I add a quadratic age variable and re-estimate all specifications of Table 4.5. I find that both age and quadratic age variables are statistically insignificant across all the specifications of Table 4.5. To keep the table manageable and better visualize the results, these results are not presented, but are available upon request from the author.

Table 4.6 Results of Infrastructural and other structural variables with foreign ownership intensity

Variables	(1)	(2)	(3)	(4)	(5)	(6)
	2SLS	IV probit	2SLS	IV probit	2SLS	IV probit
Minority foreign owned	0.160^{***}	0.213^{**}	0.107^{***}	0.149^{*}	0.157^{***}	0.196^{**}
	(0.030)	(0.106)	(0.020)	(0.088)	(0.027)	(0.086)
Majority foreign owned	0.088^{***}	0.136^{***}	0.095^{***}	0.136^{***}	0.085^{***}	0.111^{***}
	(0.010)	(0.030)	(0.008)	(0.039)	(0.012)	(0.030)
Agglomeration	0.102^{***}		0.099^{***}		0.103^{***}	
	(0.013)		(0.010)		(0.012)	
Medium Firm—MF	0.015^{**}	0.067^{***}	0.019^{***}	0.071^{***}	0.014	0.061^{***}
(20–99 workers)	(0.007)	(0.020)	(0.004)	(0.021)	(0.011)	(0.023)
Large Firm—LF	0.076^{***}	0.180^{***}	0.091^{***}	0.240^{***}	0.068^{***}	0.183^{***}
(100+ workers)	(0.016)	(0.043)	(0.024)	(0.055)	(0.025)	(0.054)
Firm age	0.001^{**}	0.001^{***}	0.000^{*}	0.001^{***}	0.001^{*}	0.001^{**}
	(0.000)	(0.0002)	(0.000)	(0.0002)	(0.000)	(0.0003)
Infrastructural problems (IP)	−0.001	−0.002				
	(0.031)	(0.039)				
Physical infra. problems (PIP)			0.022	0.013		
			(0.016)	(0.016)		
Financial infra. problems (FIP)			−0.037*	$−0.018^{*}$		
			(0.021)	(0.009)		
Skilled labor problems (SLP)	$−0.013^{**}$	−0.006	−0.007	−0.016		
	(0.006)	(0.019)	(0.014)	(0.024)		
Custom & trade reg. (CTR)	0.010	−0.033*	−0.013	$−0.018^{*}$		
	(0.016)	(0.018)	(0.012)	(0.009)		
Crime & disorder (CD)	$−0.020^{*}$	$−0.017^{***}$	$−0.039^{***}$	$−0.031^{**}$		
	(0.011)	(0.004)	(0.010)	(0.014)		
Telecom (website)					0.014	0.052^{***}
					(0.018)	(0.006)
Telecom (email)					0.027^{***}	0.037^{**}
					(0.008)	(0.015)
Observations	2063	2063	1742	1742	2199	2199
Number of countries	4	4	4	4	4	4
$\overline{R}^2$	0.65		0.66		0.65	

(continued)

Table 4.6 (continued)

Variables	(1)	(2)	(3)	(4)	(5)	(6)
	2SLS	IV probit	2SLS	IV probit	2SLS	IV probit
% of correct prediction		89.29		88.29		89.54
Wald test for exogeneity						
Infrastructure						
Chi^2 (1)		0.00				
p-value		0.978				
Physical/Financial infra						
Chi^2 (2)				3.10		
p-value				0.021		
Telecom: Chi^2 (1) p-value						13.24 0.000
Test if coefficients are significantly different: F-test (Prob > F)						
Minority versus Majority	0.037**	0.363	0.554	0.955	0.056*	0.426
MF versus LF	0.000***	0.000***	0.000***	0.000***	0.000***	0.000***

Notes See Table 4.5

of F-test are greater than the conventional 10% significance level). This implies that for the internationalization of firms, the FDI channel is substantially relevant regardless of the degree of foreign ownership. This is not consistent with the view that the majority of foreign-owned firms are the main drivers; for productivity spill overs in SSA (Demena and Murshed 2018), for productivity premium for EAC (Demena et al. 2021b; Chap. 7 of this book) or for Latin American countries (Chang and van Marrewijk 2013).

In all the previous analyses, I find the relevance of medium-sized and large-sized firms as opposed to small-sized firms for internationalization strategy. In addition, in Table 4.6, I provided additional analysis to investigate the statistical difference between medium-sized and large-sized firms. I find that firm-level internationalization strategies are mainly driven by large-sized firms (all the p-values of the F-test suggest statistically significant results). This implies that medium-sized firms are more productive than small-sized firms, and that large-sized firms are even more productive not only than small-sized firms but also those that are medium-sized firms.

Across all the specifications, our estimations of the probit model are comparable to the 2SLS. In particular, I continue to find consistently comparable and stable results of the identified impacts of the structural factors of the national investment climate and firm-level determinants of internationalization of EAC firms.

4.5 Conclusion and Policy Recommendations

This chapter focused on supply-side constraints for export market integration as experienced at the firm level. Existing studies argue that SSA countries have faced relatively fewer binding constraints in accessing external markets than other developing countries. The literature suggests that the weak investment climate in developing countries is the main reason constraining the utilization of available foreign market access. Accordingly, SSA countries' poor export performance is likely to be associated with weak export supply responses. Some of the supply-side bottlenecks are linked to investment climate that hinders strengthening supply capacity, while others are underlying economic conditions (Morris and Fessehaie 2014; Demena et al. 2021a). This is an important policy dimension as government interventions to ease such trade policy obstacles to support export competitiveness and diversification can address the key factors that are responsible for constraining supply capacity across SSA countries.

Measures to stimulate private sector development have focused on improving the investment climate or business environment (Jahari 2021). I investigate several business climate measures of the investment along individual firm characteristics on international integration using the WBES firm-level data for four countries in EAC. I first build an empirical framework with firm-level data on how investment climates related to institutional and trade policy obstacles affect international integration. Next, I demonstrate the application of more disaggregated data to capture firm-level heterogeneity aspects in explaining internationalization.

For most EAC countries, firms tend to see many areas of the investment climate as bottlenecks to business. I find that access to formal and informal finance, custom and trade regulations, and telecommunication opportunities tend to pose serious constraints for the investment climate. Unlike existing studies for SSA countries (for instance Kinda 2013), I did not find any evidence that the availability of a skilled labor force was a serious constraint to business. It might be the case that, as Gelb et al. (2011) argued, the lack of skilled labor tends to be more of a concern as the capacity of the government to enforce regulations increases and economies become more sophisticated. In terms of policy implications, policymakers should pay particular attention to design priorities with the most binding constraints to business as seen by firms across the EAC. In line with Gelb et al. (2011), firms often tend to observe serious business constraints and thus can support the design and prioritize regulatory policy reforms across the business climate. Indeed, there is no magic bullet even if a particularly binding constraint to business emerges as posing serious problems. Regardless, the current study shows that governments in EAC counties need to design policies and efforts to solve bottlenecks to business across the identified fronts focusing on access to formal and informal finance and enhanced telecommunication opportunities complemented by reforms on custom and trade regulations as well as a system of service delivery monitoring.

Regarding firm-level determinants, the study reveals that all the considered factors are substantially significant across all specification and estimation approaches.

Medium-sized firms are more likely to be exporters as opposed to small-sized firms, but large-sized firms are even more likely to be exporters compared to any other firms. Larger domestic firms can perform better because they are likely to have sufficient production space and scale to be able to counter competition in foreign markets. This is an important policy consideration and binding constraint as the vast majority of domestic firms in EAC are SMEs, employing only a few workers (Demena 2017). For instance, the median size of domestic firms operating in Uganda in 2015 is merely 15 workers (Demena and van Bergeijk 2019). Likewise, Demena and Murshed (2018) report that more than two-thirds of domestic firms in eight SSA countries are small firms, whereas in Nigeria 99% of firms employ fewer than 10 employees (McKenzie 2017).[6]

Geographical (agglomeration) dimension of firms is also an important channel of internationalization of firms, capturing some externality (positive and negative) of nearby firms in a specific region and industry. Similar results were reported for productivity externality by Demena (2016b); Demena (2017); Demena and van Bergeijk (2019). According to the theory of economic geography, the potential for the flow of information is more pronounced when firms are geographically co-located. The notion is that the existence of agglomeration economies is enhanced by the geographical concentration of economic activities (industries) (Demena and Murshed 2018). The results in this chapter are in line with the evidence that the majority of firms in SSA countries tend to concentrate in larger and capital cities where finance, infrastructure, labor force, and other institutions are well developed (Kinda 2013). One possible policy implication could be that governments should consider the geographical location/concentration of firms in a given industry in promoting investment projects.

Another important factor is that FDI is an essential dimension of firm-level internationalization strategy. This implies that foreign affiliates may enable to bridge to foreign markets either to enter new markets or to increase sales in existing markets from a host country. The implication is that to encourage firms that have relatively advanced productivity to be willing to accept a degree of foreign ownership is shown to be one of the best approaches to internationalization. The result is in line with the location advantage economic theory, the macroeconomic development approach that relies on the influence of location to explain FDI activities (e.g., Vernon, 1966). The argument is that foreign affiliates may facilitate the entry or expansion of trade to foreign markets by providing knowledge of foreign product markets, transport infrastructure, and distribution channels (Demena 2017). The result supports the product cycle theory developed by Vernon (1966) which states that a firm initially exploits foreign markets through exports, and later undertakes FDI from a host country as a product moves through its life cycle where demand sufficiently warrants new production activities. As in Vernon's argument, US firms moved to Europe where there were relatively cheaper factors of production, lower transportation costs, and higher product demand, and thus indicating the location advantages of the host country

---

[6] Similar patterns are observed for other developing counties, for instance, in Mexico, Indonesia, and India, 90% of the domestic firms employ fewer than 10 workers (Hsieh and Olken 2014).

for local and foreign market production (Demena 2017). Indeed, foreign firms may consider EAC countries as a production location for competitive advantages for instance using cheaper factors of production.

However, the extension of foreign firms' presence in a host country for international integration via the FDI channel is substantially relevant regardless of the degree of foreign ownership (majority versus minority foreign-owned firms). The findings regarding the degree of foreign ownership do not corroborate with recent studies suggesting that majority foreign-owned firms are the main drivers. For instance, for productivity spill overs in SSA (Demena and Murshed 2018), for productivity premium in EAC (Chap. 7 of this book). Beyond the region, a sample of firms from 15 Latin American countries (Chang and van Marrewijk 2013). In other words, for the current study, I can conclude that it is merely foreign ownership that matters regardless of the degree of ownership for the firm-level globalization strategy. The policy implication is that targeting minority-owned foreign subsidiaries that provides a higher level of local participation would be a sufficient condition for foreign market integration. This is also substantiated by the notion that minority ownership could potentially provide local firms to become acquainted with advanced foreign technology, as the latter allows better access to specific foreign knowledge (Demena 2017).

References

Bacchetta M (2007) Releasing export constraints: the role of governments. AERC Research Project on Export Supply Response Capacity Constraints in Africa

Chaffai M, Kinda T, Plane P (2012) Textile manufacturing in eight developing countries: does business environment matter for firm technical efficiency? J Dev Stud 48(10):1470–1488

Chang HH, Van Marrewijk C (2013) Firm heterogeneity and development: evidence from Latin American countries. J Int Trade Econ Dev 22(1):11–52

Demena BA (2016a) Does the development of private sector through promoting FDI facilitate inclusive growth? Evidence from sub-Saharan African Industries. In: Proceedings of conference on inclusive growth and poverty reduction in the IGAD region, p 22

Demena BA (2016b) FDI, spillovers and firm-level heterogeneity: identifying the transmission channels. European Trade Study Group, Conference paper no 195

Demena B (2017) Essays on intra-industry spillovers from FDI in developing countries: a firm-level analysis with a focus on Sub-Saharan Africa

Demena BA, Murshed SM (2018) Transmission channels matter: identifying spillovers from FDI. J Int Trade Econ Dev 27(7):701–728

Demena BA, van Bergeijk PAG (2017) A meta-analysis of FDI and productivity spillovers in developing countries. J Econ Surv 31(2):546–571

Demena BA, van Bergeijk PAG (2019) Observing FDI spillover transmission channels: evidence from firms in Uganda. Third World Q 40(9):1708–1729

Demena BA, Msami J, Mmari D, van Bergeijk PAG (2021a) Trade, productivity and competitiveness. African Portal and Policy brief no. 18/2021a, Research on Poverty Alleviation

Demena BA, Msami J, Mmari D, van Bergeijk PAG (2021b) Productivity premia and firm heterogeneity in Eastern Africa, ISS WP No 680

Demena BA, Msami J, Mmari D, van Bergeijk PAG (2022) Productivity premia and firm hetero-geneity in Eastern Africa. In: Demena BA, van Bergeijk PAG (eds) Trade and investment in East Africa: prospect, challenges and pathways to sustainability. Springer

Djankov S, Freund C, Pham CS (2010) Trading on time. Rev Econ Stat 92(1):166–173

Freund C, Rocha N (2011) What constrains Africa's exports? World Bank Econ Rev 25(3):361–386

Gelb A, Ramachandran V, Shah MK, Turner G (2011) What matters to African firms? The relevance of perceptions data. In: Financial inclusion, innovation, and investments: biotechnology and capital markets working for the poor, pp 197–225

Hallward-Driemeier M, Pritchett L (2015) How business is done in the developing world: deals versus rules. J Econ Perspect 29(3):121–140

Hoekman B, Shepherd B (2015) Who profits from trade facilitation initiatives? Implications for African countries. J Afr Trade 2(1–2):51–70

Hsieh CT, Olken BA (2014) The missing "missing middle." J Econ Perspect 28(3):89–108

Jahari C (2021) Business environment and enterprise competitiveness, diversification and value chain. African Portal and Policy brief no. 9/2021, Research on Poverty Alleviation

Kinda T (2010) Investment climate and FDI in developing countries: firm-level evidence. World Dev 38(4):498–513

Kinda T (2013) Beyond natural resources: horizontal and vertical FDI diversification in Sub-Saharan Africa. Appl Econ 45(25):3587–3598

Kinuthia BK (2016) Technology spillovers: Kenya and Malaysia compared. J Int Trade Econ Dev 25(4):536–569

McKenzie D (2017) Identifying and spurring high-growth entrepreneurship: experimental evidence from a business plan competition. Am Econ Rev 107(8):2278–2307

Morris M, Fessehaie J (2014) The industrialisation challenge for Africa: towards a commodities-based industrialisation path. Journal of African Trade 1(1):25–36

Stern N (2002) A strategy for development. The World Bank, Washington, DC

UNECA, Economic Commission for Africa (2015) Industrializing through trade, Economic Report on Africa, Addis Ababa, Ethiopia

van Bergeijk PAG, Fortanier F, Garretsen H, de Groot HL, Moons SJ (2011) Productivity and internationalization: a micro-data approach. De Econ 159(4):381–388

van Bergeijk PAG, van Marrewijk C (2013) Heterogeneity and development: an agenda. J Int Trade Econ Dev 22(1):1–10

van den Berg M (2015) The trade, aid, and investment nexus. In: van Bergeijk PAG (ed) To graduate or not to graduate: the case of Cape Verde. INCLUDE special report

Vernon R (1966) International investment and international trade in the product cycle. Q J Econ 80(2):190–207

World Bank Enterprise Survey (2017) Enterprise survey indicator description. Accessed 18 June 2020. https://www.enterprisesurveys.org/content/dam/enterprisesurveys/documents/Indicator-Descriptions.pdf. Accessed 18 June 2020

Chapter 5
Trade Complementarities Between Europe and Tanzania

Huda Ahmed Yussuf and Masoud Mohammed Albiman

Abstract We study the changes in comparative advantage over time of Tanzanian exports and identify opportunities for trade with Europe. Comparative advantage is measured using the Balassa index (and the Volrath index as a robustness check). Additionally, trends in intra-industry trade (both between Tanzania and the world as well as with sub-Saharan Africa) are measured using the Grubel–Loyd Index. All products studied are under Harmonized System (HS) 2-digit classification and from 2009 to 2018, inclusive. Tanzania's exports still rely heavily on raw materials such as those in groups of stone and glass, animals and vegetables. However, from 2012 onward Tanzania has gained an export advantage in intermediate goods. These intermediate exports are highly correlated with exports of textiles and clothing as well as processed vegetables. Tanzania has an opportunity to export processed fish and animal products to Europe. In addition, we find import opportunities in rubber and plastic, transportation, chemical and woods. Most of these products can be used in the production process, hence a trade agreement will lower the cost of production for local industries. Trade between Tanzania and the rest of the world is found to be inter-industry as opposed to intra-industry except for textile products. Sectors with export potential are processing of animal products, textile and leather industries.

The authors are thankful to Peter van Bergeijk and Binyam Afewerk Demena of Erasmus University, International Institute of Social Studies for technical guidance in carrying out the research work. The study was financially supported by Research on Poverty Alleviation (REPOA), the African Caribbean and Pacific Group of States (ACP Group) of this project, grant number FED/2019/408-112.

H. A. Yussuf (✉)
Muslim University of Morogoro, Morogoro, Tanzania
e-mail: hudayssf@gmail.com

M. M. Albiman
Institute of Tax Administration, Dar-es-Salaam, Tanzania

5.1 Introduction

The East African Community (EAC) is undertaking resource-based industrialization, which will increase the average share of manufacturing in the GDP of its members from 8.7% in 2012 to 25.0% in 2032.[1] Among other strategies to achieve these objectives are the promotion and development of strategic industries which have a competitive advantage and increasing their access to foreign markets. The latter is through achieving both full(er) market integration within the EAC and securing other global markets. In order to increase the market for EAC products, EAC signs trade agreements with other countries or other trade blocks.

While Tanzania is moving toward industrialization, the EU is waiting for Tanzania to sign the EU-EAC trade agreement. One of the routes to industrialization is export promotion, which is also a Tanzanian government policy priority. However, the question remains: will this trade agreement help Tanzania towards industrialization through exports? This chapter answers this question by investigating the possibilities of trade between Tanzania and Europe using the theories of comparative advantage.

Industrialization is essential for structural transformation and high-quality employment in any nation (Naudé and Szirmai 2012). Dodzin and Vamvakidis (2004) suggest that developing countries that increase their openness to trade are more likely to increase their share of industrial production at the expense of agricultural products. However, Brown and Kee (2011) found that developing countries are more hesitant to trade than developed nations and Tanzania is no different.

Industrialization has long been seen as a road towards development. Experience shows that more developed nations are characterized by a large sophisticated industrial sector. Tanzania aims to transform into a semi-industrialized nation by 2025. Policymakers believe that this can be achieved through resource-based industrialization and human development to become a competitive export-led economy. The economy is at the phase of improving the share of tech-related goods production in GDP. Between 2015 and 2020, the share of low-tech goods to improve from 17 to 29%, medium-tech from 11 to 24%, and high-tech from 2 to 6% of GDP. While the number of exporting firms was targeted to increase from 247 to 729 firms during the same period.[2]

As Tanzania intends to attain its industrialization through exports, it must build on a comparative advantage with its trading partners in these sectors (Schott 2003). This chapter aims to compute and analyse movements in comparative advantages with the rest of the world and trade complementarities of Tanzania and Europe from 2009 to 2018. This period will allow the evaluation of several intervention strategies that have been implemented from the National Five-Year Development Plan 2015/16–2020/21 as the period will provide the before and after implementation comparison.

---

[1] East African Community Industrial Policy 2021–2032 accessed from https://www.eac.int/docume nts/category/industrialization-sme-development.

[2] National Five-Year Development Plan 2015/16–2020/21 accessed from https://www.mof.go.tz/ mofdocs/msemaji/Five%202016_17_2020_21.pdf.

The remainder of this chapter is organized as follows. Section 5.2 discusses our methodology. Section 5.3 reviews Tanzania trade followed by the findings on the trends of competitive indices in Sects. 5.4 and 5.5. Section 5.6 highlights trade complementarities between Tanzania and Europe. The EU trends in Sect. 5.4 and 5.5 also involve Central Asia due to the data availability. Section 5.7 concludes.

5.2 Methodology and Data

5.2.1 Methodology

The objective of the study is to investigate (the changes in) the comparative advantages of Tanzanian exports and its trade complementarities with Europe. Comparative advantage is a concept first coined by David Ricardo. A country has a comparative advantage in a certain product if it can produce that product at lower opportunity cost than other countries. Trade complementarity between two nations exists when country A has a comparative advantage on a good for which country B has comparative disadvantage (Viner 1950). Thus complementarity exists when country A can export its commodity to country B according to this theory.

Competitiveness can be measured by the presence of a significant amount of product's exports. In this chapter, we use three indices to measure the competitiveness of Tanzanian exports. We start with the Balassa index (Balassa 1965) of Revealed Comparative Advantage (RCA) in Eq. (5.1) then the Volrath Index of Trade Advantage (RTA) in Eq. (5.3) as used by Bojnec and Fertő (2012), comparing indices from Eq. (5.1) and Eq. 5.2 to determine trade complementarities. Finally, the Grubel–Loyd index in Eq. (5.4) for the presence of intra-industry trade.

$$RXA = \left(\frac{X_a^i}{X_t^i}\right) \div \left(\frac{X_a^w}{X_t^w}\right) \tag{5.1}$$

$$RMA = \left(\frac{M_a^i}{M_t^i}\right) \div \left(\frac{M_a^w}{M_t^w}\right) \tag{5.2}$$

$$RTA_a = RXA_a - RMA_a \tag{5.3}$$

where

RTA: Relative Trade Advantage.

RXA: Revealed Export Advantage.

RMA: Revealed Import Advantage.

X: Exports.

M: Imports.

a, i, t and w: represent industry, country, total and world, respectively.

The Balassa index examines the Revealed Export Advantage, and hence, is equivalent to the *RXA*. Tanzania is considered to have an RXA in a particular industry if the share of the industry's exports in Tanzanian total exports is greater than, or equal to one, to the share of the industry's exports in the world's exports (i.e. RXA_a). The same interpretation goes for the *RMA*.

Tanzania has an *RTA* in a certain industry if RXA_a is greater than the RMA_a (i.e. *RTA* > 0) and will have a disadvantage if the *RTA* < 0. The use of *RTA* is important in this study since we are dealing with trade between regions. A region may have a vast amount of exports but if some of those exports are imported within the same region then that will deflate the actual comparative advantage between the region and the rest of the world.

With increased globalization, intra-industry trade emerged, that is, countries exporting and importing the same products, hence expanding choices and competition within countries. The presence of intra-industry trade also shows the country's participation in the global value chain. In this regard, the research also analysed movement in intra-industry trade using Grubel Lloyd (GLIndex 1971) which is computed as follows:

$$GL_i = \frac{(X_i + M_i) - (|X_i - M_i|)}{X_i + M_i} \tag{5.4}$$

where i represents a particular industry, X is export and M is import.

Hence the GL index ranges from 0 to 1, whereby 0 means there is no intra-industry trade for that particular industry, either Tanzania only imports or only exports. When GL_i is equal to 1, then Tanzania's imports and exports of that industry are equal. Following Jing (2009), intra-industry trade is reported present when GL is 0.5 and above.

5.2.2 Data

The goods are categorized using 2-digits Harmonized System (HS) classifications and downloaded from World Integrated Trade Solutions (WITS, 2018a, b, 2021). In WITS, data for the EU is grouped with Central Asia,[3] hence all exports and imports data for the EU also involve Central Asia and competitiveness measures for the EU include Central Asia. The exports and imports are analysed in two stages. First by the economic character of the product: capital goods, consumer goods, intermediate goods and raw materials. Second by the nature of the products: Animals,

---

[3] Central Asia includes five countries; Kazakhstan, Kyrgyz Republic, Tajikistan, Turkmenistan, and Uzbekistan.

chemicals, food products, hides and skins, machines and electrical appliances, metals, miscellaneous, minerals, plastic and rubber, stone and glass, textiles and clothing, transportation, vegetables and wood. The data is from 2009 to 2018.

5.3 Tanzania's Trade

In this section, we review Tanzania's trade. The section begins with Tanzania's trade with the rest of the world followed by its trade with the EU. Sect. 5.3.2 reviews Tanzania's export diversification and Sect. 5.3.3 reviews intra-industry trade between Tanzania and the rest of the world.

5.3.1 Tanzania's Openness to Trade

Trade openness is positively related to export diversification (for example, Osakwe et al. 2018; Dodzin and Vamvakidis 2004). This trade openness can be multilateral, where each country is freely trading with all countries in the world or through regional trade agreements. According to the WTO, there are 349 regional trade agreements as of 15th June 2021. Countries within a regional trade agreement have agreements to trade among themselves freely. These agreements can be through individual countries or through economic blocks, like the one pending for ratification between EAC and EU.

Tanzania has also opened up its economy to various trade blocks providing challenges and opportunities to Tanzania's productive capacity (Osakwe et al. 2018). Apart from being a member of the WTO since 1995, Tanzania has also joined other regional agreements, such as the Southern African Development Community (SADC), Common Market for East and Central Africa (COMESA), and EAC.

In 2018 GDP per capita of EAC partner states ranged from USD 261 in Burundi to USD 1,839 in Kenya. Tanzania is second to Kenya with a GDP per capita of USD 1,090. Even though geographically, Tanzania is the biggest country in EAC-6, its trade volumes within EAC are below Uganda and Kenya and just slightly above Rwanda when it comes to EAC exports in 2018. Over the past decade trade between Tanzania and EAC has grown by 20% and 14% on average annually for exports and imports, respectively. The trend, however, is interesting, as Tanzania faced a trade deficit in 2014 and decided to decrease its import in 2015, exports had also declined in 2016, leading to another decline in trade balance (see Fig. 5.1).

Apart from EAC, Tanzania also engages in multilateral trade, where the majority of trade occurs. Among the top trading partners are China, the EU, United Arab Emirates, Japan, India, Kenya and South Africa. Tanzania's main exports to these countries include minerals, cash crops such as tobacco, coffee, cashew nuts and sisal, manufactured goods, horticultural products and fish. While the main imports include

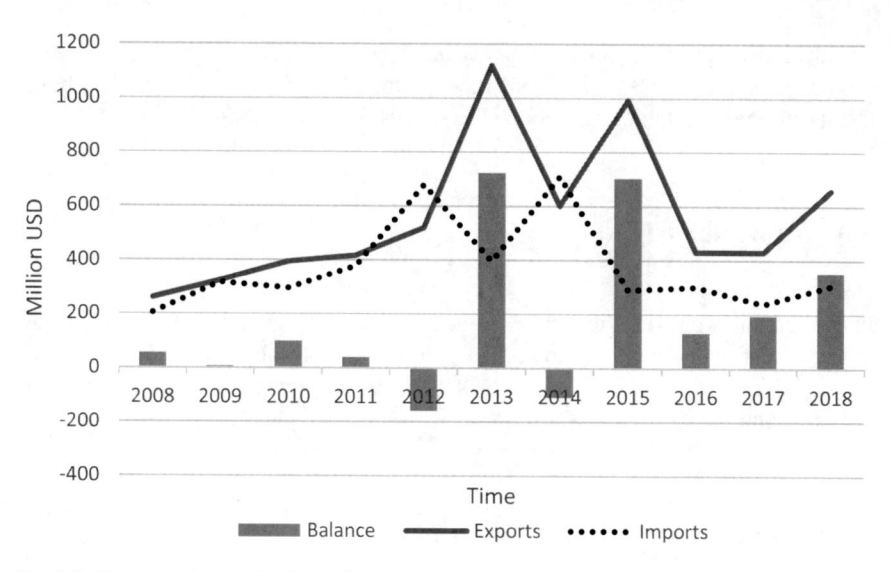

Fig. 5.1 Tanzania's trade with EAC. *Source* Authors' compilation using EAC Secretariat (2019)

transport equipment, machinery, petroleum, fertilizers, industrial raw materials, food and other consumer goods.

Europe ranks as Tanzania's third trading partner with imports worth € 837 million and exports of € 424 million in 2019. The main exports from Tanzania to Europe are live animals, vegetables, minerals and textiles. While the main imports are chemicals, base metals, machinery and transportation. A good volume of intra-industry trade, where both exports and imports appear in the same group of products is visible in foodstuff, textiles and base metals (Directorate-General for Trade 2021).

Tanzania is enjoyed a decline in its trade deficit from 2015 to 2017, which is not due to an increase in exports only but also a decrease in imports, however, the rate of decline in imports exceeds the growth of exports. As a matter of fact, just like within the EAC region, a substantial decline in imports after 2015 is also accompanied by a decrease in exports as shown in Fig. 5.2 on Tanzanian's exports and imports.

5.3.2 Export Diversification

Tanzania is a resource-rich economy and its exports are moderately diversified. According to the UNCTAD database, the export concentration index has remained stable from 2010 to 2020 ranging between 0.2 and 0.3. Export diversification can be through different goods but are in the same level of production like either primary goods, intermediate goods, or consumer goods. Tanzania resource diversification is mostly through primary products. The industrialization goal requires that exports be

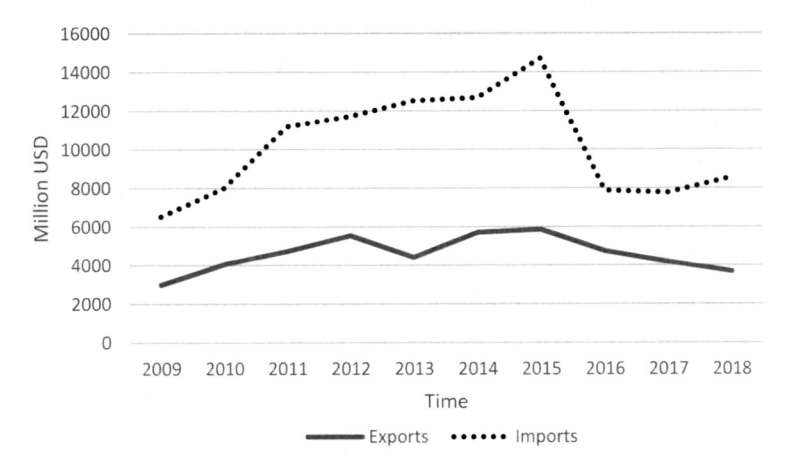

Fig. 5.2 Tanzania's total exports and imports. *Source* Authors' compilation using WITS 31st March 2021

diversified from primary to intermediate, capital and consumer goods with different levels of technology.

As of 2019 Tanzanian exports constituted 46.5% minerals and 16.7% traditional exports, that is, 63.2% of the total value of exports is from primary products. However, as Tanzania is diversifying through industrialization, 16% was for manufacturing and 6.9% were processed fish products and outputs from the horticulture industry. Among manufactured exports, only 1% was from processed traditional cash crops such as sisal products, manufactured tea and coffee and 15% were from other sectors. Table 5.1 shows that things have remained almost the same for the past 10 years. The share of manufacturing exports declined with the rise of horticultural products. The share of traditional exports has increased by 2 percentage points and the share of mineral exports (where gold is 97%) has increased by 5 percentage points.

Table 5.1 Composition of Tanzanian exports (2010 and 2019)

Exports, goods	Percent of exports	
	2010	2019
Traditional exports, (coffee, cotton, sisal, tea, tobacco, cashew nuts, cloves)	15.5	16.7
Minerals	41.5	46.5
Manufactured goods	25.6	16.0
Fish and fish products	4.0	3.4
Horticultural products	0.8	3.5
Other export products	9.0	9.0
Re-exports	3.5	4.9

Source Bank of Tanzania (2021)

Diversification is considered an essential pattern for economic development as countries find more production opportunities and create employment for their labour force. Diversification can follow the changes in comparative advantage as suggested by Heckscher–Ohlin theory or through intentional efforts by the government to support specific sectors even though defying its comparative advantage. Lectard and Rougier (2018) found that countries that defy comparative advantage become more diversified and export more sophisticated exports as compared to those following only their comparative advantage.

In both scenarios, the knowledge base and innovative capacity of the economy are crucial in reaching diversification. In the case of Tanzania, export diversification is through both scenarios. Some exports are a result of processed goods that are related to Tanzania's factor endowments such as manufactured coffee and sisal products. However, 93% of manufacturing exports are not directly related to the country's factor endowment. According to Wangwe et al. (2014), 70% of inputs used by the majority of exporting manufacturers are imported.

5.3.3 Intra-Industry Trade

Using the data from WITS as depicted in Fig. 5.3 we see that major imports are consumer goods. However, they declined after 2015 and its exports have increased in 2018. The gap between exports and imports has also decreased in 2018, showing an increase in intra-industry trade within the consumer goods industry.

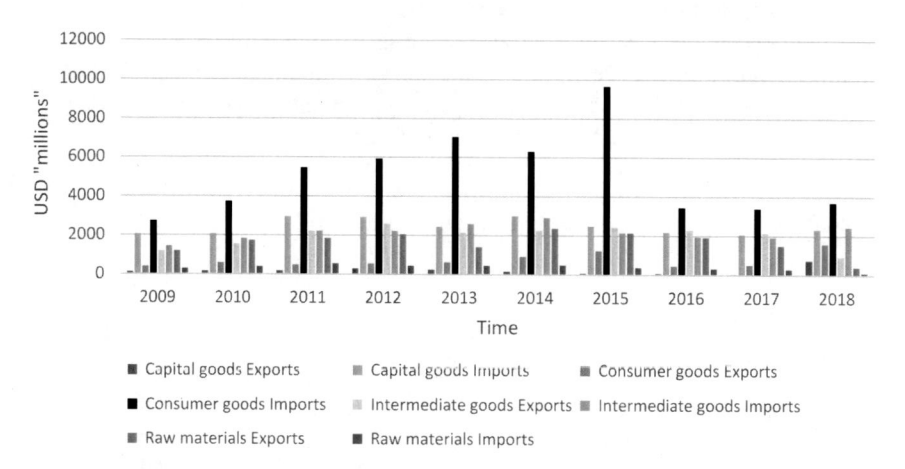

Fig. 5.3 Tanzania's trade by value chain. *Source* Authors' compilation using WITS 31st March 2021

From 2009 to 2017, exports of raw materials surpassed the imports of raw materials. In 2018, both exports and imports of raw materials declined and the difference between them has also declined. The trade balance for capital goods has also improved in 2018 due to higher exports.

From 2009 to 2017, exports and imports of intermediate goods were almost equal. In 2018, there was a decline in exports of intermediate goods while imports increased. This could be due to industrialization policies that focused on transforming raw materials and intermediate goods into capital and consumer goods which command higher market prices.

5.4 Overview of Findings

Table 5.2 summarizes the results for the entire period from 2009 to 2018 for both Tanzania and Europe and Central Asia. It is found that on average Europe and Central Asia have an export advantage in 10 groups of products, import advantage in 13 groups and trade advantage in 8 groups of products. This means there are 8 groups of products that these countries have a greater export advantage than import advantage. It is also found that there is intra-industry trade for all groups of goods.

Tanzania on other hand is found to have an export advantage in 8 groups of products and an import advantage in 7 groups. The number of goods in which Tanzania had an export advantage remained between 7 and 8 throughout except for 2014, which is 9. The average number of goods that Tanzania has a trade advantage (9) has exceeded both those with export or import advantage. These represent some of the goods that Tanzania does not necessarily have an export advantage but their share

Table 5.2 Descriptive statistics. *Source* Authors' compilation using WITS data

Competitive index	Tanzania	Europe and Central Asia
Average RXA (number of products)	8	10
Average RMA (Number of Products)	7	13
Average RTA (number of products)	9	8
Average GL (number of products)	8	21
–	–	–
Maximum RXA	10.60	1.37
Minimum RXA	0.02	0.42
Maximum RMA	4.51	1.34
Minimum RMA	0.09	0.50
Maximum RTA	10.33	0.17
Minimum RTA	−4.44	−0.43
Maximum GL	0.90	0.90
Minimum GL	0.019	0.75

of exports to the rest of the world exceeds their share of imports with the rest of the world. Intra-industry trade is seen to exist in only 8 groups on average.

The maximum value of the revealed export advantage is found to be 1.37 in Europe and 10.6 in Tanzania. In the case of Tanzania, the maximum value is far from one. This implies that the export share in the country is far greater than the export share of those commodities in the world. This value of 10.6 is found to be the *RXA* for stone and glass; this group consists of precious or semi-precious stones (HS 71) including gold. The minimum *RXA* is 0.02 in Tanzania and 0.42 in Europe and Central Asia. The gap between the maximum and minimum *RXA* is wider in Tanzania as compared to Europe and Central Asia. The very small value of 0.02 shows a very small share in the Tanzanian exports as compared to the product's export share in the world. This 0.02 is found in footwear: Tanzania produces and exports a very small share of footwear in the world market.

The maximum value of revealed import advantage (*RMA*) is 4.51 in Tanzania and 1.34 in Europe and Central Asia. The *RMA* of 1.34 shows that the product share in the imports of Europe and Central Asia is almost equivalent to the world's import share of that particular product which is animal products in our current study. The *RMA* of 4.51 in Tanzania on other hand is found in fuels, implying that the import share of fuels in Tanzania is far greater than the import share of fuels in the world. The minimum import advantage is 0.09 for Tanzania and 0.5 for Europe and Central Asia. This shows that Europe and Central Asia have a good import share for all goods while in Tanzania there are goods with a very small share of imports. The lowest RMA in Tanzania is found in raw materials.

The minimum GL for Europe and Central Asia is found to be 0.75 showing that all industries are above 0.5, as discussed intra-industry trade is present in all industries. The maximum value is 0.99, which is approximated to 1.00 in Table 5.2. Most industries displayed a GL of 0.9 and above for Europe and Central Asia.

The minimum GL for Tanzania was found to be 0.02 which indicates the absence of intra-industry trade in some industries. Most industries in Tanzania had a GL below 0.5. Even the GL for total products averaged at 0.63 indicating a low level of intra-industry trade nationwide for the entire period of study. The trend remained between 0.5 and 0.7 with exception of a small, incidental, increase in 2017. Only a handful of products were found to have GL of 0.90 and above. These products are intermediate goods, food products, textiles and clothing and vegetables. Imports and exports of intermediate goods are a good sign of progress in processing industries.

5.5   Detailed Findings

In this section, we present the trends of revealed comparative advantage, revealed trade advantage and intra-industry trade index for both Tanzania and Europe and Central Asia.

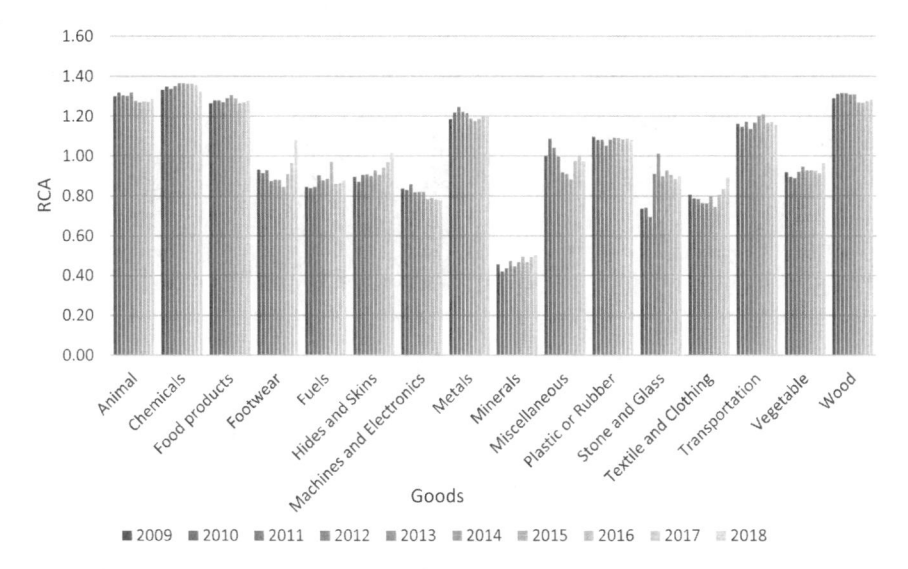

Fig. 5.4 Trend of RCA for Europe and Central Asia. *Source* Authors compilation WITS data

5.5.1 Revealed Comparative Advantage (RCA)

5.5.1.1 Trend of RCA for All Goods in Europe and Central Asia

Figure 5.4 shows the trend of revealed export advantage for 16 groups of products based on 2-digits HS classification from 2009 to 2018 for Europe and Central Asia. Products that have revealed export advantages throughout the study period are animals, chemicals, food products, metals, plastic and rubber, transportation and wood. Chemical products rank high amid the declining trend from 2013 followed by wood products. The region has recently gained an export advantage in footwear and hides and skin.

The region has lost a comparative advantage in the exports of miscellaneous and stone and glass products. The region has no comparative advantage on fuels, machines and electronics, minerals, textile and clothing and vegetable. Minerals rank the last albeit with an increasing trend.

5.5.1.2 Goods that Tanzania Has Gained RCA Over Time

Figure 5.5 shows the trend of revealed export advantage (RCA) of Tanzania from 2009 to 2018. Tanzania has consistently revealed export advantage in exports of animals, food products, stone and glass, textile and clothing and vegetables. Stone and glass (which includes gold) always ranked first followed by vegetables (which includes traditional exports of coffee, tea and cloves). Horticulture has grown rapidly

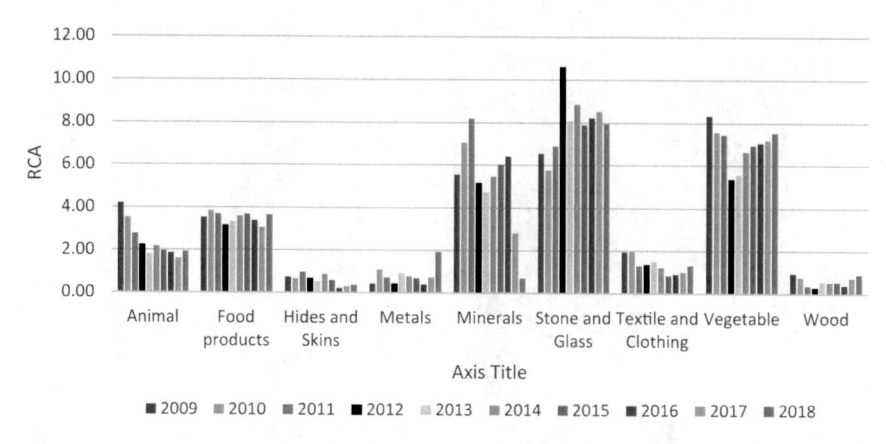

Fig. 5.5 Trends of RCA of Tanzania. *Source* Authors' compilation using WITS *data*

over the past decade increasing the share of vegetable exports.[4] This is in line with the results of Mwasha and Kweka (2009) who analysed the exports using 4 digits HS classification and found a strong RCA in coffee, tea and spices. The decline of RCA in vegetables in 2012 was not due to a decline in export levels but followed by a decline in the export share. The RCA for vegetables has continued to increase from 2012 until 2018, even though actual exports dropped in 2018. This shows that despite the export decrease, in relation to the world, Tanzania still increased revealing a comparative advantage.

Third, in rank is food products with RCA almost stable throughout the study period. The main export under this category is tobacco. Animals have shown a downward trend of RCA. In this category, Tanzania mainly relies on the export of fish which has remained rather stable from 2009 to 2018 with slight ups and downs between 150 million USD and 250 million USD. The amount of exports is greater in 2009 as compared to 2018, but it is obvious that Tanzania's share of exports in the world is dropping and if the trend continues this way it may lose its revealed comparative advantage.

Tanzania has also managed to maintain a revealed comparative advantage in textile and clothing except for 2015 and 2016. In 2017, the trend picked up. RCA in textile and clothing is a solid sign of progress for industrialization as all the products in this category have to go through some kind of processing before being exported. Noteworthy is Tanzania's emerging comparative advantage in intermediate goods of an average of 2.3 from 2012 to the end of the study period with an increasing trend. During the research period, Tanzania has gained RCA in metals and lost its advantage in minerals. Other goods that Tanzania has no export advantage on are chemicals, footwear, fuels, hides and skins, machines and electronics, miscellaneous, rubber and plastics, transportation and wood.

---

[4] https://www.freshplaza.com/article/9239162/tanzania-horti-exports-become-a-leading-subsec tor-that-drives-agricultural-growth/ *retrieved on 1st July 2021.*

Tanzania, Europe and Central Asia share an export advantage in only 2 products, animals and food products. Tanzania has a comparative advantage in stone and glass, vegetables and minerals (even though it lost RCA in 2018), in all these products Europe and Central Asia have no comparative advantage. On the other hand, there are goods that Europe and Central Asia have a comparative advantage while Tanzania has not: chemicals, metals, rubber and plastics, transportation, wood and footwear. This shows an opportunity for inter-industry trade according to the Ricardian theory of comparative advantage.

5.5.2 Revealed Trade Advantage (RTA)

5.5.2.1 Trends of RTA for All Goods in Europe and Central Asia

The RTA provides a good measure of the region's comparative advantage with the world as it filters the trade between member states. For example, a good amount of minerals exported by the Central Asian countries is imported into the EU, hence even though we found that Europe and Central Asia have revealed export advantage in minerals, it turns out their import demand is also high and the region has a trade disadvantage in minerals. As a matter of fact, according to the EU's Directorate-General for Trade[5] until 2020 even though Central Asia is not a major trading partner of the EU, it depends on the EU for 16.9% of its imports and 30.8% of its exports.

Figure 5.6 shows the trend of RTA for Europe and Central Asia on all 16 product categories in the HS 2-digit classification. The region has a strong and consistent RTA on chemicals, metals and wood. However, the RTA of metals decreases over time. The region also improved its RTA in animals, fuels and miscellaneous. Fuels have revealed trade advantage for most years except in 2010 and 2011 and *RTA* has increased substantially in 2018. Miscellaneous goods have revealed trade advantage continuously from 2016, amid a decreasing trend.

During the entire period of study, the region has displayed a trade advantage in intermediate goods. Trade advantage on capital goods was sustained until 2016 only while trade advantage on raw materials was only revealed in 2017 and 2018. The trade advantage on raw materials is due to increasing exports share of fuels and decreasing of its import share. Consumer goods had a positive *RTA* only in 2018.

The goods that Europe and Central Asia had a strong trade disadvantage on throughout the study time are footwear, hides and skin, minerals, textile and clothing and vegetables. For Europe and Central Asia even though we have seen in the section above that the region had a comparative advantage in these goods, they do have a trade advantage, hence they are more likely to be importers of these goods than exporters. Having a trade disadvantage means their revealed import advantage is greater than their revealed export advantage. The strongest trade disadvantage

---

[5] https://www.webgate.ec.europa.eu/isdb_results/factsheets/region/details_central-asia-5_en.pdf *retrieved on 25th May 2021.*

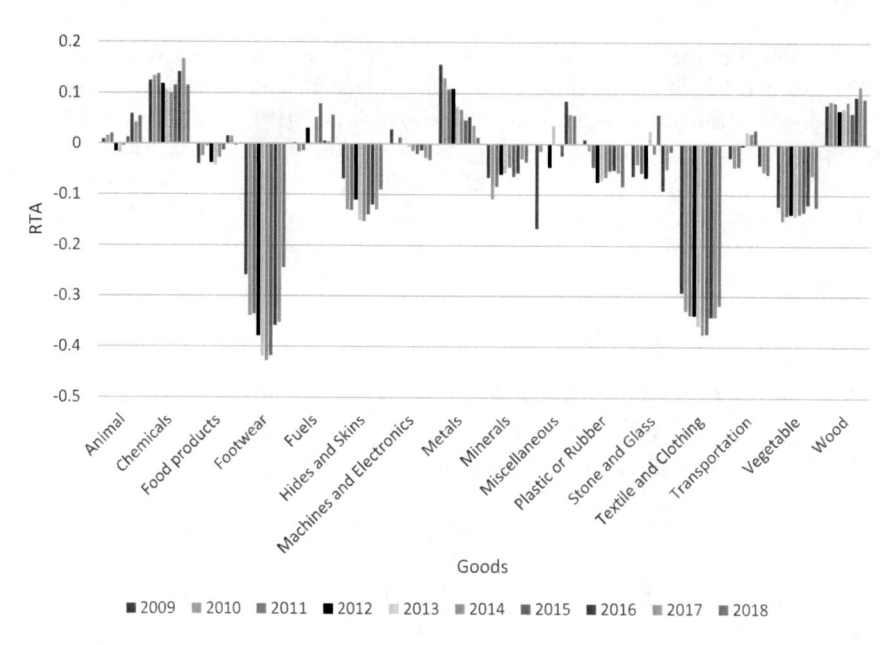

Fig. 5.6 Trends of RTA for Europe and Central Asia. *Source* Authors' compilation using WITS data

is found in consumer goods, such as footwear, textile, clothing and vegetables. However, the study shows that in 2018 Europe and Central Asia attained a trade advantage in consumer goods. This is also evident in Fig. 5.6 as there is a decline in trade disadvantage of footwear and textile and clothes.

5.5.2.2 Trends of RTA for All Goods in Tanzania

Figure 5.7 shows the trend of *RTA* of Tanzania for all 16 products from 2009 to 2018. Tanzania shows continuous trade advantage in stone and glass, vegetables, minerals, animals, food products and hides and skin. The *RTA* of animals, vegetables and food products fluctuates with some improvement in 2018. The *RTA* of stone and gold had a small decline in 2018 while that of minerals had declined substantially but remained positive. Textile and clothing had a trade advantage in all the years except for 2016. With the exception of hides and skin (which has *RTA* without export advantage), Tanzania not only had a trade advantage but also an export advantage. Hence these are goods that Tanzania can compete against the world.

Tanzania revealed trade disadvantages in chemicals, footwear, fuels, machines and electronics, miscellaneous, plastic or rubber, transportation and wood. Metals have changed its position from trade disadvantage products to trade advantage in 2018. In all these goods that Tanzania had a trade disadvantage, it also did not have

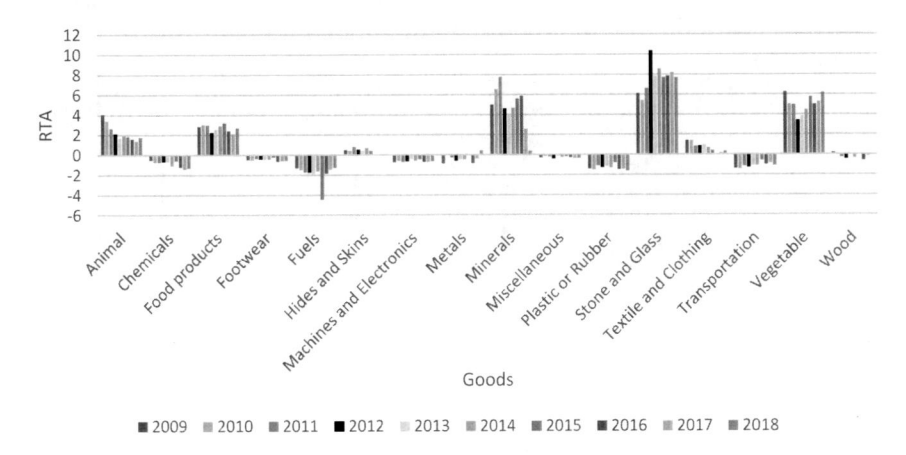

Fig. 5.7 Trends of RTA for Tanzania. *Source* Authors' compilation using WITS data

an export advantage, hence it is a net importer. Most of these goods are capital and consumer goods.

All in all, Tanzania had a trade advantage in raw materials and gained a trade advantage in intermediate goods from 2012 onwards until 2018. Trade disadvantage was continuously revealed in capital and consumer goods. Hence the growth of industrialization is still in the very early stages of processing raw materials into intermediate products.

5.5.3 The Trend of Intra-Industry Trade for All Goods in Tanzania and Europe

Figure 5.8 shows the trend of the GL index indicating the intra-industry trade for Europe and Central Asia.

The GL for Europe and Central Asia has always been above 0.5 in all groups of goods in all years. This indicates the presence of intra-industry trade in goods between Europe and Central Asia with the rest of the world. The GL has consistently been very close to 1 in animals, hides ad skin, machines and electronics, metals, rubber and plastic and wood. The rest range between 0.7 and 0.9, a minimum of 0.7 is found in minerals in 2010. The trend of intra-industry trade in footwear has an increasing trend.

The trend of intra-industry trade in Tanzania is shown in Fig. 5.9. Goods that consistently show a GL greater than 0.5 are food products, hides and skin, vegetables and wood. The GL for textile and clothing was greater than 0.5 except for 2018. Machines, metals, miscellaneous and stone and glass have revealed intra-industry trade in 2018. When we rank the averages of GL index for each product, we find

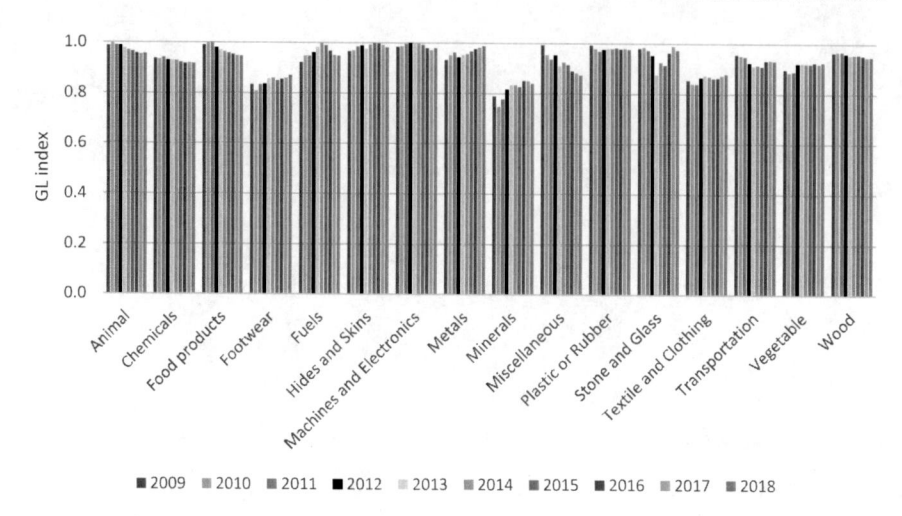

Fig. 5.8 Trend of GL Europe and Central Asia. *Source* Authors' compilation using WITS data

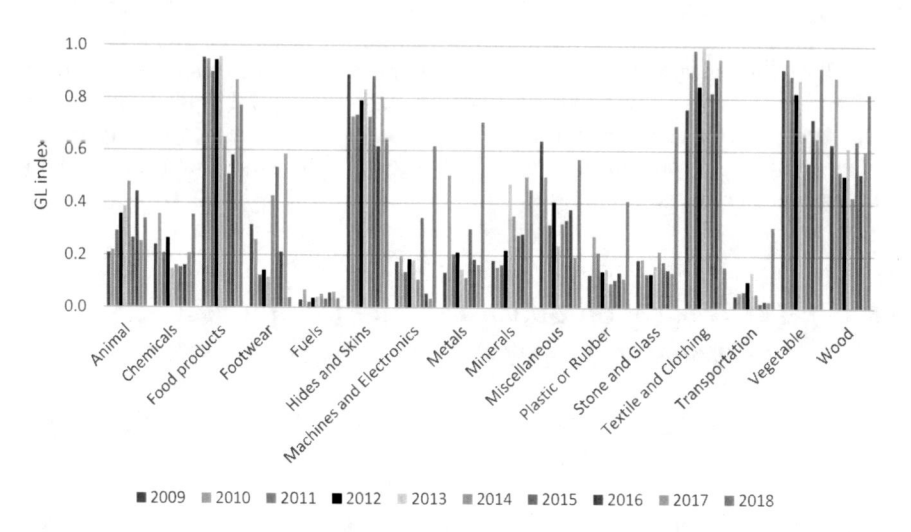

Fig. 5.9 Trends of intra-industry trade for Tanzania. *Source* Authors' compilation using WITS data

textile and clothing rank the first with an average of 0.83 (0.90 when excluding 2018), followed by food products, vegetables and hides and skin.

Goods that are consistently below 0.5 are animals, chemicals, fuels, minerals, plastic or rubber and transportation. The average GL for these products has ranged between almost zero for fuels and 0.3 for animals. The GL of below 0.5 means the country is either dominantly exporting or dominantly importing the commodity. From the previous analysis, we see that lower GL values for animals and minerals are

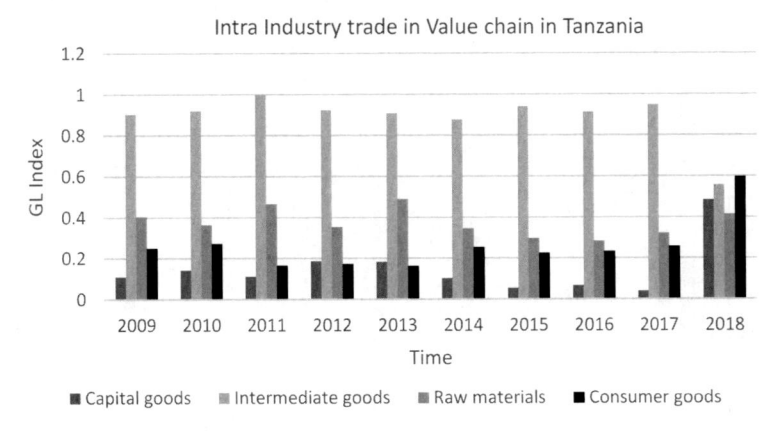

Fig. 5.10 Intra-Industry trade in Value chain in Tanzania. *Source* Authors' compilation using WITS data

associated with more exports than imports, while those of chemicals, fuels, plastic or rubber and transportation are due to the domination of imports.

Growth of industrialization is normally accompanied by a trade of goods at higher stages of the value chain, for example, import of raw materials or semi-finished goods and export of finished goods. Figure 5.10 focuses on the level of processing. We find the GL index for intermediate goods is consistently above 0.5 and averaging at 0.89 (0.92 excluding 2018). We find a substantial decline in 2018 due to a decline in exports of intermediate goods. We find the export patterns of textile and clothing also resemble the export patterns of intermediate goods and that exports of textile and clothing used 21% of exports in intermediate goods in 2009. Even though the percentage declined, the pattern remains similar except for 2017.

5.5.3.1 Robustness Check: Intra-Industry Trade Between Tanzania and Sub-Saharan Africa

Since we found very limited intra-industry trade between Tanzania with the rest of the world, it is useful to see how Tanzania performs compared the rest of the sub-Saharan countries (SSA). Figure 5.11 shows the GL indices for all classes of products from 2009 to 2018. Contrary to the previous analysis data used in this diagram consists of export and imports between Tanzania and sub-Saharan countries (prior analysis used the trade data between Tanzania and the rest of the world).

We find that, contrary to the rest of the world, intra-industry trade existed for almost all products at different years. The goods that Tanzania had revealed intra-industry trade with the rest of the world also had a GL index of above 0.5 with SSA. Wood recorded consistently above 0.5 throughout the research period with an average of 0.82, the highest being 0.995 in 2015 and the lowest being 0.527 in 2014. Food products also showed the presence of intra-industry trade for all years except

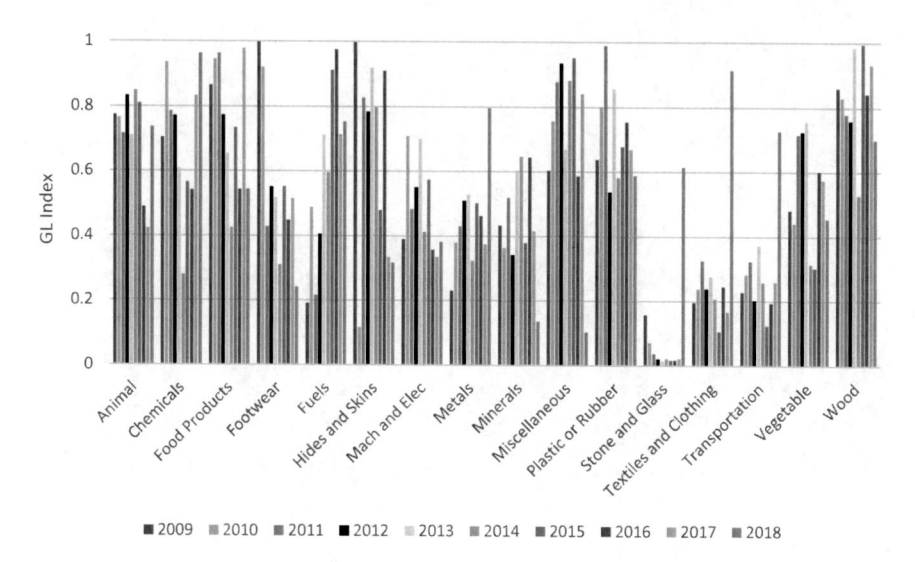

Fig. 5.11 Intra-industry trade between Tanzania and sub-Saharan countries. *Source* Authors' compilation using WITS data

2014. Vegetables and textiles on the other hand showed different results. With SSA intra-industry trade in vegetables was revealed in only 5 out of 10 years with an average of only 0.53. The GL for textiles was less than 0.5 except for 2018. As a matter of fact, in 2018 other goods that had a low GL index with SSA also improved to above 0.5 (metals, stone and glass, transportation and textile and clothing).

In addition, Tanzania goods with low GL in its trade with the world scored GL of greater than 0.5 on average with SSA. Animals had an average of 0.7 revealing intra-industry trade for all years except 2016 and 2017. Intra-industry trade was also found present in chemicals and plastic or rubber in all years (except 2014 for chemicals) with an average of 0.7. Intra-industry is also found in footwear, fuel, hides and skin and machines and electronics in different years. The intra-industry trade in hides and skin dropped significantly from 0.9 in 2016 to 0.3 in 2017 and 2018 due to improvement in exports while importation remained also the same.

This results in the presence of a significant amount of intra-industry trade between Tanzania and Sub-Saharan countries and also within the Europe and Central Asia region confirming findings by Cabral et al. (2013). They concluded that intra-industry trade increases between countries when differences in their factor endowment decrease. That is to say, countries with similar endowments like the sub-Saharan countries or European countries are more likely to engage in intra-industry trade as compared to trading between Tanzania and Europe.

5.6 Trade Complementarities Between Tanzania and Europe

Our study revealed that Europe and Central Asia have revealed import advantages in all products except in fuels, machines and electronics, minerals and stone and glass. Tanzania has revealed export advantages in animals, food products, stone and glass, vegetables and minerals (except in 2018). Hence Tanzania's exports especially animals, food products, vegetables, textiles and clothing and metals can have an import demand in Europe. Currently, according to the EU's statistics; EU 27 is ranked second in Tanzania's export destinations. The main exports so far are animals, food products and vegetables. Seeing that complementarity also exists in textiles and metals, these are the sectors that Tanzania can improve on. From the RTA analysis we also found that Tanzania has a trade advantage in hides and skin whereas Europe and Central Asia have a trade disadvantage, this is another area of potential complementarity.

The exports data show a great deal of animals' exports from Tanzania to Europe, we find that the import advantage for animals in Europe and Central Asia has not been stable. In 2010 and 2016, Europe and Central Asia *RMA* has been less than 1 and when we check the trends of RTA, we found trade advantage by Europe in several years except 2012–2014. Hence, Tanzania should look for other trading opportunities with Europe instead of reliance on live animals' exports. Food products on the other hand reveal promising trade complementarity from Tanzania to Europe as trade complementarity is shown throughout the study period. In addition, Europe and central Asia have revealed trade disadvantages for these products except for 2016 and 2017.

Complementarity in vegetables is lost in 2017 due to a loss in import advantage on the side of Europe and Central Asia (Table 5.3). Complementarity in textile and clothing has been revealed throughout the study period. This trade complementarity is backed by the revealed trade disadvantage of Europe and Central Asia.

5.6.1 Trade Complementarities from Europe and Central Asia to Tanzania

While Europe and Central Asia have revealed export advantage in 10 groups, Tanzania has revealed import advantage only in 7 groups; chemicals, fuels, metals, plastic or rubber, transportation, vegetables and wood. Table 5.4 shows these complementarities on a yearly basis. Complementarity is found in all the goods that Tanzania has RMA on except for fuel for at least some years. We found no complementarity in 2015 even though total imports have increased in that year. The import data show a decline in the goods of plastic or rubber and transportation and a sharp increase in the importation of fuel. Fuels accounted for about 50% of imports in 2015, however,

Table 5.3 Trade complementarity from Tanzania to Europe and Central Asia

Product	2009	2010	2011	2012	2013	2014	2015	2016	2017	2018
Animal	✓	✓	✓	✓	✓	✓	✓		✓	✓
Food products	✓	✓	✓	✓	✓	✓	✓	✓	✓	✓
Metals		✓								✓
Textiles and clothing	✓	✓	✓		✓	✓			✓	✓
Vegetables	✓	✓	✓	✓	✓	✓	✓	✓		
Chemicals										
Fuels										
Plastics or rubber										
Transportation										
Vegetables										
Woods										

Source Authors' compilation

Table 5.4 Trade complementarity from Europe and Central Asia to Tanzania

Product	2009	2010	2011	2012	2013	2014	2015	2016	2017	2018
Animal										
Food products										
Metals	✓	✓		✓	✓	✓		✓	✓	✓
Textiles and clothing										
Vegetables										
Chemicals						✓		✓	✓	✓
Fuels										
Plastics or rubber	✓	✓	✓	✓	✓	✓		✓	✓	✓
Transportation	✓	✓	✓	✓	✓	✓		✓		✓
Vegetables										
Woods								✓		

Source Authors' compilation

Europe and Central Asia have no revealed export advantage on fuel hence lack complementarity.

Items of plastic or rubber have revealed a complementarity throughout the study except for 2015. These items consist of both intermediate and consumer goods. However, when the goods are divided based on the level of processing, we find complementarity for consumer goods in all years and for intermediate goods only for 2009, 2010, 2014, 2016, 2017 and 2018. The complementarity is more beneficial to Tanzania's industrialization when the imported goods are capital goods, raw materials or intermediate goods because they are used in production and packaging and provide a chance for processing. Another item where we find consistent complementarity is transportation, except for 2015 and 2017. Items of transportation are aids to trade and hence facilitate the movement of goods either raw materials or finished goods. Hence services are crucial for industrialization.

Some chemicals, metals and woods are non-consumer goods and they are helpful in the industrialization process. Metals have revealed complementarity in all years except for 2011 and 2015, due to the lack of import advantage by Tanzania. Complementarity in chemicals has been revealed in the latest years of the study. Wood on other hand has a complementarity only in 2016 because that is the only year Tanzania has an import advantage in wood. Complementarity in these goods (chemicals, metals and woods) is backed by consistent trade advantage on the side of Europe and Central Asia.

5.7 Conclusion and Recommendations

Tanzania's exports still rely heavily on raw materials such as stone and glass, animals, vegetables. However, from 2012 onwards Tanzania has gained an export advantage in intermediate goods. These intermediate exports are associated with exports of textiles and clothing as well as processed vegetables. There is an opportunity for industrialization through the processing of hides and skin as we have found a trade advantage in this product, however, efforts are still needed to achieve export advantage on this product.

We find there are trade opportunities between Tanzania and Europe both in terms of exports and imports. North–south trade agreements are known for their advantages in the form of knowledge and technology spillovers. There are export opportunities to Europe in processed goods such as food products, vegetables, textile and clothing and hides and skin. Tanzania also has an opportunity to export processed fish and animal products to Europe. All these are opportunities for industrial growth by widening the market. However, these industries need to develop to produce qualities and have reasonable operating costs to be able to actually penetrate the European market.

In addition, we find import opportunities in rubber and plastic, transportation, chemical and woods. All these products can be used in the production process, hence removing trade barriers will lower the cost of production for the local industries. Caution should be taken as we found the opportunity to import consumer goods were higher than that of raw materials, capital and intermediate goods. Excessive imports of consumer goods may threaten the newly established local manufacturers.

Tanzania has excellent access to the sea and has people who are natural livestock keepers. Efforts need to be taken to see that Tanzania builds on its comparative advantage in animal products (which is a source of livelihood for many) by moving up the value chain. Presently the sector is not commercialized enough due to the lack of proper infrastructure for storage and transportation.

Our research shows an opportunity for trade in hides and skin for Tanzania both to Europe and the world, however, the sector is still small to tap these opportunities.

Efforts need to be taken to improve the export of these products, in particular, attention should be focused on improving quality.

There is an opportunity to export and expand trade with Europe and Central Asia in textile and clothing and hides and skin. However, the internal business environment for these industries should be improved so that the products meet the quality of European markets. For example, improving the availability of reliable and efficient sources of power, transport and storage.

Complementarity is found in intermediate and consumer goods. In a place where industrialization is still at an infant industry stage and poor business environment, a strong international competition on consumer goods may limit the progress of industrialization. Opening up on intermediate goods, on the other hand, is beneficial as Tanzania can process its raw materials and its finished products at a lower cost, hence growth in industrialization will be possible.

References

Balassa B (1965) Trade liberalisation and "revealed" comparative advantage 1. Manch Sch 33(2):99–123

Bank of Tanzania, Economics Statistics Publications [online] Available at: https://www.bot.go.tz/Publications/Filter/15. Accessed 1 Mar 2021

Bojnec Š, Fertő I (2012) Complementarities of trade advantage and trade competitiveness measures. Appl Econ 44(4):399–408

Bown CP, Kee HL (2011) Developing countries, new trade barriers, and the global economic crisis. Managing openness: trade and outward-oriented growth after the crisis, pp 63–83

Cabral M, Falvey R, Milner C (2013) Endowment differences and the composition of intra-industry trade. Rev Int Econ 21(3):401–418

Directorate-General for Trade 2021. Trade in goods with Tanzania, European Commission, Brussel

Dodzin S, Vamvakidis A (2004) Trade and industrialization in developing economies. J Dev Econ 75(1):319–328

EAC Secretariat 2019. East African Community Facts and Figures-2019. Arusha

Grubel HG, Lloyd PJ (1971) The empirical measurement of intra-industry trade. Econ Rec 47(4):494–517

Jing W (2009) The analysis of intra-industry trade on agricultural products of China. Front Econ China 4(1):62–75

Lectard P, Rougier E (2018) Can developing countries gain from defying comparative advantage? Distance to comparative advantage, export diversification and sophistication, and the dynamics of specialization. World Dev 102:90–110

Mwasha N, Kweka Z (2009) Tanzania in the face of international trade: the analysis of revealed comparative advantage from 2009 to 2012. Nuran Ally Mwasha, Zabibu Kweka. Tanzania in the Face of International Trade: The Analysis of Revealed Comparative Advantage from, pp 15–28

Naudé W, Szirmai A (2012) The importance of manufacturing in economic development: Past, present and future perspectives. Working Paper 2012-42, UNU-MERIT, Maastricht

Osakwe PN, Santos-Paulino AU, Dogan B (2018) Trade dependence, liberalization, and exports diversification in developing countries. J Afr Trade 5(1–2):19–34

Schott PK (2003) One size fits all? Heckscher-Ohlin specialization in global production. Am Econ Rev 93(3):686–708

Viner J (1950) The customs union issue. Stevens and Sons, London

Wangwe S, Mmari D, Aikaeli J, Rutatina N, Mboghoina T, Kinyondo A (2014) The performance of
the manufacturing sector in Tanzania: challenges and the way forward (No. 2014/085). WIDER
Working Paper
Wits.worldbank.org (2018a) Tanzania Product Exports and Imports 2018 | WITS Data. https://
www.wits.worldbank.org/CountryProfile/en/Country/TZA/Year/2018/TradeFlow/EXPIMP/Par
tner/WLD/Product/all-groups. Accessed 1 Mar 2021
Wits.worldbank.org (2018b) Europe & Central Asia Product Exports and Imports 2018
| WITS Data. https://www.wits.worldbank.org/CountryProfile/en/Country/ECS/Year/2018/Tra
deFlow/EXPIMP/Partner/WLD/Product/all-groups. Accessed 1 Mar 2021
Wits.worldbank.org (2021) Tanzania Product Exports and Imports to Sub-Saharan Africa 2018
| WITS Data. https://www.wits.worldbank.org/CountryProfile/en/Country/TZA/Year/2018/Tra
deFlow/EXPIMP/Partner/SSF/Product/all-groups. Accessed 1 Mar 2021

Chapter 6
Trade Potential and Bottlenecks in East Africa: A Gravity Approach

Binyam Afewerk Demena and Peter A. G. van Bergeijk

Abstract The stylized facts of applied gravity analysis are that regional integration has comparatively speaking progressed well in the EAC, that trade creation by far outweighs trade diversion and that EAC is the most advanced in terms of tariff liberalization. Given this existing body of knowledge, in this chapter, we focus on a relatively under-researched area where important differences exist between EAC member states, namely: the trade impact of the time and costs that firms incur when they comply with documentary requirements and border procedures. The gravity model is estimated using a panel dataset consisting of EAC, SADC, COMESA and their major trading partners for the period 2015–2018 and applying the Poisson Pseudo Maximum Likelihood (PPML) estimator. Our empirical findings highlight that reducing time and costs for documentary requirements and crossing borders is an important issue within the EAC, especially since streamlining procedures, one stop portals, reducing handling time, as well as the use of common standards that facilitate EAC internal trade flows do not require large financial investments while they do have a high payoff. Considering economic arguments as a basis to form regional entities, our findings consistently stress the need to enhance the efficacy of the various regional trading blocs. Indeed, our findings shed an optimistic light on trade-promoting effect of the tripartite free trade area (TFTA).

6.1 Introduction

From the early stages of economic integration initiatives, the focus has been not simply on reducing border taxes but on streamlining intra-trade-flows by creating common institutions, common requirements and reducing red tape. It is well known that the benefits of regional integration emerge due to a reduction of intra-trade

B. A. Demena (✉) · P. A. G. van Bergeijk
International Institute of Social Studies (ISS), Erasmus University Rotterdam, The Hague, the Netherlands
e-mail: demena@iss.nl

P. A. G. van Bergeijk
e-mail: bergeijk@iss.nl

B. A. Demena and Peter A. G. Van Bergeijk (eds.), *Trade and Investment in East Africa*, Frontiers in African Business Research, https://doi.org/10.1007/978-981-19-4211-2_6

barriers (Smith and Venables 1988), but also that significant border effects continue to be observed in internal markets. Border effects are highly significant, both in federations (such as the US or Germany) and internal markets such as the EU and also in regional economic integration areas. Reducing those barriers enhances cross-border competition that in itself is a key driver of productivity increases and thereby of long run growth. Enhanced productivity in its turn is associated with a stronger international competitive position in world markets.

It is not always straight-forward to relate the enhanced openness of regional trade initiatives to economic growth (e.g., Oloyede et al. 2021), perhaps due to sector specificity of market distortions that can, moreover, be difficult to observe. Therefore, we opt in this chapter for a more modest approach. We will focus on a necessary condition (the potential trade impact of a specific aspect of economic integration) rather than a sufficient condition (the productivity impact of market integration), also because the latter requires a general equilibrium approach while for the former a partial equilibrium approach can be used. This *inter alia* implies that our findings are more relevant for the short to medium term than for the long run when general equilibrium effects play out.[1] A benefit of our approach, however, is that our findings can be compared to recent studies that predominantly use an applied gravity approach that has developed into the standard tool for trade policy analysis regarding African integration initiatives (e.g., Dube 2021, Ejones et al. 2021, Kassa and Sawadogo 2021, Leyaro 2021, Agarwal et al. 2022). The stylized facts of applied gravity analysis are that regional integration has comparatively speaking progressed well in the EAC, that trade creation by far outweighs trade diversion and that EAC is the most advanced in terms of tariff liberalization. Given this existing body of knowledge we focus on a relatively under-researched area where important differences exist between EAC member states, namely: the trade impact of the time and costs that firms incur when they comply with documentary requirements and border procedures. As will become clear this is an important bottleneck for intra EAC trade. The costs in this cases refer to both fees and a monetary valuation of the working time involved. The time of compliance is a more readily observed variable and measures the actual time that compliance takes. The time dimension is important for perishable goods, when international value chain activities are characterized by just in time delivery and also because delays at the border hampers working capital which necessitates increased financing requirements and cost of capital. Reducing time and costs for crossing borders is an important issue within the EAC as streamlining procedures, one stop portals, reducing handling time, as well as the use of common standards that facilitate EAC internal trade flows do not require large financial investments but do have a high payoff.

The remainder of this chapter is organized as follows. Section 6.2 discusses the data and data sources with a focus on different components of the time and costs of border compliance. Section 6.3 presents the empirical strategy adopted and Sect.6.4

---

[1] See Fofack et al. (2021). Note that the general equilibrium effects reported are quite small: the production growth effect is 0.1% in their static model and 0.3% in their dynamic model.

discusses the results of the findings. Finally, Sect. 6.5 gives the conclusion and the policy implications.

6.2   Data

Our sample includes all the countries that are members of EAC, SADC and COMESA. To this sample we add the major trading partners of EAC. This sample covers 80 countries. A full list of countries under examination is provided in Appendix 6.1. The data are merged into a panel data set for the period 2015–2018.

6.2.1   Time and Cost to Export and Import

In order to estimate time and costs for documentary and border compliances that have trade-reducing impacts, we use various data sources. Our main variables of interests are survey responses regarding documentary and border compliance that will be used both in terms of time spent and cost associated with the requirements and regulations involved by all agencies for the overall process of importing, exporting or reexporting of goods and services. According to the World Bank, documentary compliance captures the time and cost associated with compliance to get, prepare, process, and submit documents during importing or exporting.[2] The aim of the survey is to measure the time and cost of the total burden related to documentary compliance in preparing and submitting the bundle of all paper or electronic documents that enable the completion of international trade. Similarly, border compliance provides the time and cost associated with the economy's customs clearance, border inspection and port handling conducted by all government agencies involved in the importing and exporting activities.[3]

We collected these secondary data from the World Bank's Doing Business database. Tables 6.1 and 6.2 provide a detailed summary on an important aspect of international trade in terms of time and cost for documentary and border compliances for exporting and importing for the period 2015–2018. Starting with the exporting time required for documentary and border compliance, Table 6.1 shows Kenya is the best performing country, as firms need less than 24 h to prepare the required documentation and to cross borders (for exporting products). In terms of cost, Rwanda (documentary compliance) and Burundi (border compliance) are the leading countries among EAC. South Sudan currently is the worst performing country in terms of the number of hours required for documentary and border compliances. The cost required to clear documents to export products from Tanzania is the highest among

---

[2] https://www.doingbusiness.org/en/data/exploretopics/trading-across-borders/score (Accessed on 25 Sept 2021).

[3] See Footnote 2.

Table 6.1 Time (hours) and cost (US $) to export for EAC countries

Year	Burundi	Kenya	Rwanda	South Sudan	Tanzania	Uganda
	Time to export for documentary compliance					
2015	120	19	42	192	120	64
2018	120	19	42	192	96	51
P.M					−20%	−20%
	Time to export for border compliance					
2015	59	28	97	146	96	85
2018	59	21	97	146	96	64
P.M		−25%				−25%
	Cost to export for documentary compliance					
2015–2018	150	191	110	194	275	102
	Cost to export for border compliance					
2015–2018	109	143	183	763	1175	209

Source The World Bank, Doing Business/Measuring Business Regulations database, accessed on Sept 25, 2021

Table 6.2 Time (hours) and cost (US $) to import for EAC countries

Year	Burundi	Kenya	Rwanda	South Sudan	Tanzania	Uganda
	Time to import for documentary compliance					
2015	180	84	48	360	264	138
2018	180	60	48	360	240	138
	Time to import for border compliance					
2015	154	180	22	179	402	154
2016	154	180	294	179	402	154
2017	154	180	86	179	402	154
2018	154	180	86	179	402	154
	Cost to import for documentary compliance					
2015–2018	1025	115	121	350	375	296
	Cost to import for border compliance					
2015–2018	1407	832	285	781	1350	447

Source The World Bank, Doing Business/Measuring Business Regulations database, accessed on Sept 25, 2021

the EAC countries, that is: it reaches as high as US $275. In contrast, in Rwanda and Uganda getting the required documents for exports is cheaper than in any other EAC member country (only at about US$100). In particular, Tanzanian exporters carry the highest burden of costs associated with border compliances for custom clearances and inspection procedures conducted by several regulatory agencies. Figure 6.1 provides

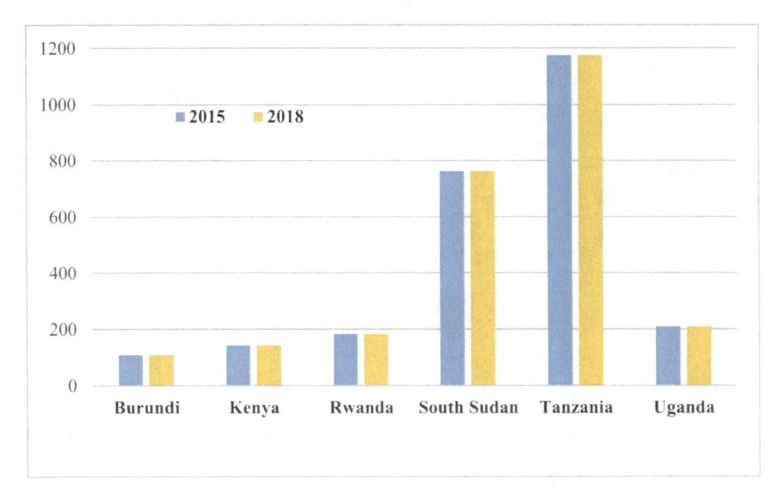

Fig. 6.1 Cost to export (US$) border compliance for EAC countries (2015 and 2018). *Source* The World Bank, Doing Business/Measuring Business Regulations database, accessed on Sept 25, 2021

a comparison of costs for border compliance to export both among the EAC-6 countries and over time. In all cases there are no changes over time, but this does not mean that the comparative burden of compliance is stable over time. Indeed, multilateral resistance factors will change when other countries reduce their costs of compliance. Regarding the border cost performance among the EAC member countries, Tanzanian exporters incur about six times higher costs than the other four EAC countries (even compared to the second worst performer, South Sudan, Tanzania has twice as high a burden).

Table 6.2 gives similar details, but from an importing perspective. The data on importing also shows substantial differences among the EAC member countries. For instance, Rwanda is best performing in terms of the number of hours required for and the cost incurred for documentary and border compliances (with Kenya taking better scores regarding cost of documentary compliance). As with exporting, Tanzania also performs poorly for imports. For instance, importers require about 400 h for border compliance, whereas in Rwanda this is only about 85 h. Figure 6.2 gives comparison over time among the EAC. The figure shows that, in 4 of the 6 EAC countries there is no improvement or change in the number of hours required to clear documentations to import over the period considered. It was only in Kenya and Rwanda there have been some changes over the period 2015–2018, inclusive.

6.2.2   Monadic and Dyadic Control Variables

Apart from an important aspect of international trade in terms of time and cost for documentary and border compliances for exporting and importing, we also included

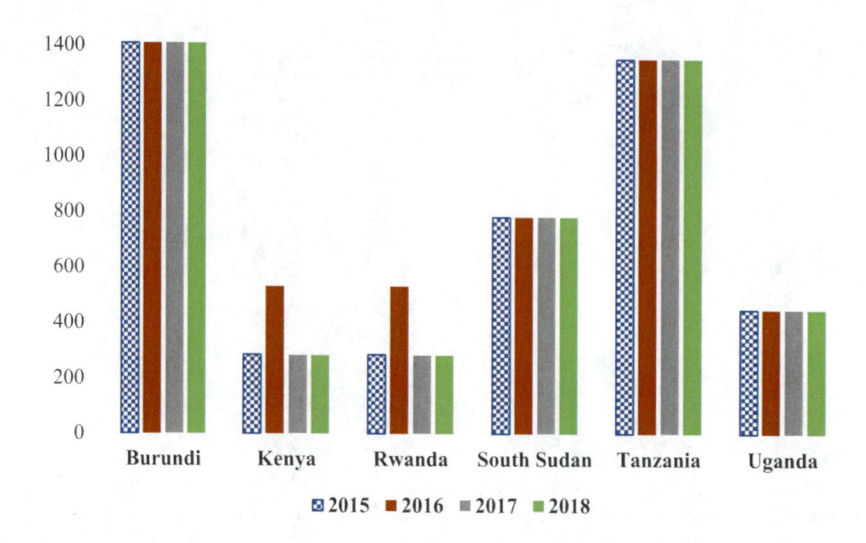

Fig. 6.2 Time to import (hours) documentary compliance for EAC countries (2015–2018). *Source* The World Bank, Doing Business/Measuring Business Regulations database, accessed on Sept 25, 2021

a set of monadic and dyadic control variables. Regarding monadic variables, these include GDP and population for the exporting and importing countries. In terms of dyadic variables, and also as additional variables of interest, we have included binary dummy variables that indicate co-membership in regional economic blocs associated with EAC. The dummy variables identify those Sub-Saharan African (SSA) countries that are considered as EAC's major trading partners that are part of the Common Market for Eastern and Southern Africa (COMESA) and Southern African Development Community (SADC). This set of dummies enables us to disentangle the impact of three of Africa's major intra-regional trading blocs, COMESA, EAC and SADC, thereby allowing the analysis of the tripartite free trade area (TFTA). In addition, we have also included a dummy for intra EU trade. For all dummy variables, the control group is a pair of countries that do not share any membership in one of the large regional economic blocks in our data set. To construct our dependent variable, we use data for bilateral trade (exports and imports) extracted from International Monetary Fund's (IMF's) Direction of Trade Statistics Database. Data on GDP and population were obtained from World Bank development indicators database. Descriptive statistics on the variables of interest are provided in Table 6.3.

Table 6.3 Summary statistics

Variables	Obs	Mean	Std. Dev	Min	Max
Adjusted trade	11,448	10.414	4.107	0	20.067
Exports	11,571	16.869	4.205	0	26.898
Log exporter GDP	12,879	25.485	2.17	20.69	30.65
Log importer GDP	12,881	25.481	2.17	20.69	30.65
Log exporter Population	12,960	16.697	1.623	11.44	21.05
Log importer Population	12,960	16.969	1.269	11.245	20.055
EAC	12,960	0.004	0.059		
SADC	12,960	0.030	0.170		
COMESA	12.960	0.040	0.195		
EU	12,960	0.083	0.276		
Log time documentary	12,960	2.425	1.955	0	5.749
Log time border	10,560	3.637	1.377	0	6.244
Log cost documentary	10,400	4.624	0.817	2.397	6.215
Log cost border	10,240	5.823	0.734	3.951	7.707

6.3 Empirical Strategy

We now proceed to build the empirical framework based on the gravity model. The gravity model is a well-established framework to study the effects of various determinants of international trade flows (van Bergeijk and Brakman 2010). This empirical gravity model has been used routinely in the trade literature and hypothesizes that bilateral trade is determined by exporter GDP (supply potential), importer GDP (market demand potential) and a set of variables representing trade facilitation and/or trade resistances (Afesorgbor 2019). Using regression analysis, the role of time to export and import, and cost to import and export are included as determinants of trade flow in facilitating or hindering bilateral trade. In this regard, documentary and border requirements are coded in terms of the respective time and costs associated with compliance and are considered as indicator variables relevant to trade facilitation to export and import for analysing the determinants of trade flow. Thus, the specification of the baseline econometric gravity equation will be as follows:

$$X_{ijt} = \alpha_0 + \alpha_{it} + \alpha_{jt} + \alpha_t + \beta_1 M_{it} + \beta_2 M_{jt} + \beta_3 D_{ijt} + \beta_4 ln\,Tim\,Doc_{it}$$
$$+ \beta_5 ln\,Tim\,Bord_{it} + \beta_6 ln\,Cost\,Doc_{it} + \beta_7 ln\,Cost\,Bord_{it} + \varepsilon_{ijt} \quad (6.1)$$

The term X_{ijt} is our dependent variable measuring the two-way (both exports and imports) trade flow between a country i and a country j at time t. α_0 is a constant term with a structural interpretation as world output. The variable $\alpha_{i(j)t}$ encompasses directional time-varying (exporter and importer) fixed-effects. According to

Anderson and van Wincoop (2003), the inclusion of the exporter-time and importer-time fixed-effects for each exporter and importer respectively, enables consideration of multilateral resistances as well as for any other potential observable and unobservable factors that vary over time that may influence trade flows (also see, Baier and Bergstrand 2007; Olivero and Yotov 2012). In principle, therefore, $\alpha_{i(j)t}$ may control for any observable and unobservable time-varying covariates. The variables $M_{i(j)t}$ are monadic factors that may affect bilateral trade for the exporter (importer) that include GDP and population at a time t. In contrast to these monadic variables, D_{ijt} dyadic factors of trade flow determinants such as capturing the presence of international borders, regional trading memberships between countries i and j for each year t. For the latter, we considered dummy variables that is equal to 1 if both exporter and importer are member of EAC, COMESA, SADC, or EU at a time t and zero otherwise.

The main variables of interest are indicators from the World Bank's Doing Business database and contain information regarding the time and costs to export and import as a result of border compliance and documentary requirement (β_4 to β_7).[4] Given the empirical framework, we addressed several econometric concerns. The first is that our variables of interest are a form of non-discriminatory trade policy. That means, a documentary requirement or border processing time/cost in the exporting country i is the same regardless of the importing country j for a given year t. In this case, any unilateral policy in an exporting country is absorbed by the exporter-time fixed effects regardless of the importing country at time t, indicating the gravity equation cannot estimate the impact of our variable of interest. This is because, any covariate that only varies at the it or jt-dimension is absorbed by the exporter or importer time-varying fixed-effects. Following best practices, we model the structural gravity equation with intra-national and international trade flows to obtain an estimate of the trade effect of documentary requirements and border-processing time/cost (Yotov et al. 2016).

The way to address this issue is to assume that there is no border processing time for trade within a country—that is: for intra-national trade. This allows to interact the border processing or documentary compliance time/cost variables with a dummy variable indicating that the trade flow is international rather than intra-national. In this case, our variable of interest (the interaction term), does have variation in the ijt-dimension, as it compares border processing time for international vs. intra-national trade flows (i.e., dependent on the exporter or importer). As it is an interaction, we will not estimate the 'base-effect' of documentary and border-processing time/cost, but instead the difference between border-processing time for international and intra-national trade flows. Hence the assumption that there is no border-processing time for intra-national trade flows is crucial, so that we can interpret the interacted coefficients β_4 to β_7 as the effect of documentary and border processing time/cost in general.[5]

---

[4] See Sect. 6.2, for the description of each of these variables.

[5] The document compliance and border processing time and cost variables are interacted with the dummy variable included in the D_{ijt} (dyadic factors), which is equal to one for *international* trade and zero for *intra-national* trade, to capture the fact that this type of policy apply only to

Another econometric concern is that trade data are known to be plagued by heteroscedasticity (Yotov et al. 2016). One way to address this issue in the gravity equation is to transform the term X_{ijt} (our dependent variable) into size-adjusted trade. According to Anderson and van Wincoop (2003), this adjustment of the dependent variable can be captured by the ratio of the trade flow to the supply potential (exporter GDP), and market demand potential (importer GDP), that is the product of the sizes of the two (exporter and importer) GDPs.[6] Moreover, since we are specifically interested in the EAC, we further distinguish between the world average border processing and documentary compliance time/cost effect and the EAC average effect.

One more empirical concern is the presence of zero trade flows. Traditionally, the gravity equation is estimated with the logarithm of international trade flows from exporter i to importer j at time t with an OLS or other estimation of the empirical specification. A well-known drawback of the log-linearized approach is that it cannot consider the information contained in the zero trade flows (Afesorgbor and van Bergeijk 2014). In our case, 11% of the trade flows has zero values which means if they are transformed into logarithmic, these observations will be simply omitted/dropped. Instead of omitting zero flows, other strategies in the literature are to use the Tobit estimator or replacing them with small arbitrary values (known as the zero plus one). However, all these strategies are known to produce inconsistent estimated parameters and thus labelled as infeasible (Yotov et al. 2016; Afesorgbor 2017). To address the presence of zero trade flows, the most convenient solution advocated by Santos Silva and Tenreyro (2006) is to estimate the gravity equation in multiplicative form rather than logarithmic transformation. This approach applies the Poisson Pseudo Maximum Likelihood (PPML) estimator to estimate the gravity model, which is also put forward as consistent in the presence of heteroskedasticity and well behaved in particular when the dataset contains large zero flows (Martínez-Zarzoso 2013). Moreover, simulations of trade flows show that the PPML estimator is the most convenient strategy in the presence of zero flows than any other approaches (Head and Mayer 2014).

6.4 Empirical Findings

This section gives the results, first, the effect of time and cost for documentary and border compliances on exports, and, second, on imports. All estimates are obtained by allowing that the "direct/partial equilibrium" effect of the border processing time (in terms of documentary and border compliance) for *EAC is different* from the world's average border processing effect. All columns use the PPML estimator. We

---

international trade so as to give the variation at ijt-dimension, whose variable is different from it (exporter time-varying dimension) or jt (importer-time varying dimension).

[6] The intuition behind this transformation is that the variance term ε_{ijt} (error) is proportional to the supply potential and market demand potential for exporter and importer respectively (Yotov et al. 2016).

follow recent studies in the literature (e.g., Olivero and Yotov 2012; Yotov et al. 2016), and estimate the gravity models with time intervals of a panel dataset using the period 2015–2018. This is also important as responses to trade policy changes will need some time to materialize, and thus will not be instantaneous.

6.4.1 Exports

Table 6.4 gives the first result, that is: the effect on exports. Columns 1 and 2 use data on time for documentary compliance and border compliance, respectively. Results in both columns differ considerably in sign and are also not significant. Column 3 adds both measures and produced an estimate with expected sign and of sufficient significance, thus indicating that the results in columns 1 and 2 suffer from omitted variable bias. Our interpretation therefore focuses on coefficients associated with estimation of our preferred model (column 3). Finally, Column 4 by way of robustness check additionally estimates the combined (interacted) effect of documentary and border compliance; the results are insignificant.

Focusing on column 3, the time for documentary compliance for the EAC is a significant trade barrier and has coefficient of −1.271 implying that a 10% decrease in the time needed for documentary compliance is associated with a 13% increase in exports of EAC countries during the period of investigation. In terms of the time required for border compliance, the effect on export is substantially lower (−0.497) as compared to documentary compliance. That is: exports can be enhanced on average by about 5% if there would be a 10% reduction on the current time spent for border processing.[7]

Table 6.5 reports even stronger effects regarding the financial costs of documentary and border compliances. Again, focusing on column 3, our variables of interest are significant and have the a priori expected sign. The cost of required documents compliance to export is significant and has a magnitude of −4.402 (a 10% decrease in cost for documentary compliance would increase exports of EAC countries on average by 44%). Similarly, the cost to export for border compliance would increase potential export of EAC countries on average by 35% associated with a 10% reduction of EAC border processing costs.

All in all, our gravity models clearly illustrate the trade limiting aspects of trade and border procedures. Reducing time and costs for crossing EAC borders (including streamlining procedures, one stop portals, reducing handling time) is an important policy issue that could substantially facilitate intra-regional trade flows of EAC countries.

To put these figures in to perspective, the world average size effect regarding cost to export for border processing is about −0.401 only, which means a 10% removal of this cost would increase exports by 4%. Comparatively, EAC countries have to

---

[7] The average border processing effect for the world has a significant effect with a magnitude of i.e., -0.962.

Table 6.4 The effect of time for documentary and border compliance on *exports*

Variables	(1)	(2)	(3)	(4)
Time-documentary—Rest of the world	0.089		0.091	
	(0.370)		(0.346)	
Time-documentary—EAC	0.365		-1.271^{**}	
	(0.387)		(0.572)	
Time-border—Rest of the world		-0.148	-0.962^{***}	
		(0.209)	(0.353)	
Time-border—EAC		-0.006	-0.497^{***}	
		(0.173)	(0.112)	
Time-documentary-border—Rest of the world				0.173
				(0.715)
Time-documentary—Border-EAC				0.394
				(0.720)
Both_EAC	4.802^{***}	4.766^{***}	4.766^{***}	4.802^{***}
	(0.316)	(0.338)	(0.338)	(0.316)
Both_SADC	3.396^{***}	3.442^{***}	3.442^{***}	3.396^{***}
	(0.314)	(0.323)	(0.323)	(0.314)
Both_COMESA	2.099^{***}	2.207^{***}	2.207^{***}	2.099^{***}
	(0.270)	(0.470)	(0.470)	(0.270)
Both_EU	2.109^{***}	1.859^{***}	1.859^{***}	2.109^{***}
	(0.136)	(0.188)	(0.188)	(0.136)
Constant term	3.842^{*}	5.762^{***}	9.941^{***}	3.470
	(2.330)	(1.083)	(1.090)	(4.338)
N	11,444	9092	9092	11,444
$\overline{R}^2$	0.661	0.663	0.663	0.661

Notes Clustered robust standard errors by country-pairs are in parentheses. $^{*}p < 0.10$, $^{**}p < 0.05$, $^{***}p < 0.01$. All estimates are obtained through allowing the "direct/partial equilibrium" effect of the border processing time (in terms of documentary and border compliance) for *EAC is different* to the average border processing effect of the world. These estimates are elasticities. The dependent variable is the size-adjusted exports. All estimates use time, export-time, and import-time fixed effects; however, these fixed effects are not included in the table for brevity. All columns use the PPML estimator. Columns 1 and 2 use data on time for documentary and border compliance respectively; Column 3 adds both these different time requirements in the same regression; and finally, Column 4 estimates the combined effect of documentary and border compliance

bear about 40% points more costs to export due to border processing. EAC exporters carry the burden of costs associated with border compliances for custom clearances and inspection procedures conducted by several regulatory agencies. Reducing time and costs for crossing borders is therefore still an important issue within the EAC. This is mainly because streamlining procedures and one stop portals would reduce handling time. At the same time, the use of common standards that facilitate EAC

Table 6.5 The effect of cost for documentary and border compliance on *exports*

Variables	(1)	(2)	(3)	(4)
Cost-documentary—Rest of the world	0.055		-1.572^{***}	
	(0.096)		(0.243)	
Cost-documentary—EAC	0.138		-4.402^{***}	
	(0.114)		(0.695)	
Cost-border—Rest of the world		-0.099	-0.401^{**}	
		(0.154)	(0.188)	
Cost-border—EAC		-0.001	-3.494^{***}	
		(0.138)	(0.653)	
Cost-documentary-Border—Rest of the world				0.026
				(0.044)
Cost-documentary-border—EAC				0.074
				(0.054)
Both_EAC	4.766^{***}	4.726^{***}	4.726^{***}	4.726^{***}
	(0.338)	(0.334)	(0.334)	(0.334)
Both_SADC	3.442^{***}	3.395^{***}	3.395^{***}	3.395^{***}
	(0.323)	(0.325)	(0.325)	(0.325)
Both_COMESA	2.207^{***}	2.189^{***}	2.189^{***}	2.189^{***}
	(0.470)	(0.468)	(0.468)	(0.468)
Both_EU	1.856^{***}	1.799^{***}	1.799^{***}	1.799^{***}
	(0.189)	(0.183)	(0.183)	(0.183)
Constant term	5.526^{***}	6.542^{***}	12.346^{***}	5.524^{***}
	(1.180)	(1.642)	(1.305)	(1.179)
N	8944	8787	8787	8787
$\overline{R}^2$	0.663	0.698	0.698	0.698

Notes See Table 6.4

internal trade flows do not require large financial investments but do have a high payoff.

6.4.2 Regional Economic Integration

Tables 6.4 and 6.5 also pay attention to four important regional economic integration areas or communities covered by our sample, namely EAC, SADC, COMESA, and EU. The estimates for trade partners in each of these blocks differ substantially in size but consistently have expected signs, implying that these regional economic blocs have a significantly positive impact on intra-area trade flows, but that the size

Table 6.6 The effect of time for documentary and border compliance on *imports*

Variables	(1)	(2)	(3)	(4)
Time-documentary—Rest of the World	-0.544^{***}		-0.309	
	(0.157)		(0.216)	
Time-documentary—EAC	-0.627^{***}		-0.813^{***}	
	(0.077)		(0.107)	
Time-border—Rest of the world		-0.855^{***}	-0.533	
		(0.198)	(0.330)	
Time-border—EAC		-0.530^{*}	-0.476^{***}	
		(0.281)	(0.104)	
Time-documentary-border—Rest of the world				-0.508^{**}
				(0.212)
Time-documentary-border—EAC				-1.095^{***}
				(0.164)
Both_EAC	3.971^{***}	3.780^{***}	3.930^{***}	3.967^{***}
	(0.374)	(0.363)	(0.400)	(0.360)
Both_SADC	3.022^{***}	3.050^{***}	3.056^{***}	3.023^{***}
	(0.294)	(0.317)	(0.317)	(0.293)
Both_COMESA	1.761^{***}	1.886^{***}	1.843^{***}	1.770^{***}
	(0.264)	(0.277)	(0.278)	(0.264)
Both_EU	2.055^{***}	1.470^{***}	1.469^{***}	2.047^{***}
	(0.125)	(0.285)	(0.285)	(0.125)
Constant term	4.504^{***}	4.504^{***}	4.504^{***}	4.504^{***}
	(1.172)	(1.172)	(1.172)	(1.172)
N	11,866	8982	8982	11,866
$\overline{R}^2$	0.737	0.742	0.743	0.737

Notes Clustered robust standard errors by country-pairs are in parentheses. $^{*}p < 0.10$, $^{**}p < 0.05$, $^{***}p < 0.01$. All estimates are obtained through allowing the "direct/partial equilibrium" effect of the border processing time (in terms of documentary and border compliance) for *EAC is different* to the average border processing effect in the world. These estimates are elasticities. The dependent variable is the size-adjusted imports. All estimates use time, export-time, and import-time fixed effects; however, these fixed effects are not included in the table for brevity. All columns use the PPML estimator. Columns 1 and 2 use data on time for documentary and border compliance respectively; Column 3 adds both these different time requirements in the same regression; and finally, Column 4 estimates the combined effect of documentary and border compliance

of the effects considerably differs. In particular, the regional economic blocs impact associated with EAC and SADC have a significantly stronger economic impact. These results are consistent with Kassa and Sawadogo (2021), who point out the drivers of these results as density of economic activity, investment in trade facilitation as well as improved quality and quantity of regional infrastructure—in particular as compared to COMESA and other African intra-regional economic blocs. Other studies that are consistent with our findings include Carrere (2006), Coulibaly (2009), and Leyaro (2021). The findings reported by Ejones et al. (2021) agree in terms of positive and significant impact but disagree on the size effect as they estimate that COMESA has generated substantially larger intraregional bilateral trade flows than the trade for EAC partner countries. Overall, the results of the four regional economic blocs are in line with the central point of creating regional integration of trade as a mechanism to enhance the capacity of local supply so as to further engage in global trade to improve market access.

Our findings seemingly contradict Candau et al. (2019), who analyse the effects of regional trade agreements (RTAs) on bilateral trade in Africa and report that there is no trade creation coming from RTAs in the years 1990–2014. Candau et al. (2019) argue that the bulk of trade creation occurred between 1955 and 1990, indicating that most gains of these RTAs have been exhausted. Earlier Longo and Sekkat (2004) for the period 1988–1997 reported in the same vein that regional trade integrations or agreements were not associated with generating trade between member countries. This paradox in the literature may reflect that the "old design" of African RTAs does not work anymore, but that "new approaches" such as currently underway in the EAC or the COMESA-EAC-SADC Tripartite free trade area do hold significant promise, provided regional integration deepens sufficiently. An alternative explanation may be the literature's exclusive focus on exports, and this motivates the next section.

6.4.3 Imports

Imports of capital goods and intermediate products are key to growth and to the development process. Exports may provide the hard currency needed for these imports, but only in this way are important. Paraphrasing Adam Smith: the sole purpose of exporting is importing.

Tables 6.6 and 6.7 take a closer look at the impacts of documentary and border compliances on imports. The results confirm the findings of Tables 6.4 and 6.5 for exports. In all the estimations, time and costs for crossing borders to import is an important issue. For instance, a 10% decrease on the time required for documentary and border compliances on imports would enhance intra-regional trade flows within EAC on average by 8% and 5% (column 3, Table 6.6). Note that the results reported in Table 6.7 on the cost to import is substantially larger in magnitude. In particular, cost of border compliance on imports within the EAC has a magnitude of −7.169 (column 3, Table 6.7). This means that a 10% decrease in cost for border compliance would increase imports within EAC countries on average by 72%. This clearly suggests that the use of common standards that facilitate intra-regional bilateral trades flows within EAC countries do have a high payoff that possibly do not require large financial investments. This result indicates that deepening of regional trading or economic blocs is a critical policy implication to utilize considerable benefits of integration.

Unlike the results for exports (Tables 6.4 and 6.5), as a robustness check, we also find that the combined time and cost for documentary and border compliance

Table 6.7 The effect of cost for documentary and border compliance on *imports*

Variables	(1)	(2)	(3)	(4)
Cost-documentary—Rest of the world	−1.235***		−0.931**	
	(0.426)		(0.452)	
Cost-documentary—EAC	−1.091***		0.628	
	(0.272)		(0.436)	
Cost-border—Rest of the world		−2.352***	−1.402**	
		(0.753)	(0.586)	
Cost-Border—EAC		−5.132***	−7.169***	
		(0.836)	(1.694)	
Cost-documentary-border—Rest of the world				−0.173***
				(0.055)
Cost-documentary-border—EAC				−0.156***
				(0.036)
Both_EAC	3.913***	3.947***	3.935***	3.921***
	(0.380)	(0.405)	(0.406)	(0.382)
Both_SADC	3.045***	3.049***	3.048***	3.045***
	(0.325)	(0.325)	(0.325)	(0.325)
Both_COMESA	1.885***	1.855***	1.857***	1.881***
	(0.283)	(0.283)	(0.282)	(0.283)
Both_EU	0.801**	0.799**	0.801**	0.801**
	(0.400)	(0.400)	(0.400)	(0.400)
Constant term	16.278***	16.278***	16.278***	16.278***
	(2.682)	(0.755)	(9.184)	(0.481)
N	8379	8379	8363	8363
$\overline{R}^2$	0.765	0.766	0.765	0.765

Notes See Table 6.6

is statistically significant as shown in column 4 of Tables 6.6 and 6.7. This is an important finding as it implies that not only individually, but also collectively the import time and cost associated with border and documentary compliances exert significantly a negative effect on bilateral trade flows.

As illustrated in Fig. 6.3 our main findings of the considered three regional economic blocs corroborate the corresponding results for exports. We thus find that these regional economic blocs have substantial effect on exports and imports. Our finding for the EAC membership is consistent with the recent study by Riedel and Slany (2019)who explore the bilateral imports within the COMESA-EAC-SADC Tripartite countries against a control group of 27 other African economies for the period 1995–2010. Riedel and Slany (2019) report a positive but insignificant relationship for the COMESA and SADC urging them to cautiously doubt the trade-promoting effect of the TFTA formed in 2011. Exploring the recent time dimension

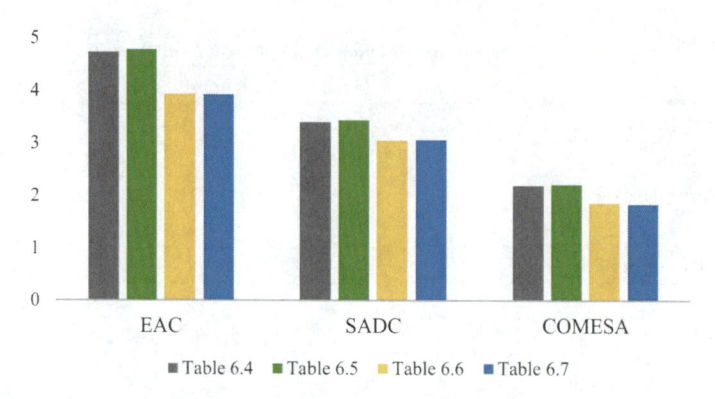

Fig. 6.3 Reported dummy variables for regional integration areas in East Africa

of the panel dataset, our study consistently suggests a much more optimistic view of the potential effectiveness of the COMESA-EAC-SADC TFTA. This is in line with Afesorgbor and van Bergeijk (2014) investigating a sample of 25 countries for the years 1980–2006 regarding multi-membership and report for ECOWAS and SADC that competing membership hampers trade agreements effectiveness. The later enables them to infer that the TFTA could resolve this. Moreover, comparing five major African intra-regional trading areas for 1980–2006, Afesorgbor (2017) finds that SADC is trade-promoting, but that COMESA membership is not significantly influencing trade. All in all, our findings consistently highlight the potential of enhancing the regional trading blocs in particular for the EAC and SADC because of their strong trade effects.

6.5   Conclusion and Policy Recommendations

This chapter shows the importance of border procedures for EAC countries. Significant costs and time are involved in documentary compliance and border procedures of exporting and importing thus creating important efficiency losses. Figure 6.4 illustrates how important these barriers to trade are.

Better management of transportation hubs such as (air)ports and border posts, reducing the costs and time of handling, as well as an efficient organization of documentary compliance (streamlining procedures, one stop portals, and the development and use of common quality standards) are therefore important for EAC countries but to a differing degree and along different dimensions. Figure 6.5 illustrates these heterogeneities by means of a radar diagram where time and costs of exporting and importing are shown for both border compliance and documentary compliance. In order to make the data comparable and also to provide a relevant benchmark all scores have been expressed in percent of the Sub-Saharan average.

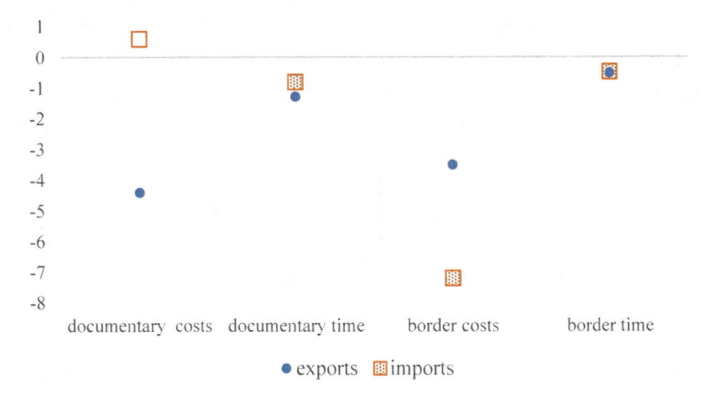

Fig. 6.4 Elasticities of exports and imports with respect to cost and time of documentary and border compliance. *Source* Tables 6.4, 6.5, 6.6 and 6.7. *Note* All elasticities are significant at the 99% confidence level with the exception of the import-elasticity of the costs of documentary compliance which is insignificant at the usual confidence levels

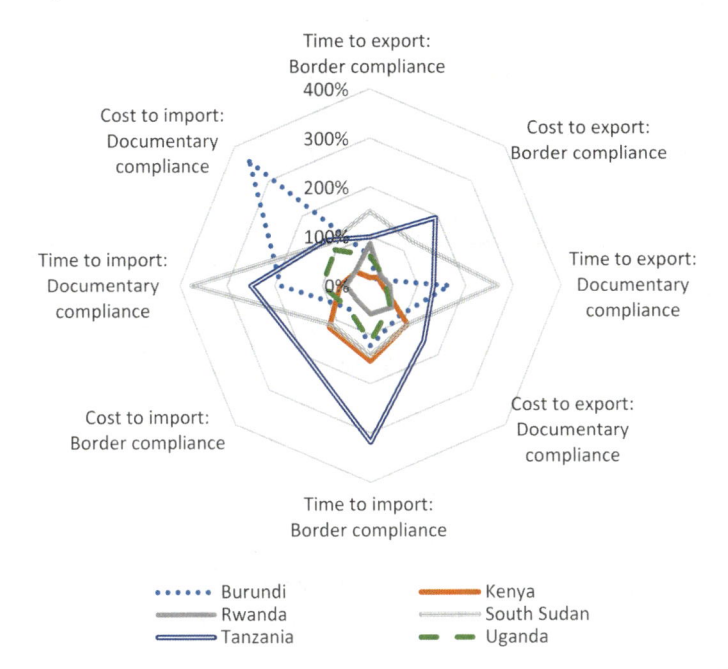

Fig. 6.5 Radar diagram of the costs (time) to cross borders (exports and imports) in percent of Sub-Saharan average (2020). *Source* Word Bank Ease of doing business dataset accessed March 29, 2022

Figure 6.5 shows that there is ample scope especially for Tanzania, South Sudan and to some extent Burundi to adjust towards Kenya's best practice. Looking beyond EAC some room for improvement would appear to exist also for Kenya because its time to import exceeds the Sub Saharan average. Such improvements, moreover, are not only directly beneficial for EAC countries that are moving towards that standard. Focussing on EAC movements towards best practice, moreover will also benefit the best performing EAC country (Kenya), because a specific trade bottleneck is just as important for an exporting as an importing country. If Tanzania, for example, reduces its time to import via the Port of Dar es Salaam, that will also help Kenyan exporters to Tanzania. This is actually a major lesson for further regional integration in the EAC: trade inefficiencies in one member country have important spill-over effects for other members. This is in a nutshell the rationale for concerted action across countries, products and markets.

Appendix 6.1

List of countries in the sample

1. Algeria	41. Japan
2. Angola	42. Kenya
3. Australia	43. Lithuania
4. Austria	44. Madagascar
5. Belgium	45. Malawi
6. Benin	46. Malaysia
7. Botswana	47. Mali
8. Brazil	48. Mauritius
9. Bulgaria	49. Mozambique
10. Burkina Faso	50. Namibia
11. Burundi	51. Netherlands
12. Cameroon	52. Niger
13. Canada	53. Nigeria
14. Central Africa Republic	54. Oman
15. Chad	55. Poland
16. China, P.R.: Mainland	56. Portugal
17. China, P.R.: Hong Kong	57. Romania
18. Comoros	58. Russian Federation
19. Congo, Dem. Rep. of	59. Rwanda
20. Côte d'Ivoire	60. Saudi Arabia
21. Croatia	61. Senegal

(continued)

(continued)

22. Cyprus	62. Seychelles
23. Czech Republic	63. Slovak Republic
24. Denmark	64. Slovenia
25. Djibouti	65. South Africa
26. Egypt	66. South Sudan
27. Estonia	67. Spain
28. Eswatini	68. Sudan
29. Ethiopia	69. Sweden
30. Finland	70. Switzerland
31. France	71. Tanzania
32. Germany	72. Tunisia
33. Ghana	73. Turkey
34. Greece	74. Uganda
35. Hungary	75. United Arab Emirates
36. India	76. United Kingdom
37. Indonesia	77. United States
38. Ireland	78. Vietnam
39. Israel	79. Zambia
40. Italy	80. Zimbabwe

References

Afesorgbor SK (2017) Revisiting the effect of regional integration on African trade: evidence from meta-analysis and gravity model. J Int Trade Econ Dev 26(2):133–153

Afesorgbor SK (2019) The impact of economic sanctions on international trade: how do threatened sanctions compare with imposed sanctions? Eur J Polit Econ 56:11–26

Afesorgbor SK, van Bergeijk PAG (2014) Measuring multi-membership in economic integration and its trade impact: a comparative study of ECOWAS and SADC. S Afr J Econom 82(4):518–530

Agarwal P, J.t Kweka and D.W. te Velde, (2022) Tanzania and the african continental free trade area, ODI briefing. Overseas Development Institute, London

Anderson JE, Van Wincoop E (2003) Gravity with gravitas: a solution to the border puzzle. Am Econ Rev 93(1):170–192

Baier SL, Bergstrand JH (2007) Do free trade agreements actually increase members' international trade? J Int Econ 71(1):72–95

Candau F, Guepie G, Schlick J (2019) Moving to autarky, trade creation and home market effect: an exhaustive analysis of regional trade agreements in Africa. Appl Econ 51(30):3293–3309

Carrere C (2006) Revisiting the effects of regional trade agreements on trade flows with proper specification of the gravity model. Eur Econ Rev 50(2):223–247

Coulibaly S (2009) Evaluating the trade effect of developing regional trade agreements: a semi-parametric approach. J Econ Integr 709–743

Dube C (2021) The role of competition reforms in unlocking international trade: evidence from africa's proposed tripartite free trade area. The Antitrust Bulletin 66(2):252–275

Ejones F, Agbola FW, Mahmood A (2021) Do regional trade agreements promote international trade? New empirical evidence from the East African Community. J Int Trade Econ Dev 30(7):1020–1053

Fofack H, Dzene R, Hussein OAM (2021) Estimating the effect of AfCFTA on intra-African trade using augmented GE-PPML. J Afr Trade 8:62–78

Head K, Mayer T (2014) Gravity equations: workhorse, toolkit, and cookbook. In: Handbook of international economics, vol 4. Elsevier, pp 131–195

Kassa W, Sawadogo PN (2021) Trade creation and trade diversion in African RECs. Policy Research Working Paper 9761. World Bank, Washington DC

Leyaro V (2021) Trade effects of the East African Customs Union in Tanzania. Working Paper 2021/55. UN WIDER, Helsinki

Longo R, Sekkat K (2004) Economic obstacles to expanding intra-African trade. World Dev 32(8):1309–1321

Martínez-Zarzoso I (2013) The log of gravity revisited. Appl Econ 45(3):311–327

Olivero MP, Yotov YV (2012) Dynamic gravity: endogenous country size and asset accumulation. Can J Econ/Rev Can D'économique 45(1):64–92

Oloyede BM, Osabuohien ES, Ejemeyovwi JO (2021) Trade openness and economic growth in Africa's regional economic communities: empirical evidence from ECOWAS and SADC. Heliyon 7.5:e06996

Riedel J, Slany A (2019) The potential of African trade integration–Panel data evidence for the COMESA-EAC-SADC Tripartite. J Int Trade Econ Dev 28(7):843–872

Santos Silva J, Tenreyro S (2006) The log of gravity. Rev Econ Stat 88(4):641–658

Smith A, Venables AJ (1988) Completing the internal market in the European Community: some industry simulations. Eur Econ Rev 32(7).1501–1525

van Bergeijk PAG, Brakman S (eds) (2010) The gravity model in international trade: advances and applications. Cambridge University Press

Yotov YV, Piermartini R, Monteiro JA, Larch M (2016) An advanced guide to trade policy analysis: the structural gravity model. UNCTAD and WTO, Geneva

Part III
Productivity and Competitiveness

Chapter 7
Productivity Premia and Firm Heterogeneity in Eastern Africa

Binyam Afewerk Demena, Jamal Msami, Donald Mmari, and Peter A.G. van Bergeijk

Abstract Productivity development is a key issue for export-driven growth and development. We use East African Community (EAC) firm-level data. Instead of focusing on single EAC partners, using the World Bank Enterprise Surveys, we investigate firm-level productivity differences for seven countries that are part of the COMESA-EAC-SADC tripartite free trade area (TFTA). Using export and ownership dimensions, we identify four types of firms: National Domestic, National Exporters, Foreign Domestic, and Foreign Exporters. We find a clear export productivity premium for national manufacturing firms and service sectors, but not for foreign-owned firms. We also find a clear foreign-ownership productivity premium for both domestic and exporting firms in manufacturing sectors but less clear in services sectors. The gap between the national export premium and the foreign-ownership premium is stronger in manufacturing firms as opposed to service sectors. Moreover, we find clear and strong productivity premia in size, training programmes, and level of development in the manufacturing firms. In the services sector, these premia are always smaller and only significant for medium-sized firms. There is no difference in experience premium between sectors in terms of both significance and magnitude of the estimated coefficients.

B. A. Demena (✉) · P. A.G. van Bergeijk
International Institute of Social Studies (ISS), Erasmus University Rotterdam, The Hague, the Netherlands
e-mail: demena@iss.nl

P. A.G. van Bergeijk
e-mail: bergeijk@iss.nl

J. Msami · D. Mmari
REPOA, Dar es Salaam, Tanzania
e-mail: jamal@repoa.or.tz

D. Mmari
e-mail: mmari@repoa.or.tz

7.1 Introduction

The economic debate on the benefits and cost of globalization has been ongoing for many years based on traditional macroeconomic analyses and reasoning. The perspective on this issue changed importantly due to applications and extensions of the New International Trade Theory building on the seminal work of Helpman and Krugman (1985) and Melitz (2003), where the focus shifted to the Micro-Economics of International Firm Activities. Accordingly, the relevance of heterogeneity across firms has become the heart of both the Micro-Economics of International Firm Activities and the New International Trade Theory (Wagner 2011).

In the past 25 years, the international trade literature radically changed by paying attention to individual firm characteristics. This literature started in 1995 by Bernard and Jensen with US firm-level data, who investigate the difference between exporters and non-exporters (Bernard and Jensen 1995).[1] They found significant economic performance differences between these two types of firms. The ensuing literature on heterogeneous firms has since seen a resurgence in other countries with the majority of empirical studies confirming their findings. However, the evolving discourse remains notable for the under-representation of important questions including the degree of firm heterogeneity and development in developing countries (van Bergeijk and van Marrewijk 2013). Underlying such lacunae has been the availability of reliable and periodic data. Recent efforts to improve the reliability of microeconomic data such as those by the World Bank Enterprise Surveys (WBES) on regional development, have enabled microeconomic analysis of firm-level productivity for many countries.

In this study, we use East African Community (EAC) firm-level data. Instead of focusing on single EAC partners, we construct a panel using WBES data and investigate the seven major intra-regional trading partners in the so-called tripartite free trade area (TFTA) that constitutes countries that are part of both the Common Market for Eastern and Southern Africa (COMESA) and the Southern African Development Community (SADC).[2] Using the WBES data, we analyse firm-level productivity for seven major intra-regional trading countries. We construct this dataset to contribute

---

[1] See Wanger (2011) for extensive survey of the empirical research on firm heterogeneity and productivity. He, summarizing studies published from 1995 to 2011, argues that the big picture that emerges after the first decade of micro-econometric research on the relationship between exporting and productivity is that exporting does not necessarily increase productivity whereas exporters are more productive than non-exporters, the latter leading to self-select more productive firms into export markets. However, underlying this partial picture is a lot of heterogeneity (regarding data characteristics, methodologies, statistical power, and coverage), and this leads Wagner (2011) to his recommendation to use a meta-analysis as a useful tool to explain heterogeneity and establish the overall underlying empirical effect.

[2] In identifying major EAC intra-regional trading partner countries that are both in the COMESA and SADC communities, we use the World Bank's World Integrated Trade Solution (WITS) statistics for trading partners, available at: https://wits.worldbank.org/CountryProfile/en/Country/TZA/Year/2018/TradeFlow/EXPIMP#. The WITS Trade Stats is a database created by the World Bank Group using data UN COMTRADE and UNCTAD TRAINS database. It has a wide range of information for bilateral trade exports, imports and tariffs covering 180 countries and regions. This construction

to the literature on productivity development and firm-level heterogeneity in five different ways.

First, this is the first study that explores whether EAC and major intra-regional trading partner exporting firms are more productive than non-exporting firms.[3] The relationship between firm-level productivity and exporting is one dimension that has received close attention (Greenaway and Kneller 2007). The existing literature on export and productivity dimensions alone can be divided into two theoretical strands, which are well recognized. The first theoretical strand focuses on self-selection: only the most productive firms enter into export markets because higher productivity is necessary to overcome the additional trade costs in exporting to foreign countries.[4] The findings on balance suggest that *pre-entry differences* between exporters and their counterparts who trade on the domestic market only support the hypothesis that more productive firms trade more. In the second strand, learning-by-exporting, firms that engage in foreign markets become more productive only after they begin to export, suggesting that *post-entry differences* should be the focus of the analysis.[5] The argument is that knowledge and information are tapped from and developed in international markets improving the export performance of the starters. In addition, firms operating in the international markets face more intense competition and thus must improve their performance to be competitive and sell their products.

Second, we extend a firm's international organization incorporating ownership dimensions, rather than putting all firms into one dimension only (i.e., export orientation only). Foreign direct investment (FDI) is another dimension of firm-level globalization strategy. FDI becomes less attractive compared to exporting when costs of entry and operation of foreign production increase, and more favourable when the foreign market size grows and costs of exporting rise (Greenaway and Kneller 2007). As argued in Chang and van Marrewijk (2013), the FDI or the foreign-ownership dimension is less recognized in the research of productivity premia. Thus, we extend the exporting internationalization literature and combine it with ownership status to create or identify four types of firms, namely: National Domestic, National Exporters, Foreign Domestic and Foreign Exporters.

Third, our analysis also covers the level of country development and four basic firm characteristics (namely: capital intensity, formal training programs, the firm size and

---

brings together three of Africa's major intra-regional trading blocs, COMESA-EAC-SADC, hence the tripartite free trade area (TFTA).

[3] In developed countries: Canada (1974–1996) Baldwin and Gu (2003), Germany (1978–1992) Bernard and Wagner (1997), Spain (1991–1996) Delgado et al. (2002), Sweden (1980–1997) Greenaway et al. (2005), UK (1988–1999) Girma et al. (2004), USA (1983–1992) Bernard and Jensen (2004). In developing countries: Chile (1990–1996) Alvarez and López (2005), Colombia (1981–1991) Fernandes and Isgut (2005), Indonesia (1990–1996) Blalock and Gertler (2004), Mexico (1986–1990) and Morocco (1984–1991) Clerides et al. (1998), Nine sub-Saharan African (1992–1996) van Biesebroeck (2005), Cameroon (1992–1995), Ghana (1991–1993), and Kenya (1992–1994).

[4] This theoretical strand of the empirical literature includes among others Melitz (2003), Helpman et al. (2004), Melitz and Ottaviano (2008), Eliasson et al. (2012).

[5] The empirical literature includes among others Clerides et al. (1998), De Loecker (2007), Chongvilaivan (2012).

age). It has been argued, for instance, that heterogeneity with respect to internalization and firm-level productivity tend to be strongest at the lowest country's development level (Mebratie and van Bergeijk 2013; Chang and van Marrewijk 2013). However, as indicated by van Bergeijk and van Marrewijk (2013) the relationship between development and firm-level heterogeneity is underexplored in the literature. They also argued that the degree of basic firm characteristics in developing countries is the other big question that is still underexplored, a point also stressed by Demena and Murshed (2018) regarding the development of productivity and different measures of firm heterogeneity (see Sect. 7.2).

Fourth, we extend our analysis to the service sectors as well. This is a broader approach than usually found in the literature as the majority of existing empirical studies regarding firm-level heterogeneity focus on the manufacturing sector only (see e.g., Lewis and Peng 2018; Chongvilaivan 2012; Mahmood 2008; van Biese-broeck 2005; Baldwin and Gu 2003). Services sectors are, however, very important for the countries in our sample: "in the majority of East African countries, real GDP growth from the supply side is driven primarily by growth in services" (African Development Bank 2019).

Fifthly, we focus on sub-Saharan Africa (SSA) countries, a region that due to lack of periodic data availability has been under researched. Chang and van Marrewijk (2013) also study firm heterogeneity and development, but for 15 developing Latin American countries for the year 2006. SSA is a very relevant area as it comprises most of the low-income countries (23 of the 29 low-income economies according to the World Bank's current classification by income).[6] There is a clear need to investigate productivity development and firm-level heterogeneity to understand what kind of productivity premia is most appropriate in general for SSA and in particular TFTA partner countries.

This chapter is structured as follows. Section 7.2 investigates the relationship between productivity development and firm heterogeneity using a review of 69 empirical studies associated with foreign ownership. Section 7.3 extensively discusses the source of the data, characteristics of the data along various dimensions and Sect. 7.4 introduces the empirical approach. Section 7.5 starts with the main results followed by further investigations and robustness checks. Finally, Sect. 7.6 concludes.

7.2   The Relationship Between Productivity and Firm Heterogeneity

The empirical and theoretical literature recognizes that firm heterogeneity regarding the degree of basic firm characteristics is important in the development of firm productivity. In this section, we explore the influence of basic firm characteristics on the outcome of firm productivity. We review a large number of published and unpublished

---

[6] The World Bank full list of current classification by income is available at: World Bank Country and Lending Groups—World Bank Data Help Desk.

Table 7.1 Firm-level heterogeneity and firm productivity

Variable	Positive and significant at 10%		Insignificant at 10%		Negative and significant at 10%		Total no.
	No	%	No	%	No	%	
Firm size	131	28	239	52	94	20	464
Export	109	40	141	52	23	8	273
Foreign ownership	466	32	740	51	244	17	1450
Capital intensity	311	33	447	48	179	19	937
R&D	39	30	67	50	26	19	132
Labour quality	346	33	499	48	202	19	1047

Source Authors' review of productivity effects reported in 1450 regressions of primary studies

empirical studies emphasizing the foreign ownership dimension alone carried out in developing countries. This review has identified 1,450 reported productivity effects associated with foreign ownership from 69 empirical dealing with 31 developing countries (for a detailed review, see Demena 2017).

Using this structured review, Table 7.1 reports how the outcome of firm productivity is associated with firm heterogeneity, illustrating how the nature of firm-specific factors play a role in enhancing the productivity effect provided included in the empirical design of the reviewed studies. For instance, 40% of the regressions that controls for export status results in the importance of firm-level exporting to enhance productivity. In contrast, the results are insignificant in 52% of the reported effects (8% for negative productivity effects). The size of the firm appears to positively influence the productivity development in 28% of the reported effects. Similarly, other basic firm characteristics related to capital intensity and the quality of labour are important factors to explain the productivity development—two-thirds of the reviewed studies report positive and significant effect. The result from Research and Development (R&D) suggests a similar trend, however, we have very small samples on this.

Table 7.1 also shows the extent of disagreement in terms of the direction and significance of the reported effects related to the foreign ownership dimension alone on productivity development. About one-third of the estimates (32%) find a positive and significant productivity effect, whereas about one in six reports a negative and significant productivity effect. The other 51% show both positive and negative but insignificant effects. Hence, despite the huge literature concerned with investigating the foreign-ownership-related productivity effects, findings in the empirical studies have generated substantially divergent results. This might be the case that some foreign firms export while others do not, hence lumping exporter and non-exporter into ownership dimension alone might hide the actual relation between heterogeneity and firm productivity development.

Another important message is that most of the reviewed studies attempted to test the productivity development associated with foreign ownership regardless of the nature of some basic firm-level heterogeneity. For instance, the reviewed studies largely ignore the heterogeneity characteristics related to the R&D, as only about 9%

of the regressions control for this difference (see also the meta-analysis of Mebratie and van Bergeijk 2013, for comparable findings). Therefore, the empirical design of the 69 studies reviewed recognizes the importance of input factors and their qualities in a production function framework but fails to include some important firm-level heterogeneity factors. Thus, the characteristics of domestic firms cannot be ignored, but rather, seem to mediate the expected magnitude, significance and sign of the productivity development. That is, the extent to which the development of productivity emerges may not appear evenly across all firms.

7.3 Data

7.3.1 Data Source and Construction

We use data obtained from the WBES. The WBES is an ongoing World Bank project designed to provide datasets using standard survey instruments. The WBES is based on a stratified random sampling of firms in participating countries. For all countries, samples are stratified along three dimensions: geographical regions, sector and firm size. The survey is administered to cover samples of representative firms from the non-agricultural formal private sector. The surveys are conducted across all geographical regions and establishment sizes (small, medium, and large) on sample of firms from the entire manufacturing sector, the services sector and transportation and construction.[7] The standardized format (i.e., the same sampling methodology and survey instruments) uses a standard set of questions, allowing for better comparisons across country and time (World Bank, 2017). In sum, the global format of the survey consists of a core questionnaire, a uniform population, and a uniform methodology.

The WBES focuses on the provision of data that allows researchers to investigate how changes in the business environment affect firm-level productivity both over time and across countries (Demena 2007). For this purpose, the data contains information on a set of individual variables, such as productivity performance, ownership status, market orientation (export status), technological behaviour and some other basic firm characteristics. Based on the objective of the study, we use data from seven major intra-regional trading countries that are part of the TFTA. These are the Democratic Republic of Congo (DRC), Kenya, Malawi, Rwanda, Tanzania, Uganda and Zambia. The data covers the period 2013–2014 and consists of firm-level information for 4,488 observations.

Table 7.2 gives the number of firm-level observations by country and sector. Leaving aside the relatively small sample from Rwanda, approximately all the countries have similar sample distribution, 12–18%. Tanzania represents the highest number of observations with 813 firm-level information, representing 18% of the

---

[7] Public utilities, government services, health care and financial services sectors are not included in the universe.

Table 7.2 Distribution of firms across countries and industries

ISIC code	Two-digit Industry	Tanzania	DRC	Kenya	Malawi	Rwanda	Uganda	Zambia	Total
		No. of Firms							
15	Food	91	37	163	45	65	118	62	581
17	Textile	37	3	38	12	1	41	9	141
18	Garment	57	37	12	16	-	13	31	166
20	Wood	20	20	8	12	9	22	24	115
22	Publishing, printing and recorded media	19	10	14	26	4	14	31	118
24	Chemicals	12	29	37	16	2	9	28	133
26	Non-metallic	14	6	12	5	3	15	40	95
28	Fabricated Metal	32	32	16	4	4	52	33	173
30	Furniture	114	44	15	14	16	54	50	308
	Other Manufacturing	75	42	87	76	41	64	90	462

(continued)

Table 7.2 (continued)

ISIC code	Two-digit Industry	Tanzania	DRC	Kenya	Malawi	Rwanda	Uganda	Zambia	Total
		No. of Firms							
Total manufacturing		*441*	*243*	*414*	*197*	*120*	*382*	*368*	*2171*
52	Retail	121	136	166	117	79	165	123	907
51	Wholesale	43	39	55	32	20	49	22	260
55	Hotel and restaurants	157	49	58	38	79	102	122	605
50	Services of motor vehicles	30	15	35	62	31	33	31	237
60	Transport storage and communication	12	26	35	24	17	9	17	140
45, 72	Other services	9	21	18	52	14	22	31	167
Total Services		*372*	*286*	*367*	*326*	*240*	*380*	*346*	*2317*
Total manufacturing and services		*813*	*529*	*781*	*523*	*360*	*762*	*720*	*4488*

Source Authors' compilation using World Bank Enterprise Surveys

Note: Other manufacturing includes manufacture of tobacco (16), leather (19), paper (21), refined petroleum products (23), plastic and rubber (25), basic metals (27), machinery and equipment (29), electronics and electrical machinery (31), precisions instruments (33), transport machines (34) and recycling (37). Other services include construction (45) and IT (72).

overall sample. Table 7.2 also provides industrial stratification designed for manufacturing industry and service sector. Manufacturing represents 48% and service sector accounts for 52%. Within these industrial stratifications, sectors are classified based on the International Standard Industrial Classification (ISIC) Rev. 3.1 2-digit classification. In total, the surveys contain 27 2-digit industries.[8] There are strong similarities in terms of industrial distribution across countries. Manufacturing of food products and beverages, furniture, other manufacturing,[9] retail, hotel and restaurants are the biggest sectors in the countries under study.

7.3.2 Descriptive Analysis

7.3.2.1 Performance in Productivity

Our main variable of interest is productivity. The WBES data does not provide a direct measure of productivity. Productivity is measured using either a direct procedure based on labour productivity, output or value added or an indirect estimate of total factor productivity (TFP).[10] There is no consensus on the appropriateness of the direct versus the indirect approach. In our case, estimation of TFP would be very much restricted due to the time dimension of our data. Thus, we opted for a direct procedure and follow Demena and Murshed (2018) and Chang and van Marrewijk (2013).[11]

We use two steps to standardize the data in local currency units (LCUs) across countries. First, we convert all monetary values to international currency—the US dollar. We use the official exchange rate for all the countries for the period of the sample year. Next, we deflate the values using the GDP deflator (i.e., in US dollars with 2000 as the base year). All data were obtained from the World Development Indicators (WDI). In doing so, the productivity observations reduced from 4,488 to 3,454 observations, due to missing data for sales value (970 observations) and total number of employees (additional 64 observations). Tables 7.3 and 7.4 report the summary statistics of productivity by country and sector, respectively. The upper part of both tables (log of productivity) show a substantial difference in productivity

---

[8] The full list of the 2-digit industry classification is available at: https://www.enterprisesurveys. org/content/dam/enterprisesurveys/documents/methodology/ES_QuestionnaireManual_2019.pdf.

[9] Other manufacturing includes manufacture of tobacco (16), leather (19), paper (21), refined petroleum products (23), plastic and rubber (25), basic metals (27), machinery and equipment (29), electronics and electrical machinery (31), precisions instruments (33), transport machines (34) and recycling (37).

[10] Studies employ a production function to estimate a firm's TFP using firm's factor inputs.

[11] Demena and van Bergeijk (2017) meta-analysis of empirical studies published in period 1986—2013 suggests the popularity of the direct procedure, with two out of five of the empirical estimates employing the direct approach. Other researchers, for instance, Mahmood (2008) point out the relevance of the direct approach (labour productivity) as it is important for living standards and wages in African context.

Table 7.3 Summary statistics for productivity by country

Country	Mean	Standard deviation	Min	Median	Max	Total no. of firms
Log of productivity						
Tanzania	6.932	1.749	1.808	6.819	16.211	476
DRC	7.521	2.359	2.315	7.157	15.732	481
Kenya	8.506	1.721	2.062	8.494	15.324	660
Malawi	7.327	1.774	1.509	7.213	13.413	348
Rwanda	7.309	2.019	2.605	7.126	15.325	360
Uganda	7.168	2.104	0.849	7.020	15.150	496
Zambia	13.866	1.333	8.285	13.001	18.147	633
Normalized productivity						
Tanzania	0.454	0.246	0	0.450	1	476
DRC	0.417	0.239	0	0.388	1	481
Kenya	0.504	0.236	0	0.508	1	660
Malawi	0.491	0.278	0	0.478	1	348
Rwanda	0.490	0.272	0	0.481	1	360
Uganda	0.488	0.269	0	0.490	1	496
Zambia	0.474	0.237	0	0.447	1	633

Source Authors' compilation using World Bank Enterprise Surveys

measures across countries and sectors. As a result of this, we employ normalized productivity (NP_{isc}) by sector and country, as given in Eq. (7.1).

$$NP_{isc} = \frac{\log(P_{isc}) - \min\log(P_{isc})}{\max\log(P_{isc}) - \min\log(P_{isc})} \qquad (7.1)$$

where P is the reported sales per total worker employed. The subscripts i, s, and c, represent firm, industry and country, respectively. In this case, $\log P_{isc}$ implies log of productivity for firm i in sector s and country c. NP_{isc}, therefore, measures normalized productivity for firm i in sector s and country c with the scale from zero to one—firms are scaled in terms of the worst and best performing for a given sector in a given country. The logic of the indicator is viewed as forming a line segment with length equal to the distance between the best- and worst-performing countries. The TFTA countries are, therefore, placed along this line segment revealing their relative potions of the indicator.

This indicator is presented in the lower part of Tables 7.3 and 7.4, allowing for a comparison of normalized productivity across sectors and countries (Chang and van Marrewijk 2013). The statistics are based on a clustered computation of seven countries (Table 7.3) and 27 industries (Table 7.4). This provides an indication of the difference in productivity distribution. For instance, countrywide, firms in Kenya are on average the most productive, whereas those in DRC are least productive (Table 7.3). Kenya is also the country with the least productivity variation across the sectors.

Table 7.4 Summary statistics for productivity by industry

Industry	Mean	Standard deviation	Min	Median	Max
Log of productivity					
Food	8.596	2.771	1.583	8.274	16.829
Textile	7.897	2.514	3.600	7.584	16.224
Garment	7.445	3.027	2.566	6.560	14.565
Wood	9.132	2.772	5.783	8.336	15.192
Publishing, printing and recorded media	7.445	3.027	2.556	6.560	14.565
Chemicals	9.524	3.428	3.242	8.458	16.984
Non-metallic	10.563	3.498	2.843	11.004	17.677
Fabricated metal	8.533	3.136	2.276	7.536	17.677
Furniture	7.904	3.216	1.808	6.819	17.899
Other manufacturing	9.594	3.094	1.583	9.015	16.761
Average manufacturing	8.732	3.155	1.509	8.164	17.899
Retail	8.404	3.005	1.857	7.776	18.147
Hotel and restaurants	8.671	3.190	2.276	7.634	17.860
Wholesale	8.762	2.902	2.315	8.334	17.716
Transport, storage & communication	8.862	3.267	0.849	8.429	17.225
Services of motor vehicles	8.732	2.977	2.681	8.153	14.527
Other Services	9.625	3.131	4.537	9.004	18.028
Average services	8.665	3.076	0.849	7.951	18.147
Normalized productivity					
Food	0.537	0.206	0	0.530	1
Textile	0.427	0.274	0	0.371	1
Garment	0.463	0.262	0	0.433	1
Wood	0.469	0.280	0	0.458	1
Publishing, printing and recorded media	0.487	0.299	0	0.477	1
Chemicals	0.504	0.288	0	0.490	1
Non-metallic	0.414	0.284	0	0.379	1
Fabricated Metal	0.510	0.278	1	0.525	1
Furniture	0.456	0.243	0	0.406	1
Other manufacturing	0.476	0.352	0	0.503	1
Average manufacturing	0.487	0.273	0	0.481	1
Retail	0.448	0.205	0	0.432	1
Hotel and restaurants	0.489	0.200	0	0.454	1
Wholesale	0.462	0.245	0	0.455	1

(continued)

Table 7.4 (continued)

Industry	Mean	Standard deviation	Min	Median	Max
Transport, storage and communication	0.490	0.278	0	0.479	1
Services of motor vehicles	0.471	0.253	0	0.444	1
Other Services	0.472	0.317	0	0.453	1
Average services	0.461	0.229	0	0.445	1

Source Authors' compilation using world bank enterprise surveys

In contrast, Malawi is the country with the highest productivity variation, suggesting the presence of larger productivity gaps between firms.

The statistics across sectors (Table 7.4) indicate that firms in the manufacture of food products and beverages are the most productive. More than half of the firms in this sector are more productive than the average firm in any sector. On average the most productive firms for food products and beverages are in Zambia and at least half of these firms have stronger productivity than firms in any country on average (Table 7.A1). Only eight firms in this sector in Tanzania are as productive as the average Zambian firms. Again, firms in this sector in DRC are the worst performing with Tanzanian firms, the second least productive. Comparisons of Tables 7.3 and 7.A1 show that firms in the manufacture of food products and beverages are better performing than the average firms in any country, suggesting the relevance of this sector for TFTA countries under study (exceptions are firms located in DRC).

Figure 7.1 shows a further relationship between firm productivity (median normalized productivity) and the level of country's development (the log of GDP per capita in PPP). As can be seen from the upward slopping line, there is a positive relationship between productivity and a country's development level—DRC in the lower left corner, Kenya in the right upper corner and the other 5 countries in between. The upward slopping line is an initial indication of a positive association between the level of country's development and productivity—countries with higher income level (more developed countries) are populated with higher productive firms. The median productivity estimates of the median productivity reported in individual countries (represented by the long-dashed line) equals 0.478, which is close to the mean of the productivity level across countries (0.474). The solid line denotes the median of all the productivity estimates. The closeness of the mean and median (Tables 7.3 and 7.4, Fig. 7.1) is an indication that there are no serious outliers in our dataset, so we do not exclude any normalized productivity estimates across the TFTA from the analysis.

7.3.2.2 Export Intensity, Firm Ownership and Firm Type

Table 7.5 gives the export intensity of the sampled firms. A firm is classified as an exporter if it exports at least 10% of its output (World Bank Enterprise, 2017).

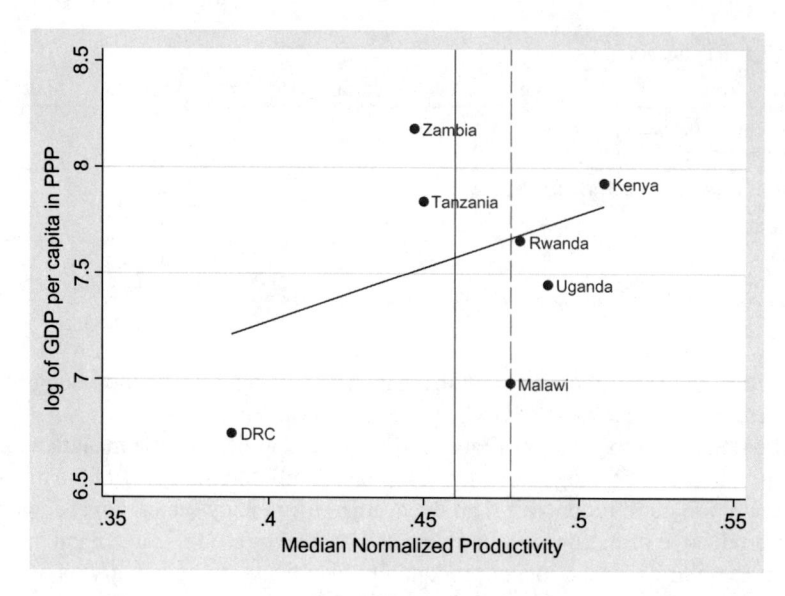

Fig. 7.1 Firm productivity and development level across the TFTA countries. *Notes:* The figure shows the relationship between firm productivity and a country's level of development. The solid vertical line represents the median of all the productivity distribution. The long-dashed line represents the median of median productivity distribution from the TFTA countries.

Table 7.5 Distribution of export intensity by country

Country	Export intensity (%)			Total no. of exporters	Total no. of firms	% of exporters
	10–20	21–60	61–100			
Tanzania	24	28	7	59	681	8.7
DRC	12	9	1	22	528	4.2
Kenya	64	60	47	171	759	22.5
Malawi	19	15	6	40	462	8.7
Rwanda	28	33	14	75	360	20.8
Uganda	37	19	8	64	733	8.7
Zambia	22	14	13	49	706	6.9
Average	29	25	14	69	604	–
Total	206	178	96	480	4229	11.4

Source Authors' compilation using World Bank Enterprise Surveys

Applying this threshold there are only 480 exporting firms, equivalent to 11.4% of the overall sample. Considering the sampled firms within each country (which depends on the relative size of the economy), Kenya and Rwanda have higher percentages of exporting firms with 23% and 21%, respectively. Conversely, the DRC and Zambia have the lowest percentage of exporting firms with 4% and 7%, respectively.

The number of exporting firms in Kenya is about threefold of the countries under study except in Rwanda. To put this figure in comparison: the total share of exporters (11.4%) is higher than the 8.0% for 8 SSA countries for the period 2006–2014 reported in Demena and Murshed (2018) and similar to the 11.5% for the 15 Latin American Countries sampled in 2006 reported in Chang and van Marrewijk (2013).

For each country, Table 7.5 also provides the export intensity in terms of the number of firms exporting certain shares of their output. Among the 480 exporters, more than two-fifths of the export is between 10 and 20% of their output, while one-third of the export is between 21 and 60% of their output (Fig. 7.2). The other one-fifth of the export is more than 60% of their output. The export intensity greatly varies across countries. Firms in the highest exporting country, Kenya, exhibit roughly similar distribution in the three categories of the percentages of firms exporting. When we look at the other countries, the export intensity pattern is slightly different for Tanzania and Rwanda. Most exporting firms in these countries are at the middle of export intensity—relatively larger proportion of firms export between 21 and 61% of their output. Moreover, the result with the lowest export share, DRC, is quite different as more than 90% of the firms export up to 60% only.

In addition to the export status, we also classify firms by ownership characteristics, i.e., whether a firm classifies as foreign or locally owned. According to the IMF (2009), an investment by foreign investor is regarded as foreign owned in which a direct investor owns at least a 10% of the ordinary share of equity or voting power in an enterprise. Our classification follows this cut-off percentage in that a firm is

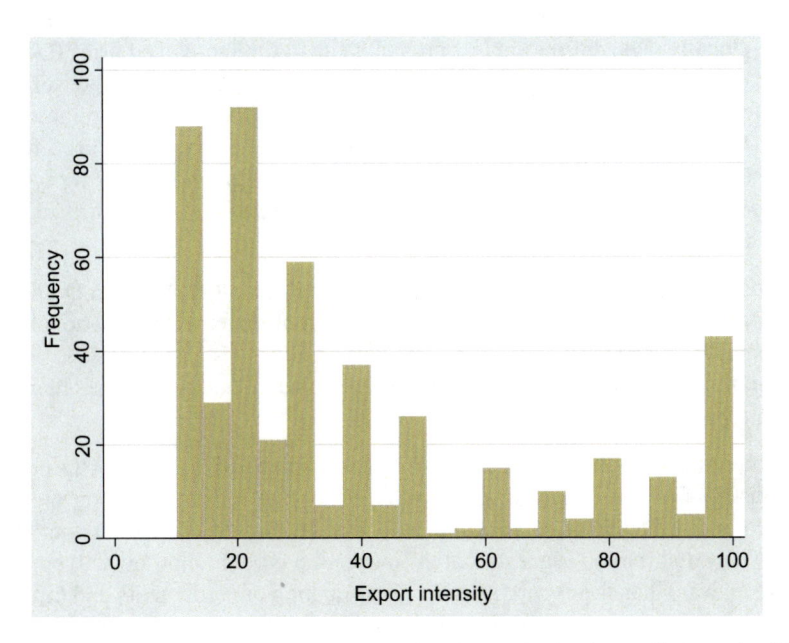

Fig. 7.2 Export intensity across the TFTA countries. *Source* Authors' compilation using World Bank Enterprise Surveys

Table 7.6 Summary statistics for firm types in the manufacturing and service sectors

Firm type	All firms	%	Manufacturing	%	Services	%
National domestic	3162	76.4	1483	72.9	1679	79.8
National exporter	320	7.7	194	9.5	126	6.0
Foreign domestic	508	12.3	254	12.5	254	12.1
Foreign exporter	148	3.6	104	5.1	44	2.1
Total	4138	100	2035	100	2103	100

Source Authors' compilation using World Bank Enterprise Surveys

classified as foreign if at least 10% of its shares are held by non-nationals. Using this classification, there are 3482 (84.1%) national and 656 (15.9%) foreign firms. Combining the two firm dimensions, i.e., export status and ownership, we distinguish four types of firms, see Table 7.6. Among the 4138 firms, most are National Domestic (76.4%) and sell their output to the domestic market. This is followed by Foreign Domestic firms in which 12.3% of the foreign firms are national/domestic market oriented. National Exporters represent 7.7%, i.e., nationally owned and export market oriented. The last 3.6% belong to Foreign Exporters—foreign owned and sales to foreign market. In terms of sector, the ordering and percentage shares are analogous when we classify firms into manufacturing and service sectors (Table 7.6).

Next, we discuss the four types of firms in terms of their productivity distribution. Exporting firms (irrespective of ownership type) are more productive than non-exporting firms (e.g., see Lin and Weng 2019; Davies and Jeppesen 2015), whereas locally owned firms are less productive than foreign-owned firms (Demena 2017). Our sampled firms confirmed this, suggesting domestic market-oriented firms (locally owned firms) are less productive than exporting firms (foreign-owned firms). The existing literature on international trade and heterogeneous firms further suggested that there is a monotonic performance hierarchy among the four types of firms identified (Kox and Rojas-Romagosa 2010). The latter is also confirmed in our sampled firms, our main hypotheses are therefore as follows:

- **Hypothesis 1**: National Exporters are more productive than National Domestic.
- **Hypothesis 2**: Foreign Domestic firms are more productive than National firms (Domestic and Exporter).
- **Hypothesis 3**: Foreign Exporters are more productive than any of the other three firm types.

Incorporating ownership status offers a more comprehensive picture of the productivity distribution. As indicated, we also find that Foreign Domestic firms are more likely to be productive than National Exporters. In this regard, the ranking of the productivity distribution suggests that the ownership type (foreign-owned) premium is more relevant than the export premium. This ranking of productivity and firm-type pattern is similar to the Dutch sampled firms in 1999–2005 reported in Kox and Rojas-Romagosa (2010) or for the 15 Latin American Countries sampled in 2006 reported in Chang and van Marrewijk (2013). We also find a similar pattern when we

Table 7.7 Summary statistics for firm types by productivity and firm size

Firm type	N	Mean	S.D	Min	Median	Max
Normalized productivity						
National domestic	2515	0.448	0.241	0	0.437	1
National exporter	290	0.535	0.269	0	0.514	1
Foreign domestic	407	0.567	0.256	0	0.565	1
Foreign exporter	128	0.598	0.287	0	0.629	1
Size by the number of workers						
National domestic	3094	31.8	127.6	1	10	4000
National exporter	314	162.5	534.1	3	50	8000
Foreign domestic	503	79.4	227.9	2	23	3500
Foreign exporter	146	211.3	543.5	5	84	5500

Source Authors' compilation using World Bank Enterprise Surveys

disaggregate the firms by the industrial type (see, Table A.2 in the Appendix). In both the upper and bottom parts of Table A.2, a clear pattern emerges also when we deal with the manufacturing and service sectors separately. All the figures in productivity differences are statistically significant at 1%. The information in Table A.2, also suggests that on average the manufacturing sector tends to be more productive than the service sector. This leads to our fourth hypothesis which compares the impact of the identified four types of firms on the development of productivity premia is significantly higher for manufacturing than services sectors.

WBES measures firm size by the number of employees (Table 7.8, definition of variables). In general, in terms of firm size, foreign-owned firms appear to be larger (Demena and Murshed 2018). In our sampled firms, we also find uniformity with this observation. The bottom part of Table 7.7 presents the identified firm types by size. On average, exporters tend to be larger in size than non-exporters. Moreover, on average Foreign Exporters tend to be larger than any other firm type. Using Table 7.7, the bottom part, therefore, we find a similar ranking pattern as the case with productivity distribution by firm type (Table 7.7 upper part), except for the reversal ranking between National Exporters and Foreign Domestic firms. Thus, our fifth hypothesis is that the larger the size of the firm the higher the productivity premia.

7.4 Empirical Approach

To develop our empirical approach to the relationship between productivity development and firm heterogeneity, we started investigating our data. The discussion of the data above suggests that there is no single dimension that can fully elucidate the difference in productivity performance of the sampled firms. In this regard, we need to simultaneously control for various other firm heterogeneities before we fully explain

Table 7.8 Definition of Variables

Variables	Description
Normalized productivity (NP_{isc})	Logarithm of a firm's annual total sales per worker (Demena 2017), normalized by sector and country
Normalized value added (NVA_{isc})	Logarithm of value added (sales — total cost of raw material and intermediate inputs) per worker (Demena and Murshed 2018), normalized by sector and country
Exports (Ex)	Firm exports (firm exports at least 10% of its outputs) (Lu et al. 2017)
National domestic (ND)	Dummy variable for nationally owned firms with domestic market-oriented (foreign participation/ownership is less than 10% with domestic sales more than 90%) (Chang and van Marrewijk 2013)
National exporter (NE)	Dummy variable for nationally owned firms with foreign market-oriented (foreign participation/ownership is less than 10% with export at least 10%) (Chang and van Marrewijk 2013)
Foreign domestic (FD)	Dummy variable for foreign-owned firms with domestic market oriented (foreign participation/ownership is at least 10% with domestic sales more than 90%) (Chang and van Marrewijk 2013;
Foreign exporter (FE)	Dummy variable for foreign-owned firms with foreign market oriented (both foreign participation/ownership and export are at least 10%) (Chang and van Marrewijk 2013;
Firm size—SS (5–19 workers)	Dummy variable if the size of the firm is small (Mebratie and Bedi 2013; Demena 2017)
Firm size—MS (20–99 workers)	Dummy variable if the size of the firm is medium (Demena and Murshed 2018)
Firm size—LS (100+ workers)	Dummy variable if the size of the firm is large (Chang and van Marrewijk 2013)
GDP per capita	Logarithm of GDP per capita, PPP corrected (van Bergeijk and van Marrewijk 2013)
Conglomerate	Dummy if the establishment is part of a large firm (subsidiary firm) (Demena 2017)
Capital city	Dummy if firms located in the capital city (Mebratie and Bedi 2013)
Firm age	Number of years in operation (Demena and van Bergeijk 2019)
Formal training	Formal training programmes for employees (Demena 2017)
Capital intensity (K/L)	The logarithm of expenditure on machinery, vehicles, and equipment per worker, normalized by sector and country (Lu et al. 2017)

the productivity performance difference. We first analyse whether exporters have significant productivity performance premium as compared to non-exporters, while controlling for various firm-level characteristics, industry and country fixed effects. Next, we distinguish the analyses according to the four identified types of firms including foreign-ownership productivity premium along the export productivity premium. Finally, we also investigate the difference in productivity performance involving other firm characteristics (e.g., firm size, development levels). The latter is vital to fully explain the difference in productivity performance by incorporating various sources of productivity premia. In doing so, we separate the model between the manufacturing and service sectors throughout the analyses and discussions.

The empirical approach is estimated using the following equation:

$$NP_{isc} = \beta_0 + \beta_1 NE_{isc} + \beta_2 FD_{isc} + \beta_3 FE_{isc} + \beta_4 MS_{isc} + \beta_5 LS_{isc} + \beta_6 GDP_{isc}$$
$$+ \alpha \sum X_{isc} + \beta_7 I_s + \beta_8 C_c + \varepsilon_{isc}$$
$$(7.2)$$

The subscripts i, s and c, represent firm, sector and country, respectively. We include industry fixed-effects (I_s) and country fixed-effects (C_c) to account for unobservable time-invariant heterogeneity in industries and countries, respectively. This addresses the econometric concerns induced by the potential omission of unobserved variables to obtain unbiased and consistent estimates (Demena 2017). We also include dummy variables for firm size (MS_{isc} and LS_{isc}), a measure of country level of development (GDP_{isc}) and a set of control variables (X_{isc}) as outlined in Table 7.8. We use the WBES classification of firm size in terms of the number of employees with the small size of the firm (SS) as a reference. Focusing on the relationship between firm heterogeneity and development, we include information related to the per capita income levels (PPP corrected) as an indicator for the level of development (van Bergeijk and van Marrewijk 2013). We follow this to test our sixth hypothesis that heterogeneity in firm-level productivity tends to be strongest at the lowest GDP per capita level, underlying the relevance of this indicator for countries under investigation. Mebratie and van Bergeijk (2013) in their meta-analysis of 30 developing and emerging markets, also find that heterogeneity is the highest at low GDP per capita levels.

Our most important variables under study are the identified four types of firms using dummy variable for the National Domestic firms as a reference, testing the first three hypotheses. The estimated coefficients for β_1, β_2 and β_3 reflect the export productivity premium among national firms, foreign-ownership productivity premium among local firms, and foreign-ownership productivity premium for exporting firms among domestic firms, respectively. Moreover, we investigate the export premium for foreign firms comparing the coefficients estimated for Foreign Exporters (β_3) and Foreign Domestic firms (β_2). In the same pattern, we examine exporting firms' foreign-ownership productivity by comparing the coefficients estimated for Foreign Exporters (β_3) and National Exporters (β_1). We test our fourth hypothesis by analysing our regression of Eq. (7.2) separately for the manufacturing and services sectors. Furthermore, we use estimated coefficients of β_4, β_5, and β_6 to test our fifth and sixth hypotheses, investigating size productivity premium for medium- and large-sized enterprises and premium for level of development, respectively. We also extend the fifth hypothesis by analysing premium for size effect by comparing the estimated coefficients for medium-sized firm (β_4) and large-sized firm (β_5). Finally, we also include a set of additional variable (X_{isc}) to complement our hypotheses testing by examining whether on-the-job training programmes and firm experience are an important component of productivity development. Accordingly, we expect that firms with a formal training programme and long experience in years since establishment to positively influence the development of productivity premia, as Demena (2017) argued they may likely have adequate production scale and space.

7.5 Estimation Results

7.5.1 Main Results: Productivity and Heterogeneity

A set of several estimations is provided. We first apply the regression regarding exporters versus non-exporters to test the export performance premium regardless of firm ownership. Table 7.9, Columns 1 and 5 report the results regarding the performance premium for exporters. Exporters enjoy a significantly larger productivity premium than non-exporters in both manufacturing and service sectors—respectively, 6 and 4-percentage-points more likely than non-exporters. Comparing the point estimates, the gap between exporters and non-exporters is strong for the manufacturing sector. The export premium for the manufacturing sector is almost about 35% as large as the service sector and the difference is statistically significant.

Next, before we estimate Eq. (7.2) testing whether the three types of firms should be included simultaneously or separately (using the National Domestic firms as a reference). The Wald test suggests statistically significant differences at the highest confidence level, indicating the simultaneous estimation of the identified types of firms. Testing our three main hypotheses, Table 7.9 Columns 2–4 and 6–8 report the results estimating Eq. (7.2) and applied to both manufacturing and service sectors separately to allow further comparison so as to test our fourth hypothesis. Regressions in Columns 2 and 6 are without a country and industry-fixed effects, whereas the regressions in Columns 3 and 7 do have country and industry-fixed effects. Columns 4 and 8 check our results in Columns 3 and 7, respectively, while controlling for the age of the firms since establishment. All columns include both conglomerate and capital city as control variables. As specified in our empirical approach, we emphasize results while controlling for industry and country fixed effects to account for unobservable time-invariant heterogeneity (Columns 3 and 7). To keep the table manageable and for clarity of illustration, we report results relating to the variables of interest.

Table 7.9 Productivity Premia: Exports, foreign ownership, firm size and development level

Variables	1	2	3	4	5	6	7	8
	Manufacturers				Services			
Exports (Ex)	0.060*** [0.019]				0.039* [0.019]			
National exporter (NE)		0.042* [0.022]	0.062** [0.023]	0.055** [0.023]		0.068*** [0.022]	0.055** [0.023]	0.055** [0.023]
Foreign domestic (FD)		0.107*** [0.020]	0.116** [0.021]	0.118*** [0.021]		0.075*** [0.017]	0.085*** [0.018]	0.090*** [0.018]
Foreign export (FE)		0.144*** [0.031]	0.144*** [0.031]	0.150*** [0.031]		0.094** [0.037]	0.093** [0.037]	0.084** [0.037]
Medium Firm—MF (20–99 workers)	0.085*** [0.015]	0.071*** [0.015]	0.072*** [0.015]	0.063*** [0.015]	0.037** [0.013]	0.037** [0.013]	0.030** [0.013]	0.029** [0.013]
Large Firm—LF (100 + workers)	0.131*** [0.020]	0.110*** [0.019]	0.108*** [0.020]	0.093*** [0.021]	0.028 [0.020]	0.026 [0.011]	0.016 [0.021]	−0.001 [0.021]
GDP per capita	0.060** (0.022)	−0.009 [0.013]	0.068** [0.022]	0.066** [0.022]	0.001** [0.021]	0.035*** [0.011]	0.005 [0.020]	−0.003 [0.020]
Firm age				0.002*** [0.0001]				0.002*** [0.0004]
Sector fixed effect	Yes	No	Yes	Yes	Yes	No	Yes	Yes
Country fixed effect	Yes	No	Yes	Yes	Yes	No	Yes	Yes
$\overline{R}^2$	0.08	0.08	0.10	0.11	0.06	0.06	0.08	0.08
Observations	1,709	1,739	1,739	1,706	1,663	1,700	1,700	1,661
Test if coefficients are significantly different: F-test (Prob > F)								
NE versus FD		0.018**	0.037**	0.014**		0.801	0.269	0.195

(continued)

Table 7.9 (continued)

Variables	1	2	3	4	5	6	7	8
	Manufacturers				Services			
FD versus FE		0.283	0.390	0.358		0.628	0.847	0.868
NE versus FE		0.004**	0.012**	0.004**		0.537	0.365	0.493
MF versus LF	0.018**	0.045**	0.073*	0.122	0.670	0.589	0.510	0.173

Notes: Robust standard errors in [] are clustered at the country level. $*p < 0.1$; $**p < 0.05$; $***p < 0.01$. The dependent variable is normalized productivity. NE versus FD reflect foreign-ownership productivity for domestic firms comparing the coefficients estimated for Foreign Domestic firm and National Exporters, whereas FD versus FE represents export premium for foreign firms comparing the coefficients estimated for Foreign Exporters and Foreign Domestic firms. NE versus FE provides foreign-ownership productivity for exporting firms comparing the coefficients estimated for Foreign Exporters and National Exporters, whereas MF versus LF signifies size productivity premium comparing medium-sized and large-sized firms

Starting with the manufacturing firms, Column 3 gives statistically positive significant effects of the three included firm types as compared to the National Domestic firms, corroborating our three main hypotheses more generally. National Domestic firms are less productive (6.2%-points) than National Exporters, which are also less productive (11.6%-points) than Foreign Domestic firms and (14.4%-points) than Foreign Exporters. The point estimates of productivity are different, and the F-test (at the bottom of Table 7.9) suggested the differences in point estimates are also statistically significant. An exception is the difference between Foreign Domestic and Foreign Exporters, suggesting our third hypothesis is only partially valid as FE are not more productive than any other firm but only ND and NE. For national manufacturing firms, we can therefore conclude that the export productivity premium is important. For foreign manufacturing firms, however, the export productivity premium is less important than the foreign-ownership productivity premium (p-value 0.390). In other words, we can conclude that Foreign Exporters are not more productive than Foreign Domestic firms, suggesting the foreign-ownership productivity premium is more important than the export productivity premium. The conclusions are consistent when we control for firm age since establishment (see, Column 4).

For service sector, Column 7, we arrive at somewhat different conclusions. Like manufacturing firms, we find that National Domestic firms are less productive (5.5%-points) than National Exporters, which are also less productive (8.5%-points) than Foreign Domestic firms and (9.3%-points) than Foreign Exporters. Although the point estimates are somewhat different and significant as compared to National Domestic firms, the comparison among the three types of firms included are not significantly different (see, F-test at the bottom of Table 7.9). This is in sharp contrast to the results of the manufacturing firms for NE versus FD and FE, thus our second and third hypotheses are only partially valid as the findings support against ND only. In sum, there is an export productivity premium for national manufacturing firms and service sectors, but not for foreign firms in both sectors. Regarding foreign-ownership, there is a significant productivity premium for both domestic and exporting firms in both manufacturing and service sectors as compared to National Domestic firms. Among exporters, foreign ownership productivity premium is not significant in the service sectors. Moreover, the gap between export premium and foreign-ownership premium is stronger in manufacturing firms as opposed to service sectors, corroborating our fourth hypothesis.

Regarding the size effects, thus testing our fifth hypothesis, for manufacturing sectors, medium-sized firms are more productive as opposed to small-sized firms and large-sized firms are even more productive. For the service sectors, results were mixed. Medium-sized firms are more productive than small-sized firms, but for large-sized firms, the effect is not significant. In addition, the point estimate difference between medium-sized and large-sized firms are statistically significant for manufacturing firms but not in services. Thus, for service sectors, our fifth hypothesis is valid for medium-sized firms only. Furthermore, the effect of medium-sized firms is stronger for manufacturing firms (the estimated magnitude is less than half in services and the difference is statistically significant, consistent with the fourth hypothesis). Looking at development levels, and thus testing the sixth hypothesis, the country's development level premium is statistically significant and larger for the manufacturing firms, but the effect in service sectors is insignificant. The latter is even negative but insignificant when we control for the experience of the firm in years (age). Regarding the experience productivity premium (Columns 4 and 8), the magnitudes are small but positive and significant, and equally important for the manufacturing and service sectors. In sum, there are clear and strong productivity premia in size and level of development in the manufacturing firms. In the service sector, these premia are always smaller and only significant for medium-sized firms. There is no difference in age productivity premium between manufacturing and service sectors in terms of both significance and magnitude of the estimated coefficients.

7.5.2 Further Investigations and Robustness Analyses

In this section, we run a set of different specifications both as further investigations and as robustness checks. This section in particular deals with the sensitivity of our main findings to the: (a) introduction of additional variables; (b) construction of the outcome variable; (c) introduction of a set of country-industry interaction fixed effects; (D) construction of the foreign ownership structure.

7.5.2.1 Introduction of Additional Variables, Country–Industry Interaction and Construction of the Outcome Variable

In this robustness check, we repeat estimation of Eq. (7.2) for three additional or alternative specifications. First, we introduce capital intensity using the logarithm of expenditure on machinery, vehicles, and equipment per worker, normalized by sector and country. The normalization procedure followed the same procedure as in Eq. (7.1) and given below:

$$Nk/l_{isc} = \frac{\log(k/l_{isc}) - \text{minlog}(k/l_{isc})}{\text{maxlog}(k/l_{isc}) - \text{minlog}(k/l_{isc})} \tag{7.3}$$

where k/l is the reported capital (expenditure on machinery, vehicles, and equipment) per total worker employed. The subscripts i, s and c, represent firm, industry and country, respectively. Nk/l_{isc} is measuring the normalized capital intensity in firm i for sector s and country c. The statistics are based on a clustered computation of 7 countries (Table 7.3) and 27 industries (Table 7.4).

In an observational study of Ugandan firms, Demena and van Bergeijk (2019) find that a formal training programme is an important component of productivity development. Testing our last hypothesis, we, therefore, include whether firms undertake formal training programmes for employees that result in an additional productivity premium. Next, we include a set of country–industry interaction fixed effects to the

Table 7.10 Robustness checks I: Capital intensity, formal training programmes and value added

Variables	1	2	3	4	5	6	7
	Manufacturers					Services	
National exporter (NE)	0.056* [0.028]	0.040* [0.020]	0.053** [0.022]	0.092*** [0.022]	0.041 [0.072]	0.052** [0.023]	0.063** [0.023]
Foreign domestic (FD)	0.136*** [0.029]	0.120*** [0.027]	0.113*** [0.021]	0.116*** [0.021]	0.146** [0.067]	0.080*** [0.018]	0.093*** [0.018]
Foreign export (FE)	0.197*** [0.031]	0.185*** [0.036]	0.142*** [0.031]	0.164*** [0.031]	0.178* [0.100]	0.084** [0.037]	0.095** [0.037]
Medium firm—MF (20–99 workers)	0.072*** [0.021]	0.064** [0.020]	0.072*** [0.015]	0.069*** [0.015]	0.094* [0.049]	0.027** [0.013]	0.031** [0.013]
Large firm—LF (100+ workers)	0.079*** [0.026]	0.086** [0.025]	0.100*** [0.021]	0.105*** [0.020]	0.068 [0.066]	0.005 [0.021]	0.046** [0.021]
GDP per capita	0.137*** [0.031]	0.085** [0.029]	0.062** [0.022]	0.181*** [0.435]	0.052 [0.071]	0.001 [0.020]	0.181 [1.664]
Capital intensity (K/L)		0.321*** [0.027]					
Formal training			0.052*** [0.014]			0.039** [0.012]	
$\overline{R}^2$	0.15	0.25	0.11	0.16	0.31	0.07	0.14
Observations	886	886	1,727	1,739	1,713	1,689	1,700
Test if coefficients are significantly different: F-test (Prob > F)							
NE versus FD	0.030**	0.020**	0.022**	0.402	0.242	0.313	0.265
FD versus FE	0.169	0.114	0.372	0.157	0.773	0.911	0.967
NE versus FE	0.012**	0.000***	0.007**	0.004**	0.224	0.442	0.440
MF versus LF	0.076*	0.347	0.128	0.060**	0.672	0.293	0.476

Notes: See Table 7.9. The dependent variable in Column 5 is the normalized value added per worker

separate industry and country dummies. Finally, we test an alternative definition to our outcome variable. This is done by replacing the sales per worker definition of labour productivity with the value added per worker. Like the labour productivity, we also adopted normalized value added per worker clustered by the 7 countries and 27 sectors. We apply this only for the manufacturing firms as the WBES does not provide data on the total cost of raw material and intermediate inputs used in production for the service sectors.

Table 7.10 gives the estimated coefficients for the various specifications outlined above. Our main findings in relation to the various productivity premium results are confirmed. Regarding capital intensity,[12] we find that more capital-intensive firms

---

[12] Since introducing the capital intensity variable reduces the sample size by about half, we first run the main specification of Column 3 in Table 7.9 excluding firms that do not report capital intensity (*K/L*) data. The result of this exercise reported in Column 1 of Table 7.10. Next, Column 2 introduces the robustness checks including capital intensity (*K/L*). Although this gives better comparison as

have a higher productivity level (Column 2). Similarly, firms undertaking formal employees training, as expected, have a higher productivity level (Column 3), concurring the results of existing studies. Furthermore, including country–sector interaction fixed effects, in Columns 4 and 7 mimic the findings of Columns 3 and 7 in Table 7.9. Regarding value added instead of labour productivity, generally, the results in Column 5 suggest that the use of either of the definitions of labour productivity does not make much difference for productivity analysis (which is consistent with Demena and Murshed 2018). Importantly, it should be noted that value-added data is more applicable for industrialized economies than in developing economies as more value additions are realized in industrialized economies (Lewis and Peng 2018). This may be attributable as we find somehow different results from value-added data—Column 5 reports insignificant premium for National Exporters and development levels.

7.5.2.2 Construction of the Foreign-Ownership Structure

In Table 7.9, we find the relevance of export productivity premium for national firms but only in the manufacturing sectors. We also find that foreign-ownership productivity premium is relevant for both exporting and domestic firms in both manufacturing and service sectors. The next question to ask is, therefore, whether the intensity of the foreign-ownership structure matters for the productivity premium. This is done by allowing broader variation in foreign-ownership in terms of majority and minority ownership. Majority foreign ownership is defined as 50% or more ownership and set the variable to zero if ownership is less than 50%. Similarly, minority foreign ownership defined as less than 50% ownership (but at least 10%).[13]

We keep the National Domestic firms as a base specification and thus we still have four types of firms except now we replace the two foreign types of firms based on the intensity of the foreign ownership. The results are presented in Table 7.11. Estimated coefficients of the three types of firms are statistically significant, suggesting the National Exporter, Minority Foreign-owned and Majority foreign-owned firms have higher productivity premium than Domestic firms in all sectors (exception is minority-owned firms in services). In general, we continued to find similar results of the main analysis (compare with Table 7.9). In addition, we find a more nuanced picture of the productivity premium. In our main results, the difference between Foreign Domestic and Foreign Exporters were never significant, but now our findings in Column 1 of Table 7.11 corroborate the view that majority foreign-owned firms are the main drivers of productivity premium than the minority foreign-owned firms (F-test, p-value 0.073). According to Demena (2017), a possible explanation

---

opposed to with large sample difference, the results are consistent (compare Column 3, Table 7.9 and Column 1, Table 7.10).

[13] Note that we did not incorporate intensity into Foreign Domestic and Foreign Exporters as no export productivity premium was found for foreign firms (Table 7.9).

Table 7.11 Robustness checks II: productivity and foreign ownership intensity

Variables	1	2	3	4	5	6	7
	Manufacturers					Services	
National exporter (NE)	0.064** [0.023]	0.038 [0.026]	0.091*** [0.022]	0.076** [0.029]	0.064* [0.037]	0.053** [0.023]	0.061** [0.023]
Minority foreign owned	0.075** [0.030]	0.135*** [0.038]	0.087** [0.030]	0.078** [0.039]	0.149** [0.052]	0.021 [0.034]	0.032 [0.033]
Majority foreign owned	0.136*** [0.021]	0.147*** [0.026]	0.149*** [0.020]	0.145*** [0.027]	0.127*** [0.035]	0.097*** [0.018]	0.103*** [0.017]
Medium Firm—MF (20–99 workers)	0.071*** [0.015]	0.063** [0.020]	0.069*** [0.015]	0.069*** [0.020]	0.081** [0.027]	0.030** [0.013]	0.031** [0.013]
Large Firm—LF (100+ workers)	0.106*** [0.020]	0.090*** [0.025]	0.110*** [0.020]	0.108*** [0.026]	0.189** [0.033]	0.018 [0.021]	0.048** [0.021]
GDP per capita	0.070** [0.022]	0.088** [0.029]	0.185 [0.434]	0.177 [0.577]	−0.189 [0.733]	0.007 [0.020]	0.182 [1.663]
Capital intensity (K/L)		0.320*** [0.027]			0.249*** [0.036]		
$\overline{R}^2$	0.10	0.25	0.18	0.89	0.82	0.07	0.11
Observations	1,739	886	1,739	1,713	883	1,700	1,700
Test if coefficients are significantly different: F-test (Prob > F)							
NE versus Minority	0.744	0.026**	0.902	0.957	0.148	0.415	0.313
Minority versus Majority	0.073*	0.778	0.059*	0.129	0.703	0.038**	0.911
NE versus Majority	0.009**	0.001**	0.032**	0.054**	0.167	0.111	0.442
MF versus LF	0.072*	0.238	0.035**	0.126	0.809	0.586	0.293

Notes: See Table 7.9. The dependent variable in Columns 4 and 5 are normalized value added per worker

could be that foreign investors may be more inclined to bring their proprietary technology with them when they have majority ownership control over subsidiary operations. However, this statistical difference in ownership intensity holds true if we don't control for capital intensity. That is, in all the reported estimates the statistical difference disappears if reported estimates incorporate capital intensity, otherwise always significant. This could indicate that the main productivity premium difference between minority- and majority-owned firms is based on capital intensity. Majority foreign-owned firms are therefore more productive than minority foreign-owned firms, and this is fully due to the higher capital intensity rather than any other potential advantage. This conclusion is similar to Chang and van Marrewijk (2013) for developing Latin American countries.

7.6 Discussion and Conclusion

We investigate firm-level productivity differences for seven intra-regional major trading partner countries that are part of the COMESA-EAC-SADC tripartite free trade area using the WBES. Incorporating export and ownership dimensions, we identify four types of firms: National Domestic, National Exporters, Foreign Domestic and Foreign Exporters. By doing so, we extend a firm's international organization by incorporating ownership dimensions, rather than putting all firms into one dimension alone. This allows us to explore the export productivity and foreign-ownership premia separately. Moreover, we complement the analysis with additional productivity premia, namely: firm size effects, country's development levels, firm experience as well as training programmes. While most existing empirical studies only focus on the manufacturing sector, we separately incorporate the service sectors in our analysis.

We find a clear and significant export productivity premium for national manufacturing firms and service sectors, but not for foreign firms in both sectors. We also find a clear foreign-ownership productivity premium for both domestic and exporting firms in manufacturing sectors but less clear in service sectors. For national manufacturing firms, we can conclude that the export productivity premium is important. For foreign manufacturing firms, however, the export productivity premium is less important than the foreign-ownership productivity premium. Foreign Exporters are thus not more productive than Foreign Domestic firms, consequently, the foreign-ownership productivity premium is more important than the export productivity premium. In terms of the literature that focused on the foreign-owned dimension alone, our foreign ownership findings contrasted with Mebratie and van Bergeijk (2013) and Mebratie and Bedi (2013), where 63 per cent of reported estimates are insignificant or negative or on average zero effects, respectively. However, our findings are consistent with the most recent body of the literature, which found that foreign ownership is likely to positively impact domestic productivity (e.g., Demena and van Bergeijk 2017; Demena and Murshed 2018).

Regarding other productivity premia, in manufacturing sectors medium-sized firms are more productive as compared to small-sized firms and large-sized firms are even more productive. For the service sectors, results were mixed. Medium-sized firms are more productive than small-sized firms, but for large-sized firms the effect is not significant. Furthermore, the effect of medium-sized firms is stronger for manufacturing firms. Looking at development levels, productivity premium is statistically significant and larger for the manufacturing firms, but the effect in service sectors is insignificant. Regarding the experience productivity premium, the results are small but positive and significant, and equally important for the manufacturing and service sectors. In sum, there are clear and strong productivity premia in size and level of development in the manufacturing firms, but results are mixed in the service sector. Leaving aside some further insights and additional findings, overall, our results corroborate with Chang and van Marrewijk (2013), who like our paper specifically investigated firm heterogeneity and productivity development, but for 15 developing Latin American countries for the year 2006.

All the above effects are consistently robust, when we introduce additional variables (for instance, capital intensity, formal training programmes); when we use value added per worker instead of labour productivity defined as sales per worker as our productivity measure; as well as the introduction of a set of country-industry interaction fixed effects rather than the separate industry and country dummies. The final question we investigate is whether the intensity of the foreign-ownership structure matters for the productivity premium. Allowing broader variation in foreign ownership, we identify intensity in terms of majority- and minority-owned foreign firms. We continued to find similar results in the main analysis with a more nuanced picture of the productivity premium. We add that the majority foreign-owned firms are more productive than minority foreign-owned firms. Initially, in line with Demena and Murshed (2018), it appears that this was because foreign investors may be more inclined to bring their proprietary technology with them when they have majority ownership control over subsidiary operations. However, controlling for potential omitted variable bias, consistent with Chang and van Marrewijk (2013) this is fully due to the higher capital intensity rather than any other potential advantage.

Based on the main objective, the findings of this paper may also have policy implications. Productivity development is a key issue for export-driven growth and development. The trade policy environment of a country with heterogeneous firms influences the size of exporter premia differently across sectors. The paper mainly focuses on the link between exports and productivity development (including other firm heterogeneities and country's development level). This narrow focus enables us to provide more robust estimations and achieve greater sectoral (manufacturing versus service), market orientation (local versus export), and ownership dimension (national versus foreign) comparability. A solid understanding of the size of the export premium and drivers of productivity development is, therefore, a prerequisite for any sound policy-oriented arguments and policy parameters for economic diplomacy and commercial trade policy.

Appendix

See Tables A.1 and A.2.

Table A.1 Normalized productivity by countries in the manufacture of food products and beverages

Country	Mean	Standard deviation	Min	Median	Max	Total no. of firms
Normalized productivity						
Tanzania	0.480	0.171	0	0.488	1	63
DRC	0.402	0.240	0	0.394	1	33
Kenya	0.529	0.149	0	0.528	1	139
Malawi	0.525	0.273	0	0.479	1	29
Rwanda	0.564	0.243	0	0.545	1	65
Uganda	0.586	0.204	0	0.577	1	81
Zambia	0.608	0.213	0	0.641	1	51

Table A.2 Productivity summary statistics for firm types by sectors

Firm type	N	Mean	S.D	Min	Median	Max
Normalized productivity—manufacturing						
National domestic	1218	0.454	0.263	0	0.447	1
National exporter	177	0.540	0.273	0	0.504	1
Foreign domestic	210	0.593	0.281	0	0.608	1
Foreign exporter	91	0.613	0.281	0	0.608	1
Normalized productivity—services						
National domestic	1588	0.458	0.229	0	0.442	1
National exporter	1049	0.472	0.244	0	0.455	1
Foreign domestic	1093	0.474	0.240	0	0.455	1
Foreign exporter	1037	0.471	0.243	0	0.454	1

References

African Development Bank (2019) East Africa Economic Outlook 2019. ADB, Abidjan

Alvarez R, López RA (2005) Exporting and performance: evidence from Chilean plants. Can J Econ/revue Canadienne D'économique' 38(4):1384–1400

Baldwin JR, Gu W (2003) Export-market participation and productivity performance in Canadian manufacturing. Can J Econ/revue Canadienne D'économique 36(3):634–657

Bernard AB, Jensen JB (2004) Exporting and Productivity in the USA. Oxf Rev Econ Policy 20(3):343–357

Bernard AB, Wagner J (1997) Exports and success in German manufacturing. Weltwirtschaftliches Archiv 133(1):134–157

Bernard AB, Jensen JB (1995) Exporters, jobs, and wages in US manufacturing: 1976–1987, *Brookings Papers on Economic Activity*. Microeconomics 1995:67–119

Blalock G, Gertler PJ (2004) 'Learning from exporting revisited in a less developed setting. J Dev Econ 75(2):397–416

Chang HH, van Marrewijk C (2013) Firm heterogeneity and development: evidence from Latin American countries. J Int Trade Econ Dev 22(1):11–52

Chongvilaivan A (2012) Learning by exporting and high-tech capital deepening in Singapore manufacturing industries, 1974–2006. Appl Econ 44(20):2551–2568

Clerides SK, Lach S, Tybout JR (1998) Is learning by exporting important? Micro-dynamic evidence from Colombia, Mexico, and Morocco. Q J Econ 113(3):903–947

Davies RB, Jeppesen T (2015) Export mode, firm heterogeneity, and source country characteristics. Rev World Econ 151(2):169–195

De Loecker J (2007) 'Do exports generate higher productivity? Evidence from Slovenia. J Int Econ 73(1):69–98

Delgado MA, Farinas JC, Ruano S (2002) Firm productivity and export markets: a non-parametric approach. J Int Econ 57(2):397–422

Demena BA (2017) Essays on intra-industry spillovers from FDI in developing countries: a firm-level analysis with a focus on Sub-Saharan Africa. PhD diss., Erasmus University, The Hague

Demena BA, Murshed SM (2018) Transmission channels matter: Identifying spillovers from FDI. J Int Trade Econ Dev 27(7):701–728

Demena BA, van Bergeijk PAG (2017) A meta-analysis of FDI and productivity spillovers in developing countries. J Econ Surv 31(2):546–571

Demena BA, van Bergeijk PAG (2019) Observing FDI spillover transmission channels: evidence from firms in Uganda. Third World Quarterly 40(9):1708–1729

Eliasson K, Hansson P, Lindvert M (2012) Do firms learn by exporting or learn to export? Evidence from small and medium-sized enterprises. Small Bus Econ 39(2):453–472

Fernandes AM, Isgut AE (2005) Learning-by-doing, learning-by-exporting, and productivity: evidence from Colombia. The World Bank

Girma S, Greenaway A, Kneller R (2004) Does exporting increase productivity? A micro econometric analysis of matched firms. Rev Int Econ 12(5):855–866

Greenaway D, Kneller R (2007) Firm heterogeneity, exporting and foreign direct investment. Econ J 117(517):F134–F161

Greenaway D, Gullstrand J, Kneller R (2005) Exporting may not always boost firm productivity. Rev World Econ 141(4):561–582

Helpman E, Melitz MJ, Stephen RY (2004) Exports Versus FDI with Heterogenous Firms. Am Econ Rev 94

Helpman E, Krugman PR (1985) Market structure and foreign trade: increasing returns, imperfect competition, and the international economy. MIT press, Cambridge

International Monetary Fund (IMF) (2009) Balance of payments and international investment position Manual 6th edition. Washington, D.C. Available at: <https://www.imf.org/external/pubs/ft/bop/2007/pdf/bpm6.pdf>. Accessed 30 June 2020

Kox HL, Rojas-Romagosa H (2010) Exports and productivity selection effects for Dutch firms. De Economist 158(3):295–322

Lewis PC, Peng F (2018) Manufacturing productivity and real consumption wages, background paper prepared for the Industrial Development Report 2018. United Nations Industrial Development Organization, Vienna

Lin SH, Weng Y (2019) Market size, productivity and product quality regarding firm heterogeneity. Economic Research-Ekonomska Istraživanja 32(1):2918–2934

Lu Y, Tao Z, Zhu L (2017) Identifying FDI spillovers. J Int Econ 107:75–90

Mahmood M (2008) Labour productivity and employment in Australian manufacturing SMEs. Int Entrep Manag J 4(1):51–62

Mebratie AD, Bedi AS (2013) Foreign direct investment, black economic empowerment and labour productivity in South Africa. J Int Trade Econ Dev 22(1):103–128

Mebratie AD, van Bergeijk PAG (2013) Firm heterogeneity and development: a meta-analysis of FDI productivity spillovers. J Int Trade Econ Dev 22(1):53–74

Melitz MJ (2003) The impact of trade on intra-industry reallocations and aggregate industry productivity. Econometrica 71(6):1695–1725

Melitz MJ, Ottaviano GI (2008) Market size, trade, and productivity. Rev Econ Stud 75(1):295–316

van Biesebroeck J (2005) Exporting raises productivity in sub-Saharan African manufacturing firms. J Int Econ 67(2):373–391 van Bergeijk PAG, van Marrewijk C (2013) Heterogeneity and development: an agenda. J Int Trade Econ Dev 22(1):1–10

Wagner J (2011) From estimation results to stylized facts twelve recommendations for empirical research in international activities of heterogeneous firms. De Economist 159(4):389–412

World Bank Enterprise Survey (2017) Enterprise survey indicator description. Available at: <https://www.enterprisesurveys.org/content/dam/enterprisesurveys/documents/Indicator-Descriptions.pdf>. Accessed 18 June 2020

Chapter 8
Export Status Changes and Firm Productivity: Evidence from EAC Countries

Gerald P. Lesseri and Kauthar S. Salum

Abstract Many developing countries are stimulating their firms to compete in world markets as part of the efforts to promote economic growth. This move is, however, driven by desirable performance characteristics that are observed among exporting firms relative to firms that sell in the domestic market only. This chapter examines whether exporting firms in Eastern African Community (EAC) countries between 2006 and 2013 exhibit characteristics that are significantly different from non-exporters and hence whether learning by exporting takes place. Similar to other countries, exporting firms in Tanzania, Kenya, Uganda and Rwanda are more productive, pay higher wages and employ more workers relative to non-exporting firms and thus an indication of export premium. In line with this, exporters exhibit higher growth of labour productivity relative to non-exporters which is an evidence of learning by exporting. A comparison of the learning effectiveness between domestic and foreign-owned firms indicates that it is the domestic firms that learn more from exporting than foreign-owned firms; that learning effects accumulate with the length of export. Thus, export promotion activities in these countries should aim at stimulating as many firms as possible to participate in international trade and tap the export premium.

8.1 Introduction

Many developing countries are stimulating their firms to compete in world markets as part of the efforts to attain export led industrialization and eventually economic growth (Van Biesebroeck 2005; Rankin et al. 2006; Babatunde 2009; Demena et al.

The authors are thankful to Peter van Bergeijk and Binyam Afewerk Demena of Erasmus University, International Institute of Social Studies for technical guidance in carrying out the research work. The study was financially supported by Research on Poverty Alleviation (REPOA), the African Caribbean and Pacific Group of States (ACP Group) of this project, grant number FED/2019/408–112.

G. P. Lesseri (✉) · K. S. Salum
University of Dar Es Salaam School of Economics (UDSoE), Dar Es Salaam, Tanzania
e-mail: lesserigerald@gmail.com; glesseri@udsm.ac.tz

2021). This move has been triggered by the advantages that a firm enjoys when it goes international including behaviour and performance changes (Silvente 2005); a lesson that has been drawn from the role trade played in the growth of high-income countries giving evidence of the linkage between export and economic growth. Trading on world markets is, however, shaped by a number of factors including among others; globalization, technology advancement and competition (MIT, POPC and UNIDO, 2012). Increased trade liberalization in recent decades and the subsequent production internationalization means that domestic firms are exposed to both internal and external competition considered necessary to foster their productivity through assimilation of improved technologies and working practices (Babatunde 2009).

While there is a general agreement that a positive correlation exists between exporting and firm performance as measured by productivity, less is agreed on the direction of causality. That is, do firms invest in raising productivity before entering the export market or higher productivity is a result of entering the export market? The former is the hypothesis of firms' self-selection into the export market or learning to export and the latter is the hypothesis of learning by exporting. The two hypotheses have been disputed and the academic debate is ongoing.

The proponents of learning to export consider that potential exporters take deliberate decisions to invest in research and development, physical and human capital as well as purchase advanced technologies before entering the export market (Harrison and Rodriguez-Clare 2010; Eliasson et al. 2012). This means that prior investment in productivity is crucial in order to cover costs that are associated with participation in international markets. On the other hand, proponents of learning by exporting consider the possibility of knowledge transfer as a result of interacting with competitors and buyers in the destination market (Pack and Page 1994; Alvarez and Lopez 2005; Newman et al. 2016a). That is the feedback from buyers helps improve product quality, design and packaging whereas competitors offer avenues for knowledge, working practices (efficiency gain in operation) and technology diffusion (Clerides et al. 1998; Pack and Page 1994; Blalock and Gertler 2004; Newman et al. 2016b).

This chapter intends to contribute to the debate by presenting and discussing the results of the econometric study of four East African Community (EAC) countries—Tanzania, Kenya, Uganda and Rwanda—on the nexus between export and firm performance. We analysed these countries using the World Bank Enterprise Surveys (WBES) datasets. Providing evidence from East Africa on international trade and firm performance is an important policy issue in line with the countries' efforts to promote export. If firms need to be highly productive before entering world markets, governments should be selective in what kind of firms they stimulate. If firms become more productive by exporting, then export promotion activities should aim at as many firms as possible.

To achieve the aforementioned objective, this chapter is organized into six sections. After Sect. 8.1 has given a background to the chapter, Sect. 8.2 gives a brief overview of export performance for EAC countries. Section 8.3 presents the ongoing theoretical and empirical debate on the nexus between export and firm productivity. Section 8.4 presents the export premia of EAC firms. Section 8.5 presents the main results of mapping export status changes and firm productivity to examine the presence of learning by exporting and its variation between domestic and foreign-owned firms. The last section concludes and provides insights on potential trade policies for the promotion of export and eventually for achieving economic transformation.

8.2 Export Performance for EAC Countries: A Brief Overview

EAC countries are among the sub-Saharan African (SSA) economies that are still striving to industrialize as part of the efforts to transform their economies. However, part of the efforts to industrialize depends on the extent of domestic firms' participation in the international market (Page et al. 2016). In recognition of the role of exports for economic development, most African countries started to open their economies to foreign trade around the 1990s in the implementation of structural adjustment reforms (Biggs and Srivastava 1996; Babatunde 2009). Before this time, the levels of industrial development and trade performance in these countries were very low. Since then countries took deliberate efforts to bring down trade barriers for purposes of influencing trade flows around the globe and expanding markets for increased benefits of globalization. Similarly, efforts to diversify exports from traditional commodities to manufactured goods and services were also done. Following the trade policy reforms, the EAC countries' merchandise and service exports performance have generally shown an increasing trend over time as indicated by their increasing share of exports to GDP (Fig. 8.1). Such an improvement regards the EAC countries as small open economies and emerging players in world trade.

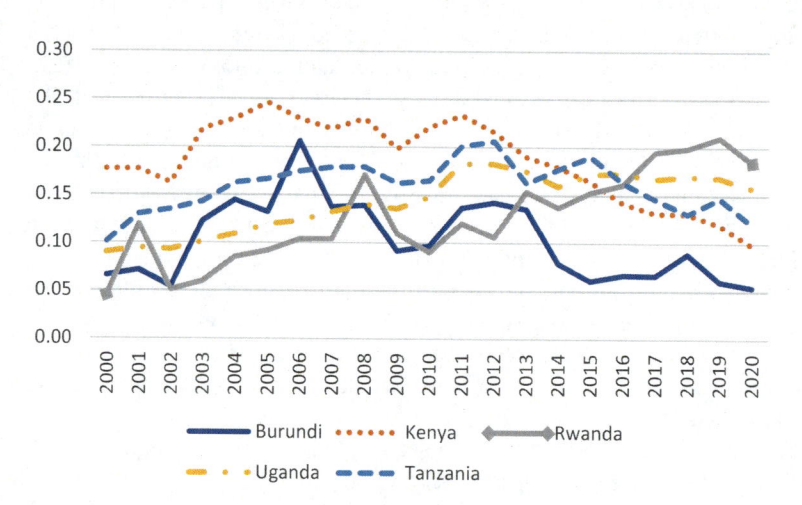

Fig. 8.1 Export Performance for EAC (per cent of GDP). *Source UNComtrade and UNCTADStat Databases (accessed in October 2021). Note No data on service exports could be obtained for the case of Burundi in 2019 and 2020*

Table 8.1 EAC countries top three merchandise export partners in 2018

Country	Export partners and percent of total exports
Tanzania	India (13.8%), South Africa (11.3%) and Switzerland (8.3%)
Kenya	Uganda (10.2%), Pakistan (10.2%) and the United States (7.8%)
Uganda	Kenya (18.1%), the United Arab Emirates (16.3%) and South Sudan (10.6%)
Rwanda	Democratic Republic of the Congo (33.7%), the United Arab Emirates (7.8%) and Switzerland (7.8%)

Source UN Statistics Division (2020)

In the early 2000s, Kenya surpassed its comparators in terms of having the highest share although recently has been overtaken by Rwanda, Uganda and Tanzania. However, all countries experienced a decreased export performance since 2019 due to the outbreak of the COVID-19 pandemic. The export partners of most of the EAC countries include a mix of countries with different levels of economic development.

The top three export partners are shown in Table 8.1.

Despite the observed increase in exports, the volume of goods and services that EAC countries export is still below a quarter of GDP. Possible reasons could be that only a few goods are manufactured in these countries or the existence of the practice of trade-restrictive regimes such as tariff and non-tariff barriers; and failure to meet the required standards for products or health regulations (Newman et al. 2016b). For example, in 2019 trade openness indices (a measure of the relative importance of international trade in goods relative to the domestic economic output of an economy) for the EAC economies were still low standing at 10.91, 11.46, 12.74 and 18.71 for Tanzania, Kenya, Uganda and Rwanda, respectively (UNCTAD 2020). To attain export-led economic growth, there is a need for these countries to address trade policy barriers that dwindle their export performance in line with the global SDG target 17.11 which aims to significantly increase the export of low-income countries.

8.3 Export and Firm Performance Debate

The fact that exporting firms possess desirable performance characteristics is undisputed, but that is not the case for the direction of causality between exporting and firm performance as it has competing explanations. One strand of the literature maintains that firms need to raise the performance indicators (notably productivity) before entering the international market (self-selection hypothesis) while the other advocates that a firm's performance increases after entering the export market (learning by exporting hypothesis). However, the two hypotheses are never mutually exclusive. This section elaborates on theoretical linkages surrounding the two strands of knowledge and provides a review of the empirical debate for the purposes of gaining more insights into the frontiers of knowledge surrounding the hypotheses.

8.3.1 Good Performance Prior to Exporting

Firms' self-selection into exporting is a more straightforward and compelling argument as is in line with the behavior of profit maximization. According to this hypothesis firms have to invest in improving productivity prior to entering the export market in order to cover extra costs associated with supplying the international market and entry costs for foreign markets. Such extra costs comprise market search costs, transit costs, modifying products to meet foreign demanded qualities, increased personnel for dealing with exportation and marketing costs (Bernard and Jensen 1999; Bernard and Wagner 1997). For such ranges of costs, only more productive firms stand a better chance to sell in the foreign market.

8.3.2 Good Performance as a Result of Exporting

The other channel of the linkage between exporting and firm performance is that firms may learn from exporting thus leading to productivity gains. The theoretical justification of causality from exporting to firm performance hinges on three reasons according to Bernard and Wagner (1997) and McKinsey (1993). First, is the increased supply or markets that make a firm benefit from increased economies of scale in production. Normally, domestic markets especially those of developing countries are small and limited to the growth of the economy meaning that only firms that enter foreign markets can enjoy higher output and sales resulting from market expansion. Second, is the increased competition as a result of supplying to meet the foreign demand. If foreign competition is more intense than domestic, then an exporting firm will increase performance efforts including investment in innovative activities in order to keep up with the pace and standards to avoid being thrown out of the market (McKinsey, 1993). Lastly, is product differentiation that results from customers' feedback covering aspects such as quality and packaging, to mention but a few. The feedback enables a firm to manufacture goods with desired qualities by foreigners which is an improvement in supply. The improvement results from technological and knowledge spillovers as foreign demanders may assist their diffusion in order to purchase in return products of the desired standards. This means that exporting serves as a conduit of technology and knowledge assimilation for domestic firms. Due to the above-outlined reasons, exporting firms will experience increased output and employment and ultimately productivity gains (Bernard and Jensen, 1999).

8.3.3 Empirical Debate

The empirical debate on the relationship between international trade and firm performance is vast and growing. It started with the ground-breaking study by Bernard and

Jensen (1995), who investigated the differences between exporters and non-exporters using US firm-level data. They found significant economic performance differences between these two types of firms. Their study did not, however, provide explanations on the direction of causality of such differences. Following the Bernard and Jensen (1995) publication, the number of studies conducted increased because more national and international firm-level data became available and an attempt was made to find evidence in respect of the two hypotheses: self-selection and learning by exporting.

The evolution of the studies on the causal effects of export and firm productivity can be divided into two periods. Firstly, is the period towards the end of the 1990s in which the direction of causality between exporting and firm performance was found to be in favour of the self-selection hypothesis (Newman et al. 2016b). It includes studies that were done in Germany (Bernard and Wagner 1997), the USA (Bernard and Jensen 1999) and Colombia (Clerides et al. 1998). These studies find that firms take conscious measures to invest in physical capital in order to raise production efficiency before they begin to export. This evidence was, however, associated with studies from developed countries. Firms in these countries operate using an advanced level of technology that is similar to their trading partners thus offering little to learn from such trade relations (Harrison and Rodriguez-Clare 2010).

Secondly, however, as data from developing countries became available, the learning by exporting hypothesis started to gain support around the 2000s. For example, Van Biesebroeck (2005) using a sample of nine SSA countries (Burundi, Cameroon, Cote d'Ivoire, Ethiopia, Ghana, Kenya, Tanzania, Zambia and Zimbabwe) found an increasing productivity gap between exporters and non-exporters after the former's entry into international market which is evidence of learning by exporting. The study applies a system GMM approach using the Regional Program on Enterprise Development (RPED) covering the period between 1992 and 1996. Similar findings were observed by Rankin et al. (2006) who found a pessimistic evidence of self-selection to exporting among five SSA (Kenya, Ghana, Tanzania, South Africa and Nigeria) using extended RPED survey data. In addition, Blalock and Gertler (2004) found a 2 percentage point increase in productivity as a result of exporting for Indonesian manufacturing enterprises. Other studies from Africa that support the learning by exporting effects include Bigsten et al. (2004) for Cameroon, Kenya, Ghana and Zimbabwe while controlling for self-selection of highly productive firms into exporting and other firm characteristics and Mengistae and Patillo (2004) for firms in Ghana, Kenya and Ethiopia.

Martins and Yang (2009) conducted a meta-analysis of 33 empirical studies to investigate the learning by exporting hypothesis. They came up with the conclusion that learning by exporting is a behaviour of firms in developing countries. The reason behind this conclusion is because of the technological gap that firms in developing countries face when compared to their counterparts in export destinations. Firms in developing countries produce using a technology that is far inside the technological frontier. Thus, exporting into foreign market provides a learning forum for them to enhance their technology, working practices and managerial skills (Pack and Page 1994; Newman et al. 2016b). Similar reasoning is given by Van Biesebroeck (2005) and Harrison and Rodriguez-Clare (2010). However, the extent of learning by exporting depends on the destination of exports. According to De Loecker (2007), learning effects are higher for developing countries that export to industrialized countries. This is because industrialized countries are innovators and users of the state-of-the-art technologies that are used in the production of goods and services.

Among the recent studies on the evidence of learning by exporting include Cruz et al. (2017) who found a productivity difference of more than 15 to 24 percentage points between firms that serve the foreign market and those that market domestically only for the case of Mozambique. Similar results from Ethiopia ranged between 8 and 19 percentage points (Siba and Gebreeyesus 2016).

The empirical findings of the relationship between export and firm performance based on the two hypotheses surrounding the field of international trade economics seem to vary by the level of economic development of a country. Based on the review, there seems to be a systematic pattern of evidence of learning by exporting hypothesis inclined more toward developing countries. This basically concerns with the ex-post performance of the exporting firm after entering the foreign market. Guided by the aforementioned observation, this chapter provides new empirical evidence of learning by exporting using firm-level data for EAC countries as a way of extending the frontiers of knowledge in the field and a guide to export promotion policies. The countries are Tanzania, Kenya, Uganda and Rwanda. Unlike Van Biesebroeck (2005) and Rankin et al. (2006) who used RPED survey data (collected between 1992 and 1996), this chapter uses analyses from a more recent data that consider a longer period of spells of trade liberalization by the four countries. Furthermore, RPED was limited in terms of scope covering only 200 manufacturing firms in four sectors namely; food stuffs, textiles and garments, wood working and metal working. In addition, Uganda and Rwanda were not part of the RPED survey. So our analysis covers both more sectors, more firms, more countries and more recent data.

8.3.4 The Data

The WBES collects data from formal registered manufacturing and services firms classified according to 4-digit industry classification codes using the United Nations ISIC Rev.3.1. It uses standardized survey instruments and a uniform sampling methodology thus providing a comparative advantage for cross-country analysis. The survey uses stratified random sampling, with strata being the business sector, size of the firm classified according to the number of employees 5–19 (small), 20–99 (medium) and 100 + (large)) and geographical location. The random sampling ensures an equal probability of inclusion in the sample of firms in various strata.

The analysis for this chapter involved a panel data set of 876 observations compiled from two waves of the survey in each country collected between 2006 and 2013. Of this total sample, Uganda has the largest share of about 45 percent followed by Tanzania (26 percent) while Kenya and Rwanda contribute about 21 and 9 percent of the total sample, respectively (Table 8.2). In each country, the number of firms that trade in a foreign market is smaller than the number that trade in the domestic market

Table 8.2 Distribution of the sample firms by country and export status

Country	Exporters		Non-exporters		Total		% panel
	All	Panel	All	Panel	All	Panel	
Tanzania	172	49	904	175	1076	224	25.6
Kenya	341	62	727	118	1068	180	20.5
Uganda	225	76	1058	320	1283	396	45.2
Rwanda	26	13	295	63	321	76	8.7
Total	764	200	2984	676	3748	876	100

Source Authors' construction from the WBES survey data

only. Combined together, only about 23 percent of the firms in the panel dataset trade in international markets.

8.4 Export Premia of EAC Firms

Existence of performance differences between exporting and non-exporting firms is the genesis of curiosity to examine whether firms learn by exporting or not. Using WBES data for firms in EAC countries the mean differences between exporters and non-exporters were computed across various indices of firm performance. The results in Table 8.3 indicate that exporting firms differ substantially from non-exporting firms in that they are; more productive as measured by labor productivity and value added, associated with foreign ownership, larger in size or employ more workers, and pay higher wages relative to firms that sell in domestic markets only. This is consistent with the recent findings by Demena (2017) for eight SSA countries. Other difference is that exporting firms are likely to be more experienced as they have more years of business operation relative to those that sell in the domestic market only.

Performance differences between exporting and non-exporting firms are also confirmed by data from other countries as presented in Table 8.4.

After observing that exporting firms are more productive relative to non-exporters using a t-test for two sample differences, we estimate a balanced panel model to measure the extent of export premium in which the dependent variable is a measure of labour productivity and the main independent variable is export dummy as specified in Eq. (8.1). We use labour productivity as a measure of firm performance because of the two waves nature of the dataset. According to Hansson and Lundin (2004) total factor productivity (TFP) tends to be more noise over a short period of time. Moreover, the popularity of the direct approach as in labour productivity was documented by Demena and van Bergeijk (2017) in a meta-analysis of empirical studies published in the period 1986 – 2013. Regardless, the best-performing enterprises will have higher productivity levels no matter which approach is used to measure productivity (Bernard and Jensen 2004; Syverson 2011; Newman et al. 2016b).

Thus, the model is specified as

Table 8.3 Characteristics of exporting firms

Variable	All firms			Exporting firms			Non-exporting firms			t-test for two sample difference
	Mean	SD	N	Mean	SD	N	Mean	SD	N	t
Labour productivity(sales)	4.86	1.64	787	5.67	1.73	192	4.60	1.52	595	8.20
Labour productivity	7.24	0.47	526	7.39	0.54	154	7.18	0.42	372	4.79
Foreign owned	0.17	0.01	871	0.32	0.03	200	0.12	0.01	671	6.81
Small firm size (5–19 employees)	0.52	0.50	876	0.22	0.42	200	0.61	0.49	676	−10.15
Medium firm size (20–99 employees)	0.33	0.47	876	0.34	0.47	200	0.32	0.47	676	0.50
Large firm size (100 + employees)	0.16	0.36	876	0.44	0.50	200	0.07	0.26	676	13.87
Firm age	17.75	12.20	874	22.86	14.66	200	16.23	10.93	674	6.93
Labour (L)	108.56	420.39	867	330.77	815.55	199	42.36	113.52	668	8.87
Average wage (wages/L)	2.75	1.27	759	3.14	1.42	183	2.63	1.20	576	4.81

Source Authors' construction from survey data

Table 8.4 Similarities of Export Premium findings with other countries

Author(s)	Publication Year	Country/Region	Performance Indicator(s)
Bernard and Jensen	1995	USA	Labour productivity, average wage, employment
Bernard and Wagner	1997	Germany	Labour productivity, average wage, employment
Isgut	2001	Colombia	Labour productivity, large-sized firms
Hansson and Lundin	2004	Sweden	Labour productivity, average wage, employment
Rankin et al.	2006	Sub-Saharan Africa	Labour productivity, employment, large-sized firms, foreign ownership
Were and Kayizzi-Mugerwa	2009	Kenya	Average wage
Demena et al.	2021	EAC	Labour productivity, value added

$$lnLP_{it} = \alpha + \beta export_{it} + \gamma_1 lnL_{it} + \gamma_2 ln(W/L)_{it} + \theta X_{it} + \pi_i + \tau_t + \rho_k + \varepsilon_{it}$$
$$(8.1)$$

where

LP_{it} is the dependent variable, measuring labour productivity.

$export_{it}$ shows firm i's export status at period t.

L_{it} is a variable for labour.

W/L_{it} is average wage.

X_{it} is a set of control variables (age of the firm, ownership status and industry of the firm).

π_i represent fixed effects of the firm (unobserved variables such as managerial ability).

τ_t represent year dummy to capture time-specific factors.

ρ_k represent country dummies.

ε_{it} is an idiosyncratic error term.

The inclusion of π_i, τ_t and ρ_k as fixed effects in the model ensures that the export premium is due to their variations within firms. Following this study's objective, the export status at time t ($export_{it}$) is the variable of interest in Eq. (8.1), whereby a statistically significant positive value for β indicates the mean labour productivity difference between exporters and non-exporters. However, there is no direction of causality warranted by Eq. (8.1). The equation shows only a correlation between exporting and productivity.

The definition and measurement of model variables are given in Table 8.5.

Before estimating the effects of export on firm performance, the Hausman test was performed to check if the coefficients of the Fixed Effects (FE) Model were statistically and significantly different from those of the Random Effects (RE) Model. The test results indicate that there is a statistical significance difference between FE and RE coefficients in favour of the FE Model. However, for reference purposes, we report both results for FE and RE models given the advantage the latter has, in that it provides the estimate of the effects of time-invariant variables, such as a comparison of results across countries.

Table 8.6 gives the results. We found a positive correlation between exporting and labour productivity. However, the FE model indicates that exporting firms are not significantly more productive than non-exporting firms. On the other hand, using the RE model, the results indicate that exporting firms are about 27 percentage points more productive than non-exporting firms. These findings demonstrate that there is an export productivity premium for firms selling in the foreign market. Furthermore, the results in Table 8.6 indicate that labour productivity increases with the average wage.

Table 8.5 Variable measurement and definition

Variable	Description
LP	Is a measure of labour productivity given as a ratio of the value of sales per employee and expressed in log form (Baldwin and Gu 2003; Silvente 2005; Demena 2017)
Export	1 if a firm export (directly and/or indirectly), 0 if it sells domestically only (Baldwin and Gu 2003; Hansson and Lundin 2004; Mengistae and Patillo 2004; Ayadi and Mattoussi, 2014)
foreign_owned	1 if a firm has foreign ownership, i.e., if at least 10% of its stake is owned by private foreign individuals, companies or organizations, 0 otherwise (Demena and Murshed 2018; Cole et al. 2010)
firm_industry	1 if a firm is manufacturing, 0 otherwise
firm_age	number of years the firm has been in operation (Mengistae and Patillo 2004; Alvarez and Lopez 2005; Silvente 2005; Demena and Bergeijk 2019). This variable was included to control for self-selection into exporting on top of also being a productivity growth influencer (Newman et al. 2016a)
Labour (L)	number of permanent and full-time employees working for the firm (Bernard and Jensen 1999, 2004; Silvente 2005; Hansson and Lundin 2004 Mengistae and Patillo 2004)
average_wage(W/L)	total wages divided by employees and expressed in log form (Bernard and Jensen 1999, 2004; Hansson and Lundin 2004)

Table 8.6 Regression results of export premium

Variable	Export Dummy	
dependent: labour productivity (ln)	FE	RE
export	0.162	0.272*
	(0.122)	(0.162)
foreign_owned	0.365	0.595***
	(0.191)	(0.147)
firm_age(ln)	−0.541	0.156*
	(0.351)	(0.092)
labour(ln)	−0.026	0.116*
	(0.061)	(0.060)
average_wage(ln)	0.563***	0.682***
	(0.076)	(0.037)
constant	5.067***	1.928***
	(0.653)	(0.085)
N	732	732
R-squared:		
within	0.303	0.277
between	0.163	0.543
overall	0.192	0.486
Number of firms	437	437

Notes Robust standard errors in parentheses clustered at country levels. Significance levels: *** $p < 0.01$, ** $p < 0.05$, * $p < 0.1$. Industry dummy, year dummy and country dummies (for RE) were included but not reported

8.5 Export Status Changes and Firm Productivity

The fact that EAC exporting firms possess desirable performance characteristics relative to non-exporters leaves us with one question. Do the firms learn from their exporting activities? The answer to this question is the focus of this section. We focus our analysis on the export market post-entry differences of firms. We use labour productivity as the measure of performance. The conceptualization of the aforementioned question leads us to presuppose that if at all productivity gains result from exporting then higher labour productivity growth rates should be observed among exporting firms after they begin to export.

To this end, our analysis adopted a simple and standard empirical approach used in many other empirical works such as Silvente (2005), Bernard and Jensen (1999), (2004), Aw et al. (2000), Alvarez and Lopez (2005) and Hansson and Lundin (2004); of mapping the export pattern of firms following their observation in the first wave to the next wave of surveys. The approach involved decomposing the growth of labour

Table 8.7 Mapping of the export pattern of firms

Variable	Definition	N
EXPORTERS	1 if a firm exported in both waves; 0 otherwise	116
ENTRANTS	1 if a firm did not export in wave I but in wave II; 0 otherwise	102
EXITERS	1 if a firm did export in wave I, but not wave II; 0 otherwise	66
NON-EXPORTERS	1 if a firm did not export in either of the waves; 0 otherwise	592
	Total	876

productivity at the firm level into continuous *EXPORTERS, ENTRANTS, EXITERS* and *NON-EXPORTERS* as defined in Table 8.7.

Thus, the model to estimate the performance of firms based on export patterns is given as

$$\Delta lnLP_{it+1} = lnLP_{it+1} - lnLP_{it}$$
$$= \alpha + \beta_1 EXPORTERS_{it} + \beta_2 ENTRANTS_{it} + \beta_3 EXITERS_{it}$$
$$+ \gamma_1 lnLP_{it} + \gamma_2 lnL_{it} + \gamma_3 ln(W/L)_{it} + \theta X_{it} + \pi_i + \rho_k + \varepsilon_{it} \quad (8.2)$$

where the dependent variable is the growth rate of labour productivity (a change in the log of labour productivity between the two waves), LP_{it} is the initial level of labour productivity included to control for self-selection of firms into exporting (Alvarez and Lopez 2005) and the other variables are as defined in Model (8.1) and Table 8.5.

The pertinent issue is the extent of percentage change in a firm's productivity due to a change in export status. Specifically, the model is geared at tracking firms that did not export in the first round of the survey but began to export in the second round of the survey (*ENTRANTS*) and the ones that exported in both waves (*EXPORTERS*). The mean labour productivity growth rates are compared with that of *NON-EXPORTERS*, which is a reference category. If only the *ENTRANTS* exhibit higher productivity growth relative to other firms, this means that improvement in firm productivity due to participation in international markets is only a short-lived effect. Alternatively, if *EXPORTERS* exhibits higher growth in labour productivity relative to other firms, then this means that firms learn continuously from exporting. The estimation also enables the tracking of productivity dynamics of firms that quit the export market (*EXITERS*) at any point in time.

8.5.1 Learning by Exporting Among EAC Firms

The results of mapping export patterns of firms between the two periods of survey to check if firms learn by exporting are presented in Table 8.8. The two main variables of interest are *ENTRANTS* and *EXPORTERS* whose coefficients came out positive

Table 8.8 Learning by exporting regression results

Variable	Learning effect	Learning heterogeneity
Outcome: lnLP(sales)	**(1)**	**(2)**
EXPORTERS	0.352	0.742*
	(0.335)	(0.309)
ENTRANTS	0.320**	0.385**
	(0.097)	(0.111)
EXITERS	−0.033	−0.073
	(0.041)	(0.136)
foreign_owned	0.539**	0.888**
	(0.138)	(0.230)
Interaction Effects		
foreign_owned exporters		−1.123*
		(0.386)
foreign_owned entrants		−0.405**
		(0.113)
foreign_owned exiters		−0.094
		(0.565)
Controls		
initial LP(ln)	−0.947***	−0.930***
	(0.052)	(0.051)
firm_age(ln)	0.315***	0.315***
	(0.025)	(0.017)
labour(ln)	0.038	0.027
	(0.036)	(0.037)
average_ wage(ln)	0.292	0.259
	(0.171)	(0.173)
constant	2.851**	2.846**
	(0.546)	(0.546)
N	349	349
R-squared	0.41	0.419

Source Authors' estimation from the WBES data

Notes Robust standard errors in parentheses clustered at the country level. Significance levels: *** $p < 0.01$, ** $p < 0.05$, * $p < 0.1$. Industry dummy and country dummies were included but not reported All independent variables were measured in the initial year the firm was observed as expected (column 1). However, only the coefficient of *ENTRANTS* is statistically significant conveying that new exporters experience higher productivity growth than firms that decide to sell in domestic markets only in line with learning by exporting hypothesis. For new exporters, participation in foreign market increases their labour productivity by 32 percentage points. The findings, although not exactly similar are comparable to those found for other countries in other studies. In Turkey, Yasar et al. (2006) found a 23 percentage points TFP difference between new exporters and non-exporting firms. Similarly, Alvarez and Lopez (2005) found a TFP difference of about 40 percentage points for new exporting firms in Chile. In Mozambique, Cruz et al. (2017) found a productivity difference ranging from 15 to 24 percentage points between exporting and non-exporting firms.

The growth of labour productivity was found to be indistinguishable between continuous exporters and non-exporters as the coefficient of *EXPORTERS* was not statistically different from zero. Lastly the productivity growth rate of firms that exit foreign market (*EXITERS*) is not statistically different from those that sell in the domestic market only. The coefficient is negative similar to findings by Hansson and Lundin (2004). This could mean that exiting the export market may be associated with a decline in productivity. The results of learning by exporting among new exporters remained robust even with labour productivity being measured from value added as indicated in Table 8.9.

8.5.2 Learning Heterogeneity Between Foreign Owned and Domestic Firms

The evidence of learning by exporting among East African firms raises another related issue to explore differential learning impacts of export between foreign-owned and domestic firms. Column (2) of Table 8.8 presents the learning heterogeneity by firm ownership as indicated by the interaction terms of export patterns and firm ownership status. The base category is domestic firms. The interaction terms, therefore, indicate the export differential learning effectiveness for foreign-owned firms relative to domestic firms.

The results for *EXPORTERS* and *ENTRANTS* show positive and statistically significant coefficients of level. This means that with the inclusion of firm ownership interaction terms in the model we are also able to find evidence of learning among continuous exporters in addition to new entrants. We found negative and statistically significant coefficients of interaction terms between *EXPORTERS* and foreign-owned firms (*EXPORTERS x foreign_owned*) and *ENTRANTS* and foreign-owned firms (*ENTRANTS x foreign_owned*). The fact that the interaction terms are statistically significant means that there is a difference in learning effects between foreign-owned and domestic firms. The marginal effect which is obtained by adding

Table 8.9 Robustness Check of Learning by Exporting

Variable	Learning Effect	Learning Heterogeneity
Outcome: lnLP(va*)	**(1)**	**(2)**
EXPORTERS	0.136	0.176
	(0.117)	(0.144)
ENTRANTS	0.211*	0.256**
	(0.110)	(0.125)
EXITERS	0.110	0.037
	(0.127)	(0.141)
foreign_owned	0.041	0.069
	(0.093)	(0.150)
Interaction Effects		
foreign_owned exporters		−0.094
		(0.216)
foreign_owned entrants		−0.176
		(0.260)
foreign_owned exiters		0.338
		(0.306)
Controls		
initial LP(ln)	−1.219***	−1.250***
	(0.162)	(0.164)
firm_age(ln)	0.062	0.057
	(0.049)	(0.049)
labour(L)	−0.022	−0.019
	(0.033)	(0.034)
average_wage(ln)	0.082**	0.080*
	(0.041)	(0.042)
constant	8.416***	8.642***
	(1.121)	(1.135)
N	173	173
R-squared	0.316	0.327

Source Authors' estimation from the WBES data

Notes *** $p < 0.01$, ** $p < 0.05$, * $p < 0.1$. Country dummies were included but not reported. All control variables were measured in the initial year the firm was observed

*va refers to value added measured as the difference between total sales and total cost of raw materials and intermediate inputs

the coefficient of interaction term to that of the level variable indicates that for continuous exporters, the difference in learning effects between domestic and foreign-owned firms is 38 percentage points, meaning that continuous domestic exporting firms learn more from their export activities than foreign-owned comparators. On the other hand, the learning effects difference between domestic and foreign new exporters is about 2 percentage points again meaning that new domestic owned exporters learn more from exporting relative to new foreign-owned exporters.

Clearly, these results indicate that although generally domestic-owned firms learn more from exporting relative to foreign-owned firms, the effects accumulate with the length of exporting. The findings that domestic owned firms learn more from exporting corroborates Sun and Hong (2011) for China while the observation that learning effects tend to accumulate with years of exporting closely mimics those of Newman et al. (2016a) for Vietnam. The explanation of these findings is in line with the theory of learning by exporting which proceeds as follows: Because of the production technology gap between local owned firms in developing countries and firms in the countries of export destinations especially those in developed countries, the latter offers a possibility of learning effect through knowledge and technology diffusion as a result of feedback from and contact with foreign consumers (Bernard and Wagner 1997; Van Biesebroeck 2005, and Harrison and Rodriguez-Clare 2010). Whereas foreign-owned firms might be producing using initially acquired advanced technology, participation in the international market offers less learning platform relative to domestic-owned firms.

8.6 Summary, Conclusions, and Policy Implications

8.6.1 Summary and Conclusions

The relationship between international trade and firm performance has attracted the interests of researchers and policymakers alike. This is because exporting firms are observed to have distinguishing performance features from those of non-exporting firms. In line with this, two hypotheses have been put forward as possible reasons for such noticeable differences: best-performing firms self-select into exporting because selling in foreign markets is associated with entry costs that can only be overcome by high productivity firms or firms learn by exporting; with the latter being more inclined with firms in low-income countries. This chapter tested the learning by exporting hypothesis using WBES data for four EAC countries (Tanzania, Kenya, Uganda and Rwanda) using data for the period between 2006 and 2013.

A correlation test between firm performance and export status found a statistically significant performance difference between exporting and non-exporting firms indicating that there exists a premium for firms that sell in international markets (see also Chap. 7 of this book). Exporting firms tend to be more productive, likely to be associated with foreign ownership, larger in size and pay higher wages relative to non-exporters. Of our interest was the higher labour productivity among exporters which was also confirmed by panel regression results. Although the Fixed Effects model found no statistical significance difference between productivity of exporters and non-exporters, the Random Effect model indicated the labour productivity premium for exporters of about 27 percentage points.

The empirical test of whether firms learn by exporting was done by mapping the export pattern of sample firms on the growth of labour productivity. It was found that both new and continuous exporters exhibit higher labour productivity growth relative to firms that remain non-exporters. This means that exporting firms learn from their exporting activities. These results were also confirmed using an alternative measure of labour productivity (from value added) at least for firms entering the export market. The findings are in line with other studies such as Alvarez and Lopez (2005), Rankin et al. (2006), Van Biesebroeck (2005), Mengistae and Patillo (2004) and Bigsten et al. (2004). The key message from the finding is that penetration of domestic firms in the international market gives them opportunities of technological and technical-know-how diffusion as a result of contact and feedback from foreign buyers. Furthermore, as the size of the domestic market is always small and only limited to the growth of local incomes, expansion to include sales in foreign markets enables firms to enjoy economies of scale and become low-cost producers, which in turn improve their competitive position in the markets (Isgut 2001; Van Biesebroeck 2005).

Comparison of learning effectiveness indicated that there is heterogeneous learning between domestic and foreign-owned firms. The learning effects among domestic-owned exporters are more pronounced than among foreign-owned exporters with the effects increasing with experience in the export market similar to findings by Sun and Hong (2011) and Newman et al. (2016a). The difference is higher (about 38 percentage points) for continuous domestic exporters relative to new domestic exporters (2 percentage points). In summary, the following three conclusions can be drawn from the analysis in this chapter; (i) firms in the EAC countries under investigation learn by exporting; (ii) learning effects accumulate with experience in export market participation; (iii) domestic firms learn more from exporting than foreign-owned firms.

8.6.2   Policy Implications

The findings in this chapter provide key policy messages to EAC countries that aspire to boost the growth of their economies through the promotion of exports. The findings clearly indicate that exporting is an integral factor for these economies to prosper. Export-led economic growth can be attained through promoting as many firms as possible to penetrate the foreign market. As Bigsten et al. (2004) and Rankin et al. (2006) put it, as the market for these economies is small and given their desire to industrialize, they can only achieve that through the promotion of export. The growth of firms that sell in domestic market only is limited to the extent of growth of local incomes which has not progressed as anticipated over the past two decades. This means that beyond trade liberalization which has been practiced since 1990s, more domestic reforms to push a number of domestic firms to participate in foreign market are needed, with East Asian economies providing a success story of export-led economic growth (see a discussion in Westphal 2002 and Belloc and Di Maio 2011). Export enhancing complementary reforms include microeconomic (direct support to current and potential exporters) and macroeconomic (functional for the whole economy). We suggest the following export promotion policies that have proven to have a positive impact on other developing countries (Belloc and Di Maio 2011):

i.   Promotion of export processing zones (EPZs) activities with China in Asia and Mauritius in Africa providing leading examples. EPZ is one form of Special Economic Zones (SEZs) which consists of a designated industrial area within a country for purposes of supporting domestic manufacturing firms to export their products by providing them with benefits and exemptions.

ii. Improving access to credits such as the establishment of a special bank to support exporters. Such loans are effective the longer the repayment period and the lower the rates. They are useful in financing fixed and working capital for domestic manufacturing firms.

iii. Establishment of export promotion agencies (EPAs) which work to influence information access to domestic manufacturing firms with the aim of increasing the volume and diversification of exports. They have an advantage in that their ownership can be by state or private or under public–private partnership (PPP). Success story countries that have managed to use EPAs to promote exports include: South Africa, Chile, Costa Rica, Argentina, Uruguay and Peru. As a caveat, is a recent note by Demena (2021) who found that the effectiveness of export promotion programmes on export performance although positive is only weak. However, the debate on the diverse findings is still live although most studies show positive effects.

iv. Lifting of trade barriers (as a way of promoting trade openness) and compliance with foreign standards of sanitary and quality. Just as Van Biesebroeck (2005) puts it one of the ways to stimulate the growth of low-income countries is to advocate for trade openness so that many firms can trade in foreign markets as frequently advocated for by the IMF and World Bank.

v.   Continued efforts to promote a conducive investment climate, e.g., investment in physical and human resources, enabling access to information, improving access to credits, promotion of investment in R&D, removal of export bureaucracy, simplification of customs procedures, etc.

References

Alvarez R, López RA (2005) Exporting and performance: evidence from Chilean plants. Can J Econ/Rev Can D'économique 38(4):1384–1400

Aw BY, Chung S, Roberts MJ (2000) Productivity and turnover in the export market: micro-level evidence from the Republic of Korea and Taiwan (China). World Bank Econ Rev 14(1):65–90

Ayadi M, Mattoussi W (2014) From productivity to exporting or vice versa? Evidence from the Tunisian manufacturing sector (No. 2014/098). WIDER Working Paper

Babatunde MA (2009) Can trade liberalization stimulate export performance in Sub-Saharan Africa. J Int Glob Econ Stud 2(1):68–92

Baldwin JR, Gu W (2003) Export-market participation and productivity performance in Canadian manufacturing. Can J Econ/Rev Can D'économique 36(3):634–657

Belloc M, Di Maio M (2011) Survey of the literature on successful strategies and practices for export promotion by developing countries

Bernard AB, Jensen JB (1995) Exporters, jobs, and wages in U.S. manufacturing: 1976–1987. Brookings Papers on Economic Activity, Microeconomics. Washington DC

Bernard AB, Jensen JB (1999) Exceptional exporter performance: cause, effect, or both? J Int Econ 47(1):1–25

Bernard AB, Jensen JB (2004) Exporting and productivity in the USA. Oxf Rev Econ Policy 20(3):343–357

Bernard AB, Wagner J (1997) Exports and success in German manufacturing. Weltwirtschaftliches Archiv 133(1):134–157

Biggs T, Srivastava P (1996) Structural aspects of manufacturing in sub-Saharan Africa: findings from a seven country enterprise survey, vol 346. World Bank Publications

Bigsten A, Collier P, Dercon S, Fafchamps M, Gauthier B, Willem Gunning J, Oduro A, Oostendorp R, Pattillo C, Söderbom M, Teal F (2004) Do African manufacturing firms learn from exporting? J Dev Stud 40(3):115–141

Blalock G, Gertler PJ (2004) Learning from exporting revisited in a less developed setting. J Dev Econ 75(2):397–416

Clerides SK, Lach S, Tybout JR (1998) Is learning by exporting important? Micro-dynamic evidence from Colombia, Mexico, and Morocco. Q J Econ 113(3):903–947

Cole MA, Elliott RJ, Virakul S (2010) Firm heterogeneity, origin of ownership and export participation. World Econ 33(2):264–291

Cruz A, Newman C, Rand J, Tarp F (2017) Learning by exporting: the case of Mozambican manufacturing. J Afr Econ 26(1):93–118

De Loecker J (2007) Do exports generate higher productivity? Evidence from Slovenia. J Int Econ 73(1):69–98

Demena BA (2017) Essays on intra-industry spillovers from FDI in developing countries: A firm-level analysis with a focus on Sub-Saharan Africa. Erasmus University, The Hague, PhD diss

Demena B, Msami J, Mmari D, van Bergeijk PAG (2021) Productivity premia and firm heterogeneity in Eastern Africa (No. 680)

Demena BA, Murshed SM (2018) Transmission channels matter: identifying spillovers from FDI. J Int Trade Econ Dev 27(7):701–728

Demena BA, van Bergeijk PAG (2017) A meta-analysis of FDI and productivity Spillovers in developing countries. J Econ Surv 31(2):546–571

Demena BA (2021) Effectiveness of export promotion programs (working paper No. 688). International Institute of Social Studies of Erasmus University Rotterdam (ISS), The Hague

Demena BA, van Bergeijk PAG (2019) Observing FDI spillover transmission channels: evidence from firms in Uganda. Third World Q 40(9):1708–1729

Demena BA, Msami J, Mmari D, van Bergeijk PAG (2022) Productivity premia and firm heterogeneity in Eastern Africa. In: Demena BA, van Bergeijk P (eds) Trade and investment in East Africa: prospect, challenges and pathways to sustainability. Springer

Eliasson K, Hansson P, Lindvert M (2012) Do firms learn by exporting or learn to export? Evidence from small and medium-sized enterprises. Small Bus Econ 39(2):453–472

Hansson P, Lundin NN (2004) Exports as an indicator on or promoter of successful Swedish manufacturing firms in the 1990s. Rev World Econ 140(3):415–445

Harrison A, Rodriguez-Clare A (2010) Foreign investment, and industrial policy for developing countries. In: Rodrik D, Rosenzweig M (eds) Handbook of development economics, vol 5. Amsterdam: North-Holland

Isgut A (2001) What's different about exporters? Evidence from Colombian manufacturing. J Dev Stud 37(5):57–82

Martins PS, Yang Y (2009) The impact of exporting on firm productivity: a meta-analysis of the learning-by-exporting hypothesis. Rev World Econ 145(3):431–445

McKinsey global institute (1993) Manufacturing productivity. McKinsey and Company. Inc., Washington, D.C.

Mengistae T, Pattillo C (2004) Export orientation and productivity in sub-Saharan Africa. IMF Staff Pap 51(2):327–353

MIT (Ministry of Industry and Trade of the United Republic of Tanzania), POPC (President's Office Planning Commission of the United Republic of Tanzania), and UNIDO (United Nations Industrial Development Organization) (2012) Tanzania Industrial Competitiveness Report *2012*. Dar es Salaam

Newman C, Rand J, Tarp F, Thi Tue Anh N (2016a) Exporting and productivity: learning from Vietnam. J Afr Econ 1–25

Newman C, Page J, Rand J, Shemeles A, Söderbom M, Tarp F (2016b) Made in Africa: learning to compete in industry. Brookings Institution Press.

Pack H, Page Jr JM (1994) Accumulation, exports, and growth in the high-performing Asian economies. In: Carnegie-Rochester Conference Series on Public Policy, vol 40. North-Holland, pp 199–235

Page J, Tarp F, Rand J, Shimeles A, Newman C, Söderbom M (2016) Manufacturing transformation: comparative studies of industrial development in Africa and emerging Asia. Oxford University Press, p 336

Rankin N, Söderbom M, Teal F (2006) Exporting from manufacturing firms in sub-Saharan Africa. J Afr Econ 15(4):671–687

Siba E, Gebreeyesus M (2016) Learning to export and learning from exporting: the case of Ethiopian manufacturing. J Afr Econ 1–23

Silvente FR (2005) Changing export status and firm performance: evidence from UK small firms. Appl Econ Lett 12(9):567–571

Sun X, Hong J (2011) Exports, ownership and firm productivity: evidence from China. World Econ 34(7):1199–1215

Syverson C (2011) What determines productivity? J Econ Lit 49(2):326–365

UN (United Nations) Statistics Division (2020) 2019 International Trade Statistics Yearbook. New York

UNComtrade Database. https://comtrade.un.org/data. Accessed 4 Oct 2021

UNCTAD (2020) UNCTADstat. https://unctadstat.unctad.org. Accessed 14 Nov 2021

UNCTADStat Databases. https://unctad.org/statistics. Accessed 4 Oct 2021

Van Biesebroeck J (2005) Exporting raises productivity in sub-Saharan African manufacturing firms. J Int Econ 67(2):373–391

Were M, Kayizzi-Mugerwa S (2009) Do exporting firms pay higher wages? Evidence from Kenya's manufacturing sector. Afr Dev Rev 21(3):435453

Westphal LE (2002) Technology strategies for economic development in a fast changing global economy. Econ Innov New Technol 11(4–5):275–320

Yasar M, Nelson CH, Rejesus R (2006) Productivity and exporting status of manufacturing firms: evidence from quantile regressions. Rev World Econ 142(4):675–694

Chapter 9
The Effect of Foreign Direct Investment and Trade Openness on the Firms' Export Competitiveness and Products Diversification Among East African Community Members

Masoud Mohammed Albiman, Huda Ahmed Yussuf, and Issa Moh'd Hemed

Authors are thankful to Peter van Bergeijk and Binyam Afewerk Demena of Erasmus University, International Institute of Social Studies for technical guidance in carrying out the research work. The study was financially supported by Research on Poverty Alleviation (REPOA), the African Caribbean and Pacific Group of States (ACP Group) of this project, grant number FED/2019/408-112

Abstract This chapter examines the effect of Foreign Direct Investment (FDI) and trade openness on competitiveness and diversification among East African Community (EAC) members. Unlike previous studies, we investigated this issue in the emerging region of EAC. This chapter uses fixed and random effects panel estimates from 2010 to 2019, inclusive. We find that the effect of FDI on a firm's export competitiveness and trade diversification is positive and statistically significant. However, the effect of trade openness is positive and statistically significant for export diversification but insignificant for export competitiveness. Results are robust to the alternative dependent variable, control variables, specifications and estimation methods. Policy reforms to improve economic freedom, technological development, and strengthening the inter-relationship of the domestic sector with FDI and trade openness are required to improve export competitiveness and diversification.

M. M. Albiman (✉)
Institute of Tax Administration, Po Box 9321, Dar-es-Salaam, Tanzania
e-mail: masoud.al-biman@tra.go.tz

H. A. Yussuf
Muslim University of Morogoro, Morogoro, Tanzania
e-mail: hudayssf@gmail.com

I. M. Hemed
Zanzibar University (ZU), Tunguu, Zanzibar, Tanzania
e-mail: issahemed@zanvarsity.ac.tz

9.1 Introduction

9.1.1 An Overview of the Study

The rise in globalization over the past 30 years has resulted in rapid changes and mobility of technologies and internationalization of production of goods and services through Foreign Direct Investment (FDI) and trade. The reasons for this shift have to do mainly with the inefficiencies of import substitution and the success of exporting in promoting economic growth (Greenaway et al. 2005). In line with these trends, Africa has witnessed a surge in FDI in recent years. For instance, FDI increased from US$5 billion in 1995 to US$48 billion in 2015 (UNCTAD, 2016). At the same time, the rise in globalization has exposed many African countries to the pressures of international trade competition.

FDI introduces new products or processes in the host country, technology diffuses to the domestic firms which are competitors in production or suppliers of inputs to the foreign companies (see, for example, Aitken et al. 1999; Kathuria 2000). It acts as a channel for technology spillover effects through transnational corporations (Demena and van Bergeijk 2019). Also, productivity and competitiveness increase among domestic manufacturing firms (Demena and Murshed 2018). Appropriation of these benefits, however, is subjected to the level of absorptive capacity of the firms, available human capital in the country and the competitive environment of industry.

Also, globalization through trade openness is thought to improve firms' efficiency through three major channels. First, it allows the exploitation of economies of scale that raises productivity. Second, globalization through trade fosters a learning process through knowledge spillovers and new technology adoption (Clerides et al. 1998; Baldwin and Gu 2003; Demena 2017). Third, export intensity improves management efficiency due to competition from abroad. Trade-in manufactures along with export-led industrialization seems to speed up development in the modern era. Indeed, Sustainable Development Goal (SDG) 9 encourages and promotes sustainable industrialization specifically promoting industrialization and innovation reflecting its importance in advancing sustainable development (UN 2015).

The recent literature on trade highlights the importance of the composition and structure of exports in driving economic growth. Hausmann et al. (2007) showed that countries that produce higher productivity goods and export sophisticated or 'high-tech' goods are more competitive in international markets and they grow faster. Notwithstanding these observations, Africa's share of global exports of high technology products remains low. For instance, while developing countries accounted for 52% of global exports of high technology products in 2014, African countries accounted for only 0.3% (UNCTAD 2015a, b, pp 23). Thus, African policymakers are confronted with the challenge of igniting export growth and enhancing export competitiveness.

Export competitiveness is important in Africa for several reasons. First, a large strand of the literature, especially on the export-led growth hypothesis, suggests that exports are the main determinants of a country's Gross Domestic Product (GDP) growth (Anwar and Nguyen 2011; Eryigit 2012). As such, African countries need to diversify their export sectors and improve the competitiveness of their exports to sustain their growth rates. Second, export diversification and increased high technology exports play an important role in reducing the vulnerability of exports to external shocks and thus help reduce the volatility of economic growth. Third, a stronger export sector helps to drive job creation, especially in the manufacturing sector. Fourth, at a microeconomic level, many arguments in favour of export-market participation have been put forward (EAC 2019, 2017). Lastly, growth in the export of sophisticated products is a key to reducing external imbalances, and macroeconomic stability, without creating debt, given the wide current account deficits of most African countries.

In this view, African economies require policies that invigorate export competitiveness to steer economic growth. Meanwhile, developing countries, faced with insufficient domestic savings, have over the years emphasized attracting FDI as a way of bridging the gap between insufficient savings and desired investment. This has raised the question of whether FDI could play a role in enhancing export competitiveness in Africa.

East Africa's economic structure and growth patterns are characterized by low industrialization. The manufacturing value added grew by just 1.7 percent from 2000 to 2016, which was less than GDP growth, reducing the manufacturing sector's share in GDP (AfDB 2019). Average manufacturing value added in GDP was just 8.1 percent, below the Sub-Saharan Africa (SSA) average of 10.3 percent in 2016. The average share of manufactured exports in total merchandise trade, 14.6 percent, also shows the region's lack of structural transformation.

The contribution of the manufacturing sector to GDP among EAC is still below 8 percent for all EAC members with the exception of Uganda which reached 16 percent in 2018 (EAC 2019). The level of competitiveness of EAC members in manufactures, in general, has been declining.[1] Employment in the manufacturing sector is still low compared to other African middle-income economies. For example, from 2018 to 2019 employment increased from 269,000 to 281,000 in Kenya, while in Tanzania it increased to 221,108 up from 139,895 (EAC 2019).

In this view, African economies require policies that invigorate export competitiveness to steer economic growth by attracting FDI, bridging the gap between insufficient savings and desired investment. Despite the strong growth of FDI and international trade in Africa, little attention has been paid to the potential role of FDI in promoting export competitiveness. This study fills a gap in the literature by using microeconomic data from the industrial sector among five EAC members.

This chapter has two main objectives. Firstly, to examine the effect of FDI inflows and trade openness on business competitiveness. Secondly to examine the impact of FDI and trade openness on firms' market diversification. The importance of this chapter is to understand the relationship between FDI and exports for manufacturing sectors that are confined to other countries but not in the East African and SSA region.

---

[1] https://www.tralac.org/news/article/8618-eastern-africa-s-manufacturing-sector-promoting-tec hnology-innovation-productivity-and-linkages.html, accessed on 10-August 2020.

So, we contribute to the literature in two ways. First, we evaluate the role of FDI on export competitiveness in the SSA region using a panel data method. Also, we use a comprehensive measure of export competitiveness (*Expy)* the sum of the weighted productivity level related to each exported product and other proxies such as the revealed comparative advantage (RCA) to investigate robustness.

This chapter continues as follows. Section 9.2 explains the performance of EAC Members in FDI, trade and manufacturing sector in different regions with EAC partner States. Section 9.3 explains the theoretical and empirical literature while Sect. 9.4 discusses the methodology of the study. Section 9.5 presents an analysis and discussion of the results while the final section provides conclusion and policy recommendations.

9.2 Performance of EAC Countries

9.2.1 Industrial Development Agenda in EAC Members

The EAC community initially was formed by three East African countries Kenya, Uganda and Tanzania between the period 1967 to 1999. Later on, from 2005 to 2016, three new members joined Rwanda, Burundi and South Sudan. Now that Democratic Republic of Congo (DRC) joined, EAC has a total of seven members. The main aims of establishing the EAC were to widen and deepen economic, social, political co-operations for the benefit of member countries.

Recently, there has been an emphasis on industrial development and contemporary development plans for many low- and middle-income countries, specifically the development of the manufacturing sector. Acknowledging the need to develop industry and to stimulate economic development, the EAC developed an industrialization strategy for 2012 to 2032.

Ambitious targets were set drawing from the EAC Industrialization Policy including: diversification of the manufacturing base, increase in local value-added in resource-based exports to at least 40% by 2032, expansion of manufacturing exports as a share of total exports to 60% and intra-regional manufacturing exports relative to total manufactured exports to at least 25% by 2032 and strengthening of research and development and technological capabilities towards the transformation of the sector through industrial upgrading. Expected long-term outcomes include Manufactured Value Added (MVA) contributing to 25% of GDP and MVA per capita reaching US$ 258 by 2032 (EAC 2017).

9.2.2 Trade Openness in Different Regions Compared to the EAC Region

For the five years (2010–2014), the total EAC exports to the rest of the world declined rapidly from US$ 3.9 billion to US$ 2.9 billion which implies a drop from 33 to 18 percent, respectively (Table 9.1). The declines in exports resulted from fallings in the price of exported goods and demand from EAC resulting from the unfavourable global economic environment. From 2015 to 2019, the EAC's total export to the rest increased marginally from 35 percent (US$ 6.1) to 41.1 percent (US$ 6.4).

The increment in total export in the EAC was attributed to increasing export volumes for agricultural products like cut flowers, coffee, tea and tobacco, due to improved weather conditions over the past two years (EAC 2017; 2019). This coupled with an increase in prices of commodities like gold and fish, supported with increasing demand, especially from China and the Far East. When viewing other economic blocks, the EAC leads in exporting merchandise with the member states compared to other economic regions as shown in Table 9.1. This implies that the EAC has a comparative advantage in exporting merchandise trade compared to other regions within South and East Africa.

9.2.3 Trend of FDI Inflows Among EAC

The FDI inflows to EAC increased from US$ 3,805.96 million posted in 2010 to US$ 3,845.56 million in 2014 (UNCTAD 2015a) (Table 9.2). This was largely driven by the significant growth of FDI into Kenya and the United Republic of Tanzania. Generally, for the period between 2010 and 2014 on average, FDI inflows increased by 19.31% (Table 9.2).

For the period 2015–2019, also FDI inflows into EAC member States increased on average by 20 percent from US$ 3.30 million to US$ 41.49 million (Table 9.3). China was the largest investor in 2019, accounting for 60 percent of FDI inflows to the region, with significant investments in construction, manufacturing and services (EAC, 2019). There was a disappointing decline in FDI inflows from 2015 to 2016 and declined again slightly from 2018 to 2019.

Generally, during 2010–2015 FDI inflows by sector were mainly concentrated in transport, communication and storage sectors followed closely by the construction and manufacturing sector (Figs. 9.1 and 9.2). FDI in the manufacturing sector became prominent during 2016–2019 compared to the period of 2010–2015. Overall, FDI inflows to the EAC were concentrated in the manufacturing, construction and services sectors.

Table 9.1 Trend of Merchandise Trade by World Regions Compared to EAC Region (in current millions US$)

Destination/Origin	2010	2011	2012	2013	2014	2015	2016	2017	2018	2019
Total EAC Exports	11,819	14,274	16,046	14,971	16,109	16,819	13,877	14,143	14,213	15,760
Intra-EAC Total Exports	2,237	2,564	3,154	3,698	3,230	2,823	2,631	2,977	3,170	3,162
COMESA	1,610	1,901	2,055	1,801	2,763	2,335	2,579	2,624	2,523	1,538
SADC	1,319	1,789	2,329	2,127	3,067	1,496	1,843	2,105	2,192	2,193
Rest of Africa	220	265	293	433	787	606	799	328	268	260
EU	2,193	2,520	2,512	2,183	2,663	2,398	2,347	2,378	2,450	2,280
USA	362	385	411	449	651	521	667	751	600	623
Total Exports to Rest of the World	3,876	4,846	5,287	4,277	2,946	6,054	5,932	5,394	5,282	6,479

Source Author's calculation from EAC (2019)

Table 9.2 FDI Inflows in EAC Region, 2010–2014 (current US$ million and Annual growth)

Country	2010	2011	2012	2013	2014	Annual average% 2010/2014
Burundi	0.78	3.36	0	7	47	5928
Kenya	1,197	1,450	1,380	1,118	820	−31
Rwanda	250	1,19	254	257	458	83
Uganda	543	894	1,205	1,096	1,058	94
Tanzania	1,813	1,229	1,799	2,087	1,416	−21
Total	3,805	3,696	4,801	3,774	3,845	1
Av. Growth	11%	−2%	29%	−215%	1%	19

Source Authors' calculations from UNCTAD *2010-2014 Date accessed 20th and 21st March 2021*

Table 9.3 FDI Inflows to EAC Region, 2015–2019 (current US$ million and Annual growth)

Country	2015	2016	2017	2018	2019	Annual average% 2015/2019
Burundi	7	0	0	0	1	−85
Kenya	619	678	1266	1625	1332	115
Rwanda	379	342	356	381	420	10
Uganda	737	625	802	1055	1266	71
South Sudan	1560	864	937	1056	1112	−28
Tanzania	0	−7	1	60	17	11,835
Total EAC	3305	2503	3364	4180	4149	25
Av. Growth	−14%	−24%	34%	24%	−0%	20

Source Authors' calculations from UNCTAD online database, 2015–2019. Date accessed 2nd and 3rd April 2021

9.2.4 Firms Export Product Diversification

Diversification of a country's productive and export structure is an important characteristic of industrial competitiveness and economic development in general. There is a positive relationship between industrial diversification and country income levels, especially at lower stages of economic development (see, Imbs and Wacziarg 2003; UNCTAD 2018; Gamariel and Hove 2019). Diversification is more important for economies such as those of the EAC, which are resource-based economies, engaged mainly in the production and exportation of primary goods.

For example, in Fig. 9.3 there is a mixed performance of EAC partner States in export product diversification. In most cases, it shows that major exports are food and beverages followed by metal and metal products. The least export is for manufactured products. This implies that the EAC region is still at an infant stage in the industrialization process.

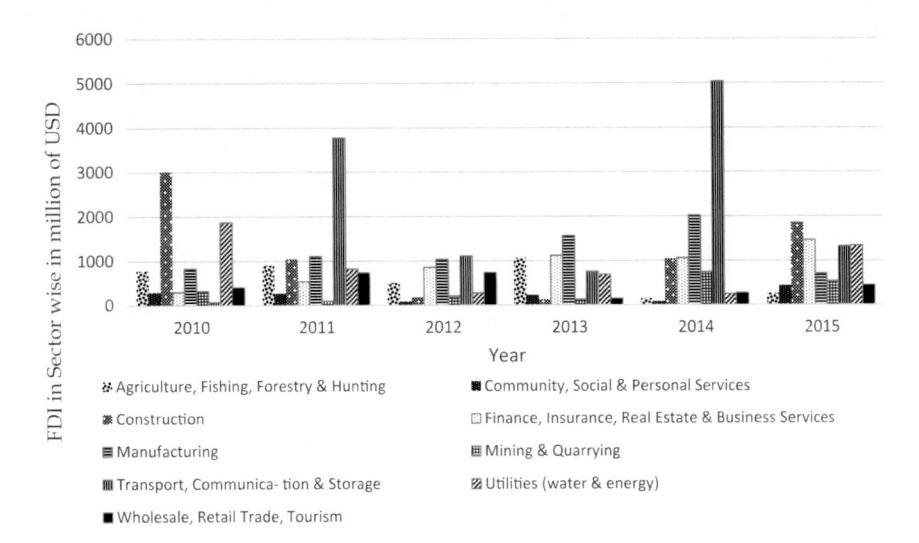

Fig. 9.1 Sectoral distribution of FDI inflows to East African Community Member States. *Source* Authors' calculations from EAC report 2010–2015 date accessed 28th and 29th March 2021

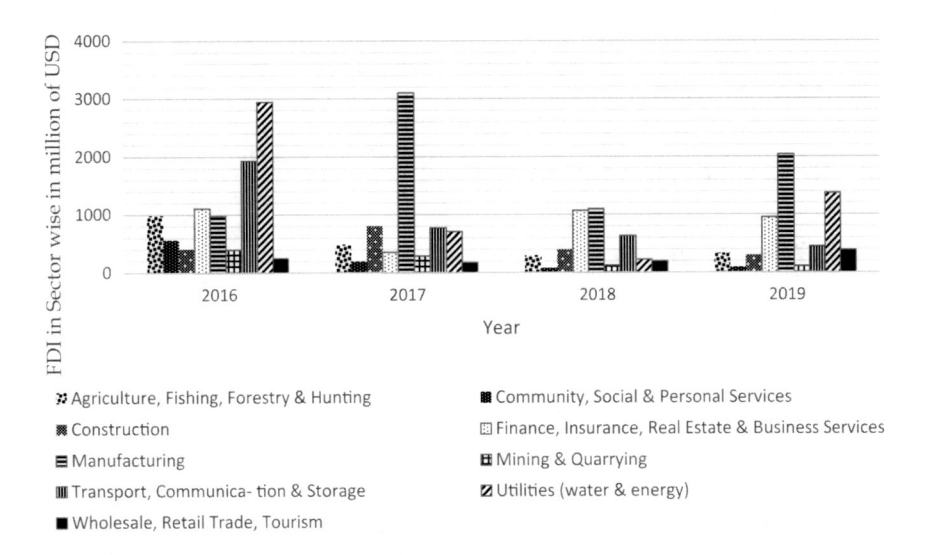

Fig. 9.2 Sectoral distributions of FDI inflows to East African Community Member States. *Source* Authors' calculations from EAC report 2015–2019

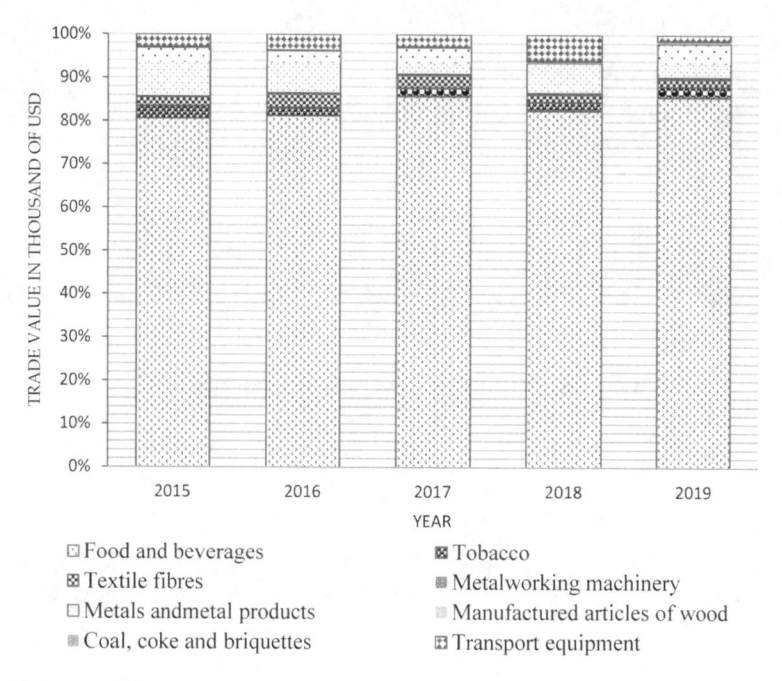

Fig. 9.3 EAC manufactured exports by sector (2014–2019). *Source* COMTRADE online database 2021 and authors' compilation

9.3 Review of Literature

9.3.1 Theoretical Literature

9.3.1.1 Export Competitiveness

The term export competitiveness can be defined as the ability of a country to produce and sell goods in qualities as required by foreign buyers, and at convenience which is better than or equal to those of other potential foreign suppliers[2] (Sharples and Milham 1990). Lotfi and Karim (2016) claimed that export competitiveness is the ability of countries to successfully integrate into the global economy. FDI can affect export competitiveness through enhancing productivity or efficiency. The efficiency and productivity can be enhanced through technology and knowledge spillover effects and the introduction of new export products and facilitating access to new and large foreign markets.

---

[2] According to this definition, export competitiveness encompasses both quantitative and qualitative factors such as quality of exports, capacity for technological innovation and degree of product specialization. However, these factors are difficult to measure in quantitative terms.

9.3.1.2 Relationship Among FDI, Trade Openness and Export Competitiveness

Ricardo (1817), in his classical trade theory, argues that a country has a comparative advantage in trade if it can produce goods at a lower relative cost than its trade partners. He insisted that relative differences in labour productivity are the basis of differences in production costs. This implies that export competitiveness is associated with price competitiveness, comparative cost advantages, factor endowments and relative labour productivity and cost differentials across nations. The Heckscher–Ohlin model extended Ricardian theory, by arguing that cost differentials are determined by differences in relative factor endowments.

Helpman and Krugman (1985) showed that the interaction between innovation in the industrialized and low-income countries and the processes of research and development, facilitates the transfer and spillover effect of technology, which in turn enhances productivity. They also insisted that economic development is one of the prerequisites for firms to continuously upgrade their production to produce more advanced products. Romer (1990) suggested a new model which indicates that productivity growth is driven largely by technological change that arises from intentional investment decisions made by profit-maximizing agents. According to Romer, the technology is labour augmenting, and enhances the research and development capital.

Borensztein et al. (1998) argued that in order to have higher productivity of FDI in a host country it must have a minimum threshold stock of human capital to absorb the advanced technologies. FDI helps to accelerate human capital development through Multinational Enterprises (MNEs) when they bring along technical assistance, training of workers and increased experience through interaction and managerial capacity building. The local firms can benefit from technological diffusion through the transmission of ideas and adopt new technologies. This can be transmitted through either vertical or horizontal spillovers, at the country, sector (industry), or firm level.

The firms' gains through vertical spillovers through the interaction with foreign firms up- or down-stream in the production chain. These can be backward spillovers (e.g., a foreign firm intentionally assists local sub-suppliers to deliver high-quality inputs and shares with them superior technology) or forward spillovers (e.g., higher quality inputs produced by foreign firms used in the production chain by the local firms) (Gamariel and Hove 2019).

Export competitiveness can also be enhanced by improving access to world markets for local exporters. The local firms can increase access to markets, increase output, lower prices and raise profitability. The local firms can increase export distribution networks and the information to access foreign markets, as a result, FDI establishes a strong niche for domestic firms to export (Markusen and Venables 1999).

However, if FDI is only concentrated on target tradable sectors, it may result in Dutch disease effects (Botta 2015, Agosin et al. 2012, UNCTAD 2018). This happens when large capital inflows may influence the appreciation of the real exchange rate in turn discouraging the competitiveness of manufacturing sectors (Sachs and Warner 1997; Botta 2015). Also, FDI through Dutch disease may also distort the balance of payments position of the host economy. The profits from FDI can be repatriated back to foreign investors, distorting the capital account and worsening the balance of payments. Profit repatriation is common to EAC members, especially in Uganda and other members (EAC 2017, 2018, 2019).

FDI inflows in some African countries are also affected by nationalist ideas from local citizens over an increment of foreign business ownership and control of the economy and there are also political influences on the host country (Moss et al. 2004). Meanwhile, it is not surprising to find evidence of restrictions through nationalizations, expropriations, ownership, rate of return, project approval requirements, financial restrictions as well as trade.

9.3.2 Empirical Literature

9.3.2.1 Direct Impact of FDI and Trade Openness on firm's Export Competitiveness

Blomström and Kokko (1996) contend that FDI improves the productivity and competitiveness of manufacturing firms, as local firms enter strategic alliances with leading foreign MNEs to expand their technology bases. Theodore (1998) suggested that FDI increased competitiveness and efficiency in the Mexican automobile export industry. Similarly, Prasanna (2010) found that FDI inflows in India led to significant increases in total and high technology-manufactured exports.

Using firm-level data, Liu (2008) and Zhang (2006)found that FDI plays a positive role in China's export performance and its effects are much larger than that of domestic capital. In addition to that, Zhang (2015) using industrial competitiveness in a large panel data set of 21 manufacturing sectors for 31 regions, claimed a positive and significant effect of FDI on China's low-tech manufacturing than on medium and high-tech industries, which are proxies for export competitiveness. Also, Greenaway et al. (2004) analysed UK firm-level data to confirm that FDI significantly increases the exporting competitiveness of domestically owned firms.

Chen et al. (2012) examined the effects of outward foreign direct investment (O-FDI) on the export competitiveness of the home-country in China. They used manufacturing data for 15 industries for the year between 1991 and 2007. The authors suggested that exports in Taiwan are positively associated with O-FDI by Taiwanese firms. However, FDI inflows were positive but insignificant. They argued that foreign-invested firms in Taiwan are not export oriented, but local market oriented. They also found that R&D–employee ratio (RDE) is insignificant throughout the sample.

Agosin et al. (2012) after using several measures of export concentration found that openness to trade induces export specialization, not export diversification. In addition, they found that higher schooling or education contributes to export diversification. UNCTAD (2018) also examined the determinants of export diversification in LDCs for the period of 2003–2015 using 145 developing countries. Generally, they found that MVA, trade openness, and FDI have a positive and significant impact on export diversification. Gamariel and Hove (2019) investigate the direct impact of FDI in the SSA region using the GMM method. The results suggest the positive and significant impact of FDI on export competitiveness while unit labour costs reduced foreign market access and lower export competitiveness.

9.3.2.2 Indirect Impact of FDI and Trade Openness on firm's Export Competitiveness Through Various Channels.

(i) Technology as transmission channel:
     The empirical literature on export productivity also identified technology as a condition for FDI to influence export productivity through technological spillover effect and diffusion. In addition to that, Javorcik (2004) using Lithuanian firm-level panel data investigated productivity and FDI spillover through backward and forward linkages. She confirmed the presence of productivity spillovers from FDI taking place through backward linkages. In contrast, Bwalya (2006) using Zambian firms found that knowledge spillovers improve firm's export competitiveness rather than technology spillovers.s
(ii) Trade openness and FDI as a conditional effect:
     Some empirical studies emphasized the importance of trade policy regimes and ownership structures as determinants of exporting firms. Balasubramanyam et al. (1996) conduct a study that covers 46 developing economies and found that the effect of FDI to host country's exports is stronger if they pursue a policy of export promotion rather than import substitution. Rădulescu and Şerbănescu (2012) also found that FDI works better in promoting export competitiveness in the tradable sector in Central and Eastern European countries. Mijiyawa (2016) used data on African countries claiming that FDI inflows positively and significantly support exports of goods and services.

It is worthy to emphasize that the effects of FDI inflows on a developing country may not necessarily be positive. UNCTAD (1999) argued that FDI could provide too few or unsuitable kinds of assets and resources for a particular economy, which would not fit with local capabilities and demand. Foreign firms may import the major proportion of higher value-added intermediate products, restricting purchases from indigenous firms to low value-added goods.

Gamariel and Hove (2019) investigate transmission channels of FDI in the SSA region using the GMM method. The results suggest that human capital and technological spillovers are the transmission channels through which FDI affects export competitiveness and the enhancement of domestic productivity. In turn, hinder local firms in the upgrading indigenous resources and capabilities.

To conclude, a larger proportion of empirical literature on FDI concentrates on its impact on economic growth or export volumes, rather than export competitiveness per se. A few empirical studies have analysed the impact of FDI on export competitiveness, with the majority of these studies focusing on the impact of FDI on productivity, and implicitly on export competitiveness. Moreover, many studies are conducted in Asia and other developing countries which left African countries unexplored. Furthermore, the effect of FDI and trade openness on export diversification is still an unexplored area, especially in African economies. This study will move further to explore the role of FDI, and trade openness on a firm's export competitiveness and diversification.

9.4   Methodology

9.4.1   Theoretical Relationship Among FDI and Trade Openness and Export Competitiveness

In a theoretical model, Helpman and Krugman (1985) show that rising intra-firm trade has significantly associated with FDI which ultimately boosts export competitiveness. Some analysts later detailed that FDI improves the export performance of the host countries by bringing new production based on modern technology and knowledge and integrating domestic production into the global corporate system (Đurić, et al. 2016)

It is pertinent to believe that FDI enhances the competitiveness of the country's exports by increasing total factor productivity (Sultan 2013; Jana et al. 2019). There is a widely accepted opinion that FDI enhances exports of the host country by augmenting domestic capital for exports, and facilitating access to new and large foreign markets, and providing training to local workforces (Zhang 2015; Gamarie and Hove, 2019). In general, FDI stimulates exports from domestic sectors through industrial linkage or spillover effects, which further instigates high-demand stimulus for domestic enterprises and results in export promotion (Harrison 1996; Fontagné 1999; UNCTAD 2018; Gamariel and Hove 2019; EAC 2019).

In light of this, several factors have been found to influence the capacity of a country's export competitiveness and diversification. Trade openness is a remarkably strong predictor of export performance in the region (Shobande 2019), i.e., enhancements in trade facilitation have boosted R&D and creativity, improving commodity efficiency and boosting the manufacturing industry's export competitiveness (Hu 2020), through the establishment of marketing and distribution channels (Farole et al. 2014).

9.4.2   Method of Analysis

The main method used for estimating the model is static linear panel analysis of Fixed Effect (FE) and Random Effect (RE). A panel data set comprises of i entities where each contains time t observations measured at year t. Hence, the entire number of observations in the panel data is it. In our study, $i = 5$ EAC members, and t is 10 years. Panel data have greater consistency and allow to control for fixed and random individual differences.

Due to the heterogeneous nature of the pooled dataset, observations for individual countries may not be independent and the usual ordinary least squares method may provide biased estimates. Hence, we deploy panel data estimation techniques (FE and RE) to control for fixed or random individual differences. The Hausman test has been applied to test for the appropriateness of FE or RE. Also, the Breuch–Pagan test has been applied in order to choose the best model. The common approaches utilized are FE and RE applied to control for fixed or random individual differences among the EAC members.

9.4.3 Model Specification

We set up two models:

$$XC_{it} = \alpha_1 FDI_{it} + \alpha_2 TO_{it} + \alpha_3 EF_{it} + \alpha_4 TECH_{it} + \alpha_5 R\&D_{it} + \alpha_6 MVA_{it} + \varepsilon$$
$$(9.1)$$

$$XD_{it} = \alpha_1 FDI_{it} + \alpha_2 TO_{it} + \alpha_3 EF_{it} + \alpha_4 TECH_{it} + \alpha_5 R\&D_{it} + \alpha_6 MVA_{it} + \varepsilon$$
$$(9.2)$$

where the subscripts t and i signify time and country. Equation 9.1 examines the impact of TO and FDI to a firm's export competitiveness (XC), proxied by the export sophistication index (*Expy*), and Eq. 9.2 investigates a firm's export diversification (XD), based on a Herfindahl–Hirschman Index (HHI). In terms of independent variables, FDI denoted as a ratio of GDP and TO refers to trade openness are explanatory variables of interest. Moreover, the study employs other control variables, including economic freedom index (EF), level of technology (TECH), research and development (R&D), and manufacturing value added (MVA). Finally, ε is the stochastic error term. The detailed descriptions of the dependent variables are elaborated below:

(i) Export Competitiveness

Export competitiveness refers to the differential between the country's export price and that of its rivals in their regular markets. On the assumption that a country's export prices do not depend on the country of destination, competitors' export prices are determined by the contribution of each country to the total supply of competing goods and the relative importance of each market in the given country's international trade (Turner and Dack, 1993). To measure the level of export competitiveness in a country, we refer to Hausmann et al. (2006) for the index of productivity of the export basket of a particular country called *Expy*. Meanwhile, we first compute an index that executes the level of export competitiveness of a product, known as *PRODY*. This index is a weighted average of the GDP per capita of the countries exporting products. Algebraically,

$$PRODY_k = \sum_j \frac{(x_{jk}/X_j)}{(x_{jk}/X_j)} Y_j \tag{9.3}$$

where in the above expression, x_{jk} is the total volume of exporting product k by country j; X_j is the volume of all exported goods of a country j, and Y_j refers to the level of country j's GDP per capita, measured as a real GDP per capita at purchasing power parity (PPP). If the values of *PRODY* for good k are large enough, it implies higher export competitiveness. The intuition of this index is that the products that are produced and exported by the wealthier countries need more advancement and a complex set of capabilities and therefore advanced economies are expected to be more competitive. The competitive level related to a country j's export *Expy* subsequently is defined as

$$Expy_j = \sum_k (x_{jk}/X_j) PRODY_K \tag{9.4}$$

Therefore, export competitiveness is expressed as a sum of the weighted productivity levels related to each exported product k, $PRODY_K$ with the weights simply denoted as the share of the products' value share in the total for the exported product of a country. This index determines the country's ability to export products that are produced domestically and exported by the wealthier countries. If the value of Expy is greater would imply that the country has the highest export competitiveness.

(ii) Export Diversification

Diversification of the exported goods refers to the (changing of the) country's export structure. This can be accomplished by altering the current commodity basket or by enhancing existing products with innovation and technology. This chapter adopts the work of Hwang (2006) and Harding and Javorcik (2011) and later introduces a measurement of export diversification based on the Herfindahl index. We start with the computation of the Herfindahl index of the shares of squared export in country i at time t using export data at the SITC 4-digit level of the United Nations.

$$Herfindahl_{it} = \left(\left(\sum_{i=1}^{N} x_{it}/X_{it} \right)^2 * 100 \right) \tag{9.5}$$

where x_{it} denotes as a value of product exported from country i and time t and X_{it} is the value of export of a given product from i at time t. Next, using this index, we compute the export diversification index;

$$(100 - Herfindahl_{it}) = Export\ Diversification\ (ED)\ Index \qquad (9.6)$$

The index of export diversification ranges between 0 and 100. The higher the value of the index being obtained, the more diversified the export basket is.

9.4.4 Data Sources

We apply a balanced panel data for 5 member countries of the EAC, namely Tanzania, Kenya, Uganda, Rwanda and Burundi.[3] The datasets contain a wide range of information for each country including export competitive index, diversification index, R&D, technology and most crucial, the share of trade openness and FDI.[4] The data period was limited by the availability of data covering 2010 to 2019 inclusive. The source of data is described in Table 9.4.

9.5 Results and Discussions

9.5.1 Summary Statistics and Correlation Matrix

Tables 9.5 summarizes the descriptive statistics. We have a total of 50 country-year observations, indicating that the panel is balanced. Almost all variables have a lower standard deviation than the mean which implies a small variation among the studied variables at the individual country level. This could be due to the fact that most of the nations that formed the EAC exhibit the common socio-economic and institutional indicators.

On average the percentage mean of trade openness (OPEN = 3.85) does vary highly compared to the inflow of FDI (FDI = 0.26). Among all variables, economic freedom has the highest mean value (EF = 5.82) followed by manufacturing value added (MVA = 2.16).

---

[3] South Sudan was not be included due to unavailability of enough data from 2010 to 2019.

[4] The lists of these variables were sourced from databases such as World Development Indicators (WDI) https://data.worldbank.org/indicator accessed on 20th, 23rd March, 2021. UNCTAD https://unctad.org/statistics accessed on 19th, 20th March 2021. Heritage foundation https://www.heritage.org/index/about accessed on 20th March 2021. UNIDO https://stat.unido.org/ accessed on 20th and 21st March 2021.

Table 9.4 Description of the variables

Variable	Description	Measurements	Previous Author	Data source	Expected sign
Export competitiveness	Sum of the weighted productivity level related to each exported products k, ($PRODY_k$) with the weights simply denoted as the share of the value of products from the total exported product in that particular country	The index of export competitiveness $EXPY$ (RCA index)	Chen et al. (2012); Gamariel & Hove (2019);	COMTRADE	
Export Diversification	Herfindahl index of the squared shares of export in country i at time t using export data, then Next, using this index, the export diversification index computed;	The index of export diversification ranges between 0 and 100	Jayaweera (2009); Iwamoto and Nabeshima (2012)	COMTRADE	+
FDI	Foreign direct inflows (US$)	Percentage FDI/GDP Total FDI in manufacturing sector	Zhang (2015); Gamariel (2019)	UNCTAD	+
Trade openness (TO)	Sum of export and import over GDP ratio in US$	Export + import/GDP ratio	Keho (2017); Huchet-Bourdon et al. (2018)	UNCTAD /World Bank	+
Economic freedom (EF)	Is an index that is designed to measure Economic Freedom. It comprises four main items: (1) rule of law, (2) government size, (3) Regulatory efficiency and (4) Open market	Range from 0 to 100	Dutta and Williamson (2016); Tran (2019)	Heritage Institute	+

(continued)

Table 9.4 (continued)

Variable	Description	Measurements	Previous Author	Data source	Expected sign
TECH	Level of technology that is embedded in industry	High-technology exports (% of manufactured exports)	Ustabaş and Ersin (2016), Kabaklarli et al. (2018)	World Bank	+
MVA	The domestic efforts in expanding the manufacturing level in the country	Manufactured Value added per year (US$)	Wako (2021)	UNIDO	+
R&D	New technology which creates the opportunity for local firms to upgrade their technological and innovative skills, thereby enhancing their export performance	The total expenditure in education as a percentage of GDP	Gamariel (2019)	World Bank	+

Data sources: Heritage Foundation. Heritage Foundation Economic Freedom Index: https://www.heritage.org/index/ accessed on 21st and 23rd March 2021.
COMTRADE. COMTRADE Statistics (Internet) accessed in https://dit-trade. International trade in goods and services based on UN Comtrade data: https://dit-trade-vis.azurewebsites.net/?reporter=834&partner=0&type=C&year=2020&flow=2 accessed on 20th and 23rd March, 2021.
UNIDO. United Nations Industrial Development. Industrail Competitiviness Index Statistics: https://stat.unido.org/database/CIP%20-%20Competitive%20Industrial%20Performance%20Index accessed on 20th and 21st March 2021.
World Bank, World Development Indicators (WDI): https://data.worldbank.org/indicator accessed on 20th and 23rd March 2021.

Table 9.5 Descriptive statistics

Variable	Mean	Std. Dev	Obs
FDI	0.26	1.83	50
OPEN	3.85	0.17	50
Epy	4.65	1.25	50
RCA	0.24	0.13	50
XD	0.75	0.05	50
R&D	1.37	0.38	50
TECH	1.48	0.85	50
EF	5.82	5.26	50
MVA	2.16	1.12	50

Source Authors Calculation

9.5.2   Selected Method of Analysis

Before selecting the appropriate method of analysis we used all three traditional panel methods, Random Effect (RE), Fixed Effect (FE) and Pooled Ordinary Least Square (POLS). To get the best model specification three tests were applied including, the Chow test between the fixed effect model and the POLS model. We also used the Breusch–Pagan (LM) test of serial correlation to gauge the best model between POLS and RE, and finally, the Hausman test was applied to capture the best model between the RE and FE model.

Generally, the results show that (See Tables 9.6, 9.7 and 9.8) FE appeared to be an appropriate technique as the value of the Hausman test and Chow test was significant across all estimated models. Therefore, FE was preferred in discussing the rest of all regressions of this chapter.

However, we also report the findings of RE also to investigate the robustness of the FE method. Finally, the estimated models are corrected for standard errors as previous results showed that the model suffered from the heteroscedasticity as the coefficient of the Breusch–Pagan test was statistically significant across all regressions.

9.5.3   Estimation Results

9.5.3.1   Impact of FDI Inflows and Trade Openness on Firms' Export Competitiveness

Table 9.6 shows the effect of FDI inflows and trade openness on export competitiveness for the EAC's Member State. The main findings are presented in Columns (1)

Table 9.6 Corrected Fixed and Random Effects: Impact of FDI and trade openness on export competitiveness

Dependent variable: export competitiveness (*LNEXPY*)

Coefficients	Fixed effect		Random effect	
	1	2	3	4
C	−0.50 [1.21]	12.06 [1.09]	-0.47 [-1.17]	1.63 [0.54]
FDI	0.15 [1.02]	NA	-0.017 [-0.55]	NA
FDI_STOCK	NA	0.24* [1.93]	NA	0.13 [1.26]
TO	−0.55 [032]	−1.02 [0.76]	−0.06 [−0.32]	−1.98 [−0.23]
MVA	0.42 [0.96]	−0.11 [−1.32]	0.763* [1.95]	0.68* [2.22]
TECH	0.09* [1.90]	0.139* [1.87]	0.28* [2.02]	0.28* [1.96]
R&D	−0.85** [2.34]	−0.38 [1.26]	−0.669* [−1.98]	−0.50 [−0.25]
EF	−0.01 [1.17]	0.02 [1.26]	−0.17* [−2.01]	−0.18** [2.65]
Breuch–Pagan test	[0.00]	[0.00]		
Chow test	[21.68]*	[17.32]*		
Hausman test			(89.29)*	(55.51)*
Breuch–Pagan test	[325]	[215.57]		
N	50	50	50	50

Note *, ** and *** imply statistically significant at 10, 5 and 1% the number within [] for the estimated parameters, Chow test and Breuch–Pagan test implies *t*-statistics, and within (….) implies chi-square value

and (2) using both FDI inflows and FDI stock[5] with the FE approach. Also, Columns (3) and (4) present the results from the RE approach.

According to the results in specification 1 (Column 1), the coefficient of FDI inflows has a positive impact on the firm's export competitiveness (FDI = 0.15) and is statistically significant.[6] Similar conclusions were reached in Paul (2011). Due to the observation of some measurement errors in international economic observations and we also run alternative regressions using FDI_Stock instead of FDI inflows (See, van Bergeijk, 1995). Meanwhile, this also serves the purpose of testing the robustness of our results. Henceforth, we substitute the FDI inflows with FDI stock as specified in Column (2) (Table 9.6) and our results still appear to have a positive effect

[5] FDI stock used to serve the purpose of robustness test.

[6] We also use sample size for the period 2009-2018 and the results remain the same (positive and significant) to conserve the space we have not reported here. The results are available upon request.

Table 9.7 Corrected Fixed and Random Effects: Impact of FDI and trade openness on export competitiveness

Dependent variable: export competitiveness (**RCA**)				
Coefficients	Fixed effect		Random effect	
	1	2	3	4
C	3.63 [0.56]	3.97 [1.12]	−1.39* [2.03]	−1.97 [1.54]
FDI	0.03* [1.98]	NA	−0.00 [064]	NA
FDI_STOCK	NA	0.00 [0.26]	NA	0.04* [1.96]
TO	−0.21 [0.47]	−0.22 [0.42]	−0.05 [0.43]	0.00 [0.62]
MVA	−0.13 [1.14]	−0.15 1.23]	0.096* [1.99]	0.11* [2.05]
TECH	0.00 [0.65]	0.00 [0953]	0.01 [0.43]	0.01 [0.86]
R&D	−0.12 [1.54]	−0.11 [1.22]	−0.02 [0.42]	−0.08 [0.03]
EF	0.00* [1.99]	0.00 [1.38]	−0.00 [139]	−0.00 [0.47]
Breuch-Pagan test	[0.00]	[0.00]		
Chow test	[13.23]*	[11.62]*		
Hausman test			(23.80)*	(22.54)*
Breuch-Pagan test	(61.95)	(53.82)		
N	50	50	50	50

Note : See Table 9.6

(FDI_STOCK = 0.24) on export competitiveness which is statistically significant. Meanwhile, FDI has a potential contribution to a firm's export competitiveness with EAC members. Prasanna (2010) for India and Gamariel and Hove (2019) for the SSA region are some of the studies that found a positive and significant effect of FDI on firms' export competitiveness. Table 9.7 shows that after using an alternative proxy of export competitiveness (RCA) shows that FDI is still positive (FDI = 0.03) with statistical significance (see Column 1).

The positive effect of FDI may be due to the involvement of EAC firms in producing manufactured products that have intra-EAC export such as food and beverage as illustrated in Figs. 9.1 and 9.2. Also, most FDI concentrate in manufacturing sectors during the period 2016–2019 as explained in Fig. 9.3. The manufacturing sector remains a leading sector in attracting foreign investment due to the introduction of an online licensing system with stringent requirements and verification.

Table 9.8 Corrected Fixed and Random Effects—Impact of FDI and trade openness on Product Diversification

Dependent variable: Export diversification, Herfindahl index (**XD**)				
Coefficients	Fixed effect		Random effect	
	1	2	3	4
C	0.06* [2.03]	−0.13 [0.53]	1.75* [2.06]	1.96* [2.08]
FDI	0.03*** [1.89]	NA	0.00	NA
FDI_STOCK	NA	0.00 [1.76]	NA	0.02* [1.96]
TO	0.08* [2.13]	0.08** [2.89]	0.02 [0.43]	−0.12 [0.63]
MVA	0.04* [1.98]	0.03 [1.46]	−0.03* [1.99]	−0.05* [2.13]
TECH	−0.01 [0.73]	−0.01 [0.24]	−0.01 [0.57]	−0.01 [1.24]
R&D	−0.00 [0.32]	0.01 [1.43]	−0.04* [2.14]	−0.00 [0.29]
EF	−0.00 [1.14]	−0.00 [0.94]	−0.01 [1.25]	−0.00 [0.24]
Breuch-Pagan test	[0.00]	[0.00]		
Chow test	[19.21}	[14.91]		
Hausman test			(27.24)	(24.94 l)
Breuch–Pagan test	(6.34)	(6.40)		
N	50	50	50	50

Note : See Table 9.6

Also, the results show that trade openness (TO) has a statistically insignificant negative effect (TO = -0.55) on the export competitiveness across all regressions (Columns 1 through 4).[7] The results are also robust as shown in Table 9.7. The insignificant impact of trade openness to export competitiveness may be linked to the fact that most developing countries, particularly EAC members either are not export-oriented or export primary products while they import expensive manufactured products and intermediate goods (Chen et al. 2012; Agosin et al. 2012, EAC 2017; UNCTAD 2018). In turn, due to stiff competitions from foreign competitors, most local exporters are losing their market due to higher cost of production (Chen et al. 2012; Agosin et al. 2012, EAC 2017; UNCTAD 2018).

Also, the negative and insignificant effect can be due to large shares of primary product exports by EAC members, they face seasonality, low value added, fluctuation of the price and poor quality. For example, Figs. 9.1, 9.2 and 9.3 show that Tanzania

---

[7] We also use sample size for the period 2009-2018 and the results remain the same (positive and significant).

and Burundi are leading exporters of primary products such as metals and food and beverage. Also, Fig. 9.3 reveals that major exports of EAC members are food and beverage (see, EAC 2017 for details).

The impact of economic freedom (EF) which also presents a potential impact of globalization on the firm's export competitiveness, appeared to have a negative (EF = -0.01) but statistically insignificant impact (see, Table 9.6 Column 1).[8] Moreover, the coefficient of technology (TECH) appears to have a positive impact on competitiveness across all regressed models. However, the results of TECH were not robust to alternative specifications within Table 9.7.

The impact of MVA has a positive impact but is statistically insignificant on the firm's export competitiveness (see Table 9.6, Columns 1 and 2). This is similar to the result found in Table 9.7. Also, R&D is statistically insignificant which is supported by several works of literature (Agosin et al. 2012; UNCTAD 2018; Gamariel and Hove 2019). In contrast, the impact of technology on a firm's export competitiveness is positive and statistically significant in Columns (1) and (2) as described in Table 9.6. However, the positive effect of TECH was no longer statistically significant in Table 9.7 as specified in Columns (1) and (2).

9.5.4 Impact of FDI Inflows and Trade Openness on Firms' Export Diversification

Table 9.8 shows the impact of FDI inflows and trade openness on product export diversification for the EAC's firms. The main results are presented in Columns (1) and (2) while Columns (3) and (4) show the results by using RE. Like the previous discussion, the variable of FDI is expressed as overall FDI inflows and by FDI_STOCK.

Starting with Column 1 the results suggest that overall FDI inflows have a positive (FDI = 0.03) and significant impact on the firm's export product diversification. Generally, the above results suggest that FDI inflow is important for EAC members if they want to diversify their export. These results are also supported by UNCTAD (2018) which has also found a positive and significant impact of FDI on export product diversification for African countries.

In addition to that, the impact of trade openness (TO) has a positive and significant (TO = 0.08) impact on the firm's export product diversification throughout all regressions (Columns 1 and 2). This implies that if EAC continues to adopt open trade policies would enhance the ability of firms to diversify their export products. Our results are consistent with Agosin et al. (2012) for developing countries and Gamariel and Hove (2019) for SSA who found a positive and significant effect of trade openness on export diversification. However, there is a need to promote trade openness in order to improve product diversification unlike the concentration of food and beverage as shown in Tables 9.1, 9.2 and 9.3.

---

[8] We ignore the results of RE model when the EF become negative and statistically significant in columns (3) and (4) as the Hausman test supported FE effect model.

According to Osakwe et al. (2018), the least developed nations with more openness to trade (based on trade intensity) have more varied export structures than those with less open trade. They also show that trade liberalization, in the form of lower tariffs, helps developing countries to diversify their export products, and the results for the developing world are promising.

The impact of economic freedom on the firm's export product diversification is negative throughout the regressions (see Columns 1 and 2) but is statistically insignificant (Table 9.8). Also, the impact of the manufactured sector through MVA on export diversification becomes positive and significant in first Column while insignificant in the second column.[9] Moreover, the impact of technology becomes insignificant with negative sign throughout all regressions. Mondal and Pant (2014) supported our results, in the case of Indian manufacturing firms for the period 2001–2006. They argued that the purchase of imported technology does not lead to export competitiveness and diversification like the presence of foreign firms. The impact of R&D is negative but not statistically significant for all regressions. The results are also supported by Mondal and Pant (2014).

9.6 Conclusion and Recommendations

This chapter examines the effect of FDI and trade openness on competitiveness and diversification among EAC Members. We apply fixed and random effects panel estimates using data from 2010 to 2019, inclusive. On the one hand, the effect of FDI on a firm's export competitiveness and trade diversification is positive and statistically significant. On the other hand, the effect of trade openness is positive and statistically significant for export diversification but insignificant for export competitiveness. Meanwhile, we recommend further improvement of both FDI and trade openness within the EAC region, which in turn would improve export competitiveness and product diversification.

It is recommended to improve the FDI linkage with EAC economic sectors. This can be achieved via three roads. First, through managing FDI inflows and FDI-related policies in order to maximize spillover effects within EAC. Second, by encouraging FDI inflows from new partners in the manufacturing sectors and establish platforms for advertisement and to exchange information. Third, to design better policies related to infrastructure so as to overcome constraints for the manufacturing sector, especially in transportation and logistics services, telecommunications and reliable power supply.

EAC members should fast-track and boost the recommendations from the EAC Industrial Competitiveness Report 2017 (EAC 2017),[10] in particular the three key

---

[9] We ignore the results of Random Effect model which show negative and statistically significant as our Hausman test prefer Fixed Effect model.

[10] The EAC report used only trend analysis of industrial competitiveness within EAC unlike our study.

policies mentioned: (a) exploiting the opportunities offered by the dynamic EAC market, (b) diversifying and upgrading through realistic, well-defined and comprehensive Strategies and (c) Strengthening of forward and backward linkages to boost industrial and overall economic growth.

This chapter concentrated on the overall FDI effect on export competitiveness and diversification and in some cases in manufacturing sectors. It is, therefore, worth also to break down this relationship into sub-sectors. For example, to examine the effect of FDI inflows from telecommunication, buildings, transportation, mining and also services on a firm's export competitiveness and diversification. Also, to examine this study by considering tri-partite economic integration is also useful (Chap. 7 of this book). For example, how this export competitiveness and diversification can be observed by using intra-trade and intra-FDI inflows among economic integration such as EAC with COMESA, or with SADC.

References

Achandi EL (2011) Effect of foreign direct investments on export performance in Uganda. Makerere University, Uganda

AfDB (2019) East Africa Economic Outlook, Macroeconomic developments and prospects, Political economy of regional integration. Africa Development Bank

Agosın MR, Alvarez R, Bravo-Ortega C (2012) Determinants of Export Diversification around the World: 1962–2000. World Econ 35(3):295–315

Aitken H, Aitken BJ (1999) Do domestic firms benefit from direct foreign investment? Evidence from Venezuela. Am Econ Rev 1:605–618

Ajayi A (2006) The influence of school type and location on resource availability and pupils learning outcome in primary schools in Ekiti State, Nigeria. Educ Thought. Accessed https://www.questia.com/library/journal/1P3-2613272731/effects-of-school-location-on-students-learning-outcomes.

Anwar S, LP Nguyen (2011) Foreign direct investment and export spillovers: evidence from Vietnam. Int Bus Rev 20:177–193

Balasubraman V, Salisu M, Sapsford D (1996) Foreign direct investment and growth in EP and is countries. Econ J 106(434):92–105. https://doi.org/10.2307/2234933

Baldwin, J. R. and Gu, W. (2003) Export-market participation and productivity performance in Canadian manufacturing. Canadian Journal of Economics 36:634–657

Blomström M, Ari Kokko A (1996) The impact of foreign investment on host countries: a review of the empirical evidence. http://elibrary.worldbank.org/doi/pdf/https://doi.org/10.1596/1813-9450-1745

Borensztein E, De Gregorio J, Lee J-W (1998) How does foreign direct investment affect economic growth? J Int Econ Elsevier 45(1):115–135

Botta A (2015) The Macroeconomics of a Financial Dutch Disease (Levy Economics Institute Working Paper No. 850)

Bwalya SM (2006) Foreign direct investment and technology spillovers: Evidence from panel data analysis of manufacturing firms in Zambia. J Dev Econ 81(2):514–526

Chen, Y., Hsu, W. C., and Wang, C. (2012) Effects of outward FDI on home-country export competitiveness: The role of location and industry heterogeneity. Journal of Chinese economic and foreign trade studies

Clerides S, Lach S, Tybout J (1998) Is learning by exporting important? Micro-dynamic evidence from Colombia, Mexico, and Morocco. Q J Econ 113(3):903–947

Demena BA (2017) Essays on intra-industry spillovers from FDI in developing countries: a firm-level analysis with a focus on Sub-Saharan Africa'. Erasmus University, The Hague, PhD diss.

Demena BA, Murshed SM (2018) Transmission channels matter: identifying spillovers from FDI'. J Int Trade Econ Dev 27(7):701–728

Demena BA, van Bergeijk PAG (2019) Observing FDI spillover transmission channels: evidence from firms in Uganda. Third World Q 40(9):1708–1729

Demena BA, Msami J, Mmari D, van Bergeijk PAG (2022) Productivity premia and firm heterogeneity in Eastern Africa. In: Demena BA, van Bergeijk P (eds) Trade and investment in East Africa: prospect, challenges and pathways to sustainability. Springer

Đurić D, Ristić J, Đurić D (2016) Foreign direct investments in the role of strengthening the export competitiveness of the Serbian economy. Econ Agric 63:531–546

Dutta, N., and Williamson, C. R. (2016) Aiding economic freedom: Exploring the role of political institutions. European Journal of Political Economy, 45, 24-38

EAC (2017) EAC trade and investment report 2017 accelerating market driven integration, East African Community, Annex VII-Draft EAC Trade Report 2017

EAC (2018) EAC trade and investmnet report. Maximizing benefits of regional integration. Accessed http://repository.eac.int/handle/11671/2041

EAC (2019) East African community trade and investment report, East Africa community

Eryiğit M (2012) The long run relationship between foreign direct investments, exports, and gross domestic product: panel data implications. Theor Appl Econ 10(10):71

Farole, T., and Winkler, D. (Eds.). (2014) Making foreign direct investment work for Sub-Saharan Africa: local spillovers and competitiveness in global value chains. World Bank Publications. https://openknowledge.worldbank.org/handle/10986/16390

Fontagné L (1999) Foreign direct investment and international trade: complements or substitutes? No 1999/3, OECD Science, Technology and Industry Working Papers, OECD Publishing

Gamariel G, Hove S (2019) Foreign direct investment and export competitiveness in Africa: investing the channels. J Afr Trade. https://doi.org/10.2991/jat.k.191115.001

Greenaway D, Sousa N, Wakelin K (2004) Do domestic firms learn to exportfrom multinationals? Eur J Polit Econ 20(4):1027–1043

Greenaway D, Guariglia A, Kneller R (2005) Do financial factors affect exporting decisions? University of Nottingham, GEP Research Paper 2005/28

Haq R (2012) The managing diversity mindset in public versus private organizations in India. Int J Hum Resour Manag 23(5):892–914

Harding T, Javorcik BS (2011) Roll out the red carpet and they will come: investment promotion and FDI inflows. Econ J 121(557):1445–1476. https://doi.org/10.1111/j.1468-0297.2011.02454

Harrison, (1996) Openness and growth: a time-series, cross-country analysis for developing countries. J Dev Econ 48(2):419–447

Hausmann R, Pritchett L, Rodrik D (2006) Growth accelerations. J Econ Growth 10:303–329

Hausmann R, Hwang J, Rodrik D (2007) What you export matters. J Econ Growth 12:1–25. https://doi.org/10.1007/s10887-006-9009-4

Helpman E, Krugman PR (1985) Market structure and foreign trade: Increasing returns, imperfect competition, and the international economy. MIT press

Hu Y (2020) Heterogeneous environmental regulations, R&D innovation and manufacturing enterprises' export technological sophistication. EconStor Preprints 222983, ZBW - Leibniz Information Centre for Economics

Huchet-Bourdon M, Le Mouël C, Vijil M (2018) The relationship between trade openness and economic growth: some new insights on the openness measurement issue. World Econ 41:59–76

Hwang J (2006) Introduction of new goods, convergence and growth, Cambridge, MA, Harvard University job market paper

Imbs J, Wacziarg R (2003) Stages of diversification. Am Econ Rev Am Econ Assoc 93(1):63–86

Iwamoto, M., and Nabeshima, K. (2012) Can FDI promote export diversification and sophistication of host countries?: dynamic panel system GMM analysis (No. 347). Institute of Developing Economies, Japan External Trade Organization

Jana SS, Sahu TN, Pandey KD (2019) Foreign direct investment and economic growth in India: a sector-specific analysis. Asia-Pac J Manag Res Innov 15(1–2):53–67. https://doi.org/10.1177/2319510X19849731

Javorcik B (2004) Does foreign direct investment increase the productivity of domestic firms? In search of spillovers through backward linkages. Am Econ Rev 94(3):605–627

Jayaweera, S. (2009) Foreign direct investment and export diversification in low income nations. Available at SSRN 1566044

John Baldwin and Wulong Gu (2003) Export-market participation and productivity performance in Canadian manufacturing. Can J Econ 36(3):634–657

Kabaklarli, E., Mangir, F., Sawhney, B. (2018) Impact of Infrastructure on Economic Growth: A Panel Data Approach Using PMG Estimator. International Review of Business and Economics, 2(2), 2

Kathuria V (2000) Productivity spillovers from technology transfer to Indian manufacturing firms. J Int Dev 12(3):343–369. https://doi.org/10.1002/(SICI)1099-1328(200004)12:3<343::AID-JID639>3.0.CO;2-R

Kutan A, Vukšić G (2007) Foreign direct investment and export performance: empirical evidence. Comp Econ Stud 49 (3):430–445

Keho, Y. (2017) The impact of trade openness on economic growth: The case of Cote d'Ivoire. Cogent Economics & Finance, 5(1), 1332820

Liu Z (2008) Foreign direct investment and technology spillovers: Theory and evidence. J Dev Econ 85(1–2):176–193

Lotfi B, Karim M (2016) Competitiveness determinants of Moroccan exports: quantity-based analysis. Int J Econ Financ 8(7):140. https://doi.org/10.5539/ijef.v8n7p140

Markusen J, Venables A (1999) Foreign direct investment as a catalyst for industrial development. Eur Econ Rev 43(2):335–356

Mijiyawa AG (2016) Does foreign direct investment promote exports? Evidence from African countries. World Econ 2(4). https://doi.org/10.1111/twec.12465

Mondal S, Pant M (2014) FDI and firm competitiveness: evidence from Indian manufacturing sector. Econ Polit Wkly XLIX(38)

Theodore M (1998) Foreign direct investment and development: The new policy agenda for developing countries and economies in transition, peterson institute for international economics. http://seaopenresearch.eu/Journals/articles/SPAS_7_3.pdf

Moss T, Ramachandran V, Shah M (2004) Is Africa's skepticism of foreign capital justified? Evidence from East African firm survey data, Centre for Global Development, Working Paper No. 41

Osakwe PN, Santos-Paulino AU, Dogan B (2018) Trade dependence, liberalization, and exports diversification in developing countries. J Afr Trade 5:19–34

Prasanna N (2010) Impact of foreign direct investment on export performance in India. J Soc Sci 24(1):65–71. https://doi.org/10.1080/09718923.2010.11892838

Rădulescu M, Şerbănescu L (2012) The impact of FDIs on exports, and export competitiveness in Central and Eastern European Countries. J Knowl Manag Econ Inf Technol

Romer PM (1990) Endogenous technological change. J Polit Econ 98(5, Part 2): S71–S102

Ricardo, D. (1817). On the principles of political economy. London: J. Murray

Sachs JD, Warner AM (2001) The curse of natural resources. Eur Econ Rev 4–6, 827–838

Sharples JA, Milham N (1990) Long-run competitiveness of Australian agriculture, foreign agricultural economic report (FAER) 147996, United States Department of Agriculture, Economic Research Service

Shobande OA (2019) Effect of economic integration on agricultural export performance in selected West African countries. Economies 7(3):79. https://doi.org/10.3390/economies

Sultan Z (2013) A causal relationship between FDI inflows and export: the case of India. J Econ Sustain Dev 4(2):20–30

Tran, D. V. (2019) A study on the impact of economic freedom on economic growth in ASEAN countries. Business and Economic Horizons (BEH), 15(1232-2020-355), 423-449

Turner P, Jozef van't dack (1993) Measuring international price and cost competitiveness. Bank for international settlemenents, Monetary and economics department. ISBN92-9131-037-9

UN (2015) Transforming our world: the 2030 Agenda for sustainable development, United Nation. Sustainabledevelopment.un.org

UNCTAD (1999) World investment report 1999, foreign direct investment and the challenge of development. United nations conference on trade and development. https://unctad.org/system/files/official-document/wir1999_en.pdf

UNCTAD (2015a) World investment Report, 2015a, reforming international investment governance, key messages and overview, United Nations conference on trade and development. https://www.imf.org/external/pubs/ft/bop/2015a/pdf/15-21.pdf

UNCTAD (2015b) Technology and innovative report 2015b: fostering innovation policies for industrial development, UNCTAD, Geneva, Switzerland, 2015b

UNCTAD (2018) World investment report, investment and new industrial policies, United Nations conference on trade and development, World investment report 2018 - investment and new industrial policies (unctad.org)

UNCTAD, UNCTAD Statistics [Internet] (2016). http://unctadstat.unctad.org

Ustabaş, A., Ersin, Ö. Ö. (2016) The effects of R&D and high technology exports on economic growth: A comparative cointegration analysis for Turkey and South Korea. In International conference on Eurasian economies (pp. 44–55)

van Bergeijk PAG (1995) The accuracy of international economic observations. Bull Econ Res 47(1):1–20

Wako, H. A. (2021) Foreign direct investment in sub-Saharan Africa: Beyond its growth effect. Research in Globalization, 3, 100054

Chen Y, Hsu W, Wang C (2012) Effects of outward FDI on home-country export competitiveness. J Chin Econ Foreign Trade Stud 5(1):56–73

Zhang KH (2006) The role of FDI in China's export performance. In: Zhang KH (ed) Chinas as the world factory. Routledge, New York

Zhang (2015) China's manufacturing performance and industrial competitiveness upgrading, international comparison and policy reflection

Chapter 10
Competitiveness of East African Exports: A Constant Market Share Analysis

Harry Thomas Silas Achentalika and Dorah Teddy Msuya

Authors are thankful to Peter van Bergeijk and Binyam Afewerk Demena of Erasmus University, International Institute of Social Studies for technical guidance in carrying out the research work. The study was financially supported by Research on Poverty Alleviation (REPOA), the African Caribbean and Pacific Group of States (ACP Group) of this project, grant number FED/2019/408-112

Abstract East African Community (EAC) exports are steadily growing. This performance of exports could be attributed to improving competitiveness despite fluctuating world trade, but also to the market focus of exporters and/or the composition of the exported commodities. This chapter focuses on competitiveness of EAC's exports using Constant Market Share analysis (CMS) to decompose EAC export growth by product category (SITC single digit level). Data is from UN Comtrade database for two periods: Period I (2009–2013) and Period II (2014–2018). The analysis focuses on disentangling the world trade effect, the commodity composition effect and the competitiveness effect. The reference group for this analysis was the world market. Findings of the study are that the world trade, commodity composition and competitiveness effects were all positively associated with increased export growth in EAC from Period I to Period II. Export growth of Standard International Trade Classification single digit-level commodities in EAC was attributed to increased demand for such products in the world market, and the commodities exported had a faster growing demand. Furthermore, there was increased competitiveness for EAC's products directed towards the selected group of reference countries.

H. T. S. Achentalika (✉) · D. T. Msuya
Refugee Services Department, Ministry of Home Affairs, Dar es salaam, Tanzania
e-mail: htsilas80@gmail.com

D. T. Msuya
NCBA Bank Tanzania, Dar es salaam, Tanzania
e-mail: dorahteddy@gmail.com

B. A. Demena and Peter A. G. Van Bergeijk (eds.), *Trade and Investment in East Africa*, Frontiers in African Business Research, https://doi.org/10.1007/978-981-19-4211-2_10

10.1 Introduction

The East African Community (EAC) is a regional intergovernmental organization of seven Partner States: The Republics of Burundi, Democratic Republic of Congo (DRC), Kenya, Rwanda, South Sudan, the United Republic of Tanzania, and the Republic of Uganda. The EAC was re-established on 30 November 1999 and entered into force on 7 July 2000 following its ratification by the original three Partner States (Kenya, Tanzania and Uganda). The Republic of Rwanda and the Republic of Burundi acceded to the EAC Treaty on 18 June 2007 and became full Members of the Community with effect from 1 July 2007. The Republic of South Sudan acceded to the Treaty on 15 April 2016 and become a full Member on 15 August 2016. The accession by DRC occurred after we finished this chapter.

The EAC-6 is home to 177 million citizens, of which over 22% are urban. With a land area of 2.5 million square kilometres and a combined Gross Domestic Product of US$ 193 billion (EAC Statistics for 2019), its realization bears great strategic economic and geopolitical significance and prospects for the renewed and reinvigorated EAC.

The EAC-6 countries cooperate in many areas one of which is to enhance the free movement of all factors of production across Partner States, cross-border infrastructure development in the region, enhancement of regional industrial development, improvement of agricultural productivity and value add. All these factors are essential for enhancing trade among the member countries and the region as a whole and facilitate firms in EAC countries to become more productive and compete in the global market.

EAC countries are geographically located in the Eastern part of Africa and have similar climatic conditions, production patterns including similar exports to other markets. While some individual countries are landlocked (Burundi, Rwanda, South Sudan and Uganda), the EAC as a whole has good access to international sea transportation routes via harbours in Kenya and Tanzania. After its formation, the export sectors of the EAC members have grown rapidly. EAC has had an increased production of exports from the years 2009–2013, inclusive (Period I) to the years 2014–2018, inclusive (Period II). The EAC member countries, are predominantly raw material producers and semi-industrialized, have invested heavily in industrialization to stimulate increases in production. Various policies and development plans aimed at increasing exports production (and ultimately aim at enhancing the free movement of all factors of production across the Partner States, (cross-border) infrastructure development in the region, enhancement of regional industrial development, improvement of agricultural productivity and value add) have been formed.

Export growth is more meaningful if it has an impact on the economic growth of countries. Most countries promote exports in light of achieving economic growth and development. The growth of the export sectors in EAC member countries is expected to translate into higher economic growth. Since 2009, a year characterized by the global economic recession and a world trade collapse, EAC exports increased, and significant economic growth of member countries could be observed.

Table 10.1 Exports as a share of GDP for EAC countries

Country/Year	Burundi	Kenya	Rwanda	Tanzania	Uganda	EAC
2009	6.6	20.0	10.4	18.2	18.7	14.8
2010	9.7	20.7	10.7	19.6	13.9	14.9
2011	8.8	21.6	12.7	21.6	12.9	15.5
2012	9.7	22.2	12.0	22.4	15.6	16.4
2013	9.1	19.9	13.5	19.0	16.6	15.6
2014	7.6	18.3	13.9	18.1	15.0	14.6
2015	5.7	16.6	13.2	17.1	12.9	13.1
2016	6.7	14.3	15.4	16.3	12.5	13.0
2017	7.4	13.2	20.5	15.1	16.7	14.6
2018	9.4	13.2	21.1	14.7	15.1	14.7

EAC's exports as a share of GDP with respective percentage growth since 2009. Data from World Bank (WB) Data accessed in December 2021

The share of export in GDP is often used as a rough measure of the importance of exports in total GDP and for the economic growth of EAC countries. The EAC experienced a slight increase in exports as a share of GDP from 2009 to 2012. A fall in exports was experienced from 2013 to 2016 but exports rose again in 2017 and 2018 (see Table 10.1). The trend of exports as a share of GDP for EAC as a whole hides the different experiences of individual member countries. Tanzania and Kenya, for example, peaked in 2012, while Rwanda has seen a steady increase in the trade to GDP ratio, presently outperforming all other EAC member countries on this measure. Burundi, Rwanda and Uganda have been experiencing an increase in exports as a share of GDP since 2015 contrary to Kenya and Tanzania which have been facing a decrease in the growth of exports as a share of GDP. These different country experiences probably reflect the fact that the integration of EAC members is far from complete.

Moreover, generally, for EAC as a whole, when the level of exports increased, the contribution to GDP decreased compared to alternative, sheltered sectors that have arguably contributed more to GDP. The pace of growth of exports is sometimes slower compared to the pace of GDP causing the share of exports in GDP to decrease. Figure 10.1 shows the trend of exports as a share of GDP in EAC since 2009. The share increased from 2009 to 2012, continuously dropping from 2013 to 2016 and rising again in 2018.

EAC has found its export partners in the past few years mainly in sub-Saharan and East African countries with its biggest importers of their products found in other regions of the world, most notably the USA, United Arab Emirates (UAE), China, India, Switzerland, Indonesia, Thailand and Germany. Furthermore, the EAC member countries export internally within the region. For example, Uganda, Burundi and Kenya have members within the EAC as one of their top five export destinations. Table 10.2 reports the values of exports of EAC and the percentage market share of

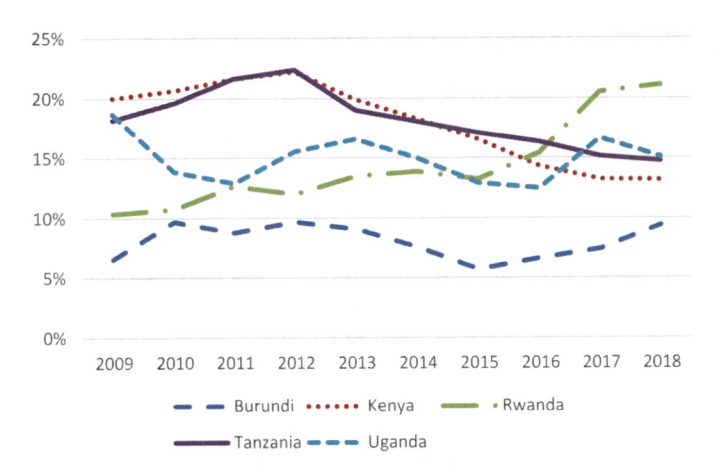

Fig. 10.1 EAC's exports as a share of GDP since 2009. *Source* World Bank (WB). Data accessed in December 2021. Figure by authors

Table 10.2 East African exports to the world as a share of total global imports

	EAC Exports	World imports	EAC Market share development (%)	World growth of imports (%)
2009	9.3	11,644		
2010	11.1	14,209	19.5	22.0
2011	7.3	17,326	−34.2	21.9
2012	8.3	17,552	13.7	1.3
2013	13.2	18,273	59.0	4.1
2014	8.7	18,288	−33.8	0.1
2015	14.7	16,023	68.9	−12.4
2016	13.7	15,549	−7.3	−3.0
2017	13.9	17,240	1.9	10.9
2018	14.0	18,907	0.4	9.7

EAC exports to the World as a percentage of World Imports. Data source: UN Comtrade and all values are reported in billions of USD. Data accessed in December 2021

these exports to global imports of Standard International Trade Classification (SITC) single-digit-level commodities. This shows whether the contribution of EAC exports in the world market for SITC single-digit commodities is increasing or decreasing. It is calculated as a change of total exports for SITC single-digit commodities over the change of total imports for the same commodities in the world market from one year to the other. The values of market share enable us to identify whether the EAC countries' exports for these products are increasing or decreasing.

The trend of market share development is depicted in Fig. 10.2. Figure 10.2 shows

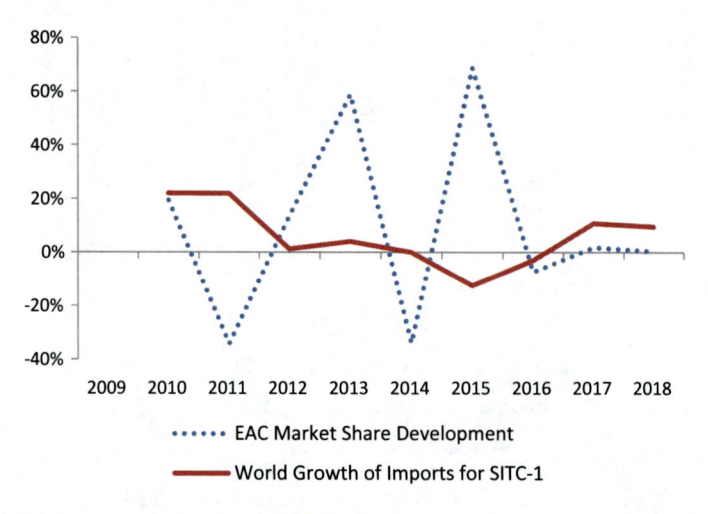

Fig. 10.2 EAC export growth and world import growth in percent (2010–2018). *Source* calculations based on UN Comtrade: Data accessed on December 2021

the trend of world imports of SITC single-digit level in one line while the other shows the trend of growth of EAC exports.

The EAC exports have not followed the development of global markets. Significant decreases in exports were experienced in 2011, 2014 and 2016, where there was a negative growth of exports compared to the years prior. −34, −33 and −7% drops in EAC exports occurred in the years 2011, 2014 and 2016, respectively. The highest growth rate of exports was experienced in 2013 and 2015 with 59% and 69% respectively. This non-linearity is the research puzzle of this chapter that we will investigate by means of a Constant Market Share (CMS) analysis.

The remainder of this chapter is organized as follows. Section 10.2 provides a summary of various studies that were reviewed, noting the authors, countries, years, methodology and the findings that were reported. Furthermore, this chapter includes the lesson learned after review and the gaps that were identified and how this study will address the gaps. Section 10.3 develops the methodology. This section explains the data sources, period under study, methods to be used for analysis, generic equations for finding effects and identification of commodities that will be considered for this study. Section 10.4 presents our findings and results. This chapter shows descriptive findings of the data, and various analytical effects that were decomposed using the CMS analysis technique. We make a decomposition into the World Trade Effect, the Commodity Composition Effect, and the Competitiveness Effect. Then we will interpret the findings in terms of competitiveness in EAC. The final session provides a discussion of the findings and draws conclusions with a view on the policy implications and offers some suggestions for policy measures that could be adapted to enhance competitiveness for EAC.

10.2   Literature Review

We provide an overview of the recent literature on applied CMS analyses in tabular format. Table 10.3 presents the authors, year of study, country and region of 32 studies, the period covered in the study, the products/commodities under the study and the major findings of these studies. The studies are grouped by region/continent. We identified the reviewed studies by searching for papers, articles and journals that used CMS analysis techniques to find the competitiveness of exports for various commodities, in different regions and countries in the world. These included Google Scholar, Academia, JSTOR and the World Bank website. The studies were published in the years 2009–2020.

These studies used CMS analysis to decompose the export performance of the countries into several parts, such as the contribution of geography, product composition and world market development. We made the following observations while reviewing these studies. First, most of the identified studies were from developed countries in Asia, Australia and Europe that all have large market shares in the global market and, more importantly, we found very few studies from an African context. We only found two studies by Ndou and Obi (2013) and Hatab (2009), This chapter aims to fill this gap in geographical coverage to some extent. Secondly, the identified studies focused mostly on a single specific product/commodity in which a country has an absolute, comparative, or competitive advantage over others in the global market. Thirdly, comparisons were made in some of the studies between countries that were competitive in the global market in a certain product.

Therefore, in this chapter, we aim to find the competitiveness of EAC exports which will generate knowledge of competitiveness and development of market share for EAC exports at the same time, checking its competitiveness in specific markets/regions in which they trade the most. The study focuses on SITC single-digit-level products hence leave room/gap for further studies on competitiveness of exports.

The next section discussed the CMS analysis in more detail and provides information about the data source and method of data collection.

10.3   Methodology

The CMS analysis is used to quantify the export performance of a country compared to the rest of the world or single foreign markets. It has the nature of an ex-post analyses, like the structural analyses carried out on national macroeconomic accounts or input–output tables. It is an accounting method for decomposing a country's growth of aggregated export shares into a competitiveness effect and a structural change effect. The technique reveals that, even if a country maintains its share of every product in every market, it can result in a decreased aggregate market share if it exports to markets that grow more slowly than the world average and/or if

Table 10.3 Major studies reviewed

Study	Country/Region	Period	Products	Findings
	Asia			
Fayaz and Ahmed (2020)	India	1980–2016	Fisheries	For most of the markets, competitiveness had been the utmost crucial driving factor of change in the market shares of Indian fish exports over the study period
Kamal et al. (2021)	Pakistan	2003 - 2017	Pharmaceutical merchandises	The empirical analysis also indicated that 'behind the border' factors confine the exports of Pakistan from reaching to its potential level
Majdalawi et al. (2020)	Jordan	2001–2012	Date export	All three components of the CMS have showed fluctuations during the studied period, mainly caused by the annual fluctuation in production and import policies of the selected importing countries from Jordan
Khaliqi et al. (2019)	Indonesia	2019	Tuna fish	Results of the estimation CMS analysis describe the effects of the most dominant influence on Indonesian tuna exports in the world market is the competitiveness effect

(continued)

Table 10.3 (continued)

Study	Country/Region	Period	Products	Findings
	Asia			
Taj and Wani (2019)	Afghanistan	2005–2017	Exports	Afghanistan was less successful in directing its geographic specialization pattern toward those regions with fast growing demand, in comparison with those commodities. Its exports remained concentrated in low and medium sectors
Maqbool et al. (2019)	Pakistan	2003–2014	Leather products	Total effect, structural effect, commodity effect, general competitive effect, specific competitive effect were positive, while average competitive effect and market effect were negative from 2003–2008. Furthermore, effects were positive, whereas competitive effect, commodity effect and general competitive effect were negative from 2009–2014

(continued)

Table 10.3 (continued)

Study	Country/Region	Period	Products	Findings
	Asia			
Bagaria and Ismail (2019)	China	2002–2014	High, medium and low technology	Export performance is mainly attributed to its competitive strength in the global market. Product structure effect, on an average, has turned out to be negative, geographical structure effect has positive impact on export performance of high-technology based exports whereas it has negative impact on export performance of low-technology and medium-technology based exports
Buana, et al. (2018)	Indonesian	2018	Canned Tuna Skipjack	Competitiveness, commodity composition and growth effect affected canned tuna export in the world market
Nanwul (2018)	Vietnam and China	2000–2014	Rice	Structural effect and growth effect have been more significant in affecting the export growth of these two parties. China rice exports have been suffered highly intense competitiveness from Vietnam's exports

(continued)

Table 10.3 (continued)

Study	Country/Region	Period	Products	Findings
	Asia			
Hutabarat (2017)	Indonesia	2017	Cassava	Maintained their share in the world market during the Global Economic Crisis, because the growth rates of dried cassava import relative quickly during the crisis
Oktaviana et al. (2017)	ASEAN	2011–2014	Tea	The major weakness of tea exports in Indonesia is competitiveness effect, while the strengths are the effect of world exports growth and the effect of market distribution
Jain (2017)	China and India	2003–2015	Cotton	Both India and China have increased their export competitiveness post Multi Fiber Agreement (MFA), however, China increased its export competitiveness more than that of India
Ahmed and Wizarat (2015)	Pakistan	2003–12	Exports	The study shows that Pakistan has the potential to increase its exports to the DMEs, but targeted diversification is required with respect to commodities and Pakistan's exports are competitive in the DMEs

(continued)

Table 10.3 (continued)

Study	Country/Region	Period	Products	Findings
	Asia			
Singh (2014)	India	1991–2011	Exports	Export performance was mainly attributed to their competitive strengths in the global export market. Negative composition effect came out as the most disturbing aspect of India's export performance. Market distribution has laid a marginally positive impact on export performance
Haque et al. (2013)	Malaysia	2000–2011	Furniture Product	Export gain of Malaysian furniture products is to a great extent a result of the size of the market as well as its competitive effect
Kaur and Nanda (2011)	India	1990–2005	Manufactured Exports	The competitiveness effect was found to be unfavourable for chemicals during the second and third sub-period and for machinery and transport equipment during the first and second sub-period

(continued)

Table 10.3 (continued)

Study	Country/Region	Period	Products	Findings
	Asia			
Sedaghat (2010)	Iran	1991–2002	Pistachio	The market distribution effect and competitiveness effect played a major role in changes in Iran's export during Period I (1996–1999), while the commodity composition effect and market distribution effect were the major sources of export changes in Period II (2000–2003)
Mahmood and Akhtar (1996)	Pakistan	1996	Exports	The market distribution and competitiveness of Pakistani exports have improved significantly
	Australia			
Liu et al. (2020)	Australia	1989–2017	Liquefied Natural Gas (LNG)	The results of the study reveal that apart from the aggregate unfavorable Market Effect and favourable Adaptation Effect, the Competitiveness Effect has contributed the most to Australia's LNG export performance over the past three decades, particularly in Australia's existing LNG markets

(continued)

Table 10.3 (continued)

Study	Country/Region	Period	Products	Findings
	Asia			
Skriner (2009)	Australia	1990–2006	Merchandise Exports	The disadvantages in competitiveness of the Austrian foreign sector have vanished, however, the market and product structure effects show negative trends after 2000
	Europe			
Backinezos et al. (2019)	Greece	2009–2018	Exports	The effect of the product composition of exports was almost neutral, while the competitiveness effect eroded more than half of the gains in the structure effect
Buturac et al. (2018)	Croatia	2010 onwards	Food industry	The analysis revealed rather disappointing results in terms of the competitive position of the Croatian food industry in the period after 2010
Pavličková (2013)	Slovakia	1999–2011	Foreign trade	Its production is competitive in the European market, although mainly in prices

(continued)

Table 10.3 (continued)

Study	Country/Region	Period	Products	Findings
	Asia			
Juhász and Wagner (2013)	Hungary	2000–2010	Agri-food	The results of the commodity (market composition) and competitiveness effects produced varied results and were not so positive
Ragacs et al. (2011)	Austria	1995–2006	Manufacturing	Competitiveness remained limited
Türkekul et al. (2010)	Turkey, Spain, Italy, Greece and Tunisia	2000–2008	Primary olive oil	Findings show that during the periods covered, Tunisia was the most competitive in the target markets. All countries showed decreased competitiveness during the periods analysed
Athanasoglou et al. (2010)	Greece	1996–2001	Exports	Considerable change in export structure, mainly the geographical structure, with a favourable effect on market shares
Cafiso (2009)	Euro Area	1996–2007	Exports	The Euro Area marginally lost export market share while France and Italy experienced greater losses in share, and Germany gained share. The structure effect had a beneficial impact on their export performance as they specialized in products and destination markets which grew relatively rapidly in comparison to the world average

(continued)

Table 10.3 (continued)

Study	Country/Region	Period	Products	Findings
	Asia			
Atış et al. (2013)	Turkey	1995–2011	Exports (SITC) Revision 3	Increase in Turkey's export performance stemmed from positive market share and commodity composition effects. The commodity adaptation effect was mostly negative during the same period
	America			
Wu et al. (2018)	US and China	2005–2012	Primary forest products	Decline of import scale and structural changes of the target markets had a negative impact on the wood products export of the two countries. The competitiveness of forest products from the United States remained stable with slight variation; however, the forest products exported by China showed a strong increasing competitive trend

(continued)

Table 10.3 (continued)

Study	Country/Region	Period	Products	Findings
	Asia			
	Africa			
Ndou and Obi (2013)	South Africa	2013	Citrus industry	Positive performance for oranges and lemons, which was linked to the industry's inherent competitiveness in the selected markets. Soft citrus quantities were almost stable to decreasing for most markets save for the Middle East, Americas and South East Asia
Hatab (2009)	Egypt	1990–2006	Cotton	The study findings revealed a high degree of geographic concentration of Egyptian cotton exports in India, Italy, the Republic of Korea, and Japan

it exports products for which demand is growing more slowly than average. The competitiveness effect is the capacity of a country to increase its market share due to competitiveness factors only, independently of structural developments in the market or in the product trade pattern. If a country only exports certain traditional products for which international demand is growing slowly compared to other products, then its total export market share of world trade will decline even if this country succeeds in maintaining its market share in traditional products. A similar reasoning holds for the geographical distribution of export markets. Therefore, a better export performance is achieved through a pattern of exports oriented towards the most dynamic markets and products in world trade.

The subsequent analysis is based on the CMS formulation proposed by Milana (1988). As already mentioned in the previous section, this method considers the information at the beginning and at the end of the observation period only. However, in the time horizon under consideration, both, a country's export structure and world exports are continuously changing. In general, such structural changes are a source of error in the analysis.

Hence, one would like to know the changes in the export shares at every observation during the period under consideration. In the past 20 years, the software applications advanced remarkably, the hardware capacity increased strongly and the quality and the availability of statistics improved. These signs of progress make the application of CMS analysis much easier today. The big advantage of this method is that the interval between initial and final observation is very small. The method helps to avoid disturbances stemming from structural changes in particular when there are many years between the initial and the final period.

The CMS analysis model that decomposes exports of EAC is as follows:

$$X^1 - X^0 = r \sum_i X_i^0 + \sum_i (r_i - r) X_i^0 + \sum_i \sum_j (r_{ij} - r_i) X_i^0 j$$

$$+ \sum_i \sum_j \left(X_i^1 j - X_i^0 j - r_{ij} X_i^0 j \right) \tag{10.1}$$

where

$X^1 - X^0$	Total Effect.
$r \sum_i X_i^0$	World Trade Effect.
$\sum_i (r_i - r) X_i^0$	Commodity Composition Effect.
$\sum_i \sum_j (r_{ij} - r_i) X_i^0 j$	Market Distribution Effect.
$\sum_i \sum_j \left(X_i^1 j - X_i^0 j - r_{ij} X_i^0 j \right)$	Competitiveness Effect.
1	final time period, i.e. the year 2018.
0	initial time period, i.e. the year 2009.
X	total EAC exports.
X_i	total exports of EAC to World i.
$X_i{}^t{}_j$	the value of EAC export of commodity i to market j at time t.

r   the rate of growth of world exports.
r_i the rate of growth of world exports of commodity
                                           i.
r_{ij} the rate of growth of world exports of commodity
                                           i in market j.

The intuition behind Eq. 10.1 is that the competitiveness effect summarizes the influence of changes in price competitiveness (i.e. the real effective exchange rate) and changes in non-price competitiveness (expressed by qualitative factors reflecting product differentiation) on EAC exports of SITC single-digit-level performance. The competitiveness effect reveals the capacity of EAC to increase its market share due to competitiveness factors only, independently of structural developments in the market or in the product trade pattern. A positive value indicates a competitive advantage of the exports of the EAC compared to the rest of the world; a negative value indicates a disadvantage.

The product composition effect defines the influence of the product specialization of EAC's exports. Small, open economies usually concentrate their industrial production on a few products only, which they also want to export. The success of specialization depends on the development of the demand in the foreign markets. If EAC specialized in products with a strong growing foreign demand, then the product composition effect will have a positive pattern. The gain in the market share will be due to the product specialization only.

The market distribution effect measures the effect stemming from the geographical breakdown of EAC's exports. If EAC's foreign trade is directed to markets, where the demand is strongly growing, the value of the market distribution effect will be positive. A negative value shows that the exports of the EAC are directed to markets in which demand is growing slower than in the rest of the world. The resulting loss in market share will stem from the market distribution of the EAC's exports only.

The data used for this chapter are derived from the United Nations Comtrade Database which is an international trade statistics database reporting global trade including exports for all countries to different regions, countries and specific groups of countries. The data that is used in this study is all manufacturing and does not include services or re-exported commodities but only those that were exported for the first time.

The data for this chapter covers the 10-year period from 2009 to 2018 inclusive. For this year the desired variables have been fully reported.[1] At the time of writing the UN Comtrade database had only fully published data for the year 2018. Therefore, for the case of CMS analysis, the dataset covered a period from (2009–2018) while for the case of descriptive analysis of the trend of trade in EAC, the same period was covered for uniformity purposes. Furthermore, for analysis purposes, this time period was divided into two periods of 5 years each; Period I which covered the

---

[1] South Sudan has not been included in the analysis because there is no data present or trade between it and other East African countries for some years and for the years for which data was reported, reliability is an issue and also the reported amounts were too small to influence the outcome/result of analysis for the other countries.

years from 2009 to 2013 (2009–2013) and Period II (2014–2018). The data covered years from 2009 when the world economic recession was fading, and economies were recovering which led to a global trade boost.

The analysis involved goods and commodities of SITC single-digit level fourth revision. In the CMS analysis we distinguish between the following ten groups.

(1)   food and live animals,
(2)   beverages and tobacco,
(3)   crude materials,
(4)   inedible except for fuels, mineral fuels etc.,
(5)   animal and vegetable oils and fats,
(6)   chemicals and related products, n.e.s.,
(7)   basic manufactures,
(8)   machinery, transport equipment,
(9)   miscellaneous manufactured articles and
(10) goods not classified elsewhere.

For the areas of analysis for CMS, the world trade of exports is subdivided into the same product categories. This enables us to find the commodity effect which is determined by the types of commodities exported.

10.4   Findings

10.4.1   Descriptive Findings

Table 10.4 shows EAC's share of exports in the world for SITC single-digit-level commodities, presenting period averages of exports of all SITC single-digit-level commodities in the two time periods. There has been an increase from Period I to Period II in total exports of 3.9%.

The highest increase being in mineral fuels, lubricants with a 61.1% increase. An increase is observed for items that are naturally produced in the East African region and where EAC has an advantage in the global market. However, a decrease was noted for commodities: crude materials, inedible products, except fuels, manufactured goods classified chiefly by material, machinery and transport equipment and commodities and transactions not classified elsewhere. These categories are mostly produced by developed industrialized countries and EAC is not much endowed with such resources as capital goods and highly trained workers.

The next step is to decompose this growth in exports of SITC single-digit-level commodities and products into various effects. The effects are: World Trade Effect which is attributed to general increased demand for such commodities from EAC in the world market. The commodity composition causes export growth as a result of growing demand for specific commodities that are produced by the country in the

Table 10.4 EAC average exports to the World for SITC 1-digit level commodities

Code	Commodity	Period I average (2009–2013)	Period II average (2014–2018)	% Change
0	Food and live animals	7.8	9.8	27
1	Beverages and tobacco	1.1	1.2	9
2	Crude materials, inedible, except fuels	4.7	3.6	−24
3	Mineral fuels, lubricants and related materials	0.9	1.4	61
4	Animal and vegetable oils, fats and waxes	0.5	0.6	27
5	Chemicals and related products, n.e.s	1.3	1.4	7
6	Manufactured goods classified chiefly by material	2.7	2.6	−6
7	Machinery and transport equipment	1.6	1.4	−15
8	Miscellaneous manufactured articles	1.2	1.8	49
9	Commodities and transactions not classified elsewhere in the SITC	4.3	3.4	−22

Source UN Comtrade and all values are reported in billions of USD. Data accessed in December 2021

world market. The market distribution effect can be distinguished into two components: (a) export growth as a result of the growth of demand for specific commodities to a specific market relative to the world market and (b) competitiveness which causes export growth as a result of increased competitiveness of EAC exports in general.

10.4.2 World Trade Effect

The World Trade Effect measures the proportion of growth in a country's export if exports of the concerned country are expected to grow at par with the world average. This means that if there is some growth/decline in the country's export, some part of this growth is attributed to the general growth/decline in world exports.

Table 10.5 presents the results of the World Trade Effect. The change in average exports of SITC single-digit level from EAC to the Rest of the World between Period I (2009–2013) and Period 2 (2014–2018) is USD 3.2 billion. This means that, generally, the average growth of exports of SITC is at the single-digit level from EAC to

Table 10.5 World Trade Effect for SITC single-digit level

	Average-Period I (2009–2013)	Average-Period II (2014–2018)
EAC Total Export to the World	9.82	13.00
Change in EAC Total Export to the World	3.18	
World Total Export	15,929.83	17,337.37
r	8.84%	
$\sum Xi^0$	2.61	
World Trade Effect $= r \sum Xi^0$	0.23	
Contribution of World Effect to EAC TE	7.25%	

All trade values are reported in billions of USD. *Data Source* UN COMTRADE Database and Calculations by Researcher. Data accessed in December 2021

the world is 7.25% contributed by the growth of exports for SITC single-digit-level products in the world.

10.4.3 Commodity Composition Effect

The Commodity Composition Effect measures if a country's export composition is concentrated in products/commodities where foreign demand is high. This effect thus checks whether the country's exports are concentrated on commodities where the demand is growing/falling with a higher/lower rate as compared to the aggregate growth rate (r) of world exports.

Table 10.6 presents the findings of the commodity composition effect. Commodity Composition Effect was found to be positively influencing the growth of exports in EAC. The value of the commodity composition effect was 81.48. This implies that the growth rate of SITC single-digit level exports by EAC was higher than the world growth rate for exports from Period I to Period II. This means that EAC has been concentrating in the production of commodities that have a high growing demand in the world market and hence has increased its exports. Due to high demand for SITC single-digit-level commodities, commodity composition effect has attributed to EAC export by USD 112 million which is equivalent to a 2.56% contribution to the total export growth of SITC single-digit level in EAC.

H. T. S. Achentalika and D. T. Msuya

Table 10.6 Commodity composition effect for SITC single-digit-level results

Code	Commodity	World average export		Ri (%)	R (%)	(Ri-R) (%)	$X°i(2009)$	$(Ri-R)X°i$
		2009–2013	2014–2018					
0	Food and live animals	937	1107	18	9	9	775.80	72.04
1	Beverages and tobacco	127	144	14	9	5	106.76	5.45
2	Crude materials, inedible, except fuels	640	626	−2	9	−11	474.13	−52.31
3	Mineral fuels, lubricants	2376	1895	−20	9	−29	88.52	−25.75
4	Animal and vegetable oils, fats and waxes	82	85	5	9	−4	48.70	−2.11
5	Chemicals and related products, n.e.s	1767	1955	11	9	2	128.61	2.28
6	Manufactured goods classified	2021	2156	7	9	−2	273.46	−5.82
7	Machinery and transport equipment	5353	6228	16	9	8	161.66	12.15
8	Miscellaneous manufactured articles	1792	2105	17	9	9	119.87	10.34
9	Goods not classified elsewhere in the SITC	835	1036	24	9	15	430.62	65.21
CCE	Commodity composition effect	$\sum(Ri - R)X°i$	81.48					
	Change in total exports							3178.55
	Contribution of CCE to TTE	2.56%						

All trade values are reported in billions of USD. Data Source: UN COMTRADE Database & Calculations by Researcher. Data accessed in December 2021.

Table 10.7 Competitiveness Effect for SITC single-digit-level of EAC Countries

Country	Competitiveness Effect (CE)
-	-
Total Competitiveness Effect to EAC Countries	100.89
Change in EAC Total Exports to the World	3178.55
Contribution of Competitiveness Effect to EAC East African Community (EAC) Total Effect	3.17%

All trade values are reported in billions of USD. *Data Source* UN COMTRADE Database and Calculations by Researcher. Data accessed in December 2021

10.4.4   Competitiveness Effect

The measurement of the change in a country's competitiveness assesses the difference between actual change in the focus country's exports and changes that would have taken place if the constant market share has been sustained in those markets by the focus country.

Table 10.7 shows the findings of the competitiveness effect. The result of competitiveness is positive which means that there is an increased competitiveness of EAC exports of SITC single-digit-level commodities directed to the world market. The value of the competitiveness effect is 100.89 from Period I to Period II marking an increase in competitiveness. This means that export growth in EAC after correction for country composition and product composition is positively associated with increased competitiveness from Period I (2009–2013) to Period II (2014–2018). The EAC has thus done better than could be expected on the basis of the development of world trade, the kind of goods that it exports and the markets that import products from the EAC.

10.5   Discussion

10.5.1   Findings

The major findings of this chapter are that changes in world trade have greatly influenced export growth in EAC countries. The increased SITC single-digit world demand has resulted in the growth of exports from EAC countries. EAC has had a greater growth rate of SITC single-digit-level exports than the growth rate of world trade. EAC exports grew by 14.7% on average while the world growth for SITC single-digit-level exports grew by 9.0% on average from Period I (2009–2013) to

Period II (2014–2018). As a result of increased demand for these exports in the world market, EAC countries benefited by increasing their exports while maintaining their initial market shares. As the economy of the world recovered from the global Great Depression (2007–2009), demand for SITC single-digit level and other raw materials increased since economies aimed at recovery by increasing production.

The commodity composition effect was found to be positive, meaning that EAC focuses its production on products characterized by a comparatively high demand growth in the world market. Most of EAC's trade consists of food and raw materials which generally are highly demanded for consumption and production of other goods. The finding that there is a positive effect of concentrating on the production of SITC single-digit level to total export growth in EAC may thus be conditioned by the high level of aggregation. Future research could investigate a greater level of detail (i.e., SITC two digits or more).

Regarding Competitiveness, the CMS findings were positive for EAC. This means that EAC has become more competitive in the world market than could be expected on the basis of the commodity composition effect. An explanation could be that EAC countries have improved the quality of their production and export through targeted industrial policies aiming at increasing production and exports and hence caused competitiveness to increase because of high rates of growth in productivity from Period I to Period II. Therefore, export growth for SITC single-digit level in EAC is attributed to its increased competitiveness in the world market by 2.2%.

10.5.2 Conclusion and Policy Implications

Trade policies played a major part in increasing EAC's competitiveness. EAC, being an economic integration area with a number of countries, has enabled the reduction of barriers to trade (such as tariffs) and easy mobilization of resources. Moreover, improved infrastructures have all together contributed to improved competitiveness. EAC trade has been increasing over the years. Export for SITC single-digit level has grown by 14.7% from Period I (2009–2013) to Period II (2014–2018). This is a result of favourable but still insufficient policies and a trade environment that is aimed at trade growth that trickles down.

The EAC integration should focus efforts on the productivity of exporting firms to increase its advantage over neighbouring countries and their competitiveness in the world market. This will increase both competitiveness and the share in trade partner markets (and the world market as a whole). On the distribution of its exports, EAC should concentrate its exports to countries where the demand growth is high in the world market than those with a slow demand growth so as to attain stronger growth in exports for its commodities. These countries include China, Switzerland, Germany, UAE, South Africa and India.

Therefore, EAC needs to focus on exports of specific goods in which it has an advantage over its neighbouring countries and partners who produce the same products in the world market. Specialization will enable the allocation of resources to produce high demand for commodities; hence helping to increase its market share and competitiveness at large in the world market.

References

Ahmad Klasra M (2005) Competitiveness of major exporting countries and Turkey in the world fishery market: a Constant market share analysis. Aquac Econ Manag 9(3):317–330

Ahmed A, Wizarat S (2015) Constant market share analysis for exports of Pakistan: case of developed market economies. Int J Sci Eng Res 6(4):172–179

Arshad FM (1997) Export performance of selected electrical and electronic products. In: Towards Management Excellence in 21st Century Asia, pp 1–22

Athanasoglou P, Backinezos C, Georgiou E an (2010) Export performance, competitiveness and commodity composition. MPRA Paper No. 31997, Munich

Atış A, Saygılı F, Kaya AA (2013) The determinants of Turkey's export performance: constant market share analysis. Erciyes Üniversitesi İktisadi Ve İdari Bilimler Fakültesi Dergisi 42:41–66

Backinezos C, Panagiotou S, Rentifi A (2019) Greek export performance: a constant market share analysis. Econ Bull 50:45–65

Bagaria N, Ismail S (2019) Export performance of China: a constant market share analysis. Front Econ China 14(1):110–130

Buana EE, Huang WC, Hanani N (2018) The export performance of Indonesian canned Skipjack in world market. Agri Soc Econ J 18(2):86–92

Buturac G, Lovrinčević Ž, Mikulić D (2018) Export competitiveness of the croatian food industry. Argumenta Oeconomica 41(2):135–155

Cafiso G (2009) The export performance of the Euro Area countries in the period 1996–2007

Djuraidin I (2017) The analysis of competitiveness and export demand of acehnese coffee in the international market. J Econ Sustain Dev 8(8)

Fayaz M, Ahmed M (2020) Fisheries exports of India: a constant market share analysis. Indian Econ J 68(1):29–39

Haque A, Anwar N, Ibrahim Z (2013) Export of furniture product from Malaysia: market prospects and challenges. J Econ Behav Stud 5(7):406–419

Hatab AA (2009) Performance of Egyptian cotton exports in international market. Agric Econ Res Rev 22(347–2016–16854):225–236

Hutabarat NA (2017) The export performance of indonesian dried Cassava in the world market. Agri Soc Econ J 17(3):134–139

Jain, M. P. (2017) Constant market share analysis of export competitiveness of cotton: A comparative study of India and China. Pacific Business Review International, 10(1), 77–84

Juhász A, Wagner N (2013) An analysis of hungarian agri-food export competitiveness. Stud Agric Econ 115(1316–2016–102799):150–156

Kamal MA, Khan S, Gohar N (2021) Pakistan's export performance and trade potential in Central Asian region: analysis based on Constant Market Share (CMS) and stochastic frontier gravity model. J Public Aff e2254

Kaur A, Nanda P (2011) Competitiveness of India's manufactured exports: a constant market share analysis. Indian J Econ Bus 10(2)

Khaliqi M, Pane TC, Fatoni RBMI (2019) Indonesian tuna position in the international market. In: IOP Conference series: earth and environmental science. IOP Publishing, vol 260, No 1, p 012024

Liu YS, Shi X, Laurenceson J (2020) Dynamics of Australia's LNG export performance: a modified constant market shares analysis. Energy Econ 89:104808

Mahmood A, Akhtar N (1996) The export growth of pakistan: a decomposition analysis. Pakistan Dev Rev 693–702

Majdalawi MA et al (2020) Improving supply chain of date palm by analyzing the competitiveness using a constant market share analysis

Maqbool MS, Anwar S, Hafeez-Ur-Rehman MT (2019) Competitiveness of the Pakistan in leather export before and after financial crises: a constant-market-share analysis. J Glob Econ 7(333):2

Milana, C. (1988) Constant-market-shares analysis and index number theory. European Journal of Political Economy, 4(4), 453–478

Nanwul DA (2018) A comparison on rice export between China and vietnam: a constant market share analysis. E3 J Bus Manag Econ 9(1):001–011

Ndou P, Obi A (2013) An analysis of the Competitiveness of the South African citrus industry using the constant market share and porter's diamond model approaches. Int J Agric Manag 2(3):160–169

Oktaviana N, Masyhuri M, Hartono S (2017) Competitiveness of tea exports in Asean: a constant market share analysis. Ilmu Pertanian (agricultural Science) 1(2):088

Pavličková V (2013) The competitiveness of slovak foreign trade in the European market. Econ Ann 58(196):7–49

Ragacs C, Resch B, Vondra, (2011) Austria's manufacturing competitiveness. Monetary Policy Econ Q 3:35–61

Sedaghat R (2010) Export growth and export competitiveness of Iran's Pistachio. Agric Trop Subtrop 43(2)

Singh K (2014) A constant market share analysis of India's export performance. Foreign Trade Rev 49(2):141–161

Skriner E (2009) Competitiveness and specialisation of the Austrian export sector: a constant-market-shares analysis. Reihe Ökonomie/Economics Series

Taj Z, Wani NUH (2019) Evaluation of Afghanistan export performance: a constant-market-share analysis approach. Management 2(2):16–40

Türkekul BM et al (2010) Competitiveness of mediterranean countries in the olive oil market. New Medit: MediterrEan J Econ, Agric Environ 9(1)(41)

Wu J, Wang J, Lin W (2016) Comparative analysis of primary forest products export in the United States and China using a constant market share model. For Prod J 66(7–8):495–503

Zhou M (2016) Analysis of the export growth impetus of chinese forest chemical products. Atlantis Press, pp 19–22

Part IV
Industries, Cooperatives and Value Chains

Chapter 11
Tanzania's Leather Value Chain: A Review of the Literature

Fauzul Muna

Abstract This chapter investigates the leather value chain in Tanzania. Tanzania has significant livestock production, which potentially provides raw materials for the leather industry. However, the contribution of the leather industry to the economy is minimal. This chapter identifies the challenges in Tanzania's leather value chain covering downstream and upstream activities. The Tanzanian government should address challenges in livestock production, slaughtering facilities, hide and skin collection, the tanning industry, and light manufacturing in order to move up the leather value chain and increase this sector's contribution to GDP. This chapter identifies best practices for leather industry development policies that are allowing China, India, Tunisia, Ethiopia, and Kenya to climb the leather value-added chain by means of a common framework underlying policies to strengthen leather industry performance. The policies include higher quality supporting facilities such as tax incentives, leather research institutes, grading institutions, innovation, and dedicated training facilities. These elements may be a vital element of Tanzania's policies for the leather industry aimed at strengthening the capacity for effective implementation of export competitiveness and diversification.

11.1 Introduction

Tanzania has experienced rapid economic growth over the last two decades. According to data from the World Bank (2020), real GDP growth was, on average, 6.3% per year, whereas per capita income grew by 3.3% annually. The agriculture sector dominates the Tanzanian economy and provides a livelihood for approximately 55% of the population (three-quarters of the poor), accounting for 29% of GDP in 2017 (World Bank 2020). Developments in this sector will have a direct impact on economic growth and poverty alleviation, particularly if Tanzania can move up the

F. Muna (✉)
International Institute of Social Studies (ISS), Erasmus University Rotterdam, The Hague, The Netherlands
e-mail: fauzulmuno@gmail.com

value chain by developing and strengthening the manufacturing of agricultural products. One of the key Tanzanian industries linked to the agriculture and manufacturing sector that has the potential to be further developed is the leather industry.

Tanzania is generously endowed with livestock. The Food and Agriculture Organisation (FAO) (2020) notes that Tanzania has the second-largest livestock production in Africa after Ethiopia, with 27.4 million head of cattle, 18.4 million head of goats, and 7.8 million head of sheep in 2019. This sector provides livelihoods for 1.7 million households (International Trade Centre 2018), contributing 7.6% to the GDP in 2018 (Ministry of Livestock and Fisheries 2019).

Large-scale livestock production potentially supplies inexpensive hides and skins to the leather industry. This potential has been recognized by policymakers and indicated by Tanzania's Five-Year Development Plan II (FYDP II), which emphasizes the leather industry as one of the priority sectors for national economic transformation. However, the leather industry in Tanzania is still underperforming, as indicated by the export earnings from this sector (Fig. 11.1), which was 0.01% of GDP in 2018. Of this percentage, the majority of exports are dominated by raw hide and skin exports, which accounted for 83.82% of total exports in 2018. Exports of leather articles accounted for 14.33% of total exports in 2018, whereas finished products such as footwear contributed to 1.84% of total exports in 2018.

This chapter aims to investigate the leather value chain in Tanzania. The remaining sections of the paper are organised as follows. Section 11.2 presents the data and methodology, followed by the leather global market trends in Sect. 11.3. Section 11.4 provides an overview of the Tanzanian leather sector. Section 11.5 discusses the Tanzanian leather value chain, followed by the trade policy in Sect. 11.6. Section 11.7 discusses regional and international comparisons, and Sect. 11.8 presents the conclusions.

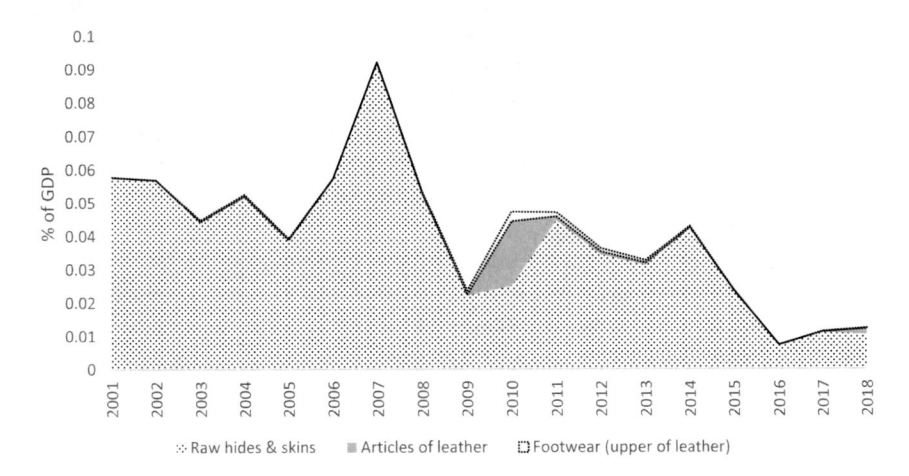

Fig. 11.1 Tanzania's raw hides and skins, leather articles, and footwear (leather upper) exports, 2001–2018 (% of GDP). *Source* Author's calculations based on International Trade Centre (ITC) and World Development Indicators (WDI) (2020)

11.2 Data and Methodology

This research employs a mixed research method combining a review of the literature and analytical descriptive statistics of secondary data. Data were collected from the International Trade Centre (ITC), Food and Agriculture Organisation (FAO), World Development Indicators (WDI), International Monetary Fund (IMF), International Growth Centre, Leather Development Fund Committee, and Tanzania Investment Centre. This study also performed a review of existing literature. The literature discussed in this chapter extends beyond academic literature, as also non-academic literature such as government documents are included.

11.3 Global Leather Market Trends

The ITC (2016) projects an increase in the demand for leather goods over the next 10 years triggered by the stable demand of leather importing countries such as the USA, Italy, and China, as well as the rapid rise of the middle class in emerging market economies such as China, Brazil, Russia, India, and South Africa. Global leather exports have more than doubled from US$50 billion in 2001 to US$112 billion in 2014. However, exports then stagnated until 2016, possibly due to the world trade slowdown. Sales began to increase again in 2016. The global financial crisis in 2007 caused a temporary decrease in the value of global leather exports from US$79 billion in 2008 to US$64 billion in 2009, but its recovery was quick and returned to the general trend in 2011.

The global raw hide and skin export are dominated by 11 countries with a share of over 60% of the world's market, as presented in Fig. 11.2, Italy, the USA, and Brazil are the top three exporting countries that accounted for over a third of the world's market in 2019. As Fig. 11.2 illustrates, the majority of countries experienced a decline between 2015 and 2019, with the biggest losses experienced by Brazil, India, and the USA, with decreases of 50%, 49%, and 47%, respectively. This decline was most likely due to the downward trend of hides prices from 87.7 cts/lb in 2015 to 39.2 cts/lb in 2019. Only Thailand and China experienced an increase from 2015 to 2019 at 8% and 6%, respectively.

Table 11.1 illustrates that global leather exports are dominated by finished products, including footwear and handbags, with 61% of total exports. Developed countries dominate exports of finished products; handbags from Italy accounted for 33% of total exports in 2019. In terms of raw material, leather further prepared after tanning and crusting had the highest percentage at 8%, followed by tanned or crust hides and skin of bovine at 3% of total exports. Table 11.2 illustrates that the global production of hides and skins is dominated by cattle, accounting for 69% of the total production in 2018, followed by sheep, goats, and buffalo, which represent 15%, 10%, and 7%, respectively.

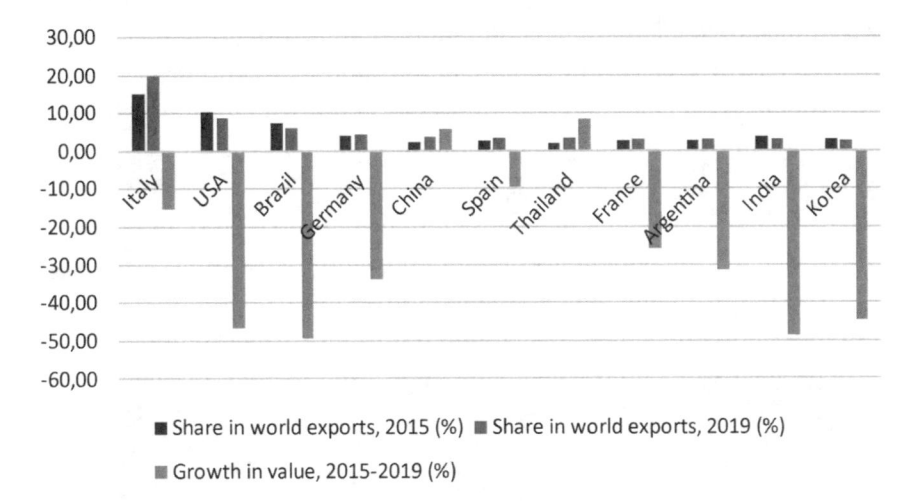

Fig. 11.2 Share and growth in value of world exporters of raw hides and skins and leather, 2015–2019 (%). *Source* ITC calculation based on the UNITSD (2020)

Table 11.1 Share in value of world leather exports by product, 2019 (%)

No	Product code	Product label	% in 2019
1	640,399	Footwear with outer soles of rubber, plastics or composition leather, with uppers of leather	27,45
2	420,221	Handbags with outer surface of leather, composition leather or patent leather	14,92
3	640,391	Footwear with outer soles of rubber, plastics or composition leather, with uppers of leather	12,35
4	4107	Leather further prepared after tanning or crusting	8,10
5	420,231	Wallets, purses, key-pouches, cigarette-cases, tobacco-pouches	4,68
6	640,359	Footwear with outer soles and uppers of leather	4,05
7	4104	Tanned or crust hides and skins of bovine "incl. buffalo" or equine animals	3,04
8	4205	Articles of leather or composition leather	2,72
9	420,310	Articles of apparel, of leather or composition leather	2,53
10	640,340	Footwear, incorporating a protective metal toecap	2,42
11		Others	17,74

Source ITC calculations based on the UNITSD (2020)

Developed countries dominate the global leather market, though there have been considerable shifts in the location of leather tanning and manufacturing. As already noted by Muchie (2000), European countries are, for example, losing markets to

Table 11.2 Share of hides and skins production by type, 2018 (%)

Type	Volume (100,000 tonnes)	%
Hides, cattle, fresh	84	68.5
Skins, sheep, fresh	19	15
Skins, goat, fresh	12	9.5
Hides, buffalo, fresh	8	7
Total	123	100

Source Food and Agriculture Organisation of the United Nations (2020)

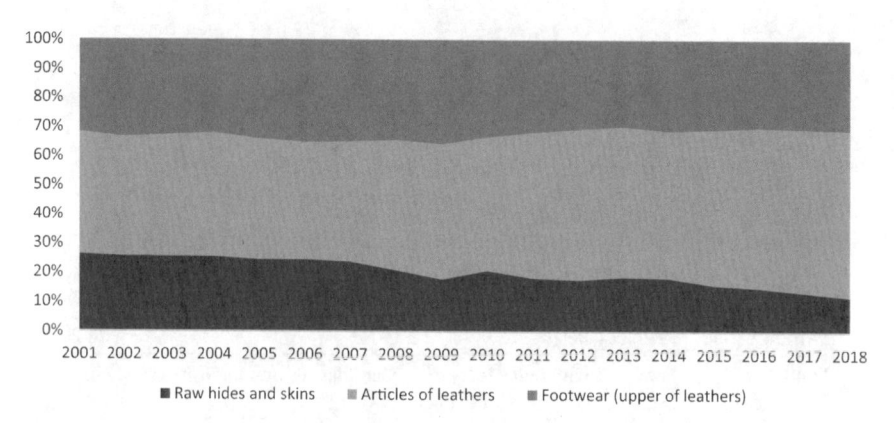

Raw hides and skins   Articles of leathers   Footwear (upper of leathers)

Fig. 11.3 Earnings from exportation of hides and leather products in developing countries, 2001–2018 (%). *Source* ITC calculations based on the UNITSD (2020)

developing countries, where production costs are lower and environmental regulations are less strict. This is also reinforced in the previous two decades, as illustrated in Fig. 11.3. The figure shows that the earnings from the exportation of raw hides and skins in developing countries have marginally risen by 0.03% from US$10.0 billion in 2001 to US$10.3 billion in 2018. Earnings from the exportation of footwear (leather uppers) in developing countries, in contrast, have increased by 108% from US$12.3 million in 2001 to US$25.6 million in 2018. These findings suggest that leather manufacturing can become an important industry in developing economies, implying that an effort to identify the challenges faced by the supply and demand of the leather industry is essential.

11.4 Overview of Tanzania Leather Industry

The leather industry in Tanzania has shrunk following privatization and market liberalization policies in the 1980s (ITC 2016). The decline has mainly occurred in light manufacturing, particularly shoes and other leather goods, which are currently being replaced by imported products (ibid). The Tanzanian tannery industry has also deteriorated since the 1980s and currently operates under installed capacity.

Policymakers in Tanzania have been attempting to revive the leather industry through a variety of policies (Lwesya 2018), including launching the Tanzania Livestock Modernization Initiatives (TLMI) (2015), the National Livestock Policy (2006), the introduction of demand-driven hides and skin curriculum for Livestock Training Institutes, a curriculum for leather processing and footwear manufacturing at technical institutions, and integrated hides, skins, and leather strategy (2007), and the United Republic of Tanzania Leather Sector Development Strategy (2016). However, these efforts have not yet shown significant results. The contribution of earnings from exports of hides and skins and the leather industry to the economy of Tanzania is minimal, accounting for only 0.01% of GDP in 2018 (ITC 2020). Figure 11.4 shows that Tanzanian raw hide, skin, and wet-blue exports have been fluctuating between US$3.6 million and US$21.06 million from 2001–2018 with a historical peak in 2014 at US$21.06 million. Leather articles and travel goods exports peaked in 2010 at US$6.19 million, though there was a decline until 2017.

Tanzania mostly exports raw materials and low value-added leather. Raw hides, skins, and wet-blue leather dominated the value of exports between 2001 and 2018, representing 94% of total exports, whereas leather articles and footwear exports represented only 6% of all exports between 2001 and 2018. Relying on raw material exports is unfavourable for the Tanzanian economy because global market prices for this commodity continue to decline from 67.9 US cts/lb in 2017 to 58.4 cts/lb in 2018 and 39.2 cts/lb in 2019. Muchie (2000) estimates that, if a company moves up to processed hides, it potentially increases its earnings by over 400%. In addition, if a company moves up to finished products, it has the chance to earn up to 10 times the value of wet-blue (Brautigam et al. 2018).

Although Tanzania has the second-largest livestock production in Africa, the country's market share in leather exports in the African region is minimal. According

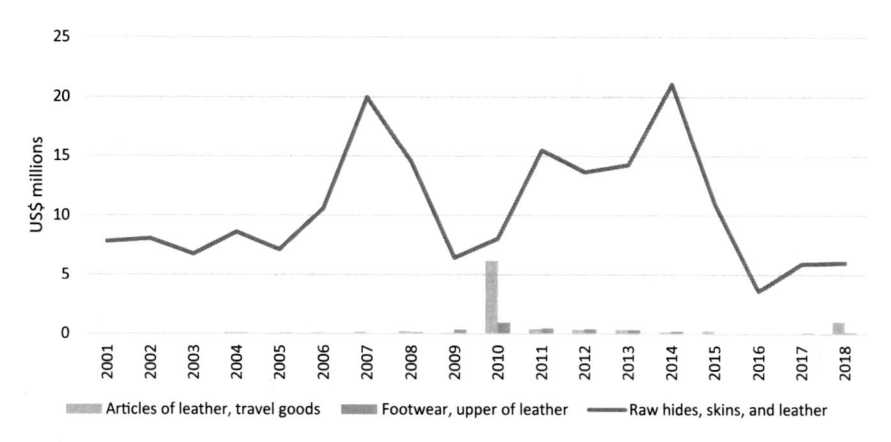

Fig. 11.4 Tanzanian leather exports, 2001–2018 (US$ millions). *Source* ITC calculations based on the UNITSD (2020)

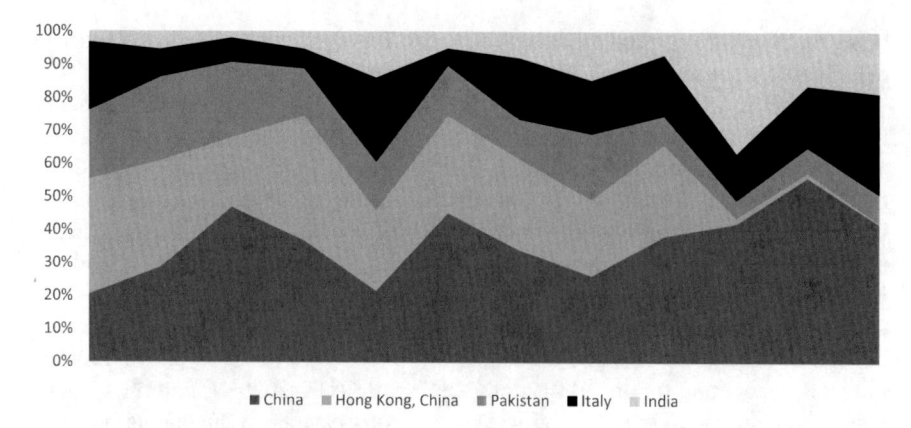

Fig. 11.5 Main export destinations for Tanzanian hides and skins, 2007–2018 (%). *Source* ITC calculation based on the UNITSD (2020)

to ITC (2020) data, Tanzania ranked 11th for hides and skins exports with a total value of US$12 million or 1.8% of total exports in 2019. South Africa was the largest hide and skin exporting country, with a share of almost a third of Africa's market in 2019. In terms of leather article exports, Tanzania ranked 25th behind Senegal and Mozambique. Tanzania ranked 19th in the footwear exports (leather upper), followed by Cameroon. Tunisia ranked first in export revenues both in leather articles and footwear, with a share of 49% and 63% of total exports in Africa in 2019, respectively.

According to ITC (2020) data, Tanzanian hides and skins exports are dominated by bovine-derived products of US$6.91 million and accounting for a third of total exports, followed by other raw hides and skins at US$3.99 million or 34% of total exports in 2019. Tanzania has had a poor export performance in leather products. In the past, these products were mostly from trunks and suitcases and peaked at slightly more than US$6 million in 2010 but declined to US$56,000 in 2019.

In terms of the destination of the exports of hides and skins, the most significant destinations are Asian markets, particularly China (including Hong Kong), Pakistan, and India. These Asian markets account for 26% of total exports in 2018 (Fig. 11.5). Italy ranked fourth, with a total share of 11% of total exports in 2018.

11.5 The Tanzanian Leather Value Chain

Discussing the leather value chain in Tanzania is intrinsically linked to the meat industry. In Tanzania, the meat industry is a household affair when there is a livestock ownership of less than 10 animals (ITC 2016). For farmers, there is no value chain for leather. Therefore, livestock production often causes animals to suffer from skin defects, making it difficult for the tanning industry to obtain quality supply of raw

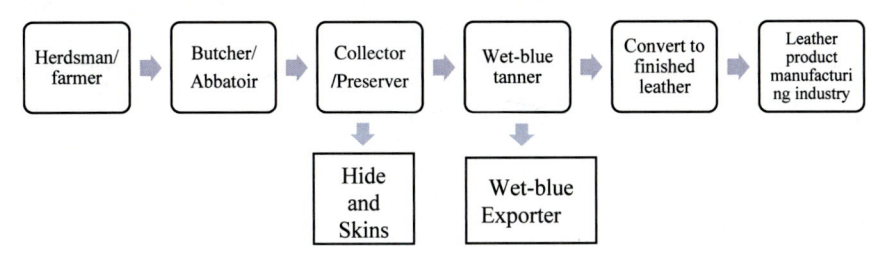

Fig. 11.6 The leather value chain in Tanzania. *Source* Based on International Growth Centre (2012) and ITC (2004)

material (ITC 2016). This section discusses the leather value chain in Tanzania, starting with supply chains in the livestock production, slaughter, and hide and skin collection. This value chain is presented in Fig. 11.6.

As described in Fig. 11.6, the leather value chain in Tanzania starts from Herdsmen/farmers that usually have livestock on a small-scale that will supply the butcher/abattoir. In the hands of collectors/preservers, hides & skins are usually exported directly as raw materials or delivered to wet-blue tanners. There are two possibilities in the wet-blue tanner: exporting as the wet-blue tanner or converting to finished leather, which will be the material for the leather manufacturing industry.

11.5.1 Livestock Production

Tanzania has the second-largest livestock production in Africa after Ethiopia, with 27 million head of cattle, 18 million head of goats, and 8 million head of sheep in 2018 (Fig. 11.7). However, the majority of livestock production is carried out traditionally on a household level with a stock of less than 10 animals (ITC 2016: 22). In terms of livestock production, 80% consists of traditional agro-pastoralists and 14% of pastoralists (China and Ndaro 2016: 56). A small percentage of livestock production is operated by the state-owned company National Ranching Company Limited (NARCO), representing approximately 7% of all livestock (China and Ndaro 2016: 55). This traditional livestock production practice often causes defects in animal skin, resulting in poor-quality hides and skins (URT 2017; Jabbar et al. 2002).

11.5.2 Slaughter

Adequate slaughtering facilities to support leather manufacturing are not available in Tanzania. Based on ITC data (2016), there are approximately 1000 slaughter slabs and 75 slaughterhouses, with a capacity of approximately 1–10 cattle per day and 100 cattle per day, respectively. These are owned both by private companies

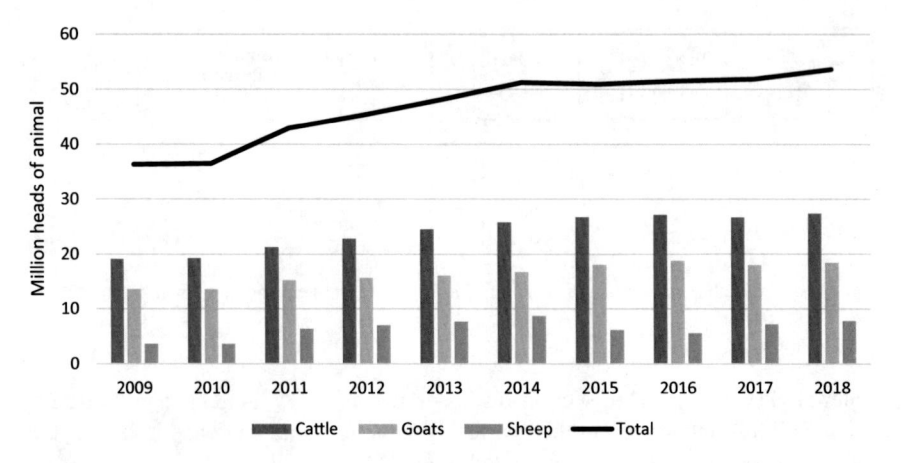

Fig. 11.7 Tanzanian livestock production, 2009–2018 (million heads of animals). *Source* Food and Agriculture Organisation of the United Nations (2020)

and local governments. Most of these slaughter facilities are simple buildings, where killing and dressing are carried out on the floor. Informal slaughterhouses also operate throughout the country with poor building conditions, hygiene, and safety. Inadequate slaughter facilities cause animal skin to be mixed with blood and faeces, which makes skin preservation difficult. In addition, slaughtering facilities in Tanzania are located far from tanneries, creating additional transportation costs and potential damage that may deteriorate hide and skin quality (China and Ndaro 2016: 55).

11.5.3 Hide and Skin (H&S) Collection

The production of H&S is low compared to livestock production. In 2018, the production of hides and skins reached 3.53 million heads of cattle, 3.63 million heads of goats, and 1.71 million heads of sheep (Fig. 11.8). ITC (2016) stated that only approximately 75% is collected, while the remaining 25% is disposed of as waste. Based on an informal discussion with the community around the Tengeru slaughterhouse, the disposed hides and skins produce an unpleasant smell, which is complained by residents. Photo narration of this situation is presented in Fig. 11.9.

Collectors obtain hides and skins from three sources, namely slaughtering locations, drying sheds, and collection centres of slaughterhouses and abattoirs. The price of the hide and skin is seasonal and varies. Approximately 10% of hides and skins are exported as raw hides and skins, whereas the rest is handed over to tanneries to be processed into wet-blue, which is subsequently exported or distributed to the local leather industry (China and Ndaro 2016).

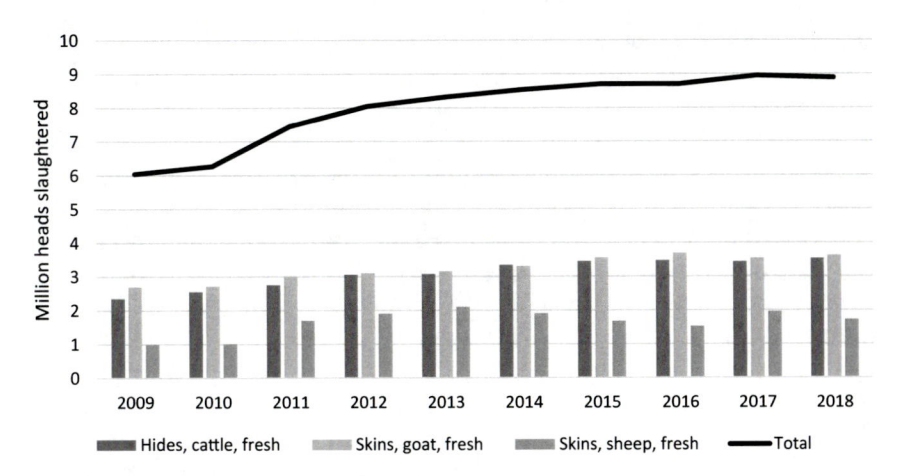

Fig. 11.8 Tanzanian production of hide & skin, 2009–2018 (equivalent to million heads slaughtered). *Source* Food and Agriculture Organisation of the United Nations (2020)

Fig. 11.9 Disposed and abandoned hides and skins at the Tengeru slaughterhouse. *Source* REPOA (Photos taken on 26/09/2019 by Cecilia China)

11.5.4 The Tanning Industry

Tanning is the process of transforming raw hides and skins into leather to prevent decay (China et al. 2020a, b). The tanning industry in Tanzania has a long tradition, and the longest-standing company is Himo Tanners, which was founded in 1895 (International Growth Centre 2012). Furthermore, the Tanzanian government established three large-scale tanneries between 1967 and 1984, with a total annual installed capacity of 2.8 million square meters of leather, namely Tanzania Tanneries (Moshi), a joint venture between Tanzania and the Swedish government built in 1968, Morogoro Tanneries, which was built in 1974 and began to operate in 1979 with financial assistance from Bulgaria, and Mwanza Tanneries, which was built in 1974 and began production in 1979 with a loan from the World Bank (International Growth Centre 2012).

Table 11.3 Selected tanneries' capacity in 2015

Company	Location	Installed annual capacity (pieces)		Installed annual capacity (Sq. ft)
		Hides	Skins	
Afro Leather Industries Ltd.	Dar es Salaam	300,000	700,000	10,650,000
Lake Trading Co. Ltd	Kibaha	90,000	420,000	4,260,000
Himo Tanners and Planters Ltd.	Moshi	90,000	900,000	6,300,000
SAK International Ltd	Arusha	450,000	900,000	15,300,000
Moshi Leather Industries Ltd.	Moshi	180,000	1,200,000	9,900,000
ACE Leather Tanzania Ltd.	Morogoro	1,200,000	3,600,000	27,450,000
Meru Tanneries Ltd.	Arusha	624,000	1,500,000	8,310,000
Xing Hua Investment Co. Ltd.	Shinyanga	900,000	2,100,000	12,700,000
Huacheng International Ltd.	Dodoma	900,000	1,500,000	9,000,000
Total		4,734,000	12,820,000	103,870,000

Source Leather Development Fund Committee (2015) in Tanzania Investment Centre (2018)

The tanning industry in Tanzania peaked in the 1980–1985 period when three government-owned companies operated at full capacity. This sector has suffered a setback since the 1990s as a result of privatization (International Growth Centre 2012). Currently, there are nine tanneries in operation in Tanzania, with a total annual capacity to process 4.7 million hides and 12.8 million skins, which is equivalent to 104 million square feet per year (Table 11.3). These tanning companies buy salted or dried hides and skins directly from slaughterhouses, collectors, or salting slabs/drying sheds (ITC 2016). However, these tanneries work well below capacity with utilization at approximately 61% for skins and 86% for hides of total annual installed capacity (Ministry of Finance and Planning 2016).

Approximately 9–10% of collected hides and skins are processed into leather; the rest is exported as raw H&S and wet-blue (China and Ndaro 2016). Production of wet-blue is still limited to approximately 170,000 hides and 720,000 skins, well below the annual collection of 2.9 million hides and 4.3 million skins (Mwangosi 2014; China and Ndaro 2016). However, Tanzania experienced an increase in imported processed leather between 2001 and 2018. Figure 11.10 shows that processed leather imported by Tanzania increased from US$23,000 in 2001 to US$97,000 in 2018 peaking in 2015 at US$292,000. Tanzania may reduce imported processed leather if it manages to increase tanning production to full capacity.

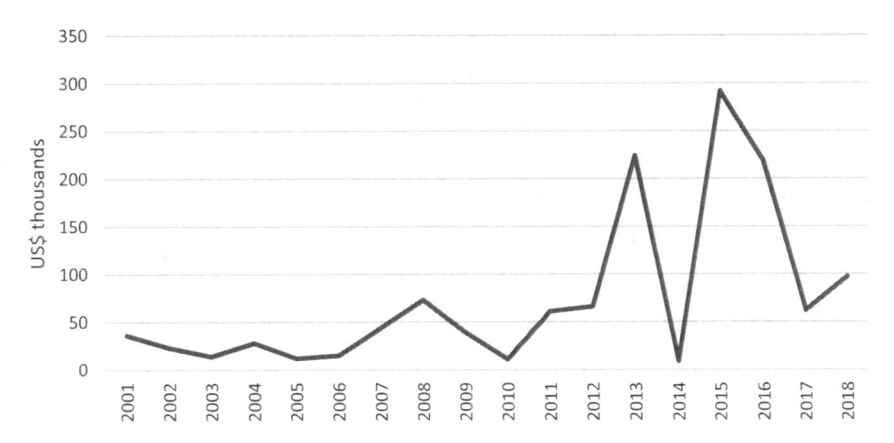

Fig. 11.10 Raw hides, skins, and leather imported by Tanzania, 2001–2018 (US$ thousands). *Source* ITC calculations based on the UNITSD (2020)

The tanning sector also faces the challenge of environmental protection standards. In most cases, effluent from tanneries exceeds the limits established by national and international standards due to a lack of and/or inefficient effluent treatment plants (Scheren et al. 1995). As much as 90% of the world's leather is chrome-tanned, which has a strong impact on water pollution (China et al. 2020a, b; Unango et al. 2019; Bacardit et al. 2014). This pollution is also common in Tanzanian tanneries, which means that many important valleys, lakes, and rivers are polluted by industrial waste (Scheren et al. 1995; China and Ndaro 2016; Mkuula 1993). Most tanneries in Tanzania are old companies that require technology upgrades to comply with international environmental standards (URT 2015; China and Ndaro 2016).

11.5.5   Leather Goods Manufacturing

The shoe industry in Tanzania began to develop in 1958, when Tanganyika Bata Shoe Company Ltd., a subsidiary of Bata Shoe International, opened a factory (International Growth Centre 2012). Furthermore, the Tanzanian government set up a state-owned shoe company Morogoro Shoe Company in 1980. During this period, the Tanzanian government nationalized Bata and changed its name to Bora. Both companies have capacities of 7 million pairs of shoes annually (International Growth Centre 2012).

The footwear industry in Tanzania peaked from 1980 to 1985 in line with the peak of the tanning industry. During this period, light manufacturing in the leather sector aimed to meet the needs of the local market, which was highly protected and inefficient compared to international standards (ITC 2004a). Footwear manufacturing declined during privatization and liberalization in the 1990s caused by limited input supply, lack of investment, severe competition from imports, lack of technology, and lack of skilled manpower (ITC 2016; China and Ndaro 2016). Leather goods manufacturing in Tanzania is in a state of collapse (ITC 2004b) and is mainly dominated by small, and medium-sized enterprises (SMEs) that can produce only 30 pairs of shoes per day due to a lack of capital needed to buy shoe making machines (Giliard and Mtengwa 2017). There are over 40 micro, SMEs and two large enterprises that produce footwear and leather products (ITC 2016).

According to the Ministry of Finance and Planning (2016), this sector is estimated to provide a livelihood for approximately 1,000 people directly. Most footwear companies in Tanzania are artisan-based and produce for the domestic market (Tanzania Export Development Strategy: Leather Sector 2004). The Tanzania footwear industry has a production capacity of 300,000 pairs per annum, while the footwear demand is estimated at 46.8 million pairs per annum (ITC 2016). The gap between production and demand is filled by imports, largely from China, Kenya, the United Arab Emirates, South Africa, and India.

China is the largest exporter of leather articles and footwear to Tanzania. As depicted in Fig. 11.11, leather article imports from China have increased from US$3 million in 2001 to US$12 million in 2018. Imported footwear from China also increased from US$3 million in 2001 to US$29 million in 2018. On the other hand, Tanzania exports raw materials to China that reached a peak of US$5.6 million in 2012. Raw materials originating from Tanzania are processed by China into finished products and exported back to Tanzania, leading to a trade deficit with China.

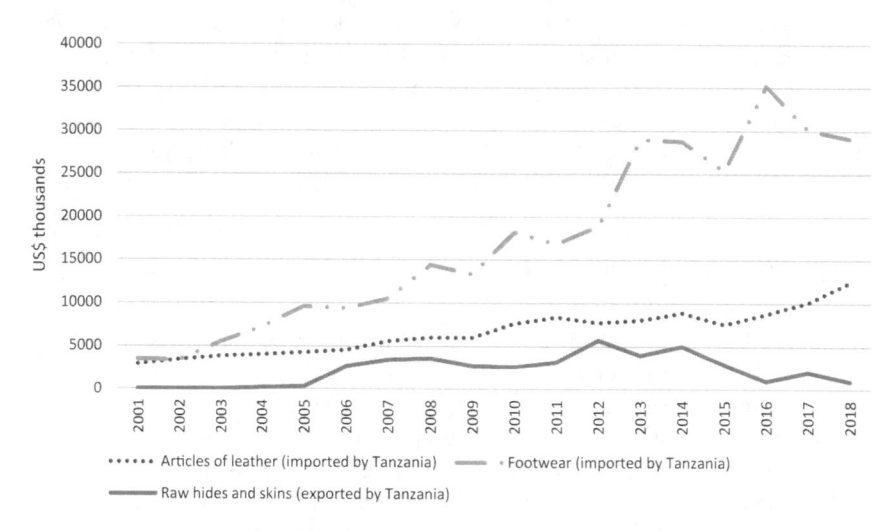

Fig. 11.11 Tanzania and China in leather exports and imports, 2001–2018 (US$ thousands). *Source* ITC calculations based on the UNITSD (2020)

11.6 Trade Policy

The leather industry in Tanzania has experienced a sharp decline since the adoption of privatization policies in the 1980s. Various obstacles are still faced in the upstream sector that means that the supply of quality raw materials is not met, and the downstream sector of the industry is not developed. Currently, Tanzania's leather industry is dependent on the exportation of raw hides and skins. Problems worsened when the light manufacturing leather industry suffered a setback, while the imports of inexpensive leather goods flooded the local market (Tairo 2019).

The Tanzanian government implemented various policies to expand the leather sector, one of which was through the application of an export levy for raw hides and skins that began in 2003. The Tanzanian government implemented a levy of 20% of the free on-board value of exports in 2003. The Levy was increased to 40% in 2007 triggered an increase in hides and raw skins smuggling to neighbouring countries, especially Kenya and Uganda. In 2012, the export levy was increased to 90% of the free on-board value (Table 11.4). The Tanzanian government also implemented a 10% levy on the free on-board price of wet- blue in June 2015.

The implementation of the export levy on raw hides and skins exports has two key objectives. First, the levy reduces the export of raw hides and skins, thus encouraging local manufacturing. Second, the funds obtained from the application of the levy (Livestock Development Fund—LDF) are used to develop the leather industry value chain through the livestock sector, tanning industry, footwear, and leather products industry, as well as vocational training (URT 2015).

No research has investigated the impact of the export levy on decreasing the export of raw hides and skins. Table 11.5 presents the collection, exports, and gap between collection and exports of cattle, goat, and sheep skins from 2003 to 2018. If the export levy has an impact on decreasing the export of raw hide and skins, the gap between collection and export will be higher after the levy has been implemented, assuming that hides and skins are used for local industry. As Table 11.5 illustrates, the implementation of an export levy of 20% in 2003 and 40% in 2007 does not seem to have had an impact on the gap between collections and exports of raw materials in 2003, 2004, 2007, and 2008. The gap between collection and export decreased in 2003 from 1.1 million cattle skins in 2003 to 991 thousand in 2004. However, this gap increased in 2012 and 2013, with an increase from 1 million in 2012 to 1.2 million cattle skins in 2013 and 1.3 million in 2012 to 3.7 million goat and sheep skins in 2013. This increase was likely due to the adoption of an export levy of 90% in 2012.

Table 11.4 Export levy on raw hides, skins, and wet-blue

	2003	2007	2012	2015
Raw hides and skins	20%	40%	90%	
Wet-blue				10%

Source ITC (2016)

Table 11.5 The collection and exports of cattle, goat, and sheep skins in Tanzania, 2003–2018

Year	Cattle skins			Goat and sheep skins		
	Collection	Export	Collection—Export	Collection	Export	Collection—Export
2003	2,437,100	1,300,000	1,137,100	6,437,790	900,000	5,537,790
2004	2,765,120	1,774,000	991,120	4,998,234	1,919,000	3,079,234
2005	1,937,215	1,400,000	537,215	2,789,230	1,797,155	992,075
2006	1,975,721	1,363,721	612,000	2,987,105	2,078,510	908,595
2007	2,168,000	1,700,000	468,000	5,995,305	1,980,530	4,014,775
2008	2,543,280	2,300,000	243,280	3,576,230	2,700,000	876,230
2009	1,223,668	982,668	241,000	6,983,998	3,469,936	3,514,062
2010	2,456,540	739,315	1,717,225	3,678,294	2,088,582	1,589,712
2011	2,378,235	1,719,506	658,729	4,978,000	1,561,000	3,417,000
2012	3,022,400	2,000,000	1,022,400	4,928,000	3,600,000	1,328,000
2013	2,567,340	1,269,060	1,298,280	6,325,525	2,582,525	3,743,000
2014	2,263,472	1,263,472	1,000,000	3,567,321	2,716,436	850,885
2015	2,543,914	1,388,139	1,155,775	5,983,210	1,020,000	4,963,210
2016	2,654,400	1,575,139	1,079,261	6,132,212	1,124,000	5,008,212
2017	2,790,561	1,215,030	1,575,531	6,643,998	928,115	5,715,883
2018	2,896,796	828,079	2,068,717	7,022,908	1,009,101	6,013,807

Source Tanzania's Economic Survey (2018)

Overall, the implementation of the export levy has still not obtained the expected results. The leather industry in Tanzania is still experiencing many problems, both upstream and downstream. The implementation of the export levy also causes the smuggling of hides and skins, mainly to countries in the region such as Kenya and Uganda. As a result, the domestic industry has suffered from a shortage of raw hides and skins, which results in a lack of investor interest in investment in the leather industry (World Footwear 2018).

11.7 Regional and International Comparisons

This section compares export performance and policies to support the leather industry in Tanzania with other countries at regional and international levels, namely China, India, Tunisia, Ethiopia, and Kenya. These countries have been selected because they are developing countries, have large livestock production, and have more advanced leather industries than Tanzania.

The five chosen countries have large livestock production with the potential to supply raw hides and skins. China and India are the largest livestock producers in the world after Brazil (FAO 2020). China produced 63 million cattle, 138 million goats, and 164 million sheep in 2018, whereas India produced 184 million cattle, 132 million goats, and 61 million sheep. In Africa, East Africa is a major livestock producer with Ethiopia and Tanzania as the first and second-largest producers. Ethiopia produced 62 million cattle, 33 million goats, and 31 million sheep in 2018, whereas Tanzania produced 27 million cattle, 18 million goats, and 7 million sheep.

China has the most impressive performance in leather and leather products exports compared to the other five countries (Table 11.6). This country ranked first in the world for exports of leather articles and footwear with a value of US$33.9 billion and US$10.7 billion in 2019, respectively. In exports of raw hides and skins, this country ranked sixth, at US$1.6 billion. India ranked eighth for exports of articles of leather and leather shoes, at US$2.5 billion and US$1.8 billion, respectively. India exported US$544 million of raw hides and skins in 2019, allowing it to rank 11th. In Africa, Tunisia has the most impressive export performance of finished leather products compared to the other three countries. Tunisia ranks 27th and 39th for exports of leather shoes and articles, respectively.

Figure 11.12 presents the share of leather exports to total exports in six countries. Leather exports in China and Tunisia make the most significant contribution to total

Table 11.6 Exports of leather and leather products in 2019

Country	Export value (US$ million)	Share of world exports (%)	Country rank
Raw hides, skins, and leather			
Tanzania	11.61	0.0591	76
China	1,614.46	8.2197	6
India	554.8	2.8247	11
Tunisia	14.66	0.0746	70
Ethiopia	71.08	0.3619	43
Kenya	30.40	0.1548	58
Leather articles			
Tanzania	0.14	0.0002	137
China	33,993.42	38.3054	1
India	2,513.32	2.8321	8
Tunisia	166.75	0.1879	39
Ethiopia	14.52	0.0164	71
Kenya	2.21	0.0025	91
Footwear, leather upper			
Tanzania	0.06	0.0001	132
China	10,719.87	19.1080	1
India	1,886.43	3.3625	8
Tunisia	357.42	0.6371	27
Ethiopia	30.62	0.0546	56
Kenya	1.84	0.0033	84

Source ITC calculation based on the UNITSD (2020)

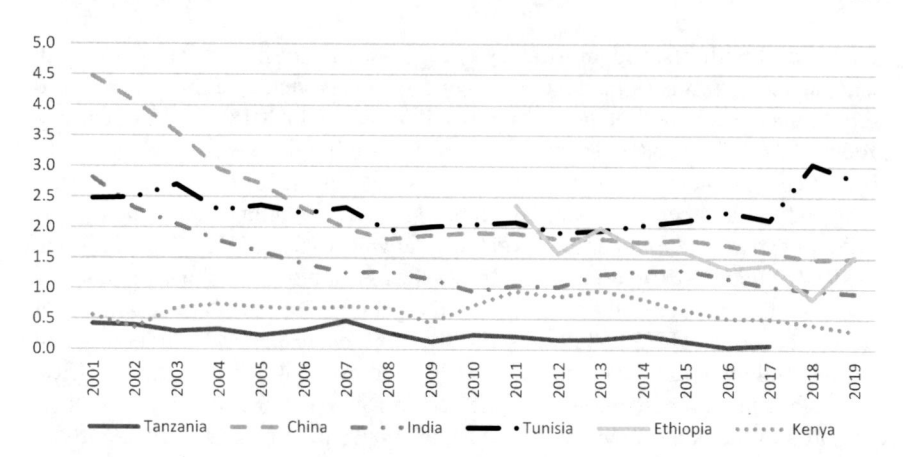

Fig. 11.12 Raw hides and skins, leather articles, and footwear (leather upper) exports, 2001–2019 (% of total exports). *Source* Calculations by the author based on International Trade Centre (ITC) and World Development Indicators (WDI) (2020)

exports. The share of leather exports in China reached 4.48% of total exports in 2001 and then saw a drop to 1.50% in 2019. In Tunisia, leather exports contributed to 2.48% of total exports in 2001, reached a peak of 3.04% of total exports in 2018, and fell to 2.79% of total exports in 2019. In Ethiopia, leather exports fluctuated from 2011 to 2019, falling from 2.37% in 2011 to 1.53% of total exports in 2019. Leather exports in India decreased sharply from 2.81% in 2001 to 0.92% of total exports in 2019. Tanzania and Kenya had a relatively similar share in leather exports in 2001, at 0.42% and 0.56% of total exports, respectively. However, in subsequent years, Kenya had a more impressive performance than Tanzania, with a peak of 0.97% of total exports in 2003, then experiencing a drop to 0.30% in 2019. The share of leather exports in Tanzania reached a peak of 0.46% of total exports in 2007, then experienced a downward trend to 0.08% of total exports in 2017.

Figure 11.13 presents the share of leather exports to GDP in six countries. The leather industry in Tunisia has the largest share of the GDP compared to the other five countries at 1.06% of GDP in 2001, peaking at 1.49% of the GDP in 2018 and then falling to 1.39% of the GDP in 2019. China ranks second with a share of 0.96% of the GDP in 2003 and then experienced a drop to 0.28% of the GDP in 2019. The share of leather exports in Ethiopia experienced a drop and fluctuations from 0.88% of the GDP in 2001 to 0.12% of the GDP in 2019. In India, the share of leather exports of the GDP fell slightly from 0.35% of GDP in 2001 to 0.17% of the GDP in 2019. In Kenya, the share of leather exports fluctuated between 0.09 and 0.21% of the GDP during 2001–2019. The share of leather exports in Tanzania stagnated from 0.06% of the GDP in 2001, peaked at 0.09% of the GDP in 2007, and decreased to 0.04% of the GDP in 2019.

Tunisia and China have the highest value chain performance compared to the other four countries. Finished products dominated leather exports in Tunisia and China at 97% and 96% of total leather exports in 2019 (Fig. 11.14). The leather industry in

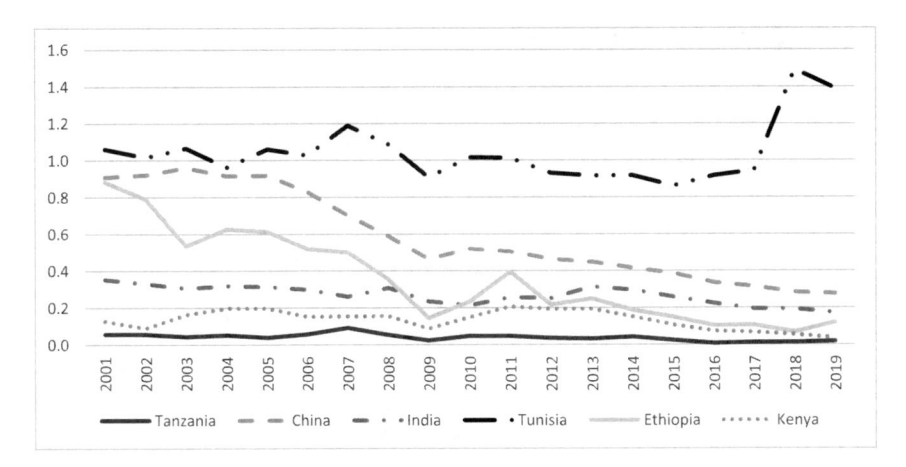

Fig. 11.13 Raw hides and skins, leather articles, and footwear (leather upper) exports, 2001–2019 (% of total GDP). *Source* Calculations by the author based on International Trade Centre (ITC) and World Development Indicators (WDI) (2020)

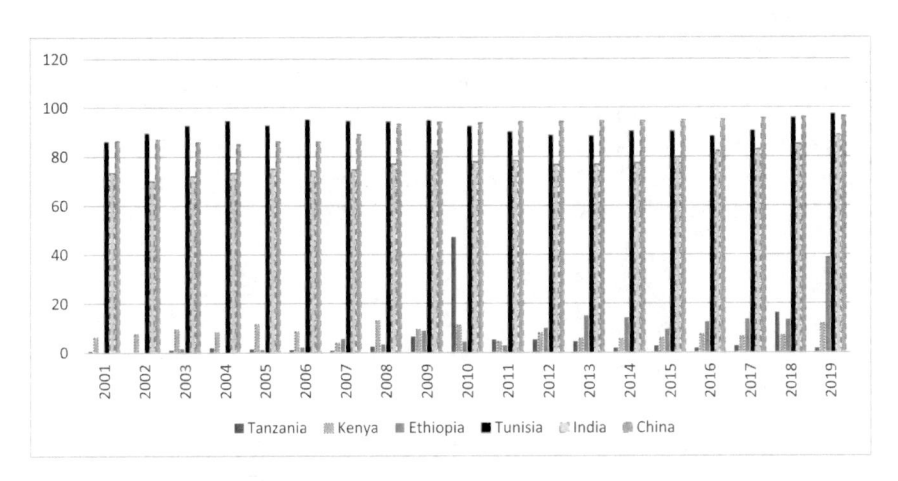

Fig. 11.14 Share of leather articles and footwear in total exports, 2001–2019 (%). *Source* ITC calculation based on the UNITSD (2020)

India has also moved to the finished industry, indicated by the share of exports of leather articles and footwear at 88% of total leather exports in 2019, up from 69% of total exports in 2002. Finished leather products in Ethiopia are still below the three countries, though the country has experienced a rapid increase from 0.04% of total leather exports in 2002 to 38% in 2019. A similar trend occurred in Kenya, which shares a border with Tanzania. Finished product exports almost doubled from 6.2% of total leather exports in 2001 to 11.74% in 2019.

11.7.1 Regional Comparisons

This section analyses the leather industry status and policies to support the leather industry in Tunisia, Ethiopia, and Kenya.

11.7.1.1 Tunisia

Tunisia does not have a large livestock production compared to the other three African countries, leading to a low rank in raw hide and skin exports in 2019. The country's production of raw hides and skins is also low compared to the other three countries in Africa. Tunisia produced 244,145 heads of cattle hide, 751,733 heads of goat skin, and 3.5 million head of skin sheep in 2018. However, Tunisia is able to maximize livestock production to support the leather industry, as indicated by the export of finished leather products from this country, which reached US$524 million or 97% of total exports from the leather sector in 2019 (Fig. 11.15).

Skilled labour at a reasonable price plays an important role in supporting the improvement of the value chain in the Tunisian leather industry. This factor cannot be separated from the existence of a vocational training system consisting of 15 institutions (FIPA-Tunisia 2020). Furthermore, the Tunisian government has provided a specific upgrading programme to 275 leather and footwear companies. The Tunisian Foreign Investment Promotion Agency (2020) claims that this programme has been able to double the productivity and exports of the companies involved. In addition, the Tunisian government has also established the National Centre of

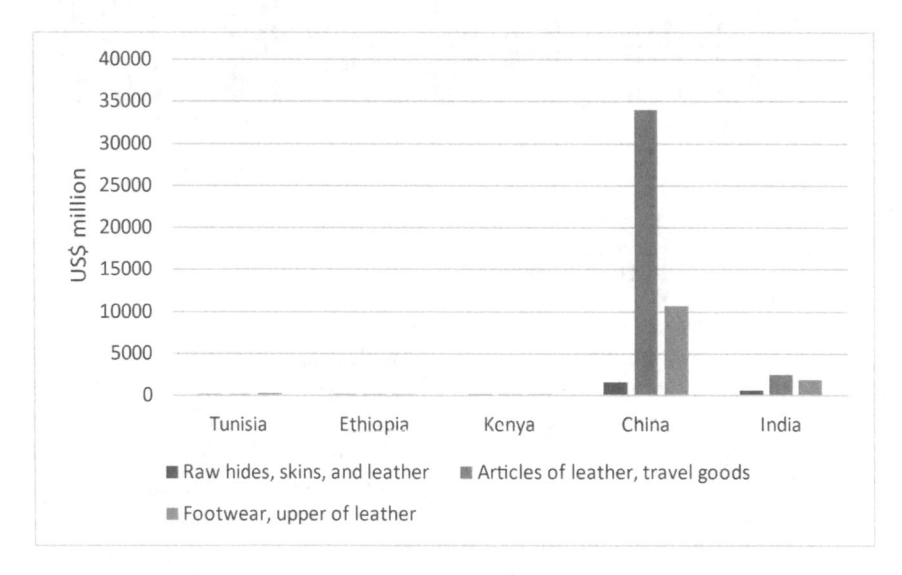

Fig. 11.15 Export of leather in five countries, 2019 (US$ millions). *Source* ITC calculation based on the UNITSD (2020)

Leather and Footwear (CNCC), which provides services to support the leather industry, including technical assistance and coaching, analysis, testing, and calibration, training, research, and development, industrial promotion, and information and communication (FIPA-Tunisia 2020).

11.7.1.2 Ethiopia

According to FAO (2020), Ethiopia produced the largest livestock in Africa with 57 million cattle, 30 million sheep, and 23 million goats in 2019. Large-scale livestock production has the potential to supply raw materials for the leather industry. In 2018, Ethiopia produced 3.7 million hides, 10 million goat skins, and 10.4 million sheep skins. The annual collection rate of hides and skins in Ethiopia is also high, reaching 10% for cattle, 33% for sheep, and 38% for goats (Alubel Abtew 2015: 231).

The performance of the finished leather industry in Ethiopia is still far behind those of China, India, and Tunisia, though it is adequate compared to its peers in Africa. Ethiopia was in the fourth position in the export of leather articles and leather footwear in the Africa region, with export values of US$14 million and US$31 million, respectively, in 2019 (Fig. 11.15). However, Ethiopia has not finished climbing the value-added chain and still exported raw hides and skins at US$69 million in 2019.

The leather industry in Ethiopia has experienced the challenges seen by Tanzania, including poor livestock management, which results in poor-quality raw material supply, low utilization of industry capacity, and a lack of skills and technology. Ethiopia has also implemented a policy to ban exports of raw hides and skins since 1986, though this policy has not been able to grow leather manufacturing in the country (Alubel Abtew 2015: 232). This ban increased illegal exports to countries that share a border with Ethiopia (Alubel Abtew 2015: 232).

However, the leather industry in Ethiopia has a more impressive performance than in Tanzania. Munchie (2000) states that the adoption of new technology is one of the key factors, which includes modernization, technology improvement, organisational change, management training and upgrading, quality control, and standards for product improvement. Brautigam et al. (2013) note that the adoption of new technology in the leather industry in Ethiopia cannot be separated from the policy to suspend the ban on foreign direct investment (FDI) across tanneries. This research has found evidence of technology transfer from FDI. European firms in Ethiopia hire technology experts from China, whereas local tanneries invite technology experts from India. This difference has ultimately improved the technology in tanneries. However, the adoption of this technology is limited to large companies. Small tanneries have a limited capacity to adopt new technology, resulting in the inability to produce high-quality leather (Brautigam et al. 2013: 3). Furthermore, the liberalization policy in the 1990s encouraged the growth of the leather industry in Ethiopia (Alubel Abtew 2015: 232).

11.7.1.3 Kenya

Kenya also has a large livestock production that has the potential to supply raw materials for the leather industry. Kenya produced 2.7 million hides, 4.8 million goat skins, and 2.8 million sheep skins in 2018. However, this number of hides and skins has not yet made a significant contribution to the Kenyan economy.

Kenya has the worst performance in both hide and skins and finished product exports compared to the other countries under examination. Kenya ranks sixth in Africa for the exportation of raw hides and skins, with a total export value of US$42 million in 2019 (Fig. 11.15). In terms of the export of articles of leather and leather shoes, Kenya ranks seventh and 14th among African countries with an export value of US$3 million and US$1 million, respectively, in 2018. However, Kenya's export performance is of a higher level than that of Tanzania.

The difference in performance between the countries may be due to the Kenyan government's support of this industry via the establishment of two research institutes, namely the Kenya Industrial Research and Development Institute (KIRDI) and Training and Production Centre for Shoe Industry (TPCSI) (KIRDI 2020; TPCSI 2020). The government is also establishing a special economic zone, the Ngoxi Kenya Leather Park at Kinanie, Machakos County, with an investment value of US$62 million (ITC 2018: 25). The leather park is expected to attract FDI in leather. Other policies such as a training centre and subsidies for workers also play an important role in building this industry (ITC 2018).

11.7.2 International Comparisons

Further to the regional comparison, this section discusses the status of the leather industry in China and India, and policies and incentives to promote the leather industry.

11.7.2.1 China

Livestock production in China is the third largest in the world after Brazil and India, countries that play a major role in supplying raw materials to the leather industry. In 2018, China produced 39.6 million head/slaughtered cattle hides, 153 million head/slaughtered goat skins, and 141 million head/slaughtered sheep skins. China has been able to utilize this large-scale livestock production to support the leather industry. China has overtaken Italy's position as the largest leather and leather product exporter in the world since 2000 (Sankar 2006). In addition, finished products dominated leather exports at US$44 billion (96%) of total leather exports in 2019 (Fig. 11.15).

Sankar (2006) states that the leather industry in China has developed rapidly since economic reforms in the 1970s linked to investment from Taiwan, financial support from Hong Kong, support from the Chinese government, and logistics and trade infrastructure. In the 1980s, Taiwan experienced a significant surge in labour costs, which caused the country to shift leather manufacturing production to China (Sankar 2006). The Chinese government facilitated this shift by providing tax incentives for joint ventures between Chinese and Taiwanese companies, such as two-year tax exemptions, a 50% discount in income tax in the third year, and ease of licensing (Sankar 2006). These incentives increased the investment value from Taiwan to 80% of the total investment in the footwear sector in the 1990s (Sankar 2006: 2474). The local government also plays an important role in providing incentives for investment in leather, for example by the Xinji municipality in the development of the Xinji Fur and Leather Trade Centre (FLTC) (Bleacher and Shue 2001). Xinji officials provided incentives as priority consumers in local banks for companies that were committed to building real estates in FLTC. These companies may borrow up to 70% of their planned building costs. In addition, the officials also provide a tax reduction and 5 year tax holiday on real estate tax.

11.7.2.2   India

The leather sector in India is one of the oldest and fast-growing industries. According to the Indian Council for Leather Export (2021), the leather industry plays an important role in India's economy, with an export value of US$5.07 billion in 2019–2020, providing jobs for 4.42 million people, particularly women. The leather value-added industry is also well developed in India. India is the second-largest footwear producer in the world after China, with a total production of 2.60 billion pairs in 2019 (Indian Council for Leather Export 2021). The country is also the second-largest exporter of leather garments, accounting for 8.46% of India's total leather exports in 2018–2019 (Indian Council for Leather Export 2021).

India has a number of advantages that have allowed it to develop the leather industry. As the second-largest livestock producer in the world after Brazil, this country has a strong supply of raw materials. In 2018, India produced 9.2 million hides, 50.4 million goat skins, and 19.1 million sheep skins. In addition, India also has a large number of tanneries, with an annual capacity of 2.5 billion sq.ft. of leathers, accounting for 13% of world leather production (Indian Council for Leather Export 2021). The leather industry is also supported by trained manpower and adequate research and development (ibid).

India has been able to take advantage of the large livestock production to develop a leather industry. India exported US$554 million raw hides and skins, US$2.5 billion articles of leather, and US$1.8 million of leather shoes in 2019. Indian leather exports are dominated by finished products, which represent 96% of total leather exports in 2019 (Fig. 11.15).

The ban on raw hide and skin exports is one of the important policies, accompanied by a policy to develop the finished leather industry divided into two phases (Muchie 2000). In the first phase (1973–1983), India increased its production capacity to convert raw materials into value-added products. In the second phase (1984–1993),

India focused on export promotion through the formation of the Council for Leather Exports (CLE), a non-profit company under the Ministry of Commerce. CLE facilitates Indian leather exporters to open new markets and expand existing markets (Muchie, 2000).

Muchie (2000) states that the policy that determined the leather industry as an export thrust sector also plays an important role in climbing the value chain. This determination allowed the leather industry to receive government assistance in meeting the needs of the labour force and bringing in much-needed foreign exchange. In addition, the role of technology is a key factor in leather industry development. The Indian government established the Central Leather Research Institute (CLRI) to support increasing the value, quality, and environmental attractiveness of this industry. This institution is also supported by a strong annual budget of US$2.3 million, with solid human resources, including 639 scientists and technologists (Muchie 2000). The Indian government has also implemented a strategy to encourage small-medium enterprises via the licensing and reservations of products (Sankar 2006). In 2002, as many as 80% or more of leather shoes were from small-scale producers (Sankar 2006).

11.8 Conclusion

The objective of this Chapter is to investigate the leather value chain in Tanzania. As noted in the Introduction section, Tanzania has a large livestock production that potentially supplies inexpensive hide and skins to the leather industry. However, the leather industry in Tanzania is still underutilized. Therefore, the country should develop and improve livestock production, slaughtering facilities, hide and skin collection, tanning facilities, and leather manufacturing in order to move up the value chain. Particular attention should be paid to the production of finished products since Tanzania does not have adequate leather manufacturing.

This report identified the best practice for leather industry development policies that allow China, India, Tunisia, Ethiopia, and Kenya to climb the leather value-added chain. Table 11.7 summarizes the key elements of the best practices in these five countries and presents the common framework underlying policies to strengthen leather industry performance. The policies include more efficient supporting facilities such as tax incentives, leather research institutes, grading institutions, innovation, and dedicated training facilities. Tanzania lacks policies in the five areas, i.e. special economic zone, leather research institutes, grading institutions, innovation, and training facilities.

The Tanzanian government may focus on adopting policies to develop a leather research institute, that has a role in grading institutions, innovation, and training facilities. China Leather Institute can be an excellent example of how a research institute becomes an epicentre of the leather industry research and development, including a standardization centre, quality supervision, and technology innovation (China Leather Institute 2022). These efforts may be a vital element of Tanzania's

Table 11.7 Quantitative and qualitative international comparison

	Tanzania	China	India	Tunisia	Ethiopia	Kenya
Share of leather exports in total exports in 2019 (%)	0.08 (2017)	1.50	0.92	2.79	1.53	0.30
Share of leather exports in GDP in 2019 (%)	0.02	0.28	0.17	1.39	0.12	0.04
Share of processed leather in exports in 2019 (%)	1.66	96.52	88.80	97.28	38.84	11.74
Special economic zone	x	✓	✓	✓	✓	Ngoxi Kenya Leather Park
Tax incentives	✓	✓	✓	✓	✓	✓
Leather Research Institute	x	*China Leather & Footwear Industrial Research Institute*	Central Leather Research Institute (CSIR)	National Centre for Leather and Footwear	Leather Industry Development Institute (LIDI)	*Kenya* Industrial *Research* and Development *Institute* (KIRDI) Training and Production Centre for Shoe Industry (TPCSI)
Grading institution	x	✓	✓	✓	✓	✓
Innovation	x	✓	✓	✓	✓	✓
Training facilities	x	✓	✓	✓	✓	✓

Source Multiple sources (2020)

policies for the leather industry aimed at strengthening capacity for the effective implementation of export competitiveness and diversification.

References

Alubel Abtew M (2015) Revealed comparative advantage of Ethiopian leather industry with selected African Economies. Int J Bus Econ Res 4(5):229. https://doi.org/10.11648/j.ijber.20150405.11

Bacardit A et al (2014) Evaluation of a new environment friendly tanning process. J Clean Prod. Elsevier Ltd., 65, pp 568–573. https://doi.org/10.1016/j.jclepro.2013.09.052

Blecher M, Shue V (2001) Into leather: state-led development and the private sector in Xinji. China Q 166:368–393. https://doi.org/10.1017/S0009443901000183

Brautigam, D., McMillan, M. and Tang, X. (2013) The role of foreign investment in Ethiopia leather value chain, Center for Economic Policy Research

Brautigam D, Weis T, Tang X (2018) Latent advantage, complex challenges: Industrial policy and Chinese linkages in Ethiopia's leather sector. China Economic Review. PEDL—Private Enterprise Development in Low-Income Countries—CEPR/DFID joint research initiative, 48, pp 158–169. https://doi.org/10.1016/j.chieco.2016.06.006

China CR, Hilonga A, Nyandoro SS, Schroepfer M, Kanth SV, Meyer M, Njau NK (2020a) Suitability of selected tannins traditionally used in leather making in Tanzania. J Clean Prod 251:119687. https://doi.org/10.1016/j.jclepro.2019.119687

China CR, Maguta MM, Nyandoro SS, Hilonga A, Kanth SV, Njau KN (2020b) Alternative tanning technologies and their suitability in curbing environmental pollution from the leather industry: a comprehensive review. Chemosphere 254:126804. https://doi.org/10.1016/j.chemosphere.2020b

China CR, Ndaro MS (2016) A review on Tanzanian leather value chain status. African J Sci Res 5(4):55–60. Available at: https://www.researchgate.net/publication/316240479_A_review_on_Ttanzanian_leather_value_chain_status

China Leather Institute (2022) Introduction of the Institute. [online] Available at: https://www.clf.cn/3067.html. Accessed 21 Feb 2022

Food and Agriculture Organisation of the United Nations (2020) FAOSTAT. [online] Available at: https://www.fao.org/faostat/en/#home. Accessed 20 July 2020

FIPA-Tunisia (n.d) Leather and Footwear Industry: A Leading and Competitive Sector. [online] Available at: <http://www.investintunisia.tn/En/strengths-of-the-sector_128_287> [Accessed 15 August 2022]

Indian Council for Leather Export (2021) Industry at a glance—council for leather exports. [online] Leatherindia.org. Available at: https://www.leatherindia.org/industry-at-a-glance/. Accessed 26 Nov 2021

International Growth Centre (2012) An enterprise map of Tanzania. Available at: https://www.theigc.org/wp-content/uploads/2012/12/An-Enterprise-Map-of-Tanzania-English.pdf

International Trade Center (2016) United republic of Tanzania leather sector development strategy 2016–2020. Popul Policy Compendium. https://doi.org/10.1007/978-1-349-07782-3_161

International Trade Centre (2004a) Tanzania export development strategy: Leather Sector

International Trade Centre (2004b) Trade map—list of supplying markets for a product imported by Tanzania, United Republic Of. [online] Trademap.org. Available at: https://www.trademap.org/Country_SelProductCountry_TS.aspx?nvpm=1%7c834%7c%7c%7c%7c%7c42%7c%7c%7c%7c2%7c1%7c1%7c1%7c2%7c1%7c2%7c1%7c1%7c1. Accessed 22 June 2020

International Trade Centre (2018) Leather value chain: leather value chain investment profile: Tanzania. Available at: https://www.allpi.int/courses-and-publications/reports/manuals/leather-manual

International Trade Centre (2020) International trade in goods—exports 2001–2019. [online] Available at: https://www.intracen.org/itc/market-info-tools/statistics-export-country-product/. Accessed 20 July 2020

Jabbar MA, Kiruthu S, Gebremedhin B, Ehui SK (2002) Essential actions to meet quality requirements of hides, skins and semi-processed leather from Africa (No. 610–2016–40461)

Kenya Leather Development Council (2020) TPCSI. [online] Available at: https://www.leatherco uncil.go.ke/tpcsi/. Accessed 19 Oct 2020

Kilimo Trust (2009) Livestock Product Value Chains in East Africa; a Scoping and Preliminary Mapping Study. Available at: https://www.kilimotrust.org/documents/working%20papers/1%20Livestock%20Product%20Value%20Chains%20in%20East%20Africa.pdf

Kenya Industrial Research And Development Institute (KIRDI) (2020) Kenya Industrial Research And Development Institute. [online] Kirdi.business.site. Available at: https://www.kirdi.business.site. Accessed 19 Octr 2020

Lwesya F (2018) Determinants of Leather and leather products exports in Tanzania. Acad J Econ Stud 4(1):133–140

Ministry of Finance and Planning (2016) National five year development plan 2016/2017–2020/2021: Nurturing industrialization for economic transformation and human development

Ministry of Livestock and Fisheries (2019) National Fisheries and Aquaculture Research Agenda (2020–2025). Available at: <https://www.mifugouvuvi.go.tz/uploads/publications/en1586943 753-RESEARCH%20AGENDA%202020%20-%202025%20(1).pdf. Accessed 22 June 2020

Mkuula S (1993) Pollution of wetlands in Tanzania. Wetlands of Tanzania, pp 85–93.

Muchie M (2000) Leather processing in Ethiopia and Kenya: lessons from India. Technol Soc 22(4):537–555. https://doi.org/10.1016/S0160-791X(00)00027-0

Mwangosi IL (2014) Analysis of leather value chain in Tanzania: the case of Mwanza City (Doctoral dissertation, The Open University of Tanzania).

Sankar U (2006) Trade liberalisation and environmental protection responses of leather industry in Brazil, China and India. Econ Politic Weekly 41(24):2470–2477. Available at: http://www.jstor.org/stable/4418354

Scheren PA, Bosboom JC, Njau KK, Lemmens AM (1995) Assessment of water pollution in the catchment area of Lake Victoria, Tanzania. J East African Res Dev 129–143

Tairo, A (2019) Italian firms to invest over $24m in Tanzania's leather sector. The East African. Retrieved from

Unango FJ, Duraisamy R, Ramasamy KM (2019) A review of eco-friendly preservative and biotannin materials using powdered barks of local plants for the processing of goatskin. IRJSE 1:13–20. https://doi.org/10.46378/irjst.2019.010103

URT (2017) Tanzania Livestock Sector Analysis 2016/2017–2031/2032. Available at: https://www.mifugouvuvi.go.tz/uploads/projects/1553602287-LIVESTOCK%20SECTOR%20ANALYSIS.pdf

URT (2015) Leather Sector Development Strategy 2016–2020. The International Trade Centre (ITC). Available at: http://unossc1.undp.org/sscexpo/content/ssc/library/solutions/partners/expo/2016/GSSD%20Expo%20Dubai%202016%20PPT/Day%202_November%201/SF%204_Room%20D_ITC/Value%20chain%20roadmaps/Tanzania/Tanzania%20Leather%20Sector%20Development%20Strategy.pdf

World Bank (2020) World Development Indicators|Databank. [online] Available at: https://www.databank.worldbank.org/source/world-development-indicators. Accessed 20 July 2020

World Footwear (2018) Tanzania: leather exports impacted by levy. Available at : https://www.worldfootwear.com/news/tanzania-leather-exports-impacted-by-levy/3300.html

FIPA-Tunisia (2020)

Chapter 12
Determinants of Horticultural Export and Welfare Impact of Smallholder Farmers: Evidence from Common Beans (*Phaseolus Vulgaris L*) Farming in Arusha Tanzania

Eliaza Mkuna

Author is thankful to Peter van Bergeijk and Binyam Afewerk Demena of Erasmus University, International Institute of Social Studies for technical guidance in carrying out the research work. The study was financially supported by Research on Poverty Alleviation (REPOA), the African Caribbean and Pacific Group of States (ACP Group) of this project, grant number FED/2019/408-112

Abstract Recent studies on horticulture production and export promotion have provided significant contributions to the overview of the production, marketing, and business-related aspects. However, the empirical relationship between horticulture export and its contribution to small-scale farmer's welfare has been somewhat neglected in the literature, despite its role in the development process being long recognized. Therefore, using quantitative analytical methods this study assessed the impact of horticulture export promotion on farmers' welfare in Arusha, Tanzania. The results of this study show that common beans farmers in Tanzania are aware of the significant role of exporting their crop rather than trading locally. Results further indicate that different socio-economic, production, and institutional factors influence both the decision and extent of farmers to export common beans. Specifically, it was observed that there is a positive impact of common beans export on farmers' consumption expenditure. The study recommends that policy attention needs to shift from supporting and regulating particular trade policies only but rather should focus on how farmers will be trained and utilize the available opportunity of the common beans export market.

Keywords Horticultural crops · Exportation · Welfare · Tanzania

E. Mkuna (✉)
Department of Economics, Faculty of Social Sciences, Mzumbe University, Morogoro, Tanzania
e-mail: ejmkuna@mzumbe.ac.tz; eliazamkuna@hotmail.com

12.1 Introduction

Economic growth is the leading goal of policymakers worldwide and is a primary aim of developing countries and a recurrent theme in the trade and development literature is the role of exports in this process (SanjuánLópez and Dawson 2010; Hernandez 2011). It is conventional wisdom among policymakers and academics that export is a key factor in promoting economic growth in developing countries (Myovella et al. 2015). However, one concern is that many developing countries are heavily dependent on primary commodity exports to developed countries (Alam and Myovella 2016). Agricultural exports therefore can play an important role in economic growth, and export-led growth from agriculture may represent optimal resource allocation for those countries that have a comparative advantage in agricultural production, particularly in Sub-Saharan African (SSA) countries. Tanzania is a well-documented example (SanjuánLópez and Dawson 2010; Lwesya 2018; Kanyangemu and Kundu 2019).

Agriculture, including horticulture, is a mainstay of development in Tanzania (Mallya 2019; Gupta 2020). The Horticulture industry in Tanzania is the fastest growing sub-sector within the agricultural sector with an annual average growth of about 9–12% per annum (Match-Maker 2017; Juma et al. 2019). This record of growth is more than double the overall annual growth rate of the agricultural sector. In 2015/2016, horticulture contributed 38% of the foreign income earned from the agriculture sector. The export value in 2015 reached US $ 545 million, compared to US $ 64 million in 2005. The Horticulture sub-sector employs about 2.5 million people, which makes the industry a major employer within the agricultural sector (Match-Maker 2017).

The horticulture industry is dominated by small-scale farmers with less than two hectares, especially in vegetable production whereby they account for about 70% of vegetable producers. Majority of these small-scale farmers are not connected to regional and international markets and therefore have limited chances to conduct export business themselves (Match-Maker 2017). Tanzania is among the world top 20 producers of fresh vegetables, although it has an insignificant position in the export of vegetables, mainly due to the current business arrangements whereby Tanzanian exporting companies are subsidiaries of large aggregation companies often based in Kenya, and these kinds of exports are not fully captured in Tanzania data (Match-Maker 2017). The horticulture sector is dominated by varieties of vegetables which include Asian vegetables, baby corn, baby marrow, beetroots, beans, cabbage, carrots and baby carrots, cauliflower, eggplant, kale, leeks, onions and shallots, okra, peas, potatoes, spinach, tomatoes, and common beans.

The common bean (*Phaseolus vulgaris L.*) is one of the principal food and cash crop legumes grown in the tropical world and most of the production takes place in developing countries (Hillocks et al. 2006). Common or French beans are by far the most important pulse crop both as a source of dietary protein and calories and as a source of farm income (Mywish et al. 2019; Mutungi et al. 2020). The crop is the most important legume in Tanzania. At least 34% of smallholder rural households cultivate the beans for its green leaves, green pods, and dry beans, and 16–41% sell part of the harvest (Stahley et al. 2019; Mutungi et al. 2019).

Studies show that Tanzania has not exploited much of its enormous export potential of horticultural produce and yet it is among the 20 biggest producers of horticultural crops in the world but does not feature among the 20 biggest exporters (Mayala and Bamanyisa 2018; Gramzow et al. 2018). Also, various challenges facing the horticultural sector have been documented that limit or inhibit export of horticulture products both on the demand and supply side (Mashindano et al. 2013). Thus, development of the horticultural sector in Tanzania, particularly promotion of its export, is needed and will offer many opportunities for investors, technology suppliers, and knowledge institutes, but at the same time challenges related to the investment climate in Tanzania will have to be addressed.

12.1.1 Problem Statement and Initial Research Questions

The findings discussed above imply a clear and undesirable mismatch between vegetable production in Tanzania and official exports from the country (Mashindano et al. 2013; Match-Maker 2017). As a consequence, the country is losing significant benefits in terms of lost employment opportunities and lost incomes. In addition, Tanzania does not seem to utilize her comparative advantage in the production of agro-based products (Mashindano et al. 2013).

Analyzing the horticulture sub-export sector's performance, with a specific focus on the determinants of horticultural exports, has attracted the interest of policymakers and scholars, particularly in developing countries (Dube et al. 2018). This is because the export of horticultural items allows many developing nations to diversify their export base, which is currently dominated by tea, coffee, and cocoa exports. If successful, developing countries will be less reliant on a small number of core products. However, recent studies on the horticulture production and export promotion have focused on various issues. One factor is the development of a horticulture extension support system for small holder farmers also with a view on influencing youth involvement in Horticulture Agribusiness in Tanzania. Another factor is the role of seed companies on horticultural production, perception of chemical usage in horticulture production, horticulture value chain, and reduction of post-harvest losses (Maginga 2019; Guijt and Reuver 2019; Ng'atigwa et al. 2020; De Blasis 2020; Samwel et al. 2020; Warra and Prasad 2020).

Notably, Tanzania's government and other stakeholders are currently promoting export in various agricultural commodities including horticultural produce. These activities have provided significant contributions to the overall production, marketing, and business-related aspects. However, the empirical relationship between horticulture export and its impact on small-scale farmer's welfare has been somewhat neglected in the literature. Therefore, this study aims to understand the link and critically assess the impact of horticulture export promotion on farmers' welfare.

12.2 Overview of Common Bean Production and Export in Tanzania

Horticulture is an important sub-sector that can exploit the potential of the country particularly the underutilized arable land of 44 million ha. The Tanzanian horticultural industry faces several universal challenges, namely, a weak production base, low productivity and quality, invisibility and marginalization, and limited access to finance, especially lack of long-term financing and investment. It also faces bottlenecks in land, policy and infrastructure, inadequate market development support, weak industry linkages, limited entrepreneurship capability, and inadequate skilled and competent human resources (URT 2010).

The common bean belongs to the legume plant foods with a long history in SSA due to their multiple benefits. Pulses and legumes, in general, can play an important role in agriculture because of their ability to biologically fix atmospheric nitrogen and to enhance the biological turnover of phosphorus; thus, they could become the cornerstone of sustainable agriculture. Due to their rich nutritional value, pulses are an important part of a balanced, healthy diet. Legumes are a good source of protein and of micronutrients such as iron and zinc (Snapp et al. 2018).

Many legume plant foods including common beans provide an important source of income as they can be sold for high prices at local or international markets. The price often reflects the nutrition packed nature of legume grains, with a high protein content. At the same time, a household survey in Malawi indicated that farmers were not always realizing a profit from legume sales, as labor inputs were high, access to good seed was poor, and legume prices varied tremendously (Snapp et al. 2002). The crop (common beans) does not get the attention it deserves from the public sector nor the opportunity to attract private sector investment due to a myriad of policy, institutional, technical, and socio-economic constraints. Legumes, particularly common beans, can play a critical role in achieving the Sustainable Development Goals (SDGs) (Ojiewo et al. 2018).

Green beans are grown as a cash crop by large-scale and smallholder farmers and more than 90% of the crops produced in Eastern Africa are exported to regional and international markets. Green bean/snap beans are an important export vegetable crop in Kenya, Tanzania, and Uganda. Market preferences for green bean pods differ with regions. Most of the snap beans produced in Eastern Africa are round and thin mainly to suit European markets. Green beans are also grown by large commercial companies for export to overseas supermarkets and for canning industries. Due to the high pod quality, packaging, and post-harvest care required for export produce, smallholder farmers are organized into groups (CIAT 2006).

According to FAO STAT (2021), Africa's production share accounts for (3.1%) which ranks third, while Europe (3.7%) ranks second and Asia (91.9%) leads the production of common beans in the world. In East Africa, Kenya is the leading producer of common beans (French bean), while Tanzania lags behind in the production. In Tanzania, common beans are grown mostly in the northern Tanzania of Moshi, Arusha, Manyara Province and little production in Morogoro Region thousands of

Year	Production (000 Tons)
2010	3200
2011	3500
2012	4200
2013	5000
2014	5745
2015	5419
2016	5800
2017	6120
2018	6440
2019	6760

Table 12.1 Production trend of green beans in Tanzania from 2010 to 2019

Source FAO STAT (2021), accessed 20/09/2021

tons (see Table 12.1). Family growers in this mountainous area use a combination of rain-fed and irrigated agriculture. Most farmers own half an hectare of land which they efficiently manage with farmyard manure. Due to the strict inspection of the crops abroad, they do not apply pesticides. Fresh French beans and different types of peas are currently the main exports in the (traditional) vegetables product group, accounting for about 50% in quantity and value (Match Maker Associates 2017).

12.2.1   Horticultural Crops Export in Tanzania

Increased horticultural produce trade between developing and high-income countries has been linked to: (1) increased foreign direct investment (FDI) in developing country horticultural sectors; (2) increased horticultural export chain consolidation and vertical coordination; and (3) increased public food safety regulations and the spread of private food standards (Van den Broeck et al. 2018). Tanzania ranks fifth worldwide in bean production and is the leading producer of beans in Africa which is produced almost entirely under intercropped systems with maize and other crops (FAOSTAT 2014; Binagwa et al. 2018). However, the main importing countries for Tanzania's green beans are the United Kingdom and European Union. Exports of green beans have fluctuated for a decade, with a peak in 2014 and in 2019 exports of 2.5 tons only (see Fig. 12.1). Despite the sluggishness in export quantity, the export value has increased significantly through the 2010/2011–2019/2020 period ending at 2,351 (000) US$ in 2019. The export value has increased by 896.19% from 2018 to 2019 although the price increased during that time due to shortage of green beans supply (FAO, 2020).

Table 12.2 Definition of variables and measurement

Variables	Definition and measurement
Dependent variables	
Participation in Export	1 If a farmer is participating in exporting common beans, 0 otherwise
Annual gross farm income	Total amount of income from the sale of the common beans (in Tshs)
Assets	Current monetary value of assets owned by a farmer he/she started since common beans farming (in Tshs)
Household expenditure	Household expenditure in Tshs. (for precision, farmers were asked to remember their expenditure on quarterly basis). These expenditures included food, non-food items, different community contributions, entertainment, and emergencies
Independent variables	
Socio-economic factors	
Age	Age of household (measured in years)
Household size	Number of members of household (count)
Experience	Farmers experience in common beans production
Gender	Gender of the respondent (farmers)
Marital status	Marital status of a farmer (1 if married, 0 = otherwise)
Education	Education level of farmers (measured in number of years in school and then categorized)
Farm season	Farmers were asked if they farm on season basis
Other business	Farmers were asked if they were engaged in other economic activities in the last season
Production as the last per season	
Total land size	Total land size owned by a farmer (acres)
Land size beans	Size of the land dedicated for common beans production (acres)
Fertilizer costs	Total costs of fertilizer (all types of fertilizers used were asked and total monetary value in Tshs. were computed)
Pesticide costs	Total costs of pesticides (all types of pesticides used were asked and total monetary value were computed)
Labor costs	Total costs used for labor (farmers were asked to remember number of labor used in each farming activities and their total costs were computed in Tshs)
Yield	Production amount (Kg)
Distance	Distance to the market
Institutional factors	
Extension	Farmers were asked if they had an access to extension services in the last season (1 yes, 2 = No)
Days	Number of days visited by extension officers

(continued)

Table 12.2 (continued)

Variables	Definition and measurement
Membership	Farmers were asked if they engaged in any farmers group/association in the last season (1 yes, 2 = No)
Credit	Farmers were asked if they had an access to credit in the last season (1 yes, 2 = No)
Contract	Farmers were asked if they engaged in contract farming in the last season (1 yes, 2 = No)
Grade	Farmers were asked if they were focusing on grade/standard compliance in the last season (1 yes, 2 = No)
Training	Farmers were asked if they had an access to marketing training/capacity building in the last season (1 yes, 2 = No)

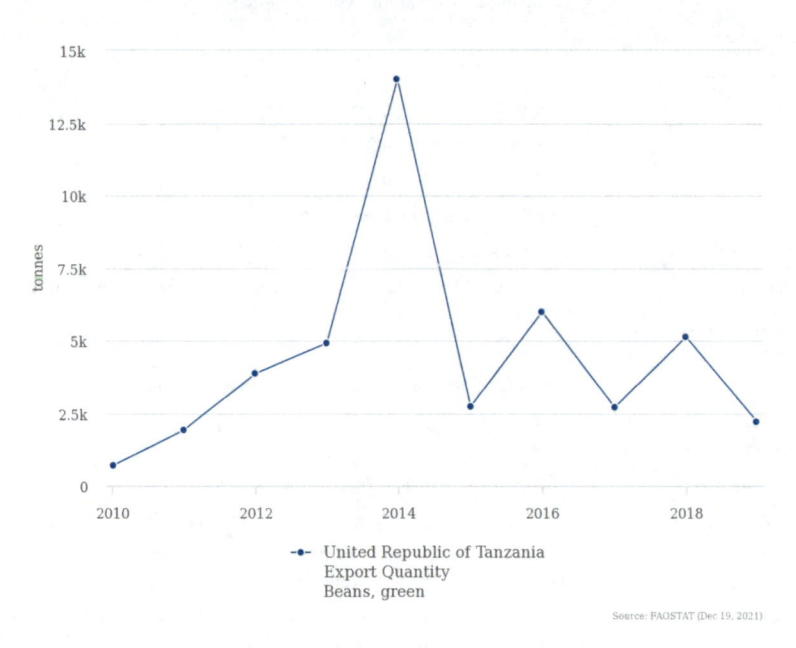

Fig. 12.1 Tanzania exportation of green beans from 2010 to 2019. *Source* FAO STAT (2021) Accessed 20/09/2021

12.3 Empirical Review of Horticultural Export

Several empirical studies on agricultural exports, particularly in the horticulture industry, have been conducted. Meme (2015) used time series data for horticultural exports, real exchange rates, agricultural GDP, real interest rates, and foreign income for a period of 30 years from 1984 to 2014 to examine the factors impacting the export of horticulture commodities in Kenya. The Cointegration error correction model was used to analyze this type of data. The findings demonstrated that the real exchange rate, agriculture GDP, and real interest rate all had a substantial impact on horticulture exports. Foreign earnings were found to be minimal in comparison to horticulture exports. The report advised the government to assess and implement policies aimed at raising agricultural GDP, achieving competitive exchange rates, and lowering lending rates to boost Kenyan horticultural exports.

Mold and Prizzon (2008) discovered that pricing had a minor impact on agricultural exports. The result of pooled regression estimates of unit price elasticity of African exports for the period 1980–2001 revealed that agricultural exports had a negative and substantial coefficient, meaning that African countries boosted agricultural exports as international prices fell.

A comparable empirical study was undertaken by Fukase and Martin (2018) to analyze agro-processing and horticultural exports in Africa. A standard Global Trade Analysis Project (GTAP) model was used to examine Changing Patterns of Processing and Exports, Global Perspective on Agricultural Processing. Also simulation scenarios were done to examine the response of processed agricultural exports from Africa to changes in protection rates and productivity growth in processing. The findings imply that escalating tariffs in export markets within the same value chains have significant consequences. Reduced protection for processed agricultural products to that of bulk agricultural products in export markets would result in a significant rise in processed agricultural product exports from Africa. Cutting agricultural protection within major African trade blocs and expanding liberalization to all trading partners and all goods will boost processed agricultural exports in a similar way.

Furthermore, Dube et al. (2018) examined the horticulture subsector's export performance in Ethiopia. The study looked at export performance from 1985 to 2016. The study also used time series data from the National Bank of Ethiopia, Ethiopia Horticulture Producer Exporters Association, Ministry of Agriculture of Ethiopia, FAOSTAT, UNCTAD, and the World Bank to examine the relationship between the series of data using the autoregressive-distributed lag (ARDL) bound test cointegration approach. There was cointegration among the data series, as demonstrated by the error correction model. The real effective exchange rate, real GDP, FDI, pricing, and the structural break all had a substantial impact on horticulture export performance in the short and long run. Only in the long run did foreign GDP and real interest rates prove to be relevant. As a result, the study recommends supportive macroeconomic measures to boost Ethiopia's horticultural export performance. Nonetheless, the analysis was country-specific, with a focus on macroeconomic and supply-side aspects.

Marwa and Manda (2021) also assessed farmers' benefit from participating in export contract farming of French beans from Kenya by using Heckman selection correction model, propensity score matching, and instrumental variable. The study found that farm size, number of extension visits, and distance between French bean farmers influenced participation in export contract farming. Also, participation in export contract farming was associated with increasing bean yield by about 17%.

Random Utility Theory

The decision to participate in horticultural exports can be analyzed as a choice problem within the random utility theoretical framework (Baiyegunhi et al. 2019). It is assumed that a utility maximizing farmer would export his/her agricultural produce if the expected net utility (welfare) from exportation (U_i^P) is greater than for non-participation (U_i^N). That is, a farmer chose to export if the expected net utility $U_i^* = U_i^P - U_i^N > 0$. The unobserved net utility can further be expressed as a function of observable elements represented in the latent variable model as follows:

$$U_i^* = \sigma Z_i + \varepsilon_i, \, U_i = 1 \text{ if } U_i^* > 0 \tag{12.1}$$

where U_i is a binary indicator variable that equals 1 for farmer in case of exportation and 0 otherwise, σ is a vector of parameters to be estimated, Z_i is a matrix of household and farm characteristics, and ε_i is an error term. The farmer's welfare indicator is measured by consumption expenditure, income from selling common beans, and assets values.

Conceptual framework

From the random utility theory above and to expand the argument of the theory, the current study seeks to know what other factors are than factor endowments that can influence the country's export, and more specifically, the horticultural produced crops. It is conceptualized that, common beans farmers in Arumeru District in Arusha are endowed with favorable resources (production factors) for common beans farming such as arable land, water, and an available market as compared to other regions in the country. However, their decision to export will depend on the net utility measured in terms of welfare that will be gained from exportation as compared to trading common beans locally. Therefore, given that these resources together with other socio-economic and institutional factors influence farmers (independent variables) to engage in common bean exports as indicated in Fig. 12.2. Thus, the study aims to understand the link between these factors and their contribution to a farmer's decision to export or not to export and if exporting what is the impact on welfare.

12.4 Methodology

This section presents the research methodologies employed. It describes research approach, design, study area, population, sample size, sampling technique, data collection, and analysis used.

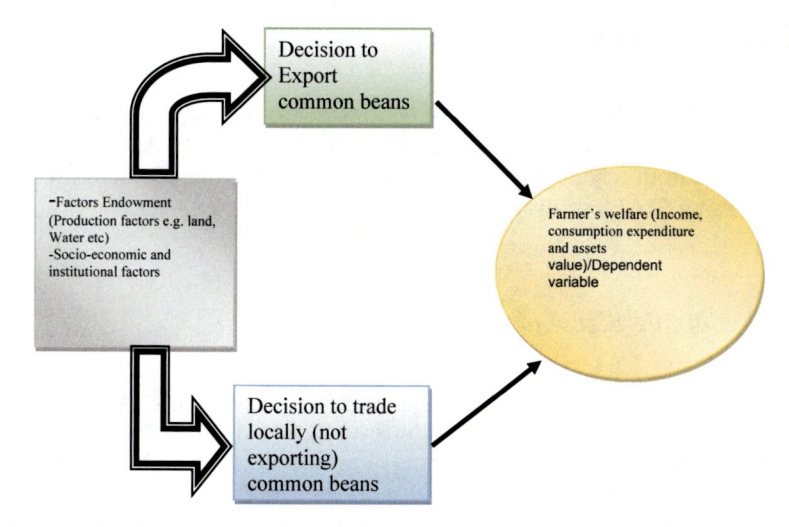

Fig. 12.2 Conceptual framework. *Source* (Author's conceptualisation)

12.4.1 Description of the Study Area

The study was conducted in Arumeru District in the Arusha Region, north of Tanzania, which is a perfect location for export because of its good connections to the major eastern African seaport of Mombasa. Moreover, the region's equatorial climate allows the cultivation of vegetables and fruit all year round. Two wards with the highest number of common beans exporters were also purposely selected which are Kikwe and Mbuguni Wards. Arumeru District is located between longitudes 35°E and 37°E and latitude 3°S. The district covers an area of 2966 km², which is 3.5% of Arusha Region. Despite its proximity to the Equator, Arusha's elevation of 1400 m amsl on the southern slopes of Mount Meru keeps temperatures relatively low and alleviates humidity. Cool dry air is prevalent for much of the year. The temperature ranges between 13 and 30 degrees Celsius, with an average of around 25 degrees. It has distinct wet and dry seasons with average annual rainfall of 654 mm (Kahimba et al. 2014).

12.4.2 Research Design

This study employed a cross-sectional design to collect data on relevant variables from a variety of common beans farmers in the study area. The information brought deeper insights and better understanding of the problems. The study reflects a mix of both qualitative and quantitative data and methodological treatments.

12.4.3 Data Collection

Data was obtained from both primary and secondary sources. Primary data was obtained using semi-structured and structured questionnaires while secondary data was obtained from literature. The data generated through the questionnaires were analyzed using STATA software.

12.4.4 Sample Size and Sampling Technique

One hundred and thirty one (131) respondents were interviewed. Out of this, 91 were engaged in common beans export while 40 were trading common beans locally. The sample size selection reflected the number of available farmers who are engaged in export as a unit of analysis with consultation of Arumeru District Agricultural Office. The lists of farmers who are exporting against those who are not exporting were sorted out with active and consistent export farmers selected. Therefore, purposive sampling (non-probability sampling) technique was used based on the intention or the purpose of study. The selected elements entail the population which only suits the best for the purpose of our study. Key informants, i.e., trade, community development officers, and agricultural extension officers were also interviewed to share general information on the institutional support for common export.

12.5 Analytical Methods

12.5.1 Socio-Economic, Institutional, and Production Factors Influencing Common Beans Export and Its Extent by Small-Scale Farmers

Probit regression model

This study employed binary probit model with the assumption that the decision by smallholder farmer to export and the intensity/extent of export are decisions which are made simultaneously. Thus, in this study, the first stage is the decision to export equation that was estimated by using a probit model as described in Eq. 12.2.

$$d_i^* = X_{1i}'\beta_i + U_i \quad U_{iN(0,1)}$$
$$1 \text{ if } d_i^* > 0 \text{ and } 0 \text{ if } d_i^* \le 0$$

$$(12.2)$$

where d_i^* the latent discrete participation choice variable that denotes binary censoring (i.e., 1 means a farmer decides to export, and 0 means otherwise). X_{1i}'

are vector of explanatory variables hypothesized to influence participation choice (i.e., socio-economic, institutional, and production factors) and d_i^* s are vectors of parameters and U_i is the standard error term.

Tobit regression model

The Tobit regression model was employed to quantify the magnitude and direction of the effects of the factors influencing common beans export. The Tobit or censored normal regression model assumes that the observed dependent variables Y_j for observations $j = 1 \ldots$ n satisfy the following:

$$Y_j = \max(Y_j^*, 0) \qquad (12.3)$$

where the $Y_j^{*'}$'s are latent variables generated by the classical linear regression model:

$$Y_j^* = \beta' X_j + U_j, \, Y_j = \begin{cases} Y_j^* \text{ if } > 0 \\ 0 \text{ if } Y_j^* \leq 0 \end{cases} \qquad (12.4)$$

where X_j denotes vector of regressors, possibly including 1 for the intercept, and β' denotes the corresponding vector of parameters. The model errors U_j are assumed to be independently normally distributed: $U_j \approx N(0, \sigma^2)$. An observation of zero on the dependent variable could mean either a "true" zero or censored data Y_j. For strictly positive values, observations would always equal Y_j^* and the true model would be linear on that range. Tobit model parameters do not directly correspond to changes in the dependent variable brought about by changes in independent variables. According to Greene (2003), the marginal effect on the intensity of market participation due to changes in the explanatory variable is given as follows:

$$\frac{\partial E\left[\frac{Y_j}{X_j}\right]}{\partial X_j} = \beta\varphi\left[\frac{\beta' X_j}{\sigma}\right] \qquad (12.5)$$

12.5.2 Modeling the Impact of Horticulture Export on Farmers Welfare

A Propensity Score Matching (PSM) approach is used to examine the impact of horticulture exports on farmers' welfare which will measure income as an indicator for welfare. The method compares the welfare of farmers who are exporting and those who are not. The parameter of interest in the estimation of the propensity score is the Average Treatment Effect on the Treated (ATT). The propensity score $p(Z_i)$ is defined as the conditional probability of farmers to export horticultural crops given pre-participation characteristics:

$$p(Z_i) \equiv Pr[L_i = |Z_i] = E[L_i|Z_i]; \ p(Z_i) = F\{h(Z_i)\} \qquad (12.6)$$

where $L_i = (0,1)$ is the indicator of mobile money-based enterprise participation, Z_i denotes a vector of pre-participation characteristics, and $F\{.\}$ can be a normal or logistic cumulative distribution. The propensity score can be predicted with either the logit or probit model. The predicted propensity scores can then be used to estimate treatment effects given the propensity score, as follows:

$$ATT = E[E\{L_i = 1, p(Z_i)\} - E\{Y_i|L_i = 0, p(Z_i)\}|L_i = 1] \qquad (12.7)$$

where Y_i^* and Y_i are two counterfactual outcomes of those who are exporting and those who are not exporting. Table 12.2 shows the variables used in the study with their definition and measurements.

12.6 Results and Discussions

12.6.1 Socio-Economic, Production, and Institutional Characteristics of Common Beans Farmers

Tables 12.3 and 12.4 present the descriptive statistics of continuous variables between farmers who are exporting common beans and those who are not exporting. These variables are categorized into demographic, market, welfare, and other factors grouped into production as the last year season. In the following sub-sections, we discuss these factors in details.

12.6.2 Socio-Economic Factors of Common Beans Farmers

Regarding age, the mean for common beans farmers who are selling locally is 48.7 higher than the mean for farmers who participate in export markets (47.5). Whereas household size is 4.2 higher for local market-oriented farmers and 3.9 for exporters. There is also mean difference in experience, but not statistically different between exporters and non-exporting farmers. Regarding gender, male exporters are more than the female exporters indicating that males are the ones who mostly export common beans while the female farmers are selling to the local market. The mean for the household head is significantly different between the two, indicating that if farmers are head of the household, they are more likely to be exporters. Furthermore, most

Table 12.3 Characteristics of farmers interviewed (continuous variables) using independent t-test

Characteristics	Mean			
Demographic factors	Exporters	Local market	Combined	t-test *(p-value)*
Age	47.5	48.7	47.9	0.5912
Household size	3.9	4.2	4	0.2389
Experience	19.4	20.8	19.8	0.4882
Production as the last per season				
Total Land size	2.02	1.8	1.9	0.1670
Land size beans	1.6	1.5	1.59	0.5967
Fertilizer costs	148,274.7	111,925	137,175.6	0.0001[c]
Pesticide costs	39,285.71	34,650	37,870.23	0.0766[a]
Labor	52,165.62	57,487.5	53,790.62	0.7133
Extension days	1.72	1.55	1.67	0.0496[b]
Number of times farmed	1.28	1	1.2	0.0003[c]
Market				
Distance to the market	39.67	24.77	35.12	0.0000[c]
Welfare factors				
Assets (Tshs)	12,700,000	653,5250	10,800,000	0.0140[b]
Expenditure (Tshs)	356,450.5	369,725	360,503.8	0.8518
Annual gross farm Income (Tshs)	3,413,718	2,574,879	2,826,531	0.0127[b]

[a, b, c]Significant at 10%, 5% and 1%. 1 USD = 2,319Tshs (June 2021)

of the farmers who are exporting had primary education level as compared to those who are trading locally.

Farmers who have other business are more likely to be exporter and the result is statistically significantly. Also, extension services are statistically significant between the two groups. However, only a small number of the respondents received extension services which provided a challenge for the government to encourage and support the extension officers in implementing their roles so as to increase farmer's participation in export markets.

12.6.3 Production Characteristics of Common Beans Farmers

Regarding production factors, land size (both total and for beans alone) and labor costs of farming activities are not statistically different between exporters and non-exporters. Among significant factors, fertilizer costs are statistically significant between the two groups implying that there is a significant relationship between fertilizer costs and probability of farmers participation in exporting common beans.

Table 12.4 Characteristics of farmers interviewed using Pearson chi-square method

Characteristics	Category	Exporters	Local	Overall	Chi-Square ($\chi2$)
Socio-economic factors					
Gender	Male	71	34	105	0.356
	Female	20	6	26	
Marital status	Married	86	39	125	0.450
	Not married	5	1	6	
Head of household	Head	70	36	106	0.079[a]
	Not head	21	4	25	
Education level	Primary	81	37	118	0.659
	Secondary	5	3	8	
	High school	1	0	1	
	Certificate	2	0	2	
	Diploma	2	0	2	
Other business	Yes	43	7	50	0.001[c]
	No	48	33	81	
Production factors					
Farm season	Yes	81	40	121	0.029[b]
	No	10	0		
Institutional factors					
Extension services	Yes	25	18	43	0.049[b]
	No	66	22	88	
Group membership	Yes	80	13	93	0.000[c]
	No	11	27	38	
Access credit	Yes	49	11	60	0.005[b]
	No	42	29	71	
Contract farming	Yes	89	7	96	0.000[c]
	No	2	33	35	
Grade/standard compliance	Yes	85	12	97	0.000[c]
	No	6	28	34	
Market training	Yes	78	3	81	0.000[c]
	No	13	37	50	

[a, b, c] Significant at 10%, 5%, and 1%

Similarly, pesticides costs are statistically significant and different between the two groups, indicating that pesticides are an important and significant aspect for farmers who are exporting common beans. The other two significant factors of production are extension days and number of times farmed.

12.6.4 Institutional Characteristics of Common Beans Farmers

Concerning institutional factors, all the variables under consideration are statistically significant between exporters and those who have local sales only. For instance, farmers who are members of any farming associations are likely to benefit from exporting activities more than those who are not members of any farm-related association. The same applies for training or capacity building for marketing as well as engaging in standard compliance is likely to enhance exporting activities.

12.6.5 Welfare Factors of the Common Beans Farmers

Looking at the included welfare factors, assets owned by farmers or households engaged in farming are all likely to enhance exporting possibilities. Similarly, the annual gross farm income is found to be statistically different between those who are engaged in exporting and domestic market. However, household-related expenditures are not likely to be different between these two groups of farmers.

12.6.6 Factors Influencing Common Beans Export

Table 12.5 presents the regression results investigating the factors that are potentially influencing extent of common beans export. We have presented the discussion as follows.

Age of a farmer

Age has a negative influence on farmers participation in common beans export and is statistically significant at a 10% level and has a marginal effect of -0.002. An increase in the age of the household would reduce the probability of farmer's participation in common beans export by 0.2%. This implies that when household age increases they become less motivated to involve agriculture as mental capacity and physical ability to do manual work decreases and youth becomes more likely to engage fully in the common bean production. This aligns with Nwaru and Iwuji (2005) who report that entrepreneurship gradually reduces as the age of the entrepreneur increases.

Household size

Household size has a negative influence on farmers participation in common beans export and is statistically significant at 5% level and has a marginal effect of −0.036. An increase of household size would reduce the probability of farmer's participation in common beans export by 3.6%. This implies that household size which indicates the number of family laborers used in production is not a crucial factor to make the

Table 12.5 Propensity score for farmers' participation in common beans export (probit model results)

Variables	Coefficient	Marginal effects	Standard error	z	P > z
Socio-economic factors					
Gender	0.206408	0.004	2.410575	0.09	0.932
Age	−0.12371	−0.002	0.071083	−1.74	0.082[a]
Marital status	−3.42952	−0.066	2.16E + 00	−1.59	0.113
Household size	−1.83563	−0.036	8.73E-01	−2.1	0.035[b]
Education level	−1.3205	−0.026	1.434762	−0.92	0.357
Experience	0.232216	0.004	0.121902	1.9	0.057[a]
Other business	−2.54162	−0.049	1.414479	−1.8	0.072[a]
Production as the last per season					
Land size beans	1.822536	0.035	2.525153	0.72	0.47
Fertilizer costs	−2.62325	−0.051	1.668951	−1.57	0.116
Labor costs	−0.49573	−0.010	0.444521	−1.12	0.265
Pesticide costs	1.667701	0.032	1.750571	0.95	0.341
Institutional factors					
Access to extension	4.663797	0.090	2.31773	2.01	0.044[b]
Group membership	4.051503	0.078	3.444391	1.18	0.239
Access credit	−5.33292	−0.103	3.534744	−1.51	0.131
Contract farming	−7.90972	−0.153	3.232005	−2.45	0.014[b]
Distance to the market	−0.03388	−0.001	0.081923	−0.41	0.679
Marketing training	−4.88869	−0.095	3.79042	−1.29	0.197
_cons	49.34772		33.99057	1.45	0.147
Log likelihood	−12.558681				
Number of obs	131				
LR chi2(17)	136.10				
Prob > chi^2	0.0000				
Pseudo-R^2	0.8442				
Outcome correctly specified	96.18%				

[a], [b]Significant at 10%, and 5%

farmers produce and export common beans since the country has never had shortage of it. This finding answers the question on the needs and essential facilities required by these households to engage fully in production to maximize export quantity. This confirms SNV (2012), focusing on the matter of poor technology and innovation among common beans farmers leading to post-harvest losses which account for significant losses in yield at farm level.

Other Business

Other business has negative influence on farmers participation in common beans export and statistically significant at 10% level and has a marginal effect of −0.049. An increased engagement in other business would reduce the probability of farmer's participation in common beans export by 4.9%. This implies that engagement of farmers in other economic activities apart from common beans production and export eases the burden of dependence on the agriculture sector which is mostly unproductive in Tanzania. This aligns with (Mishra et al. 2015) that farmer's engagement in off-farm activities enhances food security as they manage food consumption fluctuations better than a household without such an activity. Broadly speaking, the existence of alternative sources of livelihood is a key factor in under-utilization of primary source of income/livelihood in farming (Demena 2011).

Access to extension

Access to extension has positive influence on farmers participation in common beans export and is statistically significant at 5% level and has a marginal effect of 0.090. An increase in access to extension would result in 9% probability of farmer's participation in common beans export. Extension service including training for farmers is still imperative especially in common beans production which is affected by pests and diseases and intensive use of pesticides may result in non-compliance of international standards. The risks associated with the lack of compliance to the specified standards are borne by the farmer (Prowse 2012). This is consistent with the results by Okello et al. (2007). Some companies would not accept beans produced by smallholders for fear that they might violate its client's pesticide residue and hygiene standards. This concludes that extension service should be increased especially to smallholder farmers to expose them to the proper method of farming using minimum pesticides to adhere with Good Agriculture Practices (GAP).

Contract farming

Contract farming has a negative influence on farmers participation in common beans export and statistically significant at 5% level and has a marginal effect of −0.153. An increase in contract farming would reduce the probability of farmer's participation in common beans export by 15.3%. The reasons for this could be associated with the setbacks experienced in contract farming such as excessive power among buyers leading to exploitation of small holder farmers. This confirms findings by Singh (2008), arguing that buyers are violating terms of the agreement by delaying payment and deliveries to factories or by manipulating provisions of the contract. Other studies are contrary to the current findings and concluded that smallholder farmers have remained passive actors in contract farming programs. Nevertheless, the general impact on the economic gains at farm level is positive (Match Maker Associates 2006).

12.6.7 Factors Influencing farmer's Extent of Common Beans Export

Table 12.6 presents results regarding factors that are influencing extent of common beans export.

Gender

The gender of common beans farmers' was negative and statistically significant at the 5% level. This indicates that with an increase in the number of male farmers the extent of common beans export will also decrease. The implication of these findings may be drawn from the literature on the role of African women in agriculture. A

Table 12.6 Factors influencing extent of common beans export by farmers

Variables	Coefficient	Marginal effects	Std. Err	t-statistics	P > t
Socio-economic factors					
Gender	−0.046	−0.046	0.015	−3.11	0.002[b]
Age	0.000	0.000	0.001	−0.06	0.949
Marital status	0.086	0.086	0.025	3.49	0.001[c]
Household size	0.004	0.004	0.004	1.17	0.246
Education level	0.005	0.005	0.007	0.76	0.448
Experience	−0.002	−0.002	0.001	−2.91	0.004[b]
Other business	0.000	0.000	0.011	0.03	0.98
Production as the last per season					
Land size beans	−0.028	−0.028	0.012	−2.39	0.018[b]
Fertilizer costs	0.002	0.002	0.015	0.15	0.878
Pesticide costs	0.004	0.004	0.015	0.27	0.784
Labor costs	0.009	0.009	0.007	1.29	0.201
Institutional factors					
Access to extension	−0.011	−0.011	0.012	−0.89	0.377
Group membership	0.029	0.029	0.023	1.22	0.225
Access credit	−0.024	−0.024	0.015	−1.63	0.107
Contract farming	0.117	0.117	0.024	4.88	0.000[c]
Distance to the market	0.000	0.000	0.001	−0.34	0.736
Marketing training	0.045	0.045	0.025	1.77	0.08[a]
_cons 0.22712			0.243	0.93	0.353
Log likelihood	198.04				
Number of observation	131				
LR chi2(17)	157.45				
Prob > chi2	0.0000				

[a, b, c]Significant at 10%, 5% and 1%

wide variety of literature is available on the importance of agriculture to economic development in Africa and on the critical role that rural women play within this sector. Women can greatly improve food security by working as laborers on farms or as farmers, but compared to men they have fewer opportunities and resources, making it difficult to enter the sector (Human 2020; Vemireddy and Pingali 2021).

Marital status

The marital status was positive and statistically significant at the 1% level. This implies that an increase in the number of farmers who are married will lead to an increase in the extent of common beans export. One possible reason could be marriage symbolizes household responsibilities and hence influences the level of work to increase exports.

Experience

The experience of common beans farmers was negative and statistically significant at the 5% level. This may indicate that an increase in the farmers' years of experience lead to a decline in the extent of export. The possible reasons for this could be the fact that an increase in the years of farming experience at some point a farmer might be bored and would like to try another crop or venture of interest. It may also indicate that farmers discover that it is not profitable to export or returns are not worth the costs as experience increase in the years of farming.

Land size allocated for common beans

The land size allocated for common beans production was negative and statistically significant at the 5% level. This implies that an increase in the amount of land allocated for common beans export will lead to a decline in the extent of common beans export. The reasons could probably be that increasing more land space for common beans farming becomes difficult and inconvenient for smallholder farmers to manage the production given his/her capital and skills.

Contract farming

The contract farming for common beans production was positive and statistically significant at the 1% level. An increase in the level of contract farming engagement by common beans farmers will lead to an increase in the extent of export. Contract farming, a preharvest agreement between farmers and buyers, is commonly understood as a useful tool to mitigate prevalent market failures and to reduce the risks facing smallholder farmers (Bolwig et al. 2009). Contract farming is believed to improve productivity and income because it facilitates coordination between farmers and other actors in terms of production, processing, and marketing of agricultural products (Nguyen et al. 2015).

Marketing training

The marketing training for common beans production was positive and statistically significant at the 10% level. Access to market training motivates farmers to engage in exporting common beans as they become more aware of the export structure and also they learn to manage their farms for profit. The role of training in building farmers' capacity for successful agricultural development cannot be overemphasized (Antwi-Agyei and Stringer 2021). Building farmers' competences for agricultural development translates into increased demand for improved knowledge, information, and technologies (Opolot et al. 2018).

12.6.8   Impact of Common Beans Export on farmer's Welfare

Table 12.7 presents the results of the impact of common beans export on farmers' welfare with gross income from common beans, household consumption expenditure, and asset value as outcome variables.

Impact of common beans export on farmer's assets endowment

Assets were measured in terms of the value of all the durable commodities a farmer had ranging from livestock, furniture, electronics, land, tools, and equipment. Their value was estimated using current market prices. Currently, poverty debates reflect a growing interest in the importance of assets for understanding how the poor respond to shortages and shocks and generate future income and consumption (e.g., Anderson 2012; Donovan and Poole 2014). It is further argued that assets provide a better option for understanding the underlying causes and the dynamics of poverty than a focus on income or consumption variables alone (Carter and Barrett 2006; Donovan and Poole 2014). The results depict that there is no significant difference between the assets of farmers who are exporting and those who are trading. Although there is no significant difference on assets endowment, common beans farmers are likely to use part of their income from common beans production to purchase assets and this explains why they probably have more assets than their control counterparts. The insignificant difference indicates that the amount of assets owned by farmers are not directly influenced by common beans export. Thus, common beans export does not have any significant impact on the amount of assets owned by farmers.

Table 12.7   Impact of common beans export on farmers welfare: PSM results

	ATT for our outcome variables (Tshs)		
Matching estimator (algorithms)	Gross income from common beans	Household consumption expenditure	Assets value
Nearest neighbor Matching	928,000(0.644)	1,530,000 (2.273)[a]	3,990,000(1.112)
Radius matching	1,290,000(1.436)	360,000 (0.805)	4,570,000 (1.348)

Notes [a]means significant at 10% levels and *t*-values are in brackets

Impact of common beans export on farmer's income

Regarding income from common beans, there is no statistically significant difference between farmers who are exporting common beans and those who do not export. This means that they have a stream of income especially when the markets are good. As opposed to their counterparts who only depend on other types of income source, snow peas farmers have an additional source of income. This explains why they probably have more monthly net income as compared to non-snow peas growers. The results are contrary to the findings of Tolemariam and Jaleta (2010) who found that households' participation in market development intervention by coffee producers did not have a statistically significant impact on their income.

Impact of common beans export on farmer's consumption expenditure

In terms of consumption expenditure, there is a statistically significant difference between farmers who are exporting and non-exporters of common beans. Those farmers who are involved in common beans exportation are depicted to spend more money on various consumption expenditures. This could be explained by the fact that common beans exportation gives them more income compared to their counterparts. They are therefore able to afford all the basic commodities in satisfactory amounts. They can afford a good education for their children by taking them to good schools. Also, farmers who are exporting can afford both fresh and unfresh staples more frequently than farmers who are trading locally.

12.7   Conclusion and Recommendation

12.7.1   Summary and Conclusion

Common beans export has a positive impact on farmers' welfare. Allowing for interactions between common beans export and other determinants of common beans export (socio-economic, production, and institutional factors), specifically, it was observed that there is the positive impact of common beans export on farmers' consumption expenditure that does not have any significant impact on farmers' income and assets ownership. This can be interpreted as evidence that horticultural exports may have an important causal impact in terms of household welfare. Though the potential for increasing rural incomes through agricultural export is substantial, this study concluded that different socio-economic, production, and institutional factors play significant roles. The results of this study suggest that common beans farmers are aware of the significant role of exporting their crop rather than trading locally.

12.7.2 Policy Implications and Recommendations

The following policy interventions are suggested. With regard to institutional factors, capacity building (training) on common beans export should be emphasized for farmers as it has shown to positively influence the extent of common beans exportation. Policy attention needs to shift from supporting and regulating particular trade policies but rather should focus on how farmers will be trained and utilize the available opportunity of the common beans export market. Also, horticultural contract farming should be strengthened by the government and monitored by the extension officers who are with farmers to support farmers in acquiring best deals with exporting companies. Results have shown that contract farming has a potential role in increasing the extent of common beans exportation. In addition, with regard to socio-economic factors, income diversification should also be emphasized to farmers as it was found that those who were engaged in other business were also influenced to export less of the common beans as other sources of income likely to reduce the focus on common beans production.

References

Alam F, Myovella G (2016) Causality between agricultural exports and GDP and its implications for Tanzanian economy. J Econ Finance Acc 3(1):1–18

Anderson B (2012) Converting asset holdings into livelihood: an empirical study on the role of household agency in South Africa. World Dev 40(7):1394–1406

Antwi-Agyei P, Stringer LC (2021) Improving the effectiveness of agricultural extension services in supporting farmers to adapt to climate change: insights from northeastern Ghana. Clim Risk Manag 32:100304

Baiyegunhi LJS, Majokweni ZP, Ferrer SRD (2019) Impact of outsourced agricultural extension program on smallholder farmers' net farm income in Msinga, KwaZulu-Natal, South Africa. Technol Soc 57:1–7

Binagwa PH, Magdalena W, Michael K, Zakayo E, Mbiu J, Msaky J, Mdachi, M, Kasubiri F, Kisamo A, Nestory SM, Rubyogo JC (2018) Selian Agricultural Research Institute (SARI) released Seven (7) Improved Common Bean (*Phaseolus vulgaris*) Varieties January 2018. Fact Sheet 1

De Blasis F (2020) Global horticultural value chains, labour and poverty in Tanzania. World Development Perspectives 100201

Bolwig S, Gibbon P, Jones S (2009) The economics of smallholder organic contract farming in tropical Africa. World Dev 37(6):1094–1104

Carter MR, Barrett CB (2006) The economics of poverty traps and persistent poverty: an asset-based approach. J Dev Stud 42(2):178–199

CIAT (2006) http://ciat-library.ciat.cgiar.org/Articulos_Ciat/highlight31.pdf. Accessed 23 Apr 2021

Demena BA (2011) Determinants of fish catch levels in artisanal fishing in Eritrea. Master of Arts in Development Studies Research Paper, Institute of Social Studies, The Hague, The Netherlands November

Donovan J, Poole N (2014) Changing asset endowments and smallholder participation in higher value markets: evidence from certified coffee producers in Nicaragua. Food Policy 44:1–13

Dube AK, Ozkan B, Govindasamy R (2018) Analyzing the export performance of the horticultural sub-sector in ethiopia: Ardl bound test cointegration analysis. Horticulturae 4(4). https://doi.org/10.3390/horticulturae404003

FAO (2020) Trade statistics—crops, livestock products and live animal. Accessed 23 Apr 2021

FAO STAT (2021) http://www.fao.org/faostat/en/#compare. Accessed 22 Apr 2021

FAOSTAT (2014) Food and Agriculture Organization (of the United Nations), Statistics Division Available at http://faostat3.fao.org/

Fukase E, Martin W (2018) Agro-processing and horticultural exports from Africa. In: Industries without smokestacks: industrialization in Africa reconsidered, pp 90–112

Gramzow A, Batt PJ, Afari-Sefa V, Petrick M, Roothaert R (2018) Linking smallholder vegetable producers to markets-A comparison of a vegetable producer group and a contract-farming arrangement in the Lushoto District of Tanzania. J Rural Stud 63:168–179

Greene WH (2003) Econometric analysis. Pearson Education India

Guijt J, Reuver R (2019) Sowing the seed: adoption processes of good horticulture practices in northern Uganda. Wageningen Centre for Development Innovation

Gupta V (2020) A case study on economic development of Tanzania. J Int Acad Case Stud 26(1):1–16

Hernandez AR (2011) Can Asians Sustain an Export-led Growth strategy in the Aftermath of the Global Crisis? An Empirical Exploration, available online http://www.adbi.org/workingpaper/2011/12/02/4823.asia.sustain.export.growth.after.global.crisis/. Retrieved 12th April 2021

Hillocks RJ, Madata CS, Chirwa R, Minja EM, Msolla S (2006) Phaseolus bean improvement in Tanzania, 1959–2005. Euphytica 150(1):215–231

Human U (2020) Women in agriculture: a chance to improve food security. FarmBiz 6(2):9–11

Juma, I., Fors, H., Hovmalm, H.P., Nyomora, A., Fatih, M., Geleta, M., Carlsson, A.S., and Ortiz, R.O. (2019) Avocado production and local trade in the southern highlands of Tanzania: A case of an emerging trade commodity from horticulture. Agronomy, 9(11), 749

Okello JJ, Narrod C, Roy D (2007) Food safety requirements in African green bean exports and their impact on small farmers, IFPRI Discussion Paper 00737

Kahimba FC, Mutabazi KD, Tumbo SD, Masuki KF, Mbungu WB (2014) Adoption and scaling-up of conservation agriculture in Tanzania: case of Arusha and Dodoma regions. Nat Resour 5:161–176

Kanyangemu A, Kundu KK (2019) Trade performance of agricultural commodities of Tanzania. Indian J Econ Dev 15(3):427–434

Lwesya F (2018) Export diversification and poverty reduction in Tanzania. Romanian Econ J 20(68):93–110

Maginga TJ (2019) Development of horticulture extension support system for the small holder farmers: a case of Tanzania (M.Sc. Dissertation, NM-AIST)

Mallya S (2019) Factors for adoption of greenhouse farming technology among farmers-a case of Kinondoni district-Dar es salaam (Doctoral dissertation, Mzumbe University)

Marwa E, Manda J (2021) Do youth farmers benefit from participating in contract farming: evidence from French beans youth farmers in Arusha, Tanzania. International conference of agricultural economist. 17th to 21st August, 2021

Mashindano O, Kazi V, Mashauri S, Baregu S (2013) Taping export opportunities for horticulture products in Tanzania: do we have supporting policies and institutional frameworks?. ICBE-RF Report

Match Maker Associates (2006) Final report, contract farming: status and prospects for Tanzania. Report

Match Maker Associates (2017) Final report, phase 1: mapping of production of fruits and Vegetables in Tanzania. https://www.rvo.nl/sites/default/files/2017/05/Studie%20Tanzaniaanse%20T uinbouwsector%202017.pdf

Match-Maker (2017) Horticulture study, phase 1: mapping of production of fruits and vegetables in Tanzania. Final Report, p 39

Mayala NM, Bamanyisa JM (2018) Assessment of market options for smallholder horticultural growers and traders in Tanzania. Euro J Res Soc Sci 6(1):27–42

Meme SM (2015) Export performance of the horticultural sub-sector in Kenya: an empirical analysis (Doctoral dissertation, University of Nairobi)

Mishra AK, Mottaleb KA, Mohanty S (2015) Impact of off-farm income on food expenditures in rural Bangladesh: an unconditional quantile regression approach. Agric Econ 46(2):139–214

Mold A, Prizzon A (2008) Explaining Africa recent performance and limited gains from the commodity boom. Paris, France: OECD Development Centre

Mutungi C, Irungu FG, Nduko J, Mutua F, Affognon H, Nakimbugwe D, Ekesi S, Fiaboe KKM (2019) Postharvest processes of edible insects in Africa: a review of processing methods, and the implications for nutrition, safety and new products development. Crit Rev Food Sci Nutr 59(2):276–298

Mutungi C, Chamwilambo M, Masanja S, Massam C, Wayda P, Tungu J, Gaspar A, Bekunda M, Abass A (2020) Quality and storability of common beans in small-holders farm stores in Northern Tanzania: a multivariate analysis of agro-location, variety, and storage method effects. J Stored Prod Res 89:101723

Myovella GA, Paul F, Rwakalaza RT (2015) Export-led growth hypothesis: evidence from agricultural exports in Tanzania. Afr J Econ Rev 3(2):74–84

Mywish KM, Shupp R, Mishili F, Reyes B, Kusolwa P, Kudra A (2019) Willingness to pay for quality seeds: field experimental and survey data. Tanzania Bean Study, 2015–2016

Ng'atigwa AA, Hepelwa A, Yami M, Manyong V (2020) Assessment of factors influencing youth involvement in horticulture agribusiness in Tanzania: a case study of Njombe region. Agriculture 10(7):287

Nguyen AT, Dzator J, Nadolny A (2015) Does contract farming improve productivity and income of farmers?: a review of theory and evidence. J Dev Areas 49(6):531–538

Nwaru JC, Iwuji O (2005) Marketing margins and their determinants in plantain marketing in owerri agricultural zone of Imo State, Nigeria. In: Orheruata AM, Nwokoro SO, Ajayi MT, Adekunle AT, Asumugha GN (eds) Agricultural rebirth for improved production in Nigeria, proceedings of the 39th annual conference of the agricultural society of Nigeria. University of Benin, Benin City, Nigeria, pp 385–338

Ojiewo CO, Rubyogo JC, Wesonga JM, Bishaw Z, Gelalcha SW, Abang MM (2018) Mainstreaming efficient legume seed systems in Eastern Africa: challenges, opportunities and contributions towards improved livelihoods. Food and Agriculture Organization of the United Nations, Rome, p 72

Okello JJ, Swinton SM (2007) Compliance with international food safety standards in Kenya's green bean industry: comparison of a small-and a large-scale farm producing for export. Appl Econ Perspect Policy 29(2):269–285

Opolot HN, Isubikalu P, Obaa BB, Ebanyat P (2018) Influence of university entrepreneurship training on farmers' competences for improved productivity and market access in Uganda. Cogent Food Agri 4(1):1469211

Prowse M (2012) Contract farming in developing countries—a review. ADF's Research Development. Report

Samwel J, Msogoya T, Kudra A, Mtui HD, Baltazari A, Sullivan JA, Subramanian J, Mwatawala MW (2020) Pre-harvest field application effects of hexanal formulation on fruit losses in mango grown in eastern Tanzania. J Crop Improv 34(3):366–377

Sanjuán-López AI, Dawson PJ (2010) Agricultural exports and economic growth in developing countries: a panel cointegration approach. J Agri Econ 61(3):565–583

Singh S (2008) Understanding practice of contract farming in India: a small producer perspective. Working Paper, CMA, IIM, Ahmedaba

Snapp SS, Rohrbach DD, Simtowe F, Freeman HA (2002) Sustainable soil management options for Malawi: can smallholder farmers grow more legumes? Agr Ecosyst Environ 91:159–174

Snapp S, Rahmanian M, Batello C (2018) Pulse crops for sustainable farms in sub-Saharan Africa, edited by T. Calles. Rome, FAO

SNV (2012)The beans value chain in Kenya. Netherlands Development Organization

Stahley K, Slakie E, Derksen-Schrock K, Gugerty MK, Anderson CL (2019) Tanzania national panel survey LSMS-ISA: Legumes. Gates Open Res 3(205):205

Tolemariam A, Jaleta M (2010) Impact assessment of input and output market development interventions by IPMS Project: the case of Gomma Woreda, Jimma Zone (Doctoral dissertation, Haramaya University)

URT (2010) Tanzania Horticultural Development Strategy 2012–2021. Hodect Tanzania. Report

Van den Broeck G, Van Hoyweghen K, Maertens M (2018) Horticultural exports and food security in Senegal. Glob Food Sec 17:162–171. https://doi.org/10.1016/j.gfs.2017.12.00

Vemireddy V, Pingali PL (2021) Seasonal time trade-offs and nutrition outcomes for women in agriculture: evidence from rural India. Food Policy 102074

Warra AA, Prasad MNV (2020) African perspective of chemical usage in agriculture and horticulture their impact on human health and environment. In: Agrochemicals detection, treatment and remediation. Butterworth-Heinemann, pp 401–436

Chapter 13
Export Performance of the Horticultural Sub-Sector in Tanzania

William George

Abstract This chapter examines factors that influenced the performance of Tanzanian horticultural exports from 1988–2018. Data were collected from the Bank of Tanzania, the National Bureau of Statistics and the World Bank. Co-integration techniques were employed to examine the long-run relationships among the series. The results showed that the real exchange rate, agricultural gross domestic products and foreign income had significantly influenced horticultural export performance in the long-run. Real interest rates were revealed insignificant. The Error Correction Model confirmed the existence of co-integration among the series. An important policy implication is that flexibility of the exchange rate movements in line with the fundamentals of the economy is necessary. Efficient policies for the stabilization of interest rates should be put in place (e.g. ceiling on lending rates, lowering inflation rate, etc.). These are considered important policy measures to improve the horticultural export performance of Tanzania that may also be relevant for other sectors as well.

13.1 Introduction

Exports and their expansion are crucial in the process of economic growth. Export promotion has been a commercial policy issue that has attracted a lot of devotion both at national and international levels (Orindi 2011). Countries in the world are focusing on the export promotion of products mainly due to the limited local markets. The export sector of a country is crucial as a source of growth, which can be attributed to the foreign exchange earned. This is evident in the Tanzanian horticultural sub-sector which has been significant over the last decade both in the generation of foreign exchange and also in employment creation.

The horticultural sub-sector in the country has received a lot of interest from both international and local researchers, government and also donors due to its high growth rate and sustained export growth to Europe (Muendo and Tschirley 2004). The horticultural sector has significantly grown over the last decade to become the

W. George (✉)
University of Dodoma, Dodoma, Tanzania
e-mail: william.juma@udom.ac.tz

Table 13.1 Major Tanzanian trading partners for fruits and vegetables

#	Country	Share in percentage (%)
1	EU (Netherlands)	28
2	India	26
3	Kenya	17
4	United Arab Emirates	6
5	Comoros	6

Source ITC data retrieved on February 26, 2021

second biggest foreign exchange earner (after tea), employer (both directly and indirectly) and contributor to the food requirements in the country (Muhanji et al. 2011; Mutayoba 2015). Therefore, this sector needs to be studied in order to establish ways in which the sector can be further improved to continue to be a significant contributor to gross domestic product.

Tanzania's main trading partners are the Netherlands and India. Exports to these two countries add to more than half (54%) of the total export revenue of the sector. Trade with neighboring country Kenya accounts for 17%. The United Arab Emirates and Comoros each contribute six percent to the total export revenues (Table 13.1).

In Tanzania, fruit production includes mangoes, pineapples, mainly oranges among citrus fruits and bananas. Moreover, several major domestically produced and marketed vegetable crops are potatoes, onions and sweet potatoes (Table 13.2).

Sweet potato production is far vaster than originally anticipated, more than double the volume of Irish potatoes produced over that same period and much larger in Tanzania than the production in Kenya or Uganda (Table 13.3). Tanzania is reported to be the third largest producer of sweet potatoes in the world. This improved sweet potato productivity is attributed to various interventions from the government and private sector such as the development of improved sweet potato production technologies and alleviating socio-economic constraints (Kiiza et al. 2012).

The sub-sector comprises of large firms and also small scale farmers who usually sell their produce to these large farms through their marketing associations or

Table 13.2 Average production of major fruits and vegetables in Tanzania, 2010–2018

#	Fruits	Production (in MT)	Vegetables	Production (in MT)
1	Banana	3,184,832.80	Sweet potato	3,476.75
2	Mangoes, guava	422,816.70	Vegetables, fresh	1,819.71
3	Pineapple	363,910.80	Irish potatoes	1,572.54
4	Oranges	335,590.20	Tomato	374.57
5	Fresh fruits	201,566.40	Onion	140,700.00
6	Tropical fruits	50,543.30	Cabbage	67,938.00
7			Chillis and pappers, green	14,245.00

Source FAOSTAT, date accessed: 16/8/2021

Table 13.3 Vegetable and spice production of Tanzania and neighboring countries, 2010–2018 (in MT)

	Sweet potatoes	Green beans	Cloves
Kenya	822.36	39.01	2.03
United Republic of Tanzania	3,476.75	4.23	8.54
Mozambique	826.37	–	–
Rwanda	969.33	7.01	–
Uganda	1,837.97	–	–

Source FAOSTAT, date accessed: 21/7/2021

individually to brokers. The flower production and marketing chain is dominated by medium sized and large scale companies. The smallholder horticultural crop producers face many challenges mainly in production, post-harvest handling, and compliance with phytosanitary requirements, such as Global Gap regulations. In addition, access to capital by the smallholder producers is difficult. Over 90% of smallholders produce horticultural commodities but less than two percent do so directly for export (Tschirley et al. 2004; Nyange et al. 2019). Smallholders who produce for export face a lot of constraints in their efforts of seeking to remain in the sub-sector. The challenges are mainly from the increased consumer demand for quality and food safety (phytosanitary regulations) in Europe as well as from the rising numbers of supermarkets in this region.

The growth has been attributed to the increased consumption of horticultural products in Tanzania as compared to exports and this is the reason why the exports form a smaller percentage of the overall growth in the horticultural sector. Even, taking into consideration the high prices in the international market, the dominance of the local market is still evident (Tschirley et al. 2004; Simbeye 2015). The continued dominance of the local market, the slower growth rate in the export sector and constraints that smallholder farmers face in their efforts to gain access to the international markets should be addressed in order to improve the horticultural sub-sector.

13.1.1 Horticulture and the Tanzanian Economy

The horticultural sub-sector in Tanzania is the fastest growing agriculture sub-sector (Mashindano et al. 2013; TAHA, 2019). Nyange et al. (2019) argue that close to 2.5 million people are employed in both formal and informal horticultural setups. Multiplier effects can arise in horticultural production, especially in the production and packaging of production. For example, the demand for packaging materials can lead to the development of local plastic and paper manufacturing industries. The horticultural industry has helped to reduce poverty in rural areas as a result of higher incomes as compared to other crops. This is a result of forward and backward linkages. Nyairo and Backman (2009) argued that high export growth which is mostly facilitated by the increase in agricultural production is widely considered to be an important pathway to the reduction of poverty. Horticultural production provides small scale farmers with an opportunity for earning a regular income. Nyairo and Backman (2009) recognized that an increase in the production and export of horticultural products in Tanzania had resulted in increased incomes.

The analysis of available international trade data through 2018, suggests that comparing export values from fruit, vegetables and spices, the largest group is vegetables with a share of 47%. Spices follow with 37% and fruits only make up 16% of export value (Table 13.4).

Notable is the high value of spice exports. Cloves make up roughly 87% of all spice exports, with export volume averaging 1,051 MT per year and valued at USD 9.15 million per year over the most recent three years, 2016–2018. Note, however, that clove exports had fallen significantly from the levels of 2011–2014 of USD 35.65 million/year in revenue and 3,795 MT/year (averaged over four years) by the end of the decade. The COMTRADE data on black pepper exports appear to be inconsistent, showing 2014 exports of 1,302 MT valued at USD 14.6 million, with India importing 77% of the total exports at a unit price of USD 11,562 per MT. In contrast, the 2013 exports are reported at 919 MT valued at USD 146,100 (hence at a unit price of USD 159/MT). Reported exports in all of the other years of the decade of the 2010s did not exceed 112 MT (2012) and dropped to near zero in 2018. Clearly, there is an issue with the accuracy of data on black pepper. Trade data for other spices is spotty, with reports of some exports for a year or two, but not consistent exports over the decade.

Onions are the leading vegetable export crop at USD 11,915,000 followed by green beans at USD 8,278,000. Revenues for potatoes peaked in 2016 but otherwise remained well below USD 1 million per year. Export revenues for leeks increased towards the end of the decade to slightly above USD 2 million per year for 2016, 2017 and 2018 whereas revenues for tomatoes declined from USD 981,000 in 2013 to just USD 74,000 in 2018.

Oranges turn out to be the single most important exported fruit. Exports averaged 13,356 MT per year from 2010 through 2018, with nearly all exports going to Kenya in most years (with Rwanda as a minor secondary destination). The export value and unit values for orange exports to Kenya varied wildly, reported to be as high as USD 24.9 million and USD 2,250/MT in 2012, and as high as USD 22.2 million at USD 2111/MT in 2015, with far lower figures in the intervening years (USD 770,300 at USD 44/MT in 2013 and USD 489,800 at USD 42/MT in 2014).

Most other exported fruit also shows vast divergence across years between 2010 and 2018. Pineapple export revenue is reported at USD 1.0 million in 2018, a high for

Table 13.4 Distribution of Tanzanian fruit, vegetable and spices exports by value

#	Category	Percentage
1	Vegetables	47
2	Spices	37
3	Fruits	16

Source https://www.trademap.org/ accessed on 16/7/2021

the decade, while mango/guava export revenue averaged USD 280,000 and peaked at USD 2.1 million USD in 2016. Export data show modest export volumes for bananas, shipped mainly to neighboring countries (Malawi, Zambia), that reached 1,868 MT in 2016 (valued at USD 2.2 million) and 2,552 MT in 2018 (valued at USD 2.35 million). Exports of melons reached USD 293,300 in 2017, with 75% of that trade value coming from shipments of orange-fleshed melons to the UAE. Export volumes and values were far lower during the two surrounding years, 2016 and 2018, with markedly lower figures for exports to the UAE.

According to a household survey in Tanzania by Nyange et al. (2019), the households engaged in the production of horticultural crops were better off than the household which did not. In addition, a simulation exercise in the same survey showed that facilitating more households in venturing into the horticultural sector could help in reducing poverty considerably, both in rural and urban areas. Therefore it can be concluded that the horticultural sub-sector is important to the Tanzanian economy due to the foreign exchange earned by the country from horticultural exports.

13.1.2   Statement of the Problem

Horticultural production in Tanzania can be viewed as a success story, but looking generally at the percentage of horticultural exports in comparison with the total production, it is evident that the export sector constitutes only a small percentage of the total production. Between 1993 and 2016, 98% of the quantity of fruits produced and 91% of the quantity of vegetables produced were marketed locally (Mashindano et al. 2013). Over 80% of smallholders produce horticultural crops, but few do so directly for export. According to a competitiveness report by USAID (2017), Tanzania's export performance is below its potential, taking into consideration overall agricultural output, size of the economy, population, and arable land. It is indicated in the same report that horticultural exports constituted five percent of the total production. Over reliance on domestic markets has resulted in low domestic prices for the horticultural produce and hence there is a need to exploit the foreign market for horticultural commodities.

Although the horticultural export sub-sector had earlier achieved significant growth, it stagnated in the past decade. There is continued dominance of domestic horticultural production and the export sub-sector has experienced a slower growth rate (Guadagno et al. 2019). The slow growth rate in the horticultural sub-sector implies that the country has not been able to maximize the foreign exchange earned from the exports. Although much research has been carried out on the horticultural sector, few studies have empirically studied the export sector.

Tanzania implemented a number of trade and fiscal policy reforms since the mid-1980s as a way to promote export by providing incentives including abolishing export taxes/licenses and subscribing to preferential trade arrangements and treaties that provide fair access to foreign market opportunities. However, export performance has not been satisfactory. Previous studies have provided insights regarding the export performance which focused on the entire agriculture sector ignoring the fact that disaggregating the sub-sector would have a different response on export performance. For example, horticultural sub-sector and cereal sub-sectors demonstrate different export performances in Tanzania (Lipumba and Ndulu 1990). The present chapter seeks to examine the factors that influence the horticultural exports in Tanzania.

13.1.3 Research Objectives

13.1.3.1 Overall Objective

The overall objective of the study was to examine the determinants of the quantity of horticultural products exported and establish ways in which the horticultural export sub-sector could be improved so as to increase the contribution of the sector to the Gross Domestic Product (GDP) (in terms of income, employment and foreign exchange).

13.1.3.2 Specific Objectives

The specific objectives are:

(i)   To identify the relationship between agricultural GDP and export performance of the horticultural sub-sector in Tanzania
(ii) To determine the influence of real interest rate and real exchange rate on export performance of the horticultural sub-sector in Tanzania
(iii) To analyze the influence of foreign income of the trading partners on export performance of the horticultural sub-sector in Tanzania

13.1.3.3 Research Hypothesis

This study was guided by the following research hypotheses:

(a) Agricultural GDP have a positive impact on export performance of horticultural sub-sector
(b) There is a negative relationship between real interest rate and real exchange rate on export performance of horticultural sub-sector
(c) Foreign income have a positive impact on export performance of horticultural sub-sector

13.1.3.4 Significance of the Study

This study is important because the Tanzanian economy is dependent on agriculture as a source of economic growth (URT 2016). The horticultural sector is among the leading sub-sectors of agriculture in terms of income generation (Epaphra 2016). The study identified the factors which affect the performance of the horticultural sector either positively or negatively and recommended ways in which the sector could be improved. Also, the study is driven by the fact that the largest quantity of what is produced in the horticultural sector is consumed locally and the country cannot rely entirely on the domestic market because of the need to capture wider markets in order to earn more income. The horticultural export sub-sector stimulates economic growth in a number of ways e.g. linkages between production and international demand, economies of scale, and increased efficiency due to competition. In addition, when the horticultural exports increase, national goals such as the increase in GDP, rise in sectorial employment level, reduction in the trade deficit and improvement in income distribution can be realized. This study emphasizes on the horticultural sub-sector because Tanzania has a comparative advantage in the production of horticultural produce due to the agro-climatic conditions enhanced by the location of the country on the equator, which makes it possible for the production of horticultural crops throughout the year unlike competitors such as Egypt and Morocco. In addition, high dependence on one or few traditional exports e.g. coffee and tea can leave a country vulnerable to volatile international market conditions and hence the need for diversification.

13.2 Methodology

13.2.1 Data Sources and Types

Secondary data was used in this study. The data was time series from the year 1988 to 2018. This period is important as it covers the period in which the Tanzanian horticultural sub-sector had achieved a significant growth. Data on the quantity of horticultural products (fresh vegetables, fruits and flowers) exported from Tanzania was obtained from the National Bureau of Statistics (NBS). Also, the data on Tanzania's Agricultural GDP was obtained from the Economic Survey of the NBS. Data on foreign income of the major importing countries (trading partners) such as the Netherlands, India, Kenya, United Arab Emirates (UAE) and Comoros were obtained from the World Bank Development Indicators. The data on the exchange rate and real interest rate in Tanzania was obtained from the Bank of Tanzania (BOT).

13.2.2 Variables and Measurements

13.2.2.1 Volume of Horticultural Exports

Export are the dependent variable in this study. The unit of measurement is metric tons. This type of measurement had been chosen because total exports consists of a basket of goods and services therefore it was easily measured in terms of volume rather than other measurements.

13.2.2.2 Real Exchange Rate

Real exchange rate (RER) is the trade-weighted exchange rate against major trading partners computed as a product of nominal effective exchange rate and domestic consumer price index divided by foreign consumer price index. An increase in the real exchange rate makes the Tanzania's exports cheaper and competitive on the international market thereby increasing the volume of exports. A decrease in the real exchange rate makes Tanzania's exports relatively expensive and less competitive on the world market. A positive relationship between real exchange rate and volume of exports was therefore envisaged. The real exchange rate was computed as shown in Eq. 13.1.

$$RER = \sum_{i}^{n} \varepsilon_i \omega_i \tag{13.1}$$

where;

ω_i is the country i's share of trade with Tanzania and

ε_i is the real exchange rate defined in Eq. 13.2.

$$\varepsilon_i = \xi_i \times \frac{CPI_D}{CPI_F} \tag{13.2}$$

where:

ξ_i is the nominal exchange rate (how much of the trading partner's currency is needed to obtain 1 TZS,

CPI_D is the domestic consumer price index and

CPI_F is the consumer price index of the trade partner.

13.2.2.3 Foreign Income

Changes in national income in foreign countries affect the exports. This is mainly through the income effect. Income effect occurs when there is a change in consumption due to a change in real income. The income effect is clearly described by Engel curve which describes how expenditure by households on a particular good or service varies with household income. Therefore, a rise in the national income in foreign countries captured by GDP per capita will lead to an increase in foreign demand of exports as a result of income effect and a decline in national income in foreign countries will lead to a decrease in exports demanded. Therefore the income of the major trading partners as used in this study measures the absorptive capacity of those countries. An increase in the income of the trading partners will lead to an increase in the exports. Therefore the coefficient for the foreign income is expected to be positive.

13.2.2.4 Agricultural GDP

It is expected that as the agricultural GDP increases so do exports. Increases in agricultural GDP implies increased productivity in the sector. Therefore the coefficient for this variable is expected to be positive. Exports are function of output and therefore an increase in the agricultural output will lead to an increase in exports. This variable can also be explained in terms of the capacity to produce in the agricultural sub-sector. An increase in the agricultural GDP therefore implies that there is an increase in capacity to produce and hence an increase in exports.

13.2.2.5 Real Interest Rate

Real interest rate is defined as the nominal lending rate adjusted for inflation. The higher the real interest rate, the less resources are invested in the production of horticultural crops and the less the volume of exports. A negative relationship therefore was expected between horticultural exports and the real interest rate. The real interest rates were computed using Fisher's equation (Phillips 1998) as presented in Eq. 13.3.

$$RIR = LR - INF \tag{13.3}$$

where:

RIR = real interest rate,

LR = nominal lending rate and.

INF = the inflation rate.

13.2.3 Data Analysis

13.2.3.1 Descriptive Analysis

Descriptive analysis was used to assess the shape and spread of the dataset distribution of the five variables in the study. For examples, mean and median were used to give an indication of the average value of a distribution of figures. If the mean and median of each variable under study are about equal then a normally distributed data set can be expected. Standard deviation was used to measure the dispersion of a dataset relative to its mean. If the data points are further from the mean, there is a higher deviation within the data set and vice versa. Kurtosis was applied to measure whether the dataset is peaked or flat (heavy-left tailed or right tailed) in relation to a normal distribution. If the kurtosis of the variables fall in the range of -3 to 3 then the data set is normally distributed (Greene 2007). To measure symmetry or lack of symmetry of the data, the skewness test was used. A distribution is symmetric if it looks the same to the left and right of the center point. A normally distributed series falls into the acceptable range of -2 to 2 (Greene 2007). Maximum and minimum were used to measure how the values lie closer in the series.

13.2.3.2 Co-Integration Analysis

The study adopted the co-integration technique to examine the determinants of horticultural export in Tanzania. This technique is superior compared to other techniques such as panel and gravity modeling. This is because co-integration technique is able to establish the short run and long-run relationship amongst variables. Again this technique is used to estimate the unit root and co-integration test. Granger (1986) pointed out that testing for co-integration of the regression residual is imperative to avoid the possibility of producing spurious regression output. Since this study is a time series in nature it also examined the time series characteristics of the variables to be modeled, testing for stationary and co-integration of the variables.

13.2.3.3 Unit Root Test

Most time series data is usually non-stationary (the data exhibit trending behavior or non-stationarity in the mean). This implies that when estimation uses Ordinary Least Squares (OLS), spurious regression results can be yielded when time series data that is not stationary (contains unit root). In this case, the values of the time series do not fluctuate around a constant mean or with a constant variance. In spurious regression, a high R^2 is generated even if the explanatory variables have no relationship with the dependent variable. In addition, the t-statistics in spurious regression are likely to be significant even if there is no causal relationship between the dependent and the independent variables. In this case the usual t-ratios do not follow t-distribution. This implies that hypothesis testing for the regression parameters cannot be done because the results derived will be misleading. It is important to test the order of integration of each variable in a model, to establish whether it is non-stationary and how many times the variable needs to be differenced to derive stationary series. There are several ways of testing for a unit root. In this study, Phillips-Perron (1988) unit root test was used to check whether variables are stationary or not. The Philip-Perron test makes a correction to the t-statistic of the dependent variables in the autoregressive process to account for the serial correlation in random term. The null hypothesis of a unit root is rejected if the absolute value of the test statistic is greater than the critical values at the significance levels provided.

13.2.3.4 Co-Integration Test

Co-integration is vital to the analysis of the long-run relationships between time series economic variables. In this study, co-integration was tested using Engle and Granger (1987) two step approach. The first step involves applying OLS to the non-stationary variables (estimation of the long-run equation). The second step involves testing for the presence of unit root in residuals. The residuals are obtained from the long-run regression. The Augmented Dickey-Fuller (ADF) test was used to test for the unit root in the residuals. In this test the null hypothesis of co-integration is tested against the alternative hypothesis of absence of co-integration. Gujarati (2004) pointed out that if the computed absolute value of the t-statistic exceeds the Engle-Granger or Augumented Engle-Granger critical tau values, then we reject the null hypothesis of non-stationary and the alternative hypothesis of stationary will be favored.

13.2.4 Econometric Model

13.2.4.1 Estimation of Long-Run Relationship

In order to assess the relative impact of various factors on export performance, a multiplicative model was adopted in the following form (Eq. 13.4)

$$X_t = \beta_0 R_t^{\beta_1} Y_t^{f\beta_2} Ag_t^{\beta_3} I_t^{\beta_4} \varepsilon_t \qquad (13.4)$$

where:

Q_t = Quantity of horticultural exports in values in United States Dollar (USD).

β_0 = Constant.

$\beta_1 to \beta_4$ = Regression coefficients.

R_t = Real exchange rate in Tanzanian Shillings (TZS)/USD.

Y_t^f = Foreign income in USD captured by GDP per capita of major trading partners.

Ag_t = Agricultural GDP in USD over the years under study.

I_t = Real interest rate in percentage (%).

ε_t = Stochastic disturbance term.

In the estimation process, Eq. 13.4 above was linearized by use of the double-log to minimize the chance of committing specification errors and suit the time series behavior properly. Hence the transformed model is expressed in Eq. 13.5.

$$LnQ = \beta_0 + \beta_1 Ln(R_t) + \beta_2 Ln\left(Y_t^f\right) + \beta_3 Ln(Ag_t) + \beta_4 Ln(I_t) + \varepsilon_t \quad (13.5)$$

This study estimated the coefficients of long-run relationship amongst the variables using Eq. (13.3) after the regression residual found to be stationary. This was done using ADF test. Engle–Granger (1987) and Gujarati (2004) pointed out that if the regression residuals are stationary in the linear model, then coefficients are not spurious and hence representing long-run relationship amongst the variables. But if the regression residuals are non-stationary then regression coefficients obtained in the model are spurious. Thus, the coefficients in the above log linear model were interpreted as elasticity (percentage change in dependent variable due to change in the independent variable). As discussed above, the choice of the above variables is based on empirical and theoretical aspects in economics and specifically in international trade.

13.2.4.2 Estimation of an Error Correction Model

When the time series variables are co-integrated, an ECM can be adopted. Following Engle and Granger (1987) approach on co-integration, variables that are co-integrated can be modeled by an ECM. This involved running regression with first differences of dependent variable on independent variables that have been differenced once as well as one-period lagged equilibrium residuals that have been generated from the long-run (co-integrating) equation. All the variables in the error correction model are stationary. Standard hypothesis testing using t-statistics and diagnostic test for error term are also appropriate when using this model. According to Johansen (2010) since there is co-integration among dependent variable and its fundamentals, an error correction model has to be estimated by incorporating the lagged error correction term in the set of regressors. The error correction term is the residual from the static long-run regression and it joins the set of differenced non-stationary variables to be estimated to capture both short run and long-run dynamics. Following the Engel and Granger theorem, the original model (Eq. 13.5) was transformed into an error correction model. An error correction term (ECT_{t-1}) was introduced in the model and hence the final model ready for regression analysis becomes as presented in Eq. 13.6.

$$LnX = \beta_0 + \beta_1 Ln(R_t) + \beta_2 Ln\left(Y_t^f\right) + \beta_3 Ln(Ag_t) + \beta_4 Ln(I_t) + \beta_5 ECM_{t-1} + \varepsilon_t$$

$$(13.6)$$

Thus, an error correction term lagged once (ECT_{t-1}), which is the residual from the long-run equation of non-stationary variables, is included as one of the explanatory variables in the general transformed equation for the error correction model of determinants of export performance. This term captures the long-run relationship in an attempt to correct deviations from the long-run equilibrium path. The use of error correction terms helped to tie the short run behaviors of variables to its long-run. Its coefficient can be interpreted as the speed of adjustment from short run behavior to long-run equilibrium.

13.3 Results and Discussion

13.3.1 Descriptive Statistics of Variables

Table 13.5 gives the descriptive statistics of variables used in the study. Starting with the dependent variable, the quantity of horticultural exported, it has a mean of 12.22 and a median of 12.34. The mean and the median of the logarithm of exports are almost equal because the difference is very small (0.12). This implies that exports are normally distributed. The kurtosis is 1.87 which falls in the range of -3 to 3 for a normally distributed series. The maximum and minimum values are 13.24 and 10.96, respectively, implying that there are no outliers. The skewness is 0.56, suggesting the series is slightly skewed to the right. The standard deviation is 0.27, indicating

Table 13.5 Descriptive statistics of the variables

	LogQtsExp	LogR	LogRealexrate	LogFY	LogAgGDP
Mean	12.22	1.87	7.13	9.56	14.96
Median	12.34	1.90	7.64	9.57	14.96
Maximum	13.24	4.16	5.27	11.75	15.42
Minimum	10.96	−0.13	−0.44	11.23	14.77
Std Dev	0.266	0.62	0.38	0.30	1.58
Skewness	0.56	−0.80	−0.12	−0.17	−0.21
Kurtosis	1.87	2.75	2.16	1.60	2.12
Observations	22	25	22	31	31

Source Author's own computation from collected data
Where: LogQtsExp = logarithm of Quantity Exported, LogR = logarithm of real interest rate, LogRealexrate = logarithm of the real exchange rate, LogFY = logarithm of foreign income, LogAgGDP = logarithm of agricultural GDP

that the values are not wide spread out from the mean and hence there are no outliers in the dataset.

Regarding the real interest rate, the mean and the median are 1.87 and 1.90 respectively which implies that the series is normally distributed as the two measures of central tendency are almost equal. The maximum and the minimum values in this series are 4.16 and −0.13 respectively. This implies that there are no outliers as the difference between the maximum and the minimum value is not very large. The skewness and kurtosis are −0.80 and 2.75 respectively, indicating a normally distributed dataset. The standard deviation is 0.62 and thus the series is not widely spread out from the mean.

Concerning the real exchange rate, it has a mean of 7.13 and a median of 7.64. The difference between the mean and the median is 0.51 which is less than one. The maximum and the minimum values are 5.27 and −0.44 respectively, this suggests no outliers. The skewness of this series is −0.12 while the kurtosis is 2.16. Both the skewness and the kurtosis lie within the acceptable range for normal distribution. The standard deviation for this series is 0.38. Whereas the foreign income has a mean of 9.56 and a median of 9.57, almost no difference between these two measures of central tendency. The maximum value is 11.75 while the minimum value is 11.23. This is an indication that there is no outlier as the difference between the highest value and the lowest value is not big. The skewness and kurtosis for this dataset are −0.17 and 1.59 respectively which lies in the accepted range of a normally distributed dataset. The standard deviation is 0.29, implying that the data points are close to the mean.

Finally, regarding agricultural GDP, the mean and the median are 14.96 and 14.96 respectively. The two measures of central tendency are almost equal implying that the series is normally distributed. In addition the maximum and minimum values are 15.41 and 14 respectively, suggesting that there are no outliers in the dataset. The skewness for this series is −0.21 while the kurtosis is 2.12. Both the skewness and the kurtosis fall in the acceptable range for normal distribution. The standard deviation is 1.58, implying that the data points are close to the mean.

13.3.2 Stationarity Tests

The result of the Phillips-Perron (PP) tests are presented in Table 13.6. It shows that there was no stationarity in the level data for quantity of export, real exchange rate, real interest rate, foreign income and agricultural GDP. The absolute value of their tests was less than the absolute critical value of 2.96 at one percent level of significance. The null hypothesis of the presence of a unit root cannot be rejected.

The variables should be differenced due to the non-stationarity of all the variables used in the model. The first differences of the series (Table 13.7) were stationary, implying that all, the variables have one order of integration i.e. they were all integrated of degree 1 (I(1)). This indicates that the PP unit root test is an appropriate method for analyzing the long-run relationship between the series. The absolute value

Table 13.6 Phillips-Perron unit root test at the levels of the variables

Variable	Test statistic	1% Critical value
LogQtsExp	−0.803	−17.54
LogR	−12.38	−17.54
LogRealexrate	−2.03	−17.54
LogFY	−1.56	−17.54
LogAgGDP	−0.00	−17.54

Source Author's own computation from collected data

Table 13.7 Phillips–Perron (PP) unit root test at the first differences of the variables

Variable	PP Test Statistic
LogQtsExp	−38.70
LogR	−21.37
LogRealexrate	−40.22
LogFY	−39.33
LogAgGDP	−17.51

Source Author's own computation from collected data

of test statistics for variables tested was greater compared to the absolute critical values of 2.96 at a one percent level of significance. Therefore, the null hypothesis of the presence of a unit root was accepted.

13.3.3 Co-Integration Tests

The presence of co-integration among the series was tested by employing the ADF test approach. The results indicate that the critical values of −3.72 at one percent confidence levels are greater than the ADF test statistic of −4.53. This implies that there is co-integration among the series in the model. The existence of co-integration among the series aids in analyzing the long-run relationship of the factors that affected the growth of horticultural export in Tanzania.

The robust standard errors were used to correct the problem of heteroskedasticity. The $Chi^2(1) = 0.88$ and $Prob. = 0.35$. This shows $Prob. > Chi^2$ From the Breusch–Pagan test, that there is no heteroskedasticity. This indicates that the model was good enough for the study of co-integration among the variables.

13.3.4 Factors Affecting the Growth of Horticultural Sub-Sector

The model results of the long-run estimates of the factors affecting the growth perfor-mance of the horticultural sub-sector are presented in Table 13.8. The absolute value of the t-statistic determines the level of significance of a variable. From the regres-sion results of the long-run co-integrating equation, the agricultural GDP and the real exchange rate are statistically significant at 1% level of significance.

The agricultural GDP was an important variable which had significantly affected the horticultural export performance in Tanzania at 1% level of significance. Its partial elasticity was positive as expected at 1.22 in the long-run. This shows that a 1% increase in the agricultural GDP of the country will increase the export perfor-mance of the horticultural sub-sector by 1.22% in the long-run. The lag of the variable also had a significant role in explaining the export performance of the sub-sector. This confirmed that as the agricultural GDP of a country grows, more horticultural exports will be produced which will increase the possibilities of increasing horti-cultural exports. The results of this study are consistent with the empirical works of different researchers (Manji 2010; Anagaw 2013; Meme 2015).

The real exchange rate was another important variable which had significantly affected the horticultural export performance in Tanzania. The partial elasticity of horticulture exports to the change in the real exchange rate was positive as expected and significant at a 1% level of significance. The long-run coefficient value of 0.23 for the real exchange rate showed that a 1% increase (depreciation in the local currency) in the real exchange rate increased the quantity of export of horticultural crops by 0.23%. The lag of the variable also has a significant role in explaining the export performance of the sub-sector. This implies that policy measures regarding the real exchange rate have paramount importance in improving horticulture exports in the long-run. Contrasting to the findings of this study, other researchers have found that

Table 13.8 Long-run relationship (Co-integrating regression)

Variables	Coefficient	Std error	t-Statistics	(p-values)
LogR	−0.05	0.03	−1.76	0.09
LogRealexrate	0.23	0.05	4.91	0.00
LogFY	1.15	0.49	2.32	0.03
LogAgGDP	1.22	0.32	3.81	0.00
Constant	−30.50	6.16	−4.95	0.00
R-squared	0.98	Sum of squared residuals		13.68
F Statistic	321.15	Adjusted R-squared		0.98
Prob (F Statistics)	0.00	Residual sum of squares		0.27
Durbin-Watson statistic	2.17	Mean dependent variable		11.22

Source Author's own computation from collected data
Dependent Variable: LogQtsExp

the impact of the real exchange rate in explaining the export performance was revealed as insignificant or weak (Lakew 2003; Jongwanich 2007; Manji 2010; Mwinuka 2015). However, the findings of several other researchers were consistent with the results of this study (Hausmann et al. 2005; Allaro 2011; Anagaw 2013; Boansi 2013; Sawore 2015; Karamuriro 2015; Mabeta et al. 2015; Abolagba et al. 2016; Epaphra 2016). They all concluded that depreciation of the real exchange rate significantly affected the export performance of the respective countries.

The income of the importing country was also among the important variables hypothesized to influence the horticultural export performance of Tanzania. It was revealed as positive as expected and significant in the long-run at a 5% level of significance. The long-run coefficient indicated a one percent increase in foreign income of the importing countries would increase the export of horticulture by 1.15% in the long-run. This result is consistent with Sayeeda and Frank (2011); Maureen (2002); Karamuriro (2015). However, other studies had obtained a negative impact (e.g. Mabeta et al. 2015), and insignificant impact (Manji 2010; Sawore 2015) of foreign income on export performance.

The real interest rate was revealed insignificant in the long-run. The sign of the variable was shown negatively in the long-run similar to the hypothesis of the study. An increase in the real interest rate by one percent will lead to a decrease in the quantity of horticultural exports by approximately 0.05%. The insignificance of the real interest rate in influencing the horticultural exports can be attributed to the fact that the horticultural sub-sector is relatively more capital intensive as compared to other agricultural sub-sectors. For example, a significant amount of capital is required to set up green houses, cooling facilities, pack houses, and irrigation systems as well as the purchase of fertilizers, agrochemicals and other inputs. This is because when the real interest rate increases the cost of borrowing goes up thereby discouraging investors to borrow to finance their investment activities. In addition, the investors who will be already financing their loans will have less disposable income because they will be spending more on payment of interests. This will lead to a reduction in investment activities thereby resulting in a decline in the aggregate demand thereby leading to a decrease in horticultural exports. This result is inconsistent with Mabeta et al (2015). However, in the study by Meme (2015), the real interest rate had negatively influenced the horticultural export performance of Kenya.

13.3.5 Error Correction Model Estimation

The model results presented in Table 13.9, found a greater coefficient of the error-correcting term and it is statistically significant at one percent level of significance. In this model, the error correction coefficient was found with the expected sign which is negative (−1.09) which showed 109% of adjustment per annum. This confirms the existence of co-integration among the variables in the model. It also signifies that the variables in the model are adjusting faster from the short run to the long-run equilibrium. This result suggests the existence of a high speed of convergence to

Table 13.9 Error Correction Model (Short-run relationship)

Variables	Coefficients	Std error	t-Statistics	Prob
DLogR	−0.04	0.02	−1.97	0.06
DLogRealexrate	0.17	0.06	3.08	0.01
DLogFY	0 0.36	0.29	1.25	0.22
DLogAgGDP	1.21	0.37	3.22	0.00
ECT	−1.10	0.13	−8.56	0.00
Constant	0.01	0.03	0.58	0.57
R-squared	0.62	Mean dependent variable		0.07
Adjusted R-squared	0.54	S.D dependent variable		0.14
Sum of squared residuals	0.53	F-statistic		28.87
Durbin-Watson stat	1.75	Prob. (F-statistic)		0.00

Source Author's own computation from collected data
Dependent variable: LogQtsExp, Letter "D" in front of the variables is the difference operator (shows first difference) and ECT is the error correction term

long-run equilibrium amongst the variables. This finding is consistent with the result of the study by (Majeed et al. 2006).

13.4 Conclusion and Policy Implications

Overreliance on domestic markets has resulted in low domestic prices for horticultural produce and has exposed Tanzania to export earnings instability. To overcome this problem, different policy measures were taken to exploit the foreign market for horticultural commodities. Incentives have been provided for both foreign and domestic investors engaged in the horticultural sub-sector. In addition, different institutions working in the sub-sector like the Tanzania Horticultural Association (TAHA) and Exporters Association have been established to boost the horticultural sub-sector. These institutions represented the sub-sector in the country as well as internationally. Consequently, this growing sub-sector had recently become the second most important foreign earning source for the country. However, the performance of the sub-sector is far below its potential given the comparative advantages in the region. This study attempted to empirically examine the factors that affected the horticultural export performance of Tanzania, using time series data for the period between 1988 and 2018. It analyzed the influence of macroeconomic factors such as real exchange rate, real interest rate, foreign income and agricultural GDP. In testing this proposition, the ADF test was chosen to analyze the co-integration between horticultural exports and hypothesized variables. Based on the results of the study, real exchange rate, agricultural GDP and foreign income were important factors in influencing horticultural exports from Tanzania. The real interest was revealed insignificant in the long-run. These significant variables have an important policy implication in improving the horticultural export performance of the country. Therefore, the following policy implications with respect to the variables under the study are discussed:

- With regards to exchanging rate movements, there is a need to use policy instruments such as capping of interest rates to take care of interest rate differentials that may affect international capital flows. This may reduce the volatility of the exchange rate and stabilize foreign exchange earnings derived from the export of cotton and tobacco. In addition, monetary authorities in the country should formulate policies that maintain the real exchange rate at a level that is competitive for horticultural exports.
- Currently, interest rates in Tanzania are one of the highest. The government, therefore, needs to establish an agricultural development fund to provide credit at favorable and preferential rates. The interest rate charged by commercial banks and other financial institutions is very high and this discourages investors from borrowing to finance their horticultural farming. This in turn affects the performance of the horticultural sub-sector.
- It should be prioritized in terms of increased budget allocation in the sector and this will in turn raise agricultural GDP and drive the economy towards export diversification.
- To cushion the impact of changes in the income of the trading partner, the government should exploit available markets by increasing participation actively in regional integration.

Acknowledgments Author is thankful to Peter van Bergeijk and Binyam Afewerk Demena of Erasmus University, International Institute of Social Studies for technical guidance in carrying out the research work. The study was financially supported by Research on Poverty Alleviation (REPOA), the African Caribbean and Pacific Group of States (ACP Group) of this project, grant number FED/2019/408–112.

References

Abolagba EO, Abolagba OO, Omokhafe KO, Musa E, Mesike SC, Osazuwa S, Ogwuche P (2016) The performance of rubber exports in Nigeria. Glob Adv Res J Manag Bus Stud 5:347–353

Allaro HB (2011) Export performance of oilseeds and its determinants in Ethiopia. Am J Econ 1:1–14

Anagaw BK, Demissie WM (2013) Determinants of export performance in Ethiopia: VAR model analysis. Natl Mon Refereed J Res Commer Manag 2:5–94

Boansi D (2013) Competitiveness and determinants of cocoa exports from Ghana. Int J Agric Policy Res 1:236–254

Engle RF, Granger CWJ (1987) Cointegration and error correction: representation estimation and testing. Econometrica 55:251–276

Epaphra M (2016) Determinants of export performance in Tanzania. J Econ Libr 3:470–478

Granger CWJ, Engle RF (1987) Co-Integration and error correction: representation, estimation, and testing. Econometrica 55(2):251–276

Greene WH (2007) Econometric analysis. Macmillan Publishers, New York, p 134

Guadagno F, Wangwe S, Delera M, de Castro ABR (2019) Horticulture, and wood and furniture industries in Tanzania. https://www.theigc.org/wp-content/uploads/2019/11/Guadagno-et-al-2019-final-paper.pdf

Gujarati DN (2004) Basic econometrics, 4th edn. United States Military Academy, West Point. Online book, USA

Hausmann R, Pritchett L, Rodrik D (2005) Growth accelarations. J Econ Growth 10(4):303–329

International Trade Centre (ITC) (2020) Market opportunity of the horticultural products. MARKUP, the EU/EAC market access upgrade programme. EU funded

Johansen analysis of cointegration vectors SS (2010) J Econ Dyn Control 12:231–254

Jongwanich J (2007) Determinants of export performance in East and Southeast Asia; Working Paper Series, No. 106. Economic and Research Department, Asian Development Bank: Mandaluyong, Philippines.

Karamuriro HT, Karukuza WN (2015) Determinants of Uganda's export performance: a gravity model analysis. Int J Bus Econ Res 4:45–54

Kiiza B, Kisembo LG, Mwanga ROM (2012) Participatory plant breeding and selection impact on adoption of improved sweetpotato varieties in the East Africa. J Agric Sci Technol 2:673–681

Lakew B (2003) Prospects for export diversification in Ethiopia. National Bank of Ethiopia economic research department NBE staff working paper ERD/SWP/007/2003. National Bank of Ethiopia, Addis Ababa, Ethiopia

Lipumba NHI, Ndulu BJ (1990) International trade and economic development in Tanzania. In: Trade and development in Sub-Saharan Africa. Manchester University Press, Manchester

Mabeta J, Bett HK, Kiprop SK, Gutema TY (2015) Growth of Tobacco exports in Zambia: an ARDL approach. J Econ Sustain Dev 6:178–188

Manji S (2010) Export performance and determinants in Ethiopia. MPRA Paper No. 29427. Available online: https://mpra.ub.uni-muenchen.de/29427/. Accessed on 22 May 2021

Majeed, M. T., Ahmad, E., & Khawaja, M. I. (2006) Determinants of exports in developing countries [with comments]. The Pakistan Development Review, 1265–1276

Mashindano O, Kazi V, Mashauri S, Baregu S (2013) Taping export opportunities for horticulture products in Tanzania: do we have supporting policies and institutional frameworks? Economic and Social Research Foundation Dar es Salaam, Tanzania

Maureen W, Ndungu NS, Geda A, Karingi SN (2002) Analysis of Kenya's export performance: an empirical evaluation. KIPPRA (Kenya Institute for Public Policy Research and Analysis) Discussion Paper No. 22 November 2002. KIPPRA, Nairobi, Kenya

Meme SM (2015) Export performance of the horticultural subsector in Kenya—an empirical analysis. PhD thesis, University of Nairobi, Nairobi, Kenya

Muendo KM, Tschirley D (2004) Improving Kenya's domestic agricultural production and marketing system: current competitiveness of change, and challenges for the future. Working paper no 08C/2004. Tegemeo Institute of Agricultural Policy, Nairobi, Kenya

Muhanji G, Roothaert RL, Webo RC, Mwangi S (2011) African indigenous vegetable enterprise and market access for small-scale farmers in East Africa. Int J Agri Sustain 9(1):194–202

Mutayoba V (2015) Market performance and farmers' choice of marketing channels of high value crops. Int J Econ Commer, Manag 3(8):1–14

Mwinuka L, Mlay F (2015) Determinants and perfomance of sugar export in Tanzania. J Financ Econ 3:6–14

Nyairo N, Backman S (2009) Analysis of factors affecting the supply of agricultural products: market liberalization, agricultural policies, bioenergy policies, population growth, input price development, trade policies and other relevant factors. Discussion Paper No. 36. University of Helsinki, Department of Economics, Helsinki, Japan

Nyange D, Kadigi I, Muyanga M, Remen K, Kilenga P (2019) Agriculture trans-formation in Tanzania: a case of horticulture subsector. USAID, National Bureau of Statistics, Michigan State University (ASPIRES Project) and TAHA, pp 35–49

Orindi MN (2011) Determinants of the Kenyan exports: a gravity model approach. Int J Appl Econ 1(1):3–14

Phillips PCB (1998) Econometric analysis of Fisher's equation. Cowles Foundation Discussion Paper #1180, Yale University

Phillips PCB, Perron P (1988) Testing for a unit root in time series regression. Biometrika 75, 335ñ346

Sayeeda B, Frank S (2011) New Zealand Kiwifruit export performance: market analysis and revealed comparative advantage; working paper in economics 08/11. University of Waikato, Hamilton, NZ, USA

Sawore A (2015) Determinants of export trade in econometric study with special reference to Ethiopia. Int J Sci Res Index Copernic 78:132–137

Simbeye F (2015) Post harvest losses in horticulture at over 50pc. The guardian. Retrieved 28th October 2021 from http://www.dailynews.co.tz/index.php/biz/44716-post-harvest-losses-in-hor ticulture-at-over-50pc

TAHA (Tanzanian Horticultural Association) (2019) Horticulture industry in Tanzania: opportunities, challenges, and the way forward. pp 27

Tschirley D, Muendo MK, Weber TM (2004) Improving Kenya's domestic horticultural production and marketing system: current competitiveness, forces of change, and challenges for the future. Working paper no. 08B/2004. Tegemeo Institute of Agricultural Policy and Development, Nairobi, Kenya

United Republic of Tanzania (2016) Horticultural development strategy: 2016–2020

USAID (2017) Global competitiveness study: benchmarking Tanzania's horticulture sector for enhanced export competitiveness. Dar es Salaam, Tanzania: Fin

Phillips-Perron (1988)

Chapter 14
The Seaweed Sector in Zanzibar: A Multimethod Approach to Value Chain Analysis

Wahida H. Makame

Abstract Seaweed is one of Zanzibar's most important cash crops for exports with substantial livelihood (income to many poor people especially women) but as yet unrealized potential. This chapter examines the livelihood aspects of the seaweed value chain in Zanzibar in 32 villages using a multi method approach including focus group discussions, a survey, key informant interviews, and field observations. We seek to identify practices, challenges, and opportunities facing the seaweed value chain in Zanzibar and recommend policy interventions for scaling up the competitiveness of the sector. The survey involved 2290 seaweed farmers from 32 villages in 2021. Nearly half of the surveyed farmers had no formal education. This situation underlies challenges including low technology uptake and innovation, wide information and knowledge gaps, and low income and productivity. Quality, an important factor for determining price and export competitiveness, does not receive much attention as yet among seaweed farmers. Seaweed is highly impacted by climate change thus farmers move locations as the main adaptation strategy. Other challenges are weak infrastructure, high taxation, and conflicts of space between seaweed, tourism, and fishing activities. To increase export competitiveness of seaweed, Zanzibar needs to invest in education and research, quality management, tailor made trainings, and physical infrastructure. Strong coordination with stakeholders and strengthening of the policy and institutional framework are vital.

Author is thankful to Peter van Bergeijk and Binyam Afewerk Demena of Erasmus University, International Institute of Social Studies for technical guidance in carrying out the research work. The study was financially supported by Research on Poverty Alleviation (REPOA), the African Caribbean and Pacific Group of States (ACP Group) of this project, grant number FED/2019/408-112.

W. H. Makame (✉)
Ministry of Blue Economy and Fishery, Zanzibar, Tanzania
e-mail: siswahida@yahoo.com

14.1   Introduction

Zanzibar is the third country in the world in the production of *Spinosium* type of seaweed and has a long history as a significant producer of seaweed in the world. Wild seaweed farming existed for a long time. Commercial farming of red seaweed started in 1989 after two private companies imported *Eucheuma* seaweed from the Philippines and established two pilot firms at Jambiani and Paje on the island of Unguja (Msuya 2011a). Later, seaweed farming spread to other areas on Unguja and Pemba that currently accounts for 80% of total seaweed production in Zanzibar.

The archipelago of the islands of Zanzibar lies in the Indian Ocean off the coast of the Eastern Africa. Zanzibar is composed of two main sister islands which are Unguja and Pemba covering a total area of 2654 km^2 of which 1,666 km^2 are for Unguja and 988 sq km are for Pemba.[1] Zanzibar also has about 50 islets. The population of Zanzibar for the year 2020 was 1.6 million. The Zanzibar economy for the year 2020 grew at 1.3 percent (7.0 percent in 2019). For the year 2020, GDP at current prices stood at TZS 4,209 billion (US$ 1,8 billion), per capita income of 1, 870,000 (US$ 808). Zanzibar's climate is warm and humid (equatorial climate).

Zanzibar farms two main varieties of seaweeds which are *Eucheuma denticulatum* and *Kappaphycus alvarezii* commercially known as spinosum and cottonii, respectively. The cottonii is of high quality and fetches slightly higher prices than spinosum. However, Zanzibar produces high amounts of spinosium because these seaweeds can grow in shallow water. These types of seaweeds are easier for seaweed farmers of whom women constituted about 80% (Zanzibar Ministry of Agriculture, Natural Resources and Livestock 2019) to grow it. Cottonii is higher priced as compared to spinosium but prone to environmental changes and thus results in too many die-offs (Msuya 2006). Table 14.1 presents the production of two varieties of seaweeds in Zanzibar for the years 2015–2020.

Table 14.1 Seaweed production by species from 2015 to 2020

Year	Espinosium seaweed		E. Cottonii seaweed	
	Quantity	Value	Quantity	Value
	Tons	TZS. Mil	Tons	TZS. Mil
2015	16,665	9,409	58	60
2016	11,113	4,933	1	1
2017	10,955	4,382	26	35
2018	10,296	4,212	129	147
2019	9,559	5,536	104	132
2020	8,668	5201	116	186

Source Zanzibar Office of the Chief Government Statistician—OCGS, 2020

---

[1] The Revolutionary Government of Zanzibar was formed on 12th January 1964. The then two independent states, Zanzibar and Tanganyika united on 26th February 1964 to form the United Republic of Tanzania. Besides being part of the Union, Zanzibar has her own elected President, Legislature and Judiciary System (except for the court of appeal).

Seaweeds are widely used as food, production of hydrocolloids, as fertilizers and soil conditioners, animal feed, fish feed, biomass for fuel, cosmetics, wastewater treatment, and integrated aquaculture (Dennis 2003). In Zanzibar, about 99% of the seaweed is exported in raw form. Major markets for Zanzibar seaweeds are Denmark, USA, Spain, France, China, South Korea, Philippines, and Vietnam.[2] Despite being one of the priority sectors in the blue economy agenda of Zanzibar, the seaweed sub-sector has been facing many challenges including climate change, diseases, low levels of technology and value addition, lack of standards, inadequate drying facilities, low price, inadequate storage facilities, and working tools.

Upgrading the seaweed industry is the priority of the Revolutionary Government of Zanzibar under its Blue economy agenda. The sector remains to be the main source of income to many poor people especially women. Hence there is potential for programs aiming to eradicate poverty and gender empowerment. The Government has taken initiatives to upgrade the seaweed sub-sector including free provision of tools and equipment to seaweed farmers, capacity building programs, and the ongoing construction project for seaweed processing plant in Pemba. Private stakeholders as well have joined hands with the government to assist seaweed farmers and entrepreneurs. However, any interventions geared toward improving the seaweed sector need to be tailor made and fit with the environment surrounding this particular sector including the nature of seaweed farmers and the farming area. Previous research on seaweed mainly focuses on socioeconomic benefits and there are only a few studies that analyze the seaweed value chain in Zanzibar.

This chapter aims to analyze the seaweed value chain in Zanzibar and to provide policy recommendations for scaling up the competitiveness of the seaweed sector. The research seeks to answer the following questions. What are the socio characteristics of seaweed farmers in Zanzibar? What are the practices of the seaweed farming in Zanzibar? What and how are the issues affecting seaweed farming in Zanzibar? Which policy recommendations potentially scale up the competitiveness of the seaweed sector, specifically focusing on export market?

The remainder of this chapter is organized as follows: Sect. 14.2 describes the methods and methodology followed by Sect. 14.3 explaining findings and discussions whereas Sect. 14.4 presents some conclusions.

14.2 Methods and Methodology

The study uses a multimethod approach, namely, focus group discussions (FGD; Picture 14.1), key informant (KI) Interviews, survey, observation in the field (Picture 14.2), document analysis,[3] and collection and analysis of quantitative

---

[2] China, South Korea and Philippines cover 57%, 28% and 4% of world seaweed production n 2019, respectively. This is much higher than that of Zanzibar which was 0.3%. All import seaweeds from Zanzibar to complement local production.

Picture 14.1 Focus group discussion participants, village of Bweleo

Picture 14.2 Field observation (seaweed products, village of Paje)

Table 14.2 Summary of population of seaweed farmers per domain

Domain	N
Pemba (Female)	7,593
Pemba (Male)	4,112
Unguja (Female)	3,494
Unguja (Male)	328
P.M. total number of seaweed farmers in Zanzibar	15,527

primary data (survey). Prior to the survey, four FGDs were conducted in March 2021 involving 10 focus group discussants per FGD making a total of 40 focus group discussants. The FGDs were conducted in order to get initial information about the seaweed industry. The FGDs involved a mixture of both male and female seaweed farmers as well as processors. This was conducted at Paje and Bweleo villages (Unguja) and Tumbe village (Pemba). All the FGDs were recorded using voice recorder upon the consent from the respondents. The FGDs took place at respondents' business premises and homes. Information generated from the FGDs was used in preparing different topics covered in the survey questionnaire in April 2021. Next, the structured questionnaire was pre-tested to seaweed farmers at Bweleo and Chukwani villages in Unguja islands in May 2021.[4]

14.2.1 Sampling Design and Size

The survey involved a population of seaweed farmers carrying out their activities in Zanzibar. The survey population was divided into three domains which represented female farmers from Unguja and Pemba while male seaweed farmers from both Unguja and Pemba formed a single domain. The distribution of these geographical-gender domains is shown in Table 14.2.

The survey deployed a two-stage cluster sampling with probability proportional to size selection. *Shehias* (local areas) were taken as clusters where a sample of them was drawn based on their sizes during the first stage. These shehias formed the primary sampling units of the survey. There is a total of 75 shehias (out of 388 shehias) which have been identified to be the population of the topic. Out of all these shehias (clusters), 33 were selected to be included in the survey.

In the second stage of sampling, samples of seaweed farmers were selected from each shehia using a systematic selection method. The selection was made from the list of all seaweed farmers which have been recorded from each of the selected shehias. From each cluster, a sample of 50 seaweed farmers was selected. The size of the

---

[3] Textbooks, journal articles, dedicated websites and national plans governing the seaweed sector in Zanzibar were consulted.

[4] Qualitative research thus preceded the quantitative approach. However, where deemed necessary, telephone conversation was used to get clarification and collect more information from KIs after the survey had been completed.

cluster sample taken was chosen by balancing the cost and precision since lowering the sample take per cluster tends to rise the precision of the estimate, but increases the cost of enumeration due to increase in number of clusters to be selected for the study.

The sampling frame which was available for this study comprised of the individual respondents at shehia level. Analysis of this sampling frame showed large variability in terms of the number of individuals between clusters and therefore some of the clusters were selected more than once for inclusion in the survey because of their size. This was so because of the probability proportional to size selection method in which larger clusters had higher probability of being selected compared to smaller ones. Therefore, some of the clusters had multiple samples taken, that is 100, 150, or 200 depending on their size.

In order to meet requirements for the actual sample size and sample take per domain, the total sample size was slightly adjusted to the nearest multiple of 50. This adjustment resulted in a slight increase of sample size which further increased the precision of the final estimates.

The sample size for the survey was determined for each domain independently. In determining the sample size, the following parameters were used:

- Proportion of population with the characteristic of interest was unknown and thus 0.5 was used for yielding an optimum sample size;
- Margin of error was set to be 0.05;
- Design effect of the proposed design was 1.5;
- Non-response rate was assumed to be 5%;
- Since the population was known, a finite population correction (fpc) was applied to adjust the calculated sample size;
- The total sample size was the sum of the domain sample sizes.

Equation 14.1 was used to calculate the domain sample size for the survey:

$$n = \frac{Deft^2(1 - P)}{\alpha^2 P} \tag{14.1}$$

where n is the sample size, $Deft$ is the design effect, P is the proportion of target population with the characteristic of interest and α is the margin of error. Equation 14.1 yields the same sample size for whatever size of the target population. In order to take population size into consideration, a finite population correction was applied to adjust the final sample size. The finite population correction was calculated using Eq. 14.2:

$$n = \frac{n_0 N}{N + n_0} \tag{14.2}$$

where n is the adjusted sample size, n_o is the originally calculated sample size and N is the population. Applying these equations and taking into consideration the

Table 14.3 Summary of population and selected sample individuals

Domain	Net Sample Size	Sample adjusted for fpc[a]	Sample adjusted for non-response
Pemba (Female)	900	805	847
Unguja (Female)	900	716	753
Unguja & Pemba (Male)	900	739	778
Zanzibar	2,700	2,260	2,378

[a] Finite population correction

adjustment for non-response, the sample sizes for each of the three domains are presented in Table 14.3.

Adjusting the total sample size of 2,378 to the nearest multiple of 50 (which was the sample taken per cluster), this yields a total sample of 2,400 individuals. These individuals were selected from 33 clusters as explained earlier.

14.2.2 Data Collection

Based on the list of seaweed producing villages provided by the Zanzibar Ministry of Agriculture, Irrigation, Natural Resources and Livestock, a sample of villages to be surveyed was drawn wherein seaweed farmers were listed. The seaweed farmers listing exercise was conducted in May and June 2021 and involved 12 villages from Unguja and 21 villages from Pemba.[5] During the listing exercise, meetings were conducted with seaweed farmers, highlighting, among others, the purpose of research and urging the farmers to participate fully in the research. The meetings were conducted in nine villages in Unguja Islands. These villages are Kilindi, Potoa, Pongwe, Nyamanzi, Bungi, Kajengwa, Chukwani, Uzi, and Ng'ambwa and were very useful in generating more information about the seaweed industry.

Prior to data collection in the field, a three-day training for enumerators was conducted in early July 2021 at the office of the Zanzibar Ministry of Blue Economy and Fishery at Pemba to create a common understanding on the questionnaire and survey approach in general. In total, the study managed to survey a total of 2290 respondents out of a sample of 2400 respondents from 32 villages (out of sample of 33 villages in Zanzibar), making for a response rate of 95%. Importantly, during the listing exercise, it was found that farmers in Fukuchani village in Unguja no longer farmed seaweed hence the survey was not conducted in this village.

---

[5] The villages surveyed on Unguja Island were Kilindi, Bungi, Potoa, Pongwe, Nyamanzi, Muungoni, Kajengwa, Chukwani, Uzi, Urowa and Ng'ambwa and on Pemba Island Tumbe Mashariki, Tumbe Magharibi, Mtemani, Mjini Wingwi, Micheweni, Shumba Mjini, Sizini, Kinowe, Shanake, Tondooni, Makangale, Chokocho, Maziwa Ng'ombe, Kiuyu Mbuyuni, Gando, Kiuyu Minungwini, Kambini, Mchanga mdogo, Fundo and Chwale.

In particular, 1672 and 618 seaweed farmers were surveyed in Pemba and Unguja, respectively, around July, August, and November 2021. The survey questionnaires were developed in English and translated into '*Kiswahili*', the local language that was used to collect information from the respondents during the whole study. The survey questionnaire focused on the following topics: (1) socio-economic characteristics of farmers, (2) seaweed farming practices, (3) marketing information and income, (4) economic activities, (5) health and safety, (6) associations, processes and management, (7) finance, saving and credit services, (8) quality and standards, (9) the Zanzibar Seaweed Cluster Initiative (ZaSCI) and (10) challenges. The survey questionnaires took at least 30 min to complete and included both open and closed questions. The survey took place in various locations including at respondents' homes, open spaces in the villages and at the beaches. One or two days before the interview, the local leader (*sheha*) and/or seaweed committee leader was informed about the fact that the research team would be coming to their particular village. Once the research team reached the village, names of the selected farmers were announced in front of the farmers and list of names was put on the wall of the house of the local leader or any place where many people pass. This was done especially in Pemba where farmers had no access to Internet. In Unguja, the list of the selected farmers was sent to the farmers or community leaders through *WhatsApp* a few days before the start of the survey.

Face to face semi-structured interviews were conducted using '*Kiswahili language*' with at least 15 KIs (10 male and 5 female) including government officials, seaweed buyers, Zanzibar Seaweed Cluster Initiative, seaweed committee leaders, and seaweed farmers with vast knowledge and experiences in the seaweed industry. The KIs were selected using nonprobability sampling through purposive sampling. During data collection at the field, some potential KIs were identified through suggestions from farmers thus embracing a snowball method. The KIs covered the topics as outlined in the survey questionnaire and also some new ones. Topics covered under KIs with seaweed companies (buyers), for example, included (1) operation of the company's business, (2) relationships between buyers and their stakeholders (3) challenges from farmers, and (4) challenges from the institutional framework. Other topics covered under KIs with community leaders and knowledgeable person were relationships between buyers and company agents, the selling process of seaweeds, the price and markets of seaweeds. The KIs were conducted at various locations including respondents' offices and open spaces in the village. We recorded responses from KIs and observation on notebooks.

During the field work, the research team also observed various environments surrounding the seaweed industry. We observed how the farming was conducted at the sea, post-harvesting processes such as transportation, drying (Picture 14.3), measurement, and selling of seaweeds to the company agents. We also observed the way '*tie tie*' were prepared and the way seaweeds were tied on the nylon ropes. We saw different tools that were used in seaweed farming activities such as wooden pegs, iron rods, hammer, nylon ropes, drying racks, and small boats.

Picture 14.3 Sun drying of seaweeds

14.2.3   Survey Data Analysis

The quantitative data from the survey was collected through the Cispro data entry program and analyzed as descriptive statistics using the Statistical Package for the Social Science (SPSS) and Microsoft Excel. Qualitative data collected from transcripts of KI, FGDs, meetings, and observations were collected manually, summarized and analyzed. The survey also used secondary data to complement primary data.

14.3   Findings and Discussions

In this section, we first discuss the livelihood aspects of the seaweed farmers in Zanzibar. Next, we provide aspect of quality, technology, and marketing of seaweeds and the section ends with a discussion of policy issues affecting seaweed farming activities in Zanzibar.

14.3.1   Livelihoods

Agriculture, forestry, and fishing sector is the industry that engages most of the employed persons: 36% (ILFS, 2020/201) in Zanzibar. According to the *Poverty Assessment Report* by Belghith et al. (2017), more than half (56%) of the population of Zanzibar in rural areas were engaged in agriculture. The major cash crops that are grown for exports are cloves and seaweed. Seaweed is the third largest contributor to GDP preceded by clove and tourism. It is estimated that about 24,000 persons in Zanzibar are engaged in seaweed farming whereas women account for more than 80% of the total seaweed farmers (Zanzibar Ministry of Agriculture, Natural Resources and Livestock 2019).

On average, the majority of farmers spent about four to five hours per day, six days per week, and two weeks per month in seaweed farming. These are the times that were usually spent by farmers when doing seaweed activities at the sea area, for example, planting and harvesting of seaweed. However, the researcher has noticed other activities being done by seaweed farmers at home such as preparing tie tie and putting them across ropes, drying, cleaning, and packing seaweeds in the bags. The majority of seaweed farmers confirmed that seaweed farming takes place throughout the year though there are times when seaweed farming is at a high peak and times when seaweed farming is low. During stakeholders meeting, a farmer from Shanake village stated that:

In our village, seaweed can grow very well throughout the year and can die throughout the year depending on the area where the seaweed is planted) (Anonymous, Farmer, Shanake village during stakeholders meeting on 21ˢᵗ December 2021).

Being the oldest sub-sector, 80% of the surveyed seaweed farmers have been in the industry for more than six years with a highest concentration of 6–10 years. This confirms an earlier study by Ronald et al. (2015) who reported that the majority of the interviewed seaweed farmers in Zanzibar had a farming experience of 6 to 10 years. Interestingly, 77% of seaweed farmers reported to have learnt about seaweed farming for the first time by observing their colleagues during seaweed farming activities.

Seaweed farmers started seaweed farming using different sources of capital, including assistance from seaweed company (buyer), own savings, assistance from friends and relatives. More than 70% of the farmers started seaweed farming with their own savings. The amount of start-up capital for about 78% of farmers ranged between TZS 40,000 to TZS 50,000 (TZS 1000 = US $0.43). Farmers were also able to start the seaweed farming with capital below TZS. 30,000. This is because seaweed farming involves related people living in the same society. Therefore, it becomes easy for new farmers to get raw materials freely, for example, seaweed seedlings. During the introduction of seaweed farming in Zanzibar economy, some seaweed companies (buyers) were giving to farmers free farming materials such as ropes and 'tie tie' to encourage them to farm seaweeds.

The survey results showed that the proportion of males earning high quantities of seaweed per season was higher than that of females despite the fact that females constituted about 90% of the total seaweed farmers (Msuya and Hurtado 2017). This suggests that males have advantages in the industry which could be attributed to access equipment such as boats and bicycles for transporting seaweed. This situation also implies that if more men participate in the sector, production of seaweed may increase. To put this figure into perspective for other seaweed producing countries, studies have shown that both men and women have significant participation. For example, in the Philippines and the Solomon Islands, the share of men in seaweed farming 60% and 68%, respectively (Bacaltosi et al. 2012 and Kronen et al. 2010). In Indonesia, 70% of seaweed farmers were women (Wulari 2020).

Importantly, 97% of seaweed farmers confirmed that the income earned from seaweed was not satisfactory as compared to the efforts put into seaweed farming. According to a 2018 study by ZPC, Zanzibar seaweed farmers were realizing between 30 and 40% of the export price compared to farmers in the Philippines and Indonesia who earned between 60 and 70% of the export price. By the time the study was conducted, the mean price for seaweed was TZS. 596 per kilogram whereas in Indonesia in 2019, the price varied between US $0.6 and US $0.85 per kg of dried seaweed during the time of the study whereas in Philippines in 2019, dried seaweed fetched the equivalent of $1.60 per kilogram.

About 80% of the seaweed farmers were engaged in different types of economic activities apart from seaweed farming. At least 65% of seaweed farmers were engaged in small-scale agriculture followed by fishing whereby women seaweed farmers dominated small-scale agriculture while man dominated the fishing sector.

FGDs results revealed that seaweed farmers were also engaged in other small business, wage employment, handicrafts, cookery, and construction of buildings as their source of additional income. Despite having engaged in other economic activities, at least 95% of seaweed farmers across both islands considered seaweed farming as their main income activity.

14.3.2 Quality, Technology, and Marketing of Seaweeds

Seaweed farmers dried their seaweed with the help of sun, mostly on the ground (sand) or in trees (Fig. 14.3). About 71% of farmers dried their seaweed on bare land hence exposed seaweed to sand. Sun drying of seaweeds on trees was observed during the field, it was taken as an innovative approach since it is rare. Very few used local mats, plastics mats, drying racks, floors, or combination of these tools. ZPC (2018) revealed that the lack of modern drying facilities (e.g., solar driers), screeners and transportation equipment has significantly affected the quality of seaweed produced in Zanzibar. Mariño et al. (2019) for Indonesia reported that 64% of seaweed farmers used drying structures along the beach elevated from the ground while 18% placed their seaweed on the ground when their elevated drying structures are full. According to various seaweed studies, the most important quality factors for seaweeds are moisture content, seaweed maturity, and impurities. Therefore, the drying process is a very critical process for determination of the quality of seaweeds. Neish (2013) reported that the drying process determines the quality of seaweeds.

Quality is one of the determinant factors for price. Generally, the good quality product fetches the higher price. In the seaweed industry in Zanzibar, all farmers were unaware of the quality standards for seaweeds. The seaweeds were treated with no grades, and only those considered as good are bought from farmers by company agents, unlike in other seaweed producing countries which have grades with different prices. For example, in Indonesia, seaweeds affected by diseases and wet seaweeds are sold at a lower price (Zamroni et al. 2011). Moreover, all seaweed farmers confirmed that there were no set up quality standards that they were supposed to conform to during each stage of farming seaweed. Nor et al. (2017) stated that Malaysia has laid down seaweed standards on seaweed cultivation, dried seaweed, and semi-refined carrageenan.

Once dried, seaweeds are packed in bags and stored at farmers houses and/or warehouses. About 85% of seaweed farmers stored their seaweed in their houses. However, in some villages, seaweed companies have built warehouses near the sea where farmers can store their seaweed, and this was noticed especially in Pemba Island. Even in the company warehouses, seaweeds were not very well handled to ensure no contamination with sands and other contaminants.

Commercial seaweeds farming in Zanzibar existed for more than 30 years, yet the majority of farmers have been using the same way of planting seaweeds. Farmers used mainly line or off bottom methods rather than floating method despite having confirmed that planting seaweeds at high water level using floating method may help to reduce die-offs due to heat as well as contaminants thus increasing productivity. This is in line with the study by Msuya (2007) who reported that floating line method has advantage of reducing die-offs that occur using the off-bottom method.

About 87% of the farmers reported that they had not used seaweed for own consumption. Seaweed has many benefits and uses; little consumption of it meant that seaweed farmers did not benefit from medicinal properties of seaweed, taking into consideration that 60% of them got health-related seaweed problems such as overall body and joint pains. The lower level of seaweed consumption was also the result of low use of value addition technologies. The survey found that 95% of the farmers did not engage in seaweed processing and value addition technologies. Generally, all seaweed currently produced in Zanzibar are exported in raw form reducing potential incomes.

The meetings, KIIs, and FDGs results indicated that farmers lacked knowledge on the use and benefits of seaweeds. One of the farmers stated during the meeting:

we don't consume seaweed for ourselves because we don't know the use and benefits of seaweed. If seaweed have medicinal properties, those results from research should be shared to us so that we can use them for our benefits'. Other farmer commented *'we recommend to be given knowledge on value addition for seaweed so that we can produce different products for selling (Introductory Meeting at Kajengwa Village in Unguja, March 2021).*

Generally, the study found that farmers were lacking information on different aspects of seaweed. During FGDs, discussants explained that they had been told by seaweed consultant from Indonesia that those considered as 'dirties' in Zanzibar were a type of seaweed known as Glacilaria that are commercially grown in other countries including Indonesia. Since the 'dirty' is not a type of seaweed that is acceptable in the Zanzibar market, farmers continue to consider it as 'dirties' and make no use of it. The study by Shimba et al. (2021) reported that seaweed farmers in Zanzibar lacked knowledge on the competitive price of seaweed in the world market.

Zamroni et al. (2011) revealed that the seaweed industry in Indonesia faces marketing problems associated with institutional marketing, information on marketing network, and a communication gap between producers and consumers that results in seaweed not being produced in accordance with (international or domestic) standards established by the processing industry and exporters. Because of such problems, the industry can buy seaweed at low prices. In Zanzibar, there are few entrepreneurs who make different products from seaweeds such as cosmetics, body oils, and soaps and used them as food while seaweed flower are used in making cakes, snacks, bread, and juice. During FDGs, it was found that seaweed farmers at Paje and Bweleo were producing and selling different seaweed products at a premium price. The packed dried seaweed and seaweed flower at Bweleo and Paje were sold at TZS 2,000 per 250 g and TZS 10,000 per kilogram respectively. Msuya (2011a) reported that the future of seaweed farming in Zanzibar and Tanzania would depend on innovations in the farming techniques and adding value to seaweed.

The survey found that the entire processes within the seaweeds value chain seem to ignore the issue of quality. In terms of quality issues, almost all of the farmers reported that there was no institution that obliged them to conform to quality standards. Similarly, these farmers were not aware of quality aspects of seaweeds. However, some farmers seem to follow normal practices that also help in preserving the quality of seaweeds.

About 73% of the seaweed farmers sell their seaweed to private company. During the survey, it was observed that there were one or two company agents in the village that buy seaweed from the farmers. Usually a farmer is required to sell to a particular company that assists him/her. The high dependency of the seaweed farmers on a particular buyer implies the presence of a market information gap among seaweed value chain actors. Of the total farmers surveyed, no one was selling seaweeds outside Zanzibar. However, during FGDs, it was found that farmers in Unguja were able to sell their seaweed to Tanzania mainland and Kenya. The marketing structure of seaweed in Zanzibar is shown in Diagram 14.4.

In Zanzibar, some seaweed companies have strategic alliances with industries (big processors) in the seaweed export market, hence there is no middleman between the seaweed farmers and the buyers. In other seaweed producing countries, seaweed

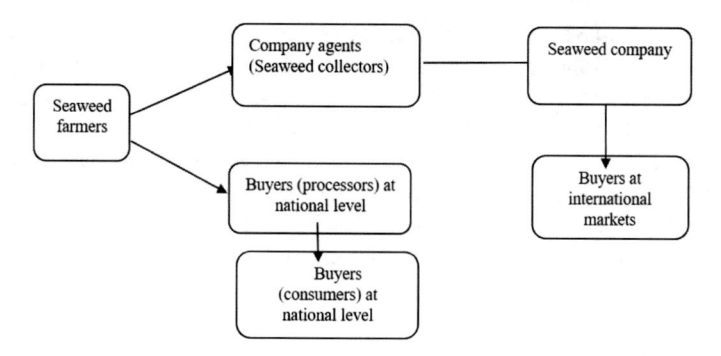

Diagram 14.4 The Marketing structure of seaweeds in Zanzibar. *Source* Author's own illustration

pass through middlemen before reaching the final market. For example, in Indonesia, farmers sell seaweed to middlemen at the district level, who, in turn, sell it to wholesalers who have warehouses or to a processing company there (Zamroni et al. 2011).

14.3.3 Issues Affecting Seaweed Farming

The seaweeds industry is impacted by climate change. According to the farmers, productivity of seaweed has severely reduced. The seaweed became rotten and die in many villages pushing farmers to always move and go farther away in the sea in search of new plantation areas. During FDGs, a farmer reported that:

'*our seaweeds get disease and die, once the seaweeds become infected, we cannot do anything, we just look at them dying, currently there are no treatment for seaweeds diseases unlike in other agricultural produces*' (Anonymous, a farmer at Tumbe village during FGDs on 28th March, 2021).

According to the Largo et al. (2020), seaweed death in Zanzibar is caused by severe epiphyte infestation coupled with high incidence of ice-ice disease.[6] To reduce the impact of climate change, farmers need to adopt deep sea water farming, promote value addition, and use of new variety of seaweeds resistant to diseases.

The discussants in FGDs meetings reported that in the past, they were planting and harvesting seaweed throughout the year. However, once after the big tsunami that hit Indonesia in 2004, farmers started to notice environmental changes that have been affecting production of seaweed. Hence, they could no longer plant and harvest seaweed throughout the year as they did before. According to them, there occurred many dirties that covered both varieties of seaweeds (spinosium and cottonii) and causing them to die. It was also reported that during sunny days (summer) there was so much heat that killed seaweed as most of them were planted at a low water level.

---

[6] Ice ice is a syndrome characterized by a whitening of the thallus in response to environmental stress, following by a secondary pathogenic infection by opportunistic strains (Ward et al. 2019). The exact pathogenesis, however, of this syndrome, which may include several bacteria and fungi species, is still unknown (Ward et al. 2019).

A proportion of 83% of the surveyed farmers confirmed to have noticed environmental changes over the past five to ten years—mainly dirties, high temperature, and strong waves. This is in line with Cleyndert et al. (2021) who reported that seaweed farmers in Zanzibar indicated that seaweed farming had been affected by changes in climatic factors over the last 20 years including increased sea temperatures, increased winds, and irregular rainfall. This also confirms study by Shimba et al. (2021) which revealed that seaweed farmers in Zanzibar reported that some water channels have dried up, farms water levels had been declining and new beaches appeared to have formed.

Quite some economic activities were reported to impact the seaweed industry. About two-third (65%) of seaweed farmers confirmed that fishing activities affected seaweed farming. Seaweed farmers reported that fishermen do their fishing in the same areas where seaweeds are planted hence destroying the seaweed firms. This situation has sometimes resulted in conflicts between seaweed farmers and fishermen.

The tourism sector was reported to affect seaweed farming especially on Unguja. This has also been confirmed during FGDs at Paje where discussants said that investors use kites for tourist gaming which hit people and pegs thus destroying their farms. The discussants further explained that previously, people used to put local mates around 20 feet from the seashore for sun drying seaweeds, but due to construction of hotels near the sea, the owners of hotel do not want to see seaweeds spread in the open space; hence they have to carry heavy (wet) seaweeds over long distances.

The discussants also reported that there were no spaces or thoroughfares in between hotels thus making them walk long distance while transporting seaweed from sea to drying and storage areas. These results confirm an earlier study by Msuya 2012a, b who reported that the growth of the tourism industry in Paje has impacted farmers access to the beaches and thus farms and hotels had built seawalls, which required farmers to walk long distances in order to access the beaches. Moreover, hotel walls had also been built in areas which had previously been used for the drying of seaweeds. Additionally, in Uroa and Pongwe villages, farmers reported that the swimming pool water coming from hotels to the sea have chemicals that cause their seaweed to decay.

Seaweed farmers at Kajengwa reported that due to construction of hotels, they had to move out of areas where they used to plant their seaweed. Farmers further explained that they could not find an open space where they could dry their sea weeds and areas where they could build a room or hut for changing clothes when they get wet in the sea. During FGDs, a discussant concluded that:

'Tourism is good, however, it should be properly managed so that it does not affect seaweeds farming (Anonymous, seaweed farmer and processor at Paje Village in Unguja during FGDs on 24th March 2021).

The main challenges reported by seaweed buyers during KI interviews were infrastructure (port congestion, roads, power), high taxation, improper handling of seaweeds by farmers, and slow handling of documentation and permits by relevant authorities in the government. The buyers reported that taxes were too high, and they sometimes did not understand why they were required to pay for a particular tax. This confirms the report by ZPC (2018) that revealed that the seaweed sector was facing multiple taxes charged by multiple authorities such as Tanzania Revenue Authority (TRA), Zanzibar Revenue Authority (ZRB), and local authorities at different stages of seaweed value chain creation. During KIIs, a seaweed buyer reported that:

Taxes are too high and multiple, it is not that we don't want to pay for taxes, we want simplification, at least there should be one stop center to pay for all taxes to avoid time loss, sometimes we do not understand why we are required to pay for a particular tax, why such a particular tax exist (Anonymous, seaweed buyer in Unguja during Key Informant Interview on 25th November, 2021).

Buyers also reported that farmers sometimes do not dry their seaweeds very well purposely to make them weigh more. They further explained that seaweeds have dirt thus increasing cost of cleaning seaweeds to the company and compromising quality of seaweeds. This is in line with Ali (2014) who revealed that buyers reported that seaweed farmers were not cleaning and drying their seaweed well. When the seaweed buyer was asked whether improper handling of seaweeds by farmers was the result of low price, the reply was:

Whether the price is high or low, seaweed farming is the farmer's business that provides income to them and spend their time on it, therefore farmers should love what they are engaged in (seaweed farming) by ensuring that what they produce is of high quality free from impurities and dried well (Anonymous, seaweed buyer in Unguja during Key Informant Interview on 25th November, 2021).

The buying company stated that the nature of Zanzibar oceans provides good quality seaweed, however the practices after harvesting may put seaweed produced in Zanzibar at risk of inferior quality. One key informant with vast experiences in seaweed business stated that:

Zanzibar seaweeds must be very competitive to get good share in the export market because Zanzibar is selling seaweeds to countries that they themselves are producing seaweeds at large quantities (Anonymous, former seaweed buyer at Wete street in Pemba during Key Informant Interview on July 2021).

14.4 Conclusions

This chapter analyzed the seaweed value chain in Zanzibar. The research sought to determine socio-economic characteristics of seaweed farmers in Zanzibar, to identify the practices of seaweed farming, to determine issues affecting seaweed farming in Zanzibar, and to propose policy recommendations for scaling up the competitiveness of the seaweed sector.

The study found that nearly half of the surveyed seaweed farmers had no formal education. This is not a good sign for farmers who are driving the very important sector of the economy. Illiteracy may be breading areas for other challenges that exist in the seaweed industry where lack of information and knowledge, low technology uptake and innovation, low income, and quality issues are ripe. Moreover, seaweed is highly impacted by climate change, leading to diseases and death of seaweed that result into lowering productivity. High taxation, unreliable infrastructure (roads, water, power), and low handling of documentations by government were the main challenges reported by seaweed buyers.

These findings suggest the need for reviewing the regulatory environment governing the seaweed subsector and formulating policies and regulations to promote the sector which includes reviving and establishing new seaweed farmers cooperatives and committees. Investing in education by introducing a training-the-trainers program to selected seaweed stakeholders at village (shehia) level and staff responsible for the seaweed sector with a detailed monitoring and evaluation framework for following up, including introducing a two-year experiment aimed at generating information, among others, by understanding clearly, for example, the best production periods and location for seaweed production, including improving farming methods and technologies, production needs, world market demand, and prices. Other policy recommendations include putting in place supporting infrastructure (power supply, water, and roads should be more reliable), investing in quality management, and strengthening collaboration and coordination among stakeholders.

Acknowledgements Special thanks should go to Dr. Salim M. Hamza, Mr. Juma Kh. Jaffar, Mr. Mohammed S. Othman, Mohammed A. Abdi, Rabia M. Omar, Aisha B. Masoud, Aisha Kh. Juma and Mohammed S. Hassan (Ministry of Blue Economy and Fishery, Zanzibar), Mr. Hamad O. Rashid, Mr. Mohamed O. Masoud, Mrs. Rehema H. Said and Mr. Yahya F. Haji (Ministry of Trade and Industrial Development, Zanzibar) and Mr. Said S. Mohammed (Ministry of Agriculture, Irrigation, Natural Resources and Livestock, Zanzibar) for support during field work. Other thanks should go to Mrs. Khadija Kh. Hamad (Technical Advisor), Mr. Abdullah O. Makame (IT), and Mr. Ali A. Shamte (Quality Assurance) from Office of Chief Government Statistician, Zanzibar. Appreciations should go to Mr. Issa Mlingoti (Former Chief Coordinator at Zanzibar Government Affairs Coordination Office—Dodoma), Mr. Khamis Sh. Mohammed, Ms. Sabra H. Makame, Mr. Azzan Kh. Iddi, local leaders (Sheha), seaweed farmers, and all those involved during the listing exercise, Focus Group Discussions (FGDs), survey, meetings, interviews, and observation. Professor Peter A.G. van Bergeijk, Dr. Binyam Afewerk Demena from ISS, and Dr. Jamal Msami from Repoa are highly appreciated for their support.

Funding This article is based on the research project titled 'Analysis of the Livelihood Aspects of Seaweed Value Chain in Zanzibar, United Republic of Tanzania' which was funded by International Institute of Social Studies (ISS) at Erasmus University, Rotterdam in Netherlands and Repoa, Dar es Salaam, Tanzania.

References

Ali NS (2014) Assessment of the market relations between smallholder seaweed farmers and buyers for poverty reduction in Zanzibar: a case of Uroa village Kusini district. Dodoma (Master's dissertation), The University of Dodoma, Dodoma.

Ana Menezes (2020) Understanding diseases and control in seaweed farming in Zanzibar. FAO Aquaculture Newsletter

Bacaltosi D, Revilla N, Castañaga R, Laguting M, Anguay G et al (2012) Gender roles in the seaweed industry cluster of Southern Philippines: the DICCEP experience Della Asian fisheries science special issue. Vol 25s, pp 251–256

Belghith NBH De Boisseson PMA (2017) Zanzibar poverty assessment (No. 120689, pp. 1-118). The World Bank

Cai J (2021) Global status of seaweed production, trade and utilization. Seaweed Innovation Forum Belize (28 May 2021). Available at: https://www.competecaribbean.org/wp-content/upl oads/2021/05/Global-status-of-seaweed-production-trade-and-utilization-Junning-Cai-FAO.pdf

Cleyndert G, Newman R, Brugere C, Cuni-Sanchez A, Marchant R (2021) Adaptation of seaweed farmers in Zanzibar to the impacts of climate change. Researchgate

de Jong Cleyndert G, Newman R, Brugere C, Cuni-Sanchez A, Marchant R (2021) Adaptation of seaweed farmers in Zanzibar to the impacts of climate change. Researchgate.

Dennis, JM (2003) A guide to the seaweed industry. FAO Fisheries Technical Paper, 441, 105pp.

Kronen, M., Meloti, A., Ponia, B., Pickering, T., Diake, S., Kama, J. and Teitelbaum, A., 2010. Gender and seaweed farming on Wagina Island, Choiseul Province in Solomon Islands. SPC Women in Fisheries Bulletin, 21, pp.3–10

Largo DB, Msuya FE, Menezes A (2020) Understanding diseases and control in seaweed farming in Zanzibar. FAO Fisheries and Aquaculture Technical Paper, (662), pp.0_1–49

Mariño M, Breckwoldta A, Teichberga M, Kasec A, Reuter H (2019) Livelihood aspects of seaweed farming in Rote Island Indonesia. Mar Policy 107:103600

Ministry of Agriculture, Natural Resources and Livestock (2019) Zanzibar agricultural sector development program (ZASDP)

Ministry of Trade and Industrial Development (2019) Zanzibar industrial policy 2019–2029

Msuya FE (2011a) The Impact of seaweed farming on the socioeconomic status of coastal communities in Zanzibar, Tanzania. World Aquac 42(3):45–48

Msuya FE (2012a) A study of working conditions in the Zanzibar seaweed farming industry. Women in Informal Employment Globalizing and Organizing U.K

Msuya FE, Shalli MS, Sullivan K, Crawford B, Tobey J, Mmochi AJ (2007) A comparative economic analysis of two seaweed farming methods in Tanzania. The sustainable coastal communities and ecosystems program. Coastal Resources Center, University of Rhode Island and the Western Indian Ocean Marine Science Association. p 27

Msuya FE, Hurtado AQ (2017) The role of women in seaweed aquaculture in the Western Indian Ocean and South-East Asia. European Journal of Phycology, 52(4), pp 482–494

Msuya FE (2006) The seaweed cluster initiative in Zanzibar, Tanzania. In: Mwamila BLM, Temu AK (eds) Proceedings of the 3rd regional conference on innovation systems and innovative clusters in Africa. Dar es Salaam, Tanzania, pp 246–260

Msuya Flower E (2012b) Women in informal employment globalizing and organizing. A study of working conditions in the Zanzibar seaweed farming industry

Neish IC, Msuya FE (2013) Seaweed value chain assessment of Zanzibar. Report submitted for UNIDO project no 13083 building seaweed processing capacities in Zanzibar and pemba: creating value for the poor

Nor AM, Gray TS, Caldwell GS, Stead SM (2017) Is a cooperative approach to seaweed farming effectual? an analysis of the seaweed cluster project (SCP) Malaysia. J Appl Phycol 29(5):2323–2337

Office of the Chief Government Statistician (OCGS) (2020) Zanzibar statistical abstract

Office of the Chief Government Statistician (OCGS) (2019/2020) Zanzibar household budget survey

Ronald B, Silayo GF, Abdalah KJ (2015) Preference sources of information used by seaweeds farmers in Unguja. Zanzibar Inter J Acad Lib Info Sci 3(4):106–116

Shimba C, Magombola DA, Ibrahim S (2021) Assessment of seaweed farming in sustaining household livelihood in East Coast District, in Zanzibar. Tanzan Eur J Phys Agric Sci

Vestling V, Forsberg V (2018) The livelihoods of female seaweed farmers: a study about women's experiences of old and new techniques of seaweed farming on Zanzibar, Tanzania. Jönköping University Bachelor thesis.

Ward, G. M., Faisan Jr, J. P., Cottier-Cook, E. J., Gachon, C., Hurtado, A. Q., Lim, P. E., ... & Brodie, J. (2020) A review of reported seaweed diseases and pests in aquaculture in Asia. Journal of the World Aquaculture Society, 51(4), 815–828

Zanzibar Planning Commission (ZPC) (2018) In-depth study to explore the best way to increase seaweed production, improve seaweed trade, value addition and processing in Zanzibar.

Zamroni A, Laoubi K, Yamao M (2011) The development of seaweed farming as a sustainable coastal management method in Indonesia: an opportunities and constraints assessment. WIT Trans Ecol Environ 150:505–516

Chapter 15
The Role of Cross-Border Cooperatives in the EAC: A Structured Review

Gerard Dushimimana

Abstract Cross-Border cooperatives are increasingly recognized for their role in improving regional trade and addressing challenges faced by small-scale cross-border traders in Africa. However, what members of these cooperatives benefit and gain from that participation remains unclear and inconclusive. This study reviewed and synthesized 15 articles that explore the role played by cross-border cooperatives in the East Africa Community (EAC). The study systematically selected and extracted English language articles published from January 2000 to August 2021 from Google scholar, applying the PRISMA 2009 protocol, and conducted a frequency analysis. The findings are twofold: on the one hand, cross-border cooperatives improved the socio-economic conditions of members according to 67% of the studies through pooling resources, reduction of transaction costs, and representation of traders in public space. On the other hand, compiled evidence indicated ambiguous outcomes with regard to specific roles of cross-border cooperatives. Therefore, future research should focus on the specific roles and effects of cross-border cooperatives on cross-border trade in EAC. The results also show that Kenya and Uganda have been covered in most studies. This suggests broadening research to other countries under-represented in the region.

15.1 Introduction

Recently, the East African Community (EAC) countries and donors have shown increasing interest in supporting cross-border traders. The focus is on small-scale traders in cooperative organizations to facilitate cross-border trade and improve the living conditions of traders. According to Asche (2021:275) Africa's economic development, particularly modern industry, necessitates regional integration. Asche pointed out that the manufacturing industry has always been associated with advanced levels of development, rather than the agricultural sector or services. Therefore,

G. Dushimimana (✉)
Department of Cooperatives Promotion and Capacity Building, at Rwanda Cooperative Agency (RCA), Kigali, Rwanda
e-mail: dugeros@gmail.com

© The Author(s), under exclusive license to Springer Nature Singapore Pte Ltd. 2022   335
B. A. Demena and Peter A. G. Van Bergeijk (eds.), *Trade and Investment in East Africa*,
Frontiers in African Business Research, https://doi.org/10.1007/978-981-19-4211-2_15

"industry needs well-integrated regions, and regions need industry for a meaningful division of labour, but neither of the two is anywhere close to realization" (Asche, 2021:275). One of the reasons is that African markets are "fragmented" (Brenton and Isik 2012).[1]

While cross-border trade has been an outstanding factor for economic growth in other regions such as East Asia, and Western Europe, African countries are yet to take full advantage of this trade (Brenton and Isik 2012). In 2017, the proportion of exports between African countries to overall Africa exports increased to 17% from 10% in 1995, which is much lower compared with Europe (69%), Asia (59%), and North America (31%) (Songwe 2019). This indicates the gap that exists in Intra African trade and why African nations need to find a solution to increase bilateral trade flows. Challenges that undermine cross-border trade include domestic and foreign policies on security, inadequate infrastructure, political instability, and change in government policies (Titeca 2009). Notably, an increasing share of African trade takes place in small-scale cross-border trade also known as informal cross-border trade (ICBT). ICBT accounts for a major share of regional cross-border trade and contributes to food security, poverty reduction, and employment for impoverished families in the medium and short run (Lesser and Moisé-Leeman 2009).

It is important to distinguish between the concepts of "informal" and "small-scale" trade. Labeling cross-border trade informal is different from illegal trade as Brenton and Soprano (2018) make a clear distinction for two main reasons. First, informal is often mistaken for illegal which provides a negative perception of the trade. Second, it misrepresents the nature of the business on the field, as traders may cross borders through both formal and informal routes interchangeably based on a range of circumstances. Additionally, due to the trade policies and political intention what is considered informal or illegal in one country can be recognized, recorded, and charged with taxes as legal in another country (Little et al. 2015). Also, traders are considered as small-scale in the EAC, if the value of traded goods is under US$ 2,000. Through the Simplified Trade Regime (STR), agreement aims to facilitate small-scale traders, products that do not exceed the threshold above are not subjected to customs duties, once they are produced within member countries and have a Simplified Certificate of Origin (SCO) (Mwanabiningo 2015).

Furthermore, implemented policies that facilitate small-scale traders at borders reflect the importance of small-scale trade in East Africa. According to Brenton et al. (2011:1) small-scale cross-border trade plays the most important role in connecting producers to markets in the Great Lakes region of Africa. Traders with limited capital view this business as a vital opportunity for income generation and job creation and they are often connected through social networks to avoid the high cost of the transaction (Nakanjako et al. 2021).

Despite the role played by small-scale Cross-border trade on economic growth and poverty alleviation in Africa (Brenton and Isik 2012:1; Titeca and Kimanuka 2012), traders engaged in cross-border trade face huge challenges that undermine

---

[1] Author is thankful to Peter van Bergeijk and Binyam Afewerk Demena of Erasmus University, International Institute of Social Studies for technical guidance in carrying out the research work.

their economic activities including but not limited to, physical and emotional abuse as well as inadequate childcare (Njikam and Tchouassi 2011), traveling times, delays at borders, spending many hours outside of their families, and tough competition with other traders (Ama et al. 2014) as well as corruption and discrimination (García Mora and Roshan 2013; Bensassi and Jarreau 2019).

These challenges put small-scale traders in a disadvantaged position compared to large traders regarding their capacity to achieve scale economies, increase bargaining power, accessing financial services, market information, and public facilities. Several authors suggest that small-scale traders in cross-border trade could solve those challenges if they are organized into collective action groups or associations, such as cooperatives (Afrika and Ajumbo 2012; Brenton et al. 2011). Cooperatives offer less privileged people the opportunity to identify probable areas for investment, encourage their members to protect their benefits, increase their participation in the public policy arena and give protection to them by turning individual risks into mutual risks (Wanyama 2016: 20).

Nevertheless, the findings of what traders benefit and gain from that participation remain unclear and inconclusive (Klopp and Trimble 2020). Empirical evidence from Van den Boogaard et al. (2021:9) suggests that traders in associations face more discrimination at borders than non-members, and these associations may potentially have a detrimental effect on traders if their activities are not supported by border officials. In addition, the level of participation of small scale cross-border traders in cooperatives, when compared to traders involved in cross-border trade, raises questions on whether those organizations have a significant impact on traders. For instance, a study by Titeca and Kimanuka (2012) in the Great Lakes region found that only 18% of traders in ICBT are members of an association or cooperative. Indeed, some data on business ownership structure from the East African region show for women (that represent 74% of small-scale traders in East Africa) most (72%) were doing business as individuals, 19% operates as an individual but also are affiliated to cooperatives while only 9% operates as full members of cooperatives (Trademark East Africa 2021).[2] It is important to point out that 90% of their income depends solely on cross-border trade (Bugingo 2018: 11).

While small-scale cross-border trade attracts a lot of attention from academics and policymakers, the role of cooperatives and other self-help organizations in this sector has been studied with less vigor although some studies exist.[3] In small-scale cross-border trade, Klopp and Trimble (2020) reviewed studies on corruption and

---

[2] Note that, the study by Mbo'o-Tchouawou et al. (2016:1) suggests almost the same participation of men and women in agriculture cross-border trading networks. Moreover, the authors also acknowledge that there are some specific activities across borders where women are more represented than men.

[3] Buang and Samah (2020) reviewed studies on factors that influence the effectiveness of the cooperative board, Soeiro and Dias (2019) focused on renewable energy cooperatives, Marcis et al. (2019) investigated the sustainability performance of agricultural cooperatives, Islam et al. (2015) and Minah et al. (2019) focused on the effects of agricultural cooperatives in developing countries, while Camargo-Benavides and Ehrenhard (2021) structured review only focused on the organization form of cooperative enterprises.

gender in East Africa, while the study by Kahiya and Kadirov (2020) in the context of sub-Saharan Africa employed a macromarketing viewpoint to depict informal cross-border trade as "substratum marketing system". Despite these studies, there is a lack of information on cooperatives in cross-border trade.

This chapter provides, to the best of our knowledge, the first structured review on the role of cross-border cooperatives in EAC countries. It aims to investigate: first, the factors that influence small-scale traders to participate in cross-border cooperatives in East Africa. This seeks to establish a foundation for determining if small-scale traders are engaged in cooperatives. Second, the socio-economic effects of participation in cross-border cooperatives on small-scale traders in East Africa. This highlights the importance of determining what sorts of advantages cross-border cooperatives give their members.

This chapter reviews and synthesizes 15 articles that explore the roles of cross-border cooperatives on small-scale traders in East Africa. Applying the PRISMA 2009 protocol, we use Google scholar to systematically select, and extract English language articles published from January 2000 to August 2021. Frequency analyses were used to investigate the findings of selected articles to produce an overview of the current knowledge base to inform evidence-based policy and suggest key areas for future research.

The remainder of this chapter is structured as follows. The following section consists of the definition, principles nature, and context of cross-border cooperatives, Sect. 15.3 discusses the methodology that has been used in this chapter. Section 15.4 presents results and discussion, and the final Sect. 15.5 concludes and suggests recommendations for future research.

15.2 Cooperative Organization: Definition, Principles, Nature, and Context

Since the establishment of cooperatives, many concepts were introduced to define a cooperative organization by researchers but the most used definition in the literature (see, e.g., Wanyama 2016; Onyilo and Adong 2019; Musahara 2012) is the one provided by the International Alliance of Cooperatives (ICA) in 1995 which refer a cooperative society as "an autonomous association of persons united voluntarily to meet their common economic, social, and cultural needs and aspirations through a jointly-owned and democratically-controlled enterprise" (ICA 1995). This definition has become more popular in the literature for several reasons. First, it's a summary of different definitions of the cooperative; second not only does it look at the economic aspect of cooperatives but also at the social and cultural aspects which make it more inclusive; third, it encompasses the values and principles of cooperatives that represent the identity of a cooperative.

Cooperatives are guided by seven international principles that were agreed upon in the congress of the International Alliance of Cooperatives in 1995. Those principles are voluntary and open membership; democratic member control; member economic participation; autonomy and independence; education, training, and information; cooperation among cooperatives and concern for the community (Wanyama 2016; ICA 1995). Those principles make cooperatives an organization that is built on the values of self-help, self-responsibility, democracy, equality, equity, and solidarity, while their members are attributed with characteristics of honesty, openness, social responsibility, and caring for others in all their activities (ICA 1995).

15.2.1 Socio-Economic Contribution of Cooperatives

Several studies attempted to show the socio-economic impact of cooperatives on poverty reduction, job creation, food security, women's empowerment, and technology adoption. It is worth saying that all those aspects are key areas for achieving sustainable development goals.

15.2.1.1 Cooperatives and Poverty Reduction

For many years cooperatives have been considered as organizations that can help to reduce poverty among members of society. One could ask what makes those members-owned enterprises special and put them in a better position of moving people from poverty. Wanyama (2016: 20) argued that cooperatives help the poor to discover business possibilities, enabling less privileged people to protect their rights and to be represented in decision-making spaces that affect them as well as protecting the members with the risk-sharing approach. This indicates how people with the same problem regardless of their means can put together a small shared capital and start an economic activity that can meet their needs. By working together and sharing ideas through general assemblies, their business may grow and increase their income. The bigger their business becomes, the more impact it has on the community.

Furthermore, Saving and Credit Cooperatives (SACCOs) and Agricultural cooperatives played a very important role in poverty reduction in East Africa. For instance, it is estimated that the life of around 5,000,000 people and 1,600,000 cooperative members depends on cooperative activities in Tanzania, which indicates their potential contribution in reducing poverty among non-members through spillover effects while also contributing to the state's social protection and development (Maghimbi 2010:32). Indeed, Rice and coffee farmers improved their income as a result of SACCOs membership in Tanzania (Maghimbi 2010:33). Similarly, in 2007, more than seven million active members of primary cooperatives in Kenya were believed to be earning their income from cooperatives (Wanyama 2009: 26) In Rwanda, the capital of cooperative members increased from approximately USD 5.1million in 2019 to approximately USD 31million in 2019 (Harelimana and Mukarukaka 2020). The increase in terms of capital implies two things. First, it is a sign that the sector is growing by accommodating more people that need to move to the upper stage of their living conditions. Second, it means that there are cooperatives whose initial investment has earned profit and as a result increased capital. Furthermore, the contribution of cooperatives to alleviate poverty is usually associated with employment opportunities generated by those organizations.

15.2.1.2 Cooperatives and Employment

Cooperatives are widely known for having a substantial impact on job creation and income generation. Develtere et al. (2008) identified three ways that cooperative societies create employment opportunities. These include: first, through direct employment for those people who are hired by cooperatives and work as their everyday employees in different capacities; second through indirect employment or self-employment for cooperatives members who find that their income depends only on cooperative activities; and third, through spillover effects for those people outside cooperatives whose occupational activities are inextricably linked to transactions performed with cooperatives such as service providers and suppliers of agricultural inputs and fertilizers to name a few.

Cooperatives have created employment in East Africa. For instance, primary cooperatives helped to establish 300,000 and 34,524 jobs in Kenya and Tanzania, respectively (Pollet 2009). Pollet estimates suggest that cooperatives employed approximately 5.5% of the total population in Kenya while employed people in government and other cooperatives-related agencies were estimated to be 3,445 and 425 in Kenya and Tanzania respectively. Similarly, in Rwanda, the estimation of full-time staff employed by U-SACCO[4] is around 3,328 (Harelimana and Mukarukaka 2020:3) while in Uganda, around 2,823 were directly employed by Cooperatives (Develtere et al. 2008). Employment opportunities created by cooperatives highlight their roles in reducing unemployment issues, especially in less developed countries.

15.2.1.3 Cooperatives and Food Security

In East Africa, like in many developing countries, the majority of people live in rural areas and depend on agriculture as their only source of income. This gives agricultural cooperatives in rural areas the potential to improve food security and nutrition. When the country is food secured, the life of people is improved through consumption, and production is sufficient to take the surplus to the markets. This contributes to both economic growth and producers' income. Indeed, nutrition among the population is improved which ensures them better health and allows them to contribute to the development of the country. Cooperatives have an important role to play in food security by increasing production and linking farmers' produce to the market. For instance, in 2004, rice cooperatives were responsible for almost all rice cultivated

---

[4] In Rwanda U-SACCOs are SACCOs that have been established in each sector (locally known as *Umurenge*) of the district all over the country. Among 437 registered SACCOs, 416 are U-SACCO.

in Rwanda with 40,148 members that produced 35% of the total demanded rice. (Nyamwasa 2008:289). This number might even be higher to date given that all rice producers in Rwanda are encouraged to be organized into Cooperatives.

Harelimana and Mukarukaka (2020:4) indicate that the role of cooperatives in food security is also observed in supplying inputs (improved seeds, fertilizers, and pesticides) which are essential for farmers to increase productivity. Though the authors did not mention the role of the government, most of the inputs are also associated with state incentives to reduce transaction costs. However, the advantage of cooperative members is that they are in a position to be facilitated by the state to get inputs quickly and easily because they are organized, while for non-members it might be quite expensive and take time. Indeed, with training and experience, most cooperatives provide extension services and produce improved seeds for their members which are also essential to increase productivity. Additionally, by working with financial institutions cooperatives are able to borrow money to purchase enough seeds and fertilizers as well as purchase insurance for their crops to limit the risk associated with climate change while for non-members this might be a challenge.

Furthermore, several scholars argued that cooperative membership is essential for the rapid adoption of technology. For instance, Demena (2011) in a study on artisanal fishing in Eritrea, found that cooperative membership and availability of loans are factors influencing the adoption of advanced technology in fishing. Similarly, Abebaw and Haile (2013) revealed that cooperatives were essential to trigger the rapid use of agricultural technologies by smallholder farmers in Ethiopia. The use of technology in most developing countries, especially in Africa is still a problem that traders and farmers are facing and that undermines the development of their activities. However, cooperative organizations can solve this problem if they are given support through different initiatives such as training and access to finance. Technology adoption is also an important factor for influencing young people to join cooperatives (Demena 2011) and participate in food production which is important for food security and nutrition.

15.2.1.4 Cooperatives and Women Empowerment

In Africa and many other developing countries, women are often left out of economic activities that generate income because of the dominant patriarchal society. This created inequality between men and women in different sectors such as governance, employment, and participation in the decision-making arena. Consequently, discrimination against girls and women has continued to be common in certain areas. However, we are now seeing an immense contribution of cooperatives to women empowerment that has already taken a remarkable step. Cooperatives have become a vital tool for women to improve their joint action and expand their business skills and capabilities. For example, in Tanzania, the number of women who are members of financial cooperatives increased from 86,000 to more than 375,000 between 2005 and 2010 which gives them a representation of 43% of the total membership (Majurin 2012). Obtaining membership in SACCOs implies using financial services such as deposits, savings, and borrowing, thus one becomes financially included. Similarly in Rwanda with 52% of women in the total population (Kaitesi 2020), their participation in the cooperative movement is estimated to be 45% (Harelimana and Mukarukaka 2020). Likewise, in Uganda, a survey conducted in 55 agricultural cooperatives revealed a significant rise in the number of women engaged in those cooperatives (Wanyama 2016).

Regarding the participation of women in leadership, a survey indicates that female participation in the boards of SACCOs varies from 24% in Kenya to 65% in Tanzania, while the average in East Africa is 44% (Majurin 2012). In addition, cooperatives have given women a space to discuss social-related issues among them (Kaitesi 2020). Therefore, cooperatives have a big role in promoting gender equality, providing employment opportunities to women, and increasing the representation of women in decision-making spaces. Although the number of women in cooperatives is generally still much lower compared to men (Majurin 2012), cross-border cooperatives show the opposite picture (Harelimana and Mukarukaka 2020).

15.2.2 Cross-Border Cooperatives

Cross-border Cooperatives are emerging organizations in cross-border communities that provide services across borders and link producers and traders to the regional markets. They also play an important role in accelerating regional integration. According to a recent study by Lloyd-Ellis and Nordstrom (2021) in East Africa, regional integration can help countries to specialize in producing services and commodities to enjoy the advantage of economies of scale that can be increased with the facilitation of effortless crossing of people on the border. Indeed, cooperatives can play an important role to achieve economies of scale, adoption, and use of ICT, reduce asymmetric information on the market, and link producers to regional markets. However, the challenge is that few findings are available to prove their impact and connection with trade (Lloyd-Ellis and Nordstrom 2021). One of the reasons there is limited evidence on the impact of cross-border cooperatives, is that most of those cooperatives and other self-help groups involved in cross-border trade consist of small-scale cross-border traders which are more difficult to observe statistically. The economic contribution of small-scale cross-border trade is often underestimated and as a result, actors involved in such trade do not get the attention they deserve (Malaba and Chipika 2012).

Cooperatives involved in cross-border trade may differ depending on whether they are legally registered or not, or whether they are formal or informal. However, they share similarities of being organized groups created, owned, and controlled by members that have the same problems and challenges, doing the same economic activity while they strive to improve their living conditions. According to Develtere et al. (2008: 41) "being a cooperative in the name is less important than being an open and democratically structured group of people who jointly carry out economic activities to the benefit of all members of the group and, by extension, the whole society" In this chapter, we use 'cross-border cooperative' to refer to all collective action groups involved in cross-border trade.

15.3 Methodology and Characteristics of the Literature

15.3.1 Introduction

To investigate the role played by cross-border cooperatives in Eastern Africa, a structured review was conducted following PRISMA (The Preferred Reporting Items for Systematic Reviews and Meta-Analyses) 2009 to retrieve, integrate, and report the available evidence (Moher et al. 2009). The protocol was utilized during the determination of factors that influence small-scale traders to participate in cross-border cooperatives and evaluation of the effect of participation on their members in East Africa (Table A.1). Overall data collection took 3 months (June–August 2021).

15.3.2 Search Strategy

To conduct the systematic review, we utilized a systematic web search to locate and review studies on cross-border cooperatives in EAC. We used the Google Scholar database as it gives access to a large collection of academic and grey (working papers, reports etc.) literature. Our search strategy is not confined to specific roles or variables because the goal of this study is to offer a comprehensive evaluation of all existing evidence. Moreover, our search method comprised a variety of keywords connected with Boolean operators "AND", "OR", and truncation "*" to find the variation in the keywords.

This resulted in the following broad keywords: "Cross-border trade*" (cooperatives OR co-operatives OR coops OR networks OR associations) AND "small-scale traders" AND members* AND participation AND (income OR revenues) AND ("East* Africa" OR Kenya OR Uganda OR Tanzania OR Rwanda OR Burundi OR "South Soudan"). Based on practical considerations the search strategy was limited to English language papers published from January 2000 to August 31, 2021.[5] In addition, the reference lists of the retrieved papers were inspected, to locate any missing studies. Identified articles were then exported to Microsoft Excel for the removal of duplicates, screening, and further processing.

---

[5] The Treat to revive EAC that was signed in November 1999. Hence, there is a possibility for articles published in early 2000 that talk about regional trade.

15.3.3 Article Selection and Data Extraction

The selection of studies was done based on articles electronically available in the English language.[6] These include books, book chapters, articles, review papers, working papers, and policy briefs. These publications were framed within any, some, or all the East African countries with a focus on self-help groups involved in regional trade. We exclude studies outside Eastern Africa; unreliably extracted data, overlapping data, and duplicates; newspaper articles, opinion papers, master's theses, abstract only papers, conferences, and editorials; and articles with incomplete texts.

The selection and extraction of studies followed a two-step process. The first step entailed an inclusive query electronic search on Google scholar which identified 362 studies. All the duplicates with the same author, year, and titles were removed and this resulted in 329 studies. Next, using title screening, 283 articles were excluded since they were not relevant to this specific study or region under study (for example because they discuss cooperatives at the local level or in regions other than EAC). The second step entailed reviewing and screening abstracts and where necessary full texts on the remaining 46 studies.

After a careful assessment and screening of texts, 32 other studies were dropped (Table A.2). Of these, 17 studies were dropped based on the unavailability of full texts and relevance to the study based on the inclusion criteria, while one was dropped since the year of publication was 1997 and fell under the exclusion criteria, and 14 articles framed outside East Africa were also dropped. Additional manual search on Google scholar identified 1 article after a citation tracking process. The selection and extraction process ended with a final 15 studies for the analysis (Table 15.1). Figure 15.1 gives the schematic flowchart that was followed in the selection procedure.

15.3.4 Limitations

The systematic review has two main limitations. One of the limitations is associated with the exclusion criteria utilized when compiling studies. Studies done in languages other than English were excluded. Also, the literature does not allow to move beyond a structured review. For example, it was not possible to apply a meta-analysis or qualitative comparative analysis because the studies selected are very heterogeneous in terms of study designs, timelines, and outcome measures. Given the still limited number of studies on cross-border cooperatives in East Africa, a meta-analysis thus is not possible.

---

[6] Physical publications could not be consulted since this research was done during the COVID-19 pandemic and lockdowns prohibited visits to libraries most of the time. Notably, some countries in East Africa use languages other than English which might have brought in a holistic exploration into the cross-border cooperatives in East Africa but their inclusion was not possible due to the time and cost required to gather and translate studies.

Table 15.1 Characteristics of the included studies

#	First author and year	Source	Location	Sample characteristics	Design	Key findings
1	Titeca and Kimanuka (2012)	*International Alert*	DRC, Burundi, Rwanda and Uganda	900 traders in each site and 6 focus groups	Quantitative and qualitative research design	Traders lack proper organizations. A small number of traders are members of cooperatives. The majority of non-members would like to become members but lack the capacity
2	Mbo'o-Tchouawou et al. (2016)	Regional Strategic Analysis and Knowledge Support System (ReSAKSS)	East Africa (Kenya, Tanzania, and Uganda)	363 traders, 4 borders	Mixed methods (qualitative and quantitative)	Almost equal participation of men and women in trading networks in agricultural cross border trade
3	García Mora and Roshan (2013)	World Bank	Democratic Republic of Congo (DRC), and Rwanda	628 traders and 66 border officials, 2 borders	Qualitative and Quantitative (2 months of survey and one month of interview and focus group	20% of traders are members of associations and average membership fees in Rwanda is US$ 18 and US$ 8 for Congolese traders

(continued)

Table 15.1 (continued)

#	First author and year	Source	Location	Sample characteristics	Design	Key findings
4	Parshotam and Balongo (2020)	South African Institute of International Affairs (SAIIA)	Kenya and Uganda	9 interviews (traders and government officials)	Qualitative	Cross-border traders' associations raised women's profiles and provided them with an important chance to raise their voices and have their problems solved
5	Nakanjako et al. (2021)	Eastern Africa Social Science Research Review	Kenya and Uganda	70 local and migrant traders and government officials	Qualitative (12 months of ethnographic field research)	Engagement in cross-border trade is influenced by migrant social networks, survival needs, prospects in the border, and weak enforcement of cross-border trade guidelines
6	Croke et al. (2020)	World Bank (working paper)	Rwanda and DRC	314 cross border traders	Randomized control trial	Training does not affect traders' membership in associations

(continued)

Table 15.1 (continued)

#	First author and year	Source	Location	Sample characteristics	Design	Key findings
7	Brenton, et al. (2011)	*World Bank*	Rwanda and Burundi	181 cross border trades, 58 border stakeholders	Quantitative	Lower participation of women in cross-border traders' cooperatives. Representation of traders in public arena is essential for the poor to move the informal economy
8	Nugent and Soi (2020)	Journal of Eastern African Studies	Kenya, Uganda & Rwanda	15 OSBPS	Qualitative	cooperatives increase awareness of crossing borders through official routes and represent their members' interests
9	Ng'asike et al. (2020)	Springer	Kenya & Somalia	Secondary data from the livestock department	Qualitative and quantitative research design	supporting traders' associations and the introduction of reforms can improve small and medium traders' living conditions and reduce their vulnerability in livestock cross border trade

(continued)

Table 15.1 (continued)

#	First author and year	Source	Location	Sample characteristics	Design	Key findings
10	Bugingo, (2018)	BRIDGES AFRICA	Rwanda	63 cooperatives, over 3,000 members	Qualitative	cooperative members improved their knowledge and abilities, as well as had access to capital and markets in nine major border areas
11	Pavanello, (2010)	Overseas Development Institute (Working paper)	Kenya and Ethiopia	Review of the literature and secondary quantitative data	Quantitative and Structure-Conduct-Performance Framework	cooperatives provide a significant potential to lower transaction costs and add value to the weak value chain of livestock cross border trade
12	Akaezuwa et al. (2020)	*Columbia School of International and Public Affairs (SIPA)*	Kenya and Uganda	11 stakeholders, women traders, and government officials	Literature reviews and qualitative interviews	Associations play a critical role in empowering women in cross border trade

(continued)

Table 15.1 (continued)

#	First author and year	Source	Location	Sample characteristics	Design	Key findings
13	Golub (2015)	*Handbook on Trade and Development*	Kenya, Ethiopia and Somalia	Case studies from East Africa and West Africa	Qualitative and quantitative analysis, case studies	The role of kinship networks to access information and finance, meet contract requirements, reduce transaction cost and integration of regional market is of great importance in ICBT
14	Kawala et al. (2018)	*Journal of Agricultural Science*	Uganda and Kenya	115 fish traders, 4 key informants, and 2 focus groups	Quantitative and qualitative	Membership in a fish marketing organization is associated with formal or informal trading routes

(continued)

Table 15.1 (continued)

#	First author and year	Source	Location	Sample characteristics	Design	Key findings
15	Titeca (2020)	*UNDP Africa Borderlands Centre*	Uganda & DRC	Secondary data and 3 border points	Quantitative and qualitative research	Associations support traders who have suffered losses due to accidents, theft, or damage of their goods through small loans and sometimes are involved in lobbying appropriate authorities to solve their issues. They have also helped traders to reduce the consequences of Covid-19

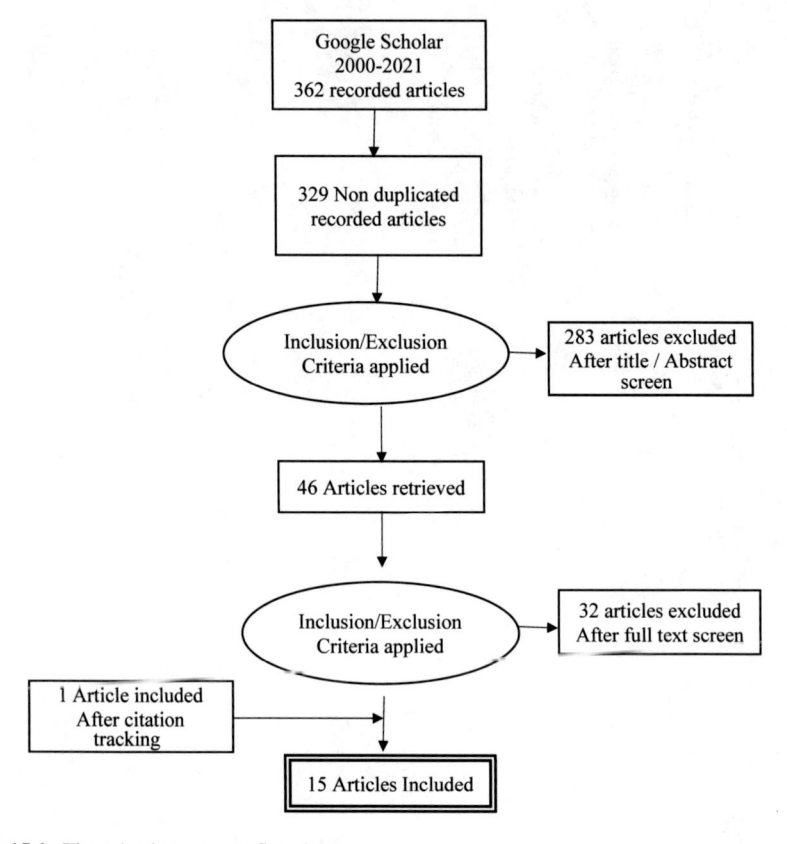

Fig. 15.1 The selection process flowchart

Since this systematic review draws information and results from diverse studies, disciplines, and methodologies, a single criterion for quality could not be established. The resources and articles utilized were appraised individually and selected for inclusion based on applicability and credibility. The selection was independently reviewed and cross checked by the supervisors of my MA Thesis at the International Institute of Social Studies (for details see, Dushimimana 2021).

15.4   Results

This section of the chapter presents the systematic review results. Results are divided into three main parts: studies and article characteristics, the general assessment of factors that influence small-scale traders to participate in cross-border cooperatives and the socio-economic effect of participation in cross-border cooperatives on small-scale traders in East Africa.

15.4.1 Descriptive Studies Characteristics

Table 15.1 presents the characteristics of the included studies. The articles on borders between Kenya and Uganda had the highest percentage—27% accounting for four studies. Articles focusing on borders between DRC, Rwanda, Uganda, and Burundi, as well as borders between DRC and Rwanda had the second-highest share with two studies accounting for 13% for each. DRC shares borders with five EAC countries and is among the main trading partners of these countries therefore, cross-border small-scale trade is common, forming one of the reasons several studies came from this region. The borders between Kenya and Somalia as well as Kenya and Ethiopia had one study each. There is also one study covering Kenya, Ethiopia, and Somalia. Studies conducted in the horn of Africa mainly focus on small-scale traders involved in livestock cross-border trade which is the most important business activity in the area (Golub 2015).

In terms of studies from a single country, Rwanda had one study. Meanwhile, no specific study from South Sudan, which is also a member of EAC, was documented. While there is one study on cross-border trade in agriculture that focuses on Tanzania, Kenya, and Uganda (Fig. 15.2).

Regarding the research design of the included studies, 53% (n = 8) applied the mixed methods approach, 33% (n = 5) adopted a qualitative-method design while 13% (n = 2) used the quantitative approach to investigate the role played by cooperatives in cross-border trade. The common issues investigated by the included articles were the role of cooperatives on the socio-economic condition of traders including farmers and women involved in business activities across borders. Almost 67% (n = 10) of the studies reviewed investigated the socio-economic effect of participation

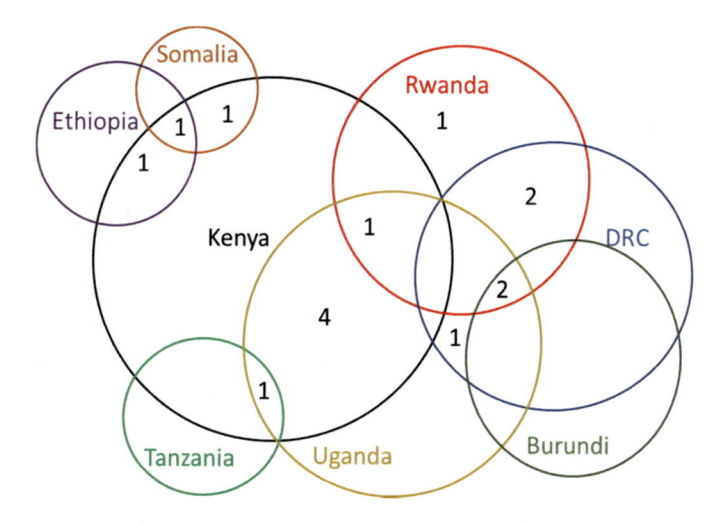

Fig. 15.2 Distribution of articles based on geographical area

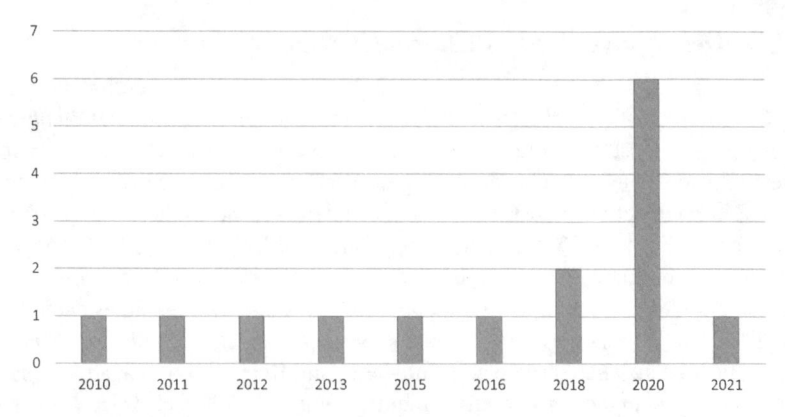

Fig. 15.3 Distribution of articles based on year of publication

in cross-border cooperatives on small-scale traders, while 33% (n = 5) investigated the factors influencing membership in cross-border cooperatives.

The findings from the analysis and assessment displayed variability in the number of study participants, the data collection, and evaluation methods. However, the specific characteristics showed some similarities with the majority being small-scale traders, women in trade, and farmers engaged in small-scale cross-border trade in the region. The largest study had more than 900 participants, whereas more than 47% (n = 7) of the articles had less than 300 participants reviews.

Regarding the publication year of the studies, the largest number of articles was published in 2020, accounting for 40% ($n = 6$). This implies that the topic is recently evolving, and small-scale cross-border trade lively debated in recent years (Fig. 15.3).

15.4.2   *Factors Influencing Small-Scale Traders' Participation in Cooperatives.*

Among the included studies, 33% (n = 5) investigated the participation of small-scale traders in cooperatives. Three studies (20%) revealed lower participation of small-scale traders in cooperatives while one study indicates equal participation of traders in trading networks. The lower level of participation of traders in cooperatives is explained by their lack of proper organization, lack of awareness of those enterprises, and limited capacity of traders who want to become members (Titeca and Kimanuka 2012).

Furthermore, cooperatives facilitate traders to grow their capital through large-scale purchases and increase their bargaining power which helps their members to influence prices in the market (Titeca and Kimanuka 2012). As a result, members of cooperatives are likely to increase their income based on their high capital and ability to direct prices at the market and play an important role to attract non-members.

Meanwhile, the training of small-scale traders might not influence traders to join cooperatives as revealed by one study in this review (Croke et al. 2020).

15.4.3 The Socio-Economic Effect of Participation in Cooperatives

Among 15 studies, 67% (n = 10) discuss the socio-economic effect of cooperative and other self-help groups' membership on small-scale traders. Of these, 27% of studies (n = 4) discuss economic effects such as reduction of transaction cost, access to finance and market information as well as the increase of capital through pooling resources. The study by Golub (2015) found that kinship networks are essential in ICBT to access information and finance, meet contract requirements, reducing transaction costs while they promote the integration of the regional market. Meanwhile, 13% of studies (n = 2) discuss the role played by cross-border cooperatives in helping traders to cross borders through official routes and to move from informal to formal trading. The study by Kawala et al. 2018 suggests that membership in fish marketing organizations is associated with formal or informal trading routes. In other words, cross-border cooperatives can play an important role in formalizing informal cross-border trade.

Furthermore, 20% of studies (n = 3) discussed the social effects of participating in cross-border cooperatives such as representing traders in the decision-making space, protecting traders' interests, and helping them to increase their knowledge and skills. The study by Akaezuwa et al. (2020) suggests that participation in cooperatives and other social associations empowered small-scale traders, especially women who were low-income earners thus enabling them to deal with the challenges they face in cross-border trade. Similarly, trader's associations play an important role to protect members' interests by lobbying appropriate officials to address their concerns and raise funds to organize social events such as weddings and funerals for their members (Titeca 2020). This resonates with the findings from previous studies. Cooperatives also improved the living conditions of small and medium traders by reducing their vulnerability in the cross-border trade in livestock in East Africa (Ng'asike et al. 2020). Despite the importance of social capital in traders' organizations which is essential for traders to move from informal to formal trading, one study (7%) indicates that informal cross-border trade is influenced by "migrants' social networks". This indicates how social networks instead of leading small-scale traders to more organized trade can rather be an opportunity to attract other traders in informal cross-border trade.

15.5 Conclusions and Suggestions for Future Research

This study investigates two research questions using a systematic review on the role of cross-border cooperatives on small-scale trade in Eastern Africa. Overall, there is a recent increase in studies that explore cross-border cooperatives using various research methods and focusing on a variety of outcomes. Also, reviewed studies focus on some EAC countries or border areas depending on considerable accessibility, as well as the historical economic significance of the border area. The results show that most studies have focused on Kenya and Uganda. There are also significant studies conducted between DRC and other East African countries. This points to the necessity to extend more research on the specific roles and effects of cross-border cooperatives to other borders and countries in the region as well as the use of different methodologies such as quantitative methods.

While gender represents an important aspect of small-scale cross-border trade, it is important to point out increasing research with a gender perspective that explores the role played by cross-border cooperatives in helping small-scale traders who are women to access finance and market information (Bugingo 2018). This highlights the role played by cross-border cooperatives to promote women who are under-represented in most of the cooperatives and require more support and initiatives to improve women's status in society.

The findings suggest that the reasons for participation so far have been under investigation (only one-third of the studies have paid attention to the drivers of membership in cross-border cooperatives). The study findings also supported the fact that on the one hand, lower levels of knowledge about cooperatives, and the poor organization associated with a limited capacity of traders are among barriers of cross-border cooperatives membership. On the other hand, challenges faced by traders accessing finance, increasing their bargaining power, and representation of traders' interest influence small-scale traders to join cooperatives. However, the training of small-scale traders who are not members of cooperatives does not affect traders' participation in associations or cooperatives.

Additionally, most of the small-scale traders have challenges of lower capital, according to reviewed studies, which constrain traders from paying the membership fees required to join cross-border cooperatives. There is a need to facilitate traders to get financial support and link them to financial institutions. This will allow small-scale traders to increase their capital and provide them with an opportunity to join different traders' organizations. However, this must go along with acknowledgment and recognition of small-scale cross-border trade as well as improving the working environment at borders. It is also important to improve the management and leadership cooperatives to increase trust among members and accountability.

Meanwhile, slightly more than two-thirds of the studies reviewed discussed the effect of participation in cross-border cooperatives on small-scale traders. Our results displayed multiple effects ranging from social to economic effects. Starting with the latter, cross-border cooperatives proved to be essential for their members to increase their income through pooling resources and bulk purchases. Two reviewed studies showed how through cooperatives, traders received support that helped them to access the capital and market information which improved traders living conditions and reduce their vulnerability. Likewise, self-help groups in cross-border trade played an important role in reducing transaction costs for small-scale traders as revealed by two studies reviewed (see Golub 2015; Pavanello 2010). Additionally, members of cooperatives have the advantage of negotiating higher prices on the market and building networks easily with other cooperatives or associations which help members to locate markets for their products across the national borders. Indeed, cooperative members receive money from contributions and savings from their respective cooperatives in terms of dividends and bonuses as well as financial support from their partners and stakeholders. Since cooperative members can increase their income through various ways, more mobilization and sensitization are needed for all small-scale cross-border traders to access these benefits.

Looking at social effects, three studies discussed the role played by cross-border cooperatives in representing traders in public policy space (see Akaezuwa et al. 2020; Nugent and Soi 2020; Titeca 2020). Small-scale traders are often vulnerable to cross-border policies, regulations, and reforms, more specifically women who make up the majority in small-scale cross-border trade. However, cross-border cooperatives are increasingly helping to address those problems by representing traders in the decision-making spaces at the same time empowering traders to raise their concerns and protect their interests. This study also indicates that participation in cooperatives improved women's participation in trade and helped them to deal with gender-based violence. As revealed by two reviewed studies, cooperatives increased awareness of crossing borders through official routes and help traders to gradually move from informal to formal trading (Kawala et al. 2018).

To sum up, this chapter systematically reviewed studies that explored cross-border cooperatives and small-scale trade in East Africa published in the English language between January 2000 and August 2021. The evidence consolidated in our systematic review showed that challenges associated with informal trade and small-scale cross-border trade were the main influence on the cooperative's participation. After a consolidated assessment, it was also evident that participation in cooperatives helped in improving the socio-economic condition of women, farmers, and small-scale traders who are engaged in cross-border trade. Cross-border cooperatives also play a critical role in alleviating poverty in the region, promoting socio-economic growth and regional integration. More interventions and support that target cross-border cooperatives and small-scale traders are needed to improve cross-border trade and maximize trading benefits and opportunities available across borders.

The findings from our systematic review show the roles of cooperatives and the significance of small-scale cross-border trade in East Africa. This information is critical in policy formulation by governments, business leaders, and small-scale traders. However, the compiled evidence indicated ambiguous outcomes with regards to specific roles of cross-border cooperatives. The study also did not indicate the role of cooperatives in specific countries in East Africa. Therefore, future research should focus on the specific roles and effects of cross-border cooperatives on trade in specific East African countries.

Appendix

See Tables A.1 and A.2.

Table A.1 PRISMA checklist (Moher et al. 2009)

Item no	Section/topic	Checklist item	Reported in page
1	TITLE	Identify the report as a systematic review, meta-analysis, or both	333
2	ABSTRACT	Provide a structured summary including, as applicable: background; objectives; data sources; study eligibility criteria, participants, and interventions; study appraisal and synthesis methods; results; limitations; conclusions and implications of key findings; systematic review registration number	333
3	INTRODUCTION Rationale	Describe the rationale for the review in the context of what is already known	333 - 335
4	Objectives	Provide an explicit statement of questions being addressed with reference to participants, interventions, comparisons, outcomes, and study design	336
5	METHODS Protocol and registration	Indicate if a review protocol exists, if and where it can be accessed (e.g., Web address), and, if available, provide registration information including registration number	Not exist
6	Eligibility criteria	Specify study characteristics (e.g., PICOS, length of follow-up) and report characteristics (e.g., years considered, language, publication status) used as criteria for eligibility, giving rationale	341 - 342

(continued)

Table A.1 (continued)

Item no	Section/topic	Checklist item	Reported in page
7	Information sources	Describe all information sources (e.g., databases with dates of coverage, contact with study authors to identify additional studies) in the search and date last searched	341
8	Search	Present full electronic search strategy for at least one database, including any limits used, such that it could be repeated	341
9	Study selection	State the process for selecting studies (i.e., screening, eligibility, included in systematic review, and, if applicable, included in the meta-analysis)	342
10	Data collection process	Describe method of data extraction from reports (e.g., piloted forms, independently, in duplicate) and any processes for obtaining and confirming data from investigators	342
11	Data items	List and define all variables for which data were sought (e.g., PICOS, funding sources) and any assumptions and simplifications made	342
12	Risk of bias in individual studies	Describe methods used for assessing risk of bias of individual studies (including specification of whether this was done at the study or outcome level), and how this information is to be used in any data synthesis	N/A
13	Summary measures	State the principal summary measures (e.g., risk ratio, difference in means)	N/A
14	Synthesis of results	Describe the methods of handling data and combining results of studies, if done, including measures of consistency	N/A

(continued)

Table A.1 (continued)

Item no	Section/topic	Checklist item	Reported in page
15	Risk of bias across studies	Specify any assessment of risk of bias that may affect the cumulative evidence (e.g., publication bias, selective reporting within studies)	N/A
16	Additional analyses	Describe methods of additional analyses (e.g., sensitivity or subgroup analyses, meta-regression), if done, indicating which were pre-specified	N./A
17	RESULTS Study selection	Give numbers of studies screened, assessed for eligibility, and included in the review, with reasons for exclusions at each stage, ideally with a flow diagram	349
18	Study characteristics	For each study, present characteristics for which data were extracted	350 - 351
19	Risk of bias within studies	Present data on risk of bias of each study and, if available, any outcome level assessment	N/A
20	Results of individual studies	For all outcomes considered	Table 15.1
21	Synthesis of results	Present results of each meta-analysis done, including confidence intervals and measures of consistency	N/A
22	Risk of bias across studies	Present results of any assessment of risk of bias across studies	N/A
23	Additional analysis	Give results of additional analyses	N/A
24	DISCUSSION Summary of evidence	Summarize the main findings including the strength of evidence for each main outcome; consider their relevance to key groups	353 - 354
25	Limitations	Discuss limitations at study and outcome level	342
26	CONCLUSIONS Future research implications	Provide a general interpretation of the results in the context of other evidence, and implications for future research	353 - 354

Table A.2 Reports of excluded studies with justification

#	Author(s), title, journal/publisher and publication year	Source	Justification for exclusion
1	Ackello-Ogutu, C. and Echessah, P., (1997) "Unrecorded cross-border trade between Kenya and Uganda". Technical paper, 59	Google Scholar	Published earlier than 2000
2	Titeca, K., (2012). "Tycoons and contraband: informal cross-border trade in West Nile, north-western Uganda". Journal of Eastern African Studies, 6(1), pp.47–63	Google Scholar	Membership participation in cooperatives is not included
3	Van den Boogaard, V., Prichard, W. and Jibao, S. (2021) "Norms, Networks, Power and Control: Understanding Informal Payments and Brokerage in Cross-Border Trade in Sierra Leone," Journal of Borderlands Studies, 36(1), pp. 77–97. https://doi.org/10.1080/08865655.2018.1510333	Google Scholar	Framed outside East Africa
4	Ogalo, V., (2010) "Informal cross-border trade in EAC: Implications for regional integration and development". Research Paper: CUTS Geneva Resource Centre	Google Scholar	The study does not include findings on cross border cooperatives
5	Little, P., (2005) "Unofficial trade when states are weak: The case of cross-border commerce in the Horn of Africa". United Nations University (UNU)	Google Scholar	The role of cross border Cooperatives on livestock traders is missing
6	Little, P.D., Tiki, W. and Debsu, D.N., (2015) "Formal or informal, legal or illegal: The ambiguous nature of cross-border livestock trade in the Horn of Africa". Journal of Borderlands Studies, 30(3), pp.405–421	Google Scholar	Effect of Cooperatives on livestock traders is missing
7	Siu, J., (2020) "Formalizing Informal Cross-Border Trade: Evidence from One-Stop-Border-Posts in Uganda". Available at SSRN 3,854,156	Google Scholar	The study does not include findings on cross border cooperatives

(continued)

Table A.2 (continued)

#	Author(s), title, journal/publisher and publication year	Source	Justification for exclusion
8	Lesser, C. and Moisé-Leeman, E., (2009)." Informal cross-border trade and trade facilitation reform in Sub-Saharan Africa". OECD trade policy working paper no. 86. OECD report	Google Scholar	Framed beyond East Africa
9	Livani, T. and Solotaroff, J.,(2019) "Promoting Women's Participation in Cross-border Trade in South Asia". ANTYAJAA: Indian Journal of Women and Social Change, 4(1), pp.9–32	Google Scholar	Framed outside East Africa
10	Schomerus, M. and Titeca, K., (2012) "Deals and dealings: inconclusive peace and treacherous trade along the South Sudan-Uganda border". Africa Spectrum, 47(2–3), pp.5–31	Google Scholar	Study does not include findings of cross border cooperatives
11	Titeca, K. and Flynn, R., (2014) "Hybrid Governance," Legitimacy, and (ii) legality in the Informal Cross-Border Trade in Panyimur, Northwest Uganda. African Studies Review, 57(1), pp.71–91	Google Scholar	Study does not include findings on cross border cooperatives
12	Oduol, J.B.A., Mithöfer, D., Place, F., Nang'ole, E., Olwande, J., Kirimi, L. and Mathenge, M., (2017) "Women's participation in high value agricultural commodity chains in Kenya: Strategies for closing the gender gap". Journal of rural studies, 50, pp.228–239	Google Scholar	Not relevant
13	Gallien, M., (2020) "Informal institutions and the regulation of smuggling in North Africa". Perspectives on Politics, 18(2), pp.492–508	Google Scholar	Framed outside East Africa
14	Dzawanda, B., Nicolau, M.D., Matsa, M. and Kusena, W.,(2021) „Livelihood outcomes of informal cross border traders prior to the rise of the virtual cash economy in Gweru, Zimbabwe". Journal of Borderlands Studies, pp.1–20	Google Scholar	Framed outside East Africa

(continued)

Table A.2 (continued)

#	Author(s), title, journal/publisher and publication year	Source	Justification for exclusion
15	Oduol, J.B.A., Mithöfer, D., Place, F., Nang'ole, E., Olwande, J., Kirimi, L. and Mathenge, M., (2017) "Women's participation in high value agricultural commodity chains in Kenya: Strategies for closing the gender gap". Journal of rural studies, 50, pp.228–239	Google Scholar	Not relevant
16	Kodero, C.U., (2020) "Development Without Borders? Informal Cross-Border Trade in Africa. In The Palgrave Handbook of African Political Economy" (pp. 1051–1067). Palgrave Macmillan, Cham	Google Scholar	Framed beyond East Africa
17	Dhliwayo, S., (2017) "Export experience and key success factors in cross-border trade: evidence from Southern Africa". Acta Commercii, 17(1), pp.1–9	Google Scholar	Framed outside East Africa
18	Peberdy, S. and Crush, J., (2001) "Invisible trade, invisible travellers: The Maputo Corridor spatial development initiative and informal cross-border trading". South African Geographical Journal, 83(2), pp.115–123	Google Scholar	Framed outside East Africa
19	Tuluy, H., (2016) "Regional economic integration in Africa". Global Journal of Emerging Market Economies, 8(3), pp.334–354	Google Scholar	Framed beyond East Africa
20	Robinson, A.L., (2016) "Internal Borders: Ethnic-based market segmentation in Malawi". World Development, 87, pp.371–384	Google Scholar	Framed outside East Africa
21	Sitko, N.J., Burke, W.J. and Jayne, T.S., (2018) "The quiet rise of large-scale trading firms in East and Southern Africa". The Journal of Development Studies, 54(5), pp.895–914	Google Scholar	Not relevant

(continued)

Table A.2 (continued)

#	Author(s), title, journal/publisher and publication year	Source	Justification for exclusion
22	Little, P.D., Debsu, D.N. and Tiki, W., (2014) "How pastoralists perceive and respond to market opportunities: The case of the Horn of Africa". Food policy, 49, pp.389–397	Google Scholar	Participation in cooperatives and effect of cooperatives on traders is not included
23	Asche, H., (2021) "The Reality of African Trade Integration—Challenges of Implementation. In Regional Integration, Trade and Industry in Africa" (pp. 35–56), Springer	Google Scholar	Framed beyond East Africa
24	Klopp, J.M. and Trimble, M., (2020) "Corruption, gender, and small-scale cross border trade in East Africa: A review". Working Paper No. 10	Google Scholar	This is a structured review study and can not be included
25	Poulton, C., Kydd, J. and Dorward, A., (2006) "Overcoming market constraints on pro-poor agricultural growth in Sub-Saharan Africa". Development policy review, 24(3), pp.243–277	Google Scholar	Framed beyond East Africa and not conducted in cross border trade
26	Zeller, W., (2009) "Danger and opportunity in Katima Mulilo: a Namibian border boomtown at transnational crossroads". Journal of Southern African Studies, 35(1), pp.133–154	Google Scholar	Framed outside East Africa
27	Mutopo, P., (2011) "Women's struggles to access and control land and livelihoods after fast-track land reform in Mwenezi District, Zimbabwe". Journal of Peasant Studies, 38(5), pp.1021–1046	Google Scholar	Framed outside East Africa
28	Pedersen, P.O., (2005) "The development of the informal small-enterprise sector in Eastern and Southern Africa: From import substitution to structural adjustment" (No. 2005: 11). DIIS Working Paper	Google Scholar	Participation in cooperatives and effect of cooperatives on traders is not included

(continued)

Table A.2 (continued)

#	Author(s), title, journal/publisher and publication year	Source	Justification for exclusion
29	Verweijen, J. and Marijnen, E., (2018) "The counterinsurgency/conservation nexus: guerrilla livelihoods and the dynamics of conflict and violence in the Virunga National Park, Democratic Republic of the Congo". The Journal of Peasant Studies, 45(2), pp.300–320	Google Scholar	Not relevant
30	Lam, Y., Fry, J.P. and Nachman, K.E., (2019) "Applying an environmental public health lens to the industrialization of food animal production in ten low-and middle-income countries". Globalization and health, 15(1), pp.1–20	Google Scholar	Not relevant
31	Kuhanen, J., (2010) "Challenging power and meaning outlining the popular epidemiology of HIV and AIDS in Rakai, Uganda", c. 1975–1990. African Journal of AIDS Research, 9(1), pp.81–94	Google Scholar	Not relevant
32	Eriksson Baaz, M., Olsson, O. and Verweijen, J., (2018) „Navigating 'taxation'on the Congo River: the interplay of legitimation and 'officialisation'". Review of African Political Economy, 45(156), pp.250–266	Google Scholar	Famed outside East Africa and not relevant

References

Abebaw D, Haile MG (2013) The impact of cooperatives on agricultural technology adoption: empirical evidence from Ethiopia. Food Policy 38(1):82–91. https://doi.org/10.1016/j.foodpol.2012.10.003

Afrika JGK, Ajumbo G (2012) Informal cross border trade in Africa: implications and policy recommendations. Africa Economic Brief, vol 3, Issue 10. Africa Development Bank

Akaezuwa V, Chakraborty A, Chang B, Manian S, Prabhakar A, Sriram S, Zhu C (2020) Ethical cross-border trading between Kenya and Uganda by women-led micro and small enterprises. Columbia School of International Affairs

Ama NO, Mangadi KT, Ama HA (2014) Exploring the challenges facing women entrepreneurs in informal cross-border trade in Botswana. Genderin Management 29(8):505–522. https://doi.org/10.1108/GM-02-20140018

Asche H (2021) The reality of African trade integration—challenges of implementation. In: Regional integration, trade and industry in Africa. Springer, pp 35–56

Bensassi S, Jarreau J (2019) Price discrimination in bribe payments: evidence from informal cross-border trade in West Africa. World Develop 122:462–480. https://doi.org/10.1016/j.worlddev.2019.05.023

Brenton P, Isik G (2012) De-fragmenting Africa: deepening regional trade integration in goods and services. World Bank Publications

Brenton P, Soprano C (2018) Small-scale cross-border trade in Africa: why it matters and how it should be supported. International centre for trade and sustainable development. BRIDGES, AFRICA 7(4)

Brenton P, Bucekuderhwa CB, Hossein C, Nagaki S, Ntagoma JB (2011) Risky business: poor women cross-border traders in the Great Lakes Region of Africa. Africa Trade Policy Note, 11. DC: World Bank, Washington

Buang M, Samah AA (2020) Systematic review of factors influencing the effectiveness of the co-operative board. REVESCO: Revista de estudios cooperativos (136), pp 107–126

Bugingo EM (2018) Empowering women by supporting small-scale cross border trade. International centre for trade and sustainable development. BRIDGES, AFRICA, 7(4)

Camargo Benavides AF, Ehrenhard M (2021) Rediscovering the cooperative enterprise: a systematic review of current topics and avenues for future research. VOLUNTAS: Int J Volunt Nonprofit Org (20210308). doi:https://doi.org/10.1007/s11266021-00328-8.

Croke K, Garcia Mora ME, Goldstein M, Mensah E, O'Sullivan M (2020) Up before dawn: experimental evidence from a cross-border trader training at the democratic republic of Congo–Rwanda Border. World Bank Policy research working paper (9123)

Demena BA (2011) Determinants of fish catch levels in artisanal fishing in Eritrea. Master's thesis presented at the international institute of social studies. The Hague, The Netherlands

Develtere, Patrick, Pollet I, Wanyama F (2008) Cooperating out of poverty. The renaissance of the African cooperative movement. ILO, Geneva

Dushimimana G (2021) Exploring cross-border cooperatives and small-scale traders in Eastern Africa with a focus on Rwanda: what matters and why? Master's thesis presented at the international institute of social studies. The Hague, The Netherlands

García Mora ME, Roshan S (2013) Barriers, risks, and productive potential for small-scale traders in the Great Lakes Region. In: Brenton P, Gamberoni E, Sear C (eds) Women and trade in Africa: realizing the potential. World Bank, Washington, D.C

Golub S (2015) Informal cross-border trade and smuggling in Africa. In: Morrissey O, López RA, Sharma K (eds) Handbook on trade and development. Edward Elgar, Cheltenham, UK, pp 179–209

Harelimana JB, Mukarukaka B (2020) contribution of cooperatives to social economic development in Rwanda. Open Access J Biog Sci Res 1(3):1–5.

ICA (1995) The international co-operative alliance statement on co-operative identity. Rev Int Co-Oper 88(3):3–4

Islam S, Mazariegos V, Nagarajan G, Zaman L (2015) Effects of farmer cooperatives on expanding agricultural markets in developing countries: a systematic review. Social Impact. USDA

Kahiya E, Kadirov D (2020) Informal cross border trade as a substratum marketing system: a review and conceptual framework. J Macromark 40(1):88–109. https://doi.org/10.1177/0276146716719897115

Kaitesi Katabarwa J (2020) Policy mapping: women's economic empowerment in Rwanda. Report. International Development Research Centre

Kawala M, Hyuha TS, William E, Walekwa P, Elepu G, Kalumba SC (2018) Determinants for choice of fish market channels: the case of Busia (Uganda/Kenya) border. J Agric Sci 10(8)

Klopp JM, Trimble M (2020) Corruption, gender, and small-scale cross border trade in east Africa: a review. Working paper no. 10

Lesser C, Moisé-Leeman E (2009) Informal cross-border trade and trade facilitation reform in Sub-Saharan Africa. OECD Trade Policy Working Paper No. 86. OECD, Paris

Little PD, Tiki W, Debsu DN (2015) Formal or informal, legal or illegal: the ambiguous nature of cross-border livestock trade in the Horn of Africa. J BordLands Stud 30(3):405–421. https://doi.org/10.1080/08865655.2015.1068206

Lloyd-Ellis H, Nordstrom A (2021) Trade, poverty and food security: a survey of recent research and its implications for East Africa. Economics Department, Queen's University Working Paper 1460

Maghimbi S (2010) Cooperatives in Tanzania mainland: revival and growth, Working paper no. 14, CoopAFRICA. International Labour Organization, Dar Es Salaam Office, Tanzania

Majurin E (2012) How women fare in East African cooperatives: the case of Kenya, Tanzania and Uganda. ILO, Dar Es Salaam

Malaba JA, Chipika JT (2012) A gender assessment of African regional economic communities databases to identify gaps in capturing the activities of women in informal cross border trade. United Nations Economic Commission for Africa

Marcis J, Bortoluzzi SC, de Lima EP, da Costa SEG (2019) Sustainability performance evaluation of agricultural cooperatives' operations: a systemic review of the literature. Environment, development and sustainability: a multidisciplinary approach to the theory and practice of sustainable development vol 21, 3rd edn, pp 1111–1126. doi:https://doi.org/10.1007/s10668-018-0095-1.

Mbo'o-Tchouawou M, Karugia J, Mulei L, Nyota H (2016) Assessing the participation of men and women in cross-border trade in agriculture: Evidence from selected East African countries. Working Paper No. 38, Regional Strategic Analysis and Knowledge Support System (ReSAKSS)

Minah M, Carletti AMP, Dohmwirth C (2019) Literature review (paper one): systematic literature review of agricultural cooperative effects on their members: what kinds of benefits they offer and for whom. Effects of agricultural cooperatives on members in developing countries: studies on pricing and inclusion, p 22

Moher D et al (2009) Preferred reporting items for systematic reviews and meta analyses: the prisma statement. BMJ (clinical Research Ed.) 339:2535. https://doi.org/10.1136/bmj.b2535

Musahara H (2012) Perspectives on cooperatives with reference to Rwanda, ILO working paper, No 13. International Labour Office, Kampala

Mwanabiningo N (2015) Deriving maximum benefit from small-scale cross border trade between DRC and Rwanda, Report. TradeMark East Africa and International Alert

Nakanjako R, Onyango EO, Kabumbuli R (2021) Positioning migrants in in-formal cross border trade: the case of Busia, Uganda-Kenya border. East Afr Soc Sci Res Rev 37(1):123143. https://doi.org/10.1353/eas.2021.0005

Ng'asike PO, Stepputat F, Njoka JT (2020) Livestock trade and devolution in the Somali-Kenya transboundary corridor. Pastoralism: research, policy, and practice 10(1). doi:https://doi.org/10.1186/s13570-02000185-y.

Njikam O, Tchouassi G (2011) Women in informal cross-border trade: empirical evidence from Cameroon. Int J Econ Financ 3:202–213. https://doi.org/10.5539/ijef.v3n3p202

Nugent P, Soi I (2020) One-stop border posts in East Africa: state encountersof the fourth kind. J Eastern Afr Stud 14(3):433–454. https://doi.org/10.1080/17531055.2020.1768468

Nyamwasa JD (2008) Jump-starting the Rwanda cooperative movement. In: Develtere P, Pollet I, Wanyama F (eds) Cooperating out of poverty: the renaissance of the African cooperative movement. International Labor Office, Geneva

Onyilo F, Adong A (2019) Agricultural cooperative marketing and credit policy re-form in Uganda: an opportunity for poverty reduction. African J Food Agricul Nutrition Develop 19(1):1415614170. https://doi.org/10.18697/AJFAND.84.BLFB1008

Parshotam A, Balongo S (2020) Women traders in East Africa: the case study of the Busia One-Stop Border Post. South African Institute of International Affairs (SAIIA), Occasional Paper 305

Pavanello S (2010) Livestock marketing in Kenya–Ethiopia border areas: a baseline study. Humanitarian policy group (HPG) working paper. Overseas Development Institute (ODI), UK

Pollet I (2009) Cooperatives in Africa: the age of reconstruction–synthesis of a survey in nine African countries. ILO Office for Kenya, Somalia, Tanzania and Uganda, Dar es Salaam

Soeiro S, Dias MF (2019) Renewable energy cooperatives: a systematic review. 16th international conference on the European energy market (EEM), pp 1–6. doi:https://doi.org/10.1109/EEM.2019.8916546

Songwe V (2019) Intra-African trade: a path to economic diversification and inclusion. In: Coulibaly BS (ed) Foresight Africa. Top priorities for the continent in 2019. The Brookings institution, Washington, DC, pp 97–116

Titeca K (2009) The changing cross-border trade dynamics between Northwestern Uganda, North-eastern Congo and Southern Sudan. Crisis States research centre working papers series No 2 (63). Crisis States Research Centre, London School of Economics, London, UK

Titeca K, Kimanuka C (2012) Walking in the dark: informal cross-border trade in the Great Lakes Region. Technical report. International Alert, London

Titeca K (2020) Informal cross-border DRC-Uganda border. UNDP Africa Borderlands Centre, Nairobi

Trademark East Africa (2021) The effects of Covid-19 on women cross border traders in East Africa Report. https://eassi.org/wpcontent/uploads/2021/03/Report-on-the-Effects-of-COVID19-onWomen-Cross-Border-Traders-in-East-Africa.pdf

Van den Boogaard V, Prichard W, Jibao S (2021) Norms, networks, power and control: understanding informal payments and brokerage in cross border trade in Sierra Leone. J BordLands Stud 36(1):7797. https://doi.org/10.1080/08865655.2018.1510333

Wanyama FO (2016) Cooperatives and the sustainable development goals. A contribution to the post-2015 development debate. International Labour Organization, Geneva

Wanyama F (2009) Surviving liberalisation: the cooperative movement in Kenya. CoopAFRICA working paper no 10. International Labour Organisation, Geneva

Index